God Yes

Atheism No

A Philosophical Journey To Christian Faith

Steve Lagoon

God Yes / Atheism No:

A Philosophical Journey to Christian Faith
Copyright © 2019 All Rights Reserved
By Steve Lagoon

All Scripture quotations are from the New International Version unless otherwise noted.

Dedication

I dedicate this work to my wonderful family including my wife Sherry, and my children: Kyle, Briana, Kellen, Hannah, Corrine, and Keenan.

To my mother Marie Lagoon.

To all those I am honored to serve with on the board of Religion Analysis Service.

And to my dear friends Steve Devore, and Paul and Diane Klevann.

Contents

Introduction

I am writing this book to share why I believe in God, and more specifically, the God of the Judeo-Christian Bible. It is not an exhaustive study, nor do I hope the reader will find it exhausting to read.

The reader will find that I have used extensive and often long quotations. I have done this for several reasons. As much as is practical, I wanted readers to hear the original authors in their own voices to avoid inaccuracies or mischaracterizations.

I am using footnotes for the convenience of the reader.

This is simply my journey, my investigation of the God question, that I share with the reader. In so doing, I have tried to honor the Socratic principle concerning the value of the examined life and the spirit of these words from Bertrand Russell:

> "Philosophy, though unable to tell us with certainty, what is the true answer to the doubts which it raises, is able to suggest many possibilities which enlarge our thoughts and free them from the tyranny of custom. Thus, while diminishing our feeling of certainty as to what things are, it greatly increases our knowledge as to what they may be; it removes the somewhat arrogant dogmatism of those who have never travelled into the region of liberating doubt, and it keeps alive our sense of wonder."[1]

I am also reminded of the statement about philosophy sometimes attributed to Ralph Waldo Emerson:

---

[1] Bertrand Russell, *The Value of Philosophy* in *Introduction to Philosophy: Classical and Contemporary Readings*, Fourth Edition, Edited by John Perry, Michael Bratman & John Martin Fischer, Oxford UK (Oxford University Press, 2007) 10.

"A little philosophy turns one away from religion, but that deeper understanding brings one back."[2]

A fuller statement was made by Francis Bacon:

"A little philosophy inclineth a man's mind to atheism; but depth in philosophy bringeth men's minds about to religion. For while the mind of men looketh upon second causes scattered, it may sometimes rest in them and go no further; but when it beholdeth the chain of them, confederate and linked together, it must needs fly to Providence and Deity."[3]

I agree wholeheartedly with this statement by Yeager Hudson:

"Some people fear that a philosophical scrutiny of religious beliefs might undermine their faith. But surely, we are inclined to say, a faith with any substantial intellectual substance should stand up to rational scrutiny, and a faith that can be destroyed by an honest search for the truth is not worth defending."[4]

One of the ideals of pure science is to follow the facts wherever they lead. This dispassionate search for the truth has been called "the view from nowhere."[5] It is my challenge to the reader to consider the material that

[2]Ralph Waldo Emerson, quoted by John Perry, *A Dialogue on Personal Identity and Immortality* in *Introduction to Philosophy: Classical and Contemporary Readings*, Fourth Edition, Edited by John Perry, Michael Bratman & John Martin Fischer, Oxford UK (Oxford University Press, 2007) 375 .

[3]Francis Bacon, *Essays. On Atheism*, as quoted in *The Great Quotations*, Compiled by George Seldes, Secaucus NJ (Castle Books, 1978) 72.

[4]Yeager Hudson, *The Philosophy of Religion*, Mountain View CA (Mayfield Publishing Company, 1991) Preface, XI.

[5]Hilary Rose, *Colonizing the Social Sciences,* chapter in Alas*, Poor Darwin: Arguments Against Evolutionary Psychology*, Edited by Hilary Rose & Steven Rose, New York (Harmony Books, 2000) 138.

follows with the openness to follow the facts wherever they lead, even if they lead to the gates of heaven!

"Two things fill my mind with ever-increasing wonder and awe. The more often and more intensely the reflection dwells on them: the starry heavens above me and the moral law within me"

Immanuel Kant

(from the conclusion of *The Critique of Practical Reason*)

Section One: Setting the Stage for the Journey

Chapter 1: Setting the Stage

I am writing this book with the intent of sharing why I am personally convinced of God's existence, most particularly as expressed in the Bible of Christianity.

I will give my reasons for believing in what the atheist Kai Nielsen called a "metaphysical blockbuster,"[6] the proposition that an infinite personal God exists and is transcendent over the universe He has created. I have yielded to what atheist Paul Kurtz called "The Transcendental Temptation, the temptation to believe things unseen because they satisfy needs and desires."[7]

That is, I am convinced the God of the classical Christian confessions is real and rules over the universe, having all the attributes normally ascribed to him in Christian theology including His omnipotence and omniscience.

I want to respond to those who sincerely reject the belief in God, and who consider such belief as no more than mere superstition. Nietzsche asked the question: "What if God himself is proving to be our longest lie?"[8] Likewise, Kai Nielsen asserted:

---

[6]Kai Nielsen, *Atheism & Philosophy*, Amherst NY (Prometheus Books, 2005) 22.

[7]Paul Kurtz, *Why Do People Believe or Disbelieve*, in Timothy Moy, *The Galileo Affair*, in *Science and Religion: Are They Compatible?*, Paul Kurtz, Editor, Amherst New York (Prometheus Books, 2003) 282.

[8]Friedrich Nietzsche, *The Gay Science*, in *Existentialism Basic*

"There is no reason, no intellectual justification or moral need to believe in God. I am convinced that religious beliefs should belong to the tribal folklore of mankind and there is no more need to believe in God than there is to believe in Santa Claus or the Easter Bunny."[9]

Matt Young agreed with Nielsen,

"I conclude that the evidence in favor of a purposeful creator, let alone a benevolent God, is so weak as to be virtually nonexistent."[10]

Surely such comments can only be hyperbole, for as we shall see, there are weighty reasons indeed why so many of the greatest intellects of history have been believers in God. Given the ubiquitous nature of God belief, it can be nothing but sophistry to compare the belief in God with belief in fairytales, the Easter Bunny, and Santa Claus.[11]

I hope to show that belief in God does not qualify one for the psychiatrist's office as the atheistic scientist Richard Dawkins suggested:

"Richard Dawkins set the tone. In his seminal 1976 work *The Selfish Gene*, he defined faith as 'a kind of mental illness.'"[12]

Writings, Second Edition, Charles Guignon & Derk Pereboom, Indianapolis/Cambridge (Hackett Publishing Company, Inc, 2001) 151.

[9]Kai Nielsen, *Atheism & Philosophy*, 147.

[10]Matt Young, *Science and Religion in an Impersonal Universe*, in *Science and Religion: Are They Compatible?*, Paul Kurtz, Editor, Amherst New York (Prometheus Books, 2003) 348.

[11]No disrespect intended to the historical Saint Nicholas, the fourth century bishop of Myra and servant of Jesus Christ.

[12]David Marshall, *The Truth Behind the New Atheism: Responding to the Emerging Challenge to God and Christianity,* Eugene OR (Harvest House Publishers, 2007) 16.

Where I'm coming from

By way of self-disclosure, I would identify myself as somewhere between an Evangelical and a Fundamentalist Christian (fundagelical!). Still more specifically, I am of a conservative of Baptist persuasion or confession.

What this means doctrinally is that I believe in the fundamental doctrines of the Christian faith. These include the belief that there is one God (monotheism); that within the nature of the one God, there are three distinct persons: the Father, the Son, and the Holy Spirit (the Trinity); that Jesus is fully God and fully man; in His virgin birth; in His atoning sacrifice for the sins of the world; in His miracles; in His bodily resurrection from the dead; in His bodily ascension to heaven, and in His future literal and visible second coming to earth.

Some of these can be known through natural theology, the use of our God-given reason to study the world. Others can only be known by special revelation in the Bible.

The inerrancy of the Bible

Underlying all these doctrines is my commitment to the inerrancy of the Scriptures. The idea is that if God has inspired the Bible (which Christians affirm), it follows that it would be without error when received. It is difficult to understand why God would inspire a message, indeed the most important message ever given to man, filled with errors.

I suggest that it is quite reasonable, despite what you might hear otherwise, to be committed to both critical scholarship and biblical inerrancy.

An anonymous wit said of Nietzsche:

"God is dead—Nietzsche

Nietzsche is dead—God"[13]

Nietzsche, the Madman, and the Death of God

A great place to begin is with the powerful thoughts of the atheist philosopher Friedrich Nietzsche, and particularly his *Parable of the Madman* harkening the death of God. Timothy Morgan said:

> "When I say no one should be an atheist without first wrestling with Nietzsche, it is because he was one of the few to fully embrace all the implications of a naturalist worldview."[14]

Yes, Nietzsche, perhaps better than anyone else showed the startling implications of a world without God. Kerry Walters described Nietzsche's powerful account announcing the death of God:

> "In one of his most gripping and famous parables, Friedrich Nietzsche tells the story of the 'madman' who wandered through the streets 'in the bright morning hours' holding up a lighted lantern and repeatedly crying 'I seek God! I seek God!' Townspeople laughed, mockingly asking him whether God was hiding or had gotten lost somewhere in the cosmos. Finally losing patience at their gibes, the madman shouts out that *he'll* tell the people where God is.

[13]*Random House Webster's Quotationary*, Leonard Roy Frank, Editor, New York (Random House, 2001) 50.
[14]Timothy Morgan, *Thank God for Atheists: How the Greatest Skeptics Led Me to Faith*, Eugene OR (Harvest House Publishers, 2015) 72.

'We have killed him—you and I. All of us are his murderers.' And then he forced his way into a nearby church and struck up a requiem for the late deity, insisting that churches had now become 'the tombs and sepulchers of God.'"[15]

In the Gay Science, Nietzsche said:

"The greatest recent event—that 'God is dead,' that the belief in the Christian God has become unbelievable— already begins to cast its first shadows on Europe."[16]

Let us hear Nietzsche's *Parable of the Madmen* in his own words:

"Have you not heard of that madman who lit a lantern in the bright morning hours, ran to the market place, and cried incessantly: 'I seek God! I seek God!' -- As many of those who did not believe in God were standing around just then, he provoked much laughter. 'Has he got lost?' asked one. 'Did he lose his way like a child?' asked another. 'Or is he hiding? Is he afraid of us? Has he gone on a voyage? Emigrated?' -- Thus they yelled and laughed.
    The madman jumped into their midst and pierced them with his eyes. 'Whither is God?' he cried; 'I will tell you. *We have killed him* -- you and I. All of us are his murderers. But how did we do this? How could we drink up the sea? Who gave us the sponge to wipe away the entire horizon? What were we doing when we unchained this earth from its sun? Whither is it moving now? Whither are we moving? Away from all suns? Are we not plunging continually? Backward, sideward, forward, in all directions? Is there still any up or down? Are we not straying, as through an infinite nothing? Do we not feel the

[15]Kerry Walters, *Atheism: A Guide for the Perplexed*, New York (The Continuum International Publishing Group Inc, 2010) 10.
[16]Friedrich Nietzsche, *The Gay Science*, in *Existentialism Basic Writings*, Second Edition, Charles Guignon & Derk Pereboom, Indianapolis/Cambridge (Hackett Publishing Company, Inc, 2001) 149.

breath of empty space? Has it not become colder? Is not night continually closing in on us? Do we not need to light lanterns in the morning? Do we hear nothing as yet of the noise of the gravediggers who are burying God? Do we smell nothing as yet of the divine decomposition? Gods, too, decompose. God is dead. God remains dead. And we have killed him.'

'How shall we comfort ourselves, the murderers of all murderers? What was holiest and mightiest of all that the world has yet owned has bled to death under our knives: who will wipe this blood off us? What water is there for us to clean ourselves? What festivals of atonement, what sacred games shall we have to invent? Is not the greatness of this deed too great for us? Must we ourselves not become gods simply to appear worthy of it? There has never been a greater deed; and whoever is born after us -- for the sake of this deed he will belong to a higher history than all history hitherto.'

Here the madman fell silent and looked again at his listeners; and they, too, were silent and stared at him in astonishment. At last he threw his lantern on the ground, and it broke into pieces and went out. 'I have come too early,' he said then; 'my time is not yet. This tremendous event is still on its way, still wandering; it has not yet reached the ears of men. Lightning and thunder require time; the light of the stars requires time; deeds, though done, still require time to be seen and heard. This deed is still more distant from them than the most distant stars -- *and yet they have done it themselves.*'

It has been related further that on the same day the madman forced his way into several churches and there struck up his *requiem aeternam deo.* Led out and called to account, he is said always to have replied nothing but: 'What after all are these churches now if they are not the tombs and sepulchers of God?'"[17]

---

[17]Friedrich Nietzsche, *The Gay Science, The Portable Nietzsche*, Walter Kaufmann, Editor. New York (Penguin Books, 1982) 95-96.

Wow! Nietzsche powerfully captures the dramatic implications of atheistic thought on human civilization. His words are prophetic of the increasingly secular nature of society and the corrupting influence of atheistic naturalism on every area of our lives.

Nietzsche deserves credit for so profoundly describing what is at place in the question of the existence of God. Nevertheless, that God is dead is reminiscent of Mark Twain's quip that "the reports of my death are greatly exaggerated" and how much more is that true of the living God. At least, that is what I hope to defend here.

It may be that for all his philosophical bravado, Nietzsche may have personally struggled with the question of the existence of God, as a letter to his sister seems to indicate:

> "But what if God lives, and I have doomed myself to destruction because I have separated myself from Him?"[18]

Perhaps Nietzsche is a microcosm of modern-man, having developed critical arguments against the belief in God, yet, unable to shake the belief from one's own soul, or from the culture in general. Indeed, the atheist Victor Stenger is perplexed at the continued belief in God:

> "What is amazing is that in this sophisticated modern-age so many still cling to primitive, archaic images from the childhood of humanity."[19]

---

[18]*Random House Webster's Quotationary*, Leonard Roy Frank, Editor, New York (Random House, 2001) 49.

[19]Victor J. Stenger, *God: The Failed Hypothesis, How Science Shows That God Does Not Exist*, Amherst New York (Prometheus Books, 2007) 40.

Perhaps, this should tell Stenger that the arguments for God's existence are more compelling that he is willing to face. That is the testimony of Francis Collins, one of the great scientists of our age, who directed the Human Genome Project: "At the same time, I had reached the conclusion that faith in God was much more compelling than the atheism I have previously embraced."[20]

Charles Guignon and Derk Pereboom described not only Nietzsche's, but really the secular view of life in general with these words:

> "They were able to embrace life on its own terms, with its ceaseless ebb and flow, its risks and uncertainties, and they did so with neither nostalgia for a Garden that never was nor fantasies about a future that can never be."[21]

Socrates' challenge to explore ultimate truth

One thing is clear; many keep themselves so busy that they have little time to reflect upon the more philosophical or spiritual questions of life. I plead with the reader to consider well the words of Socrates (as reported by Plato) as he reflected upon the meaning of life in the face of his impending death sentence:

> "Men of Athens, I honour and love you; but I shall obey God rather than you, and while I have life and strength I shall never cease from the practice and teaching of philosophy, exhorting any one whom I meet and saying to him after my manner: You my friend—a citizen of the

---

[20]Francis S. Collins, *The Language of God: A Scientist Presents Evidence for Belief,* New York (Free Press, 2006) 198.

[21] Charles Guignon and Derk Pereboom, *Existentialism: Basic Writings,* Second Edition, Indianapolis IN (Hackett Publishing Company, Inc, 2001) 100.

great and mighty Athens—are you not ashamed of heaping up the greatest amount of money and honour and reputation, and caring so little about wisdom and truth and the greatest improvement of the soul."[22]

So, Socrates admonished us to seriously consider life's most profound questions; to live the examined life. Further, he calls us to do so with humility:

"I went to one who had the reputation of wisdom, and observed him . . . and the results were as follows. When I began to talk with him, I could not help thinking that he was not really so wise, although he was thought wise by many, *and still wiser by himself,* and thereupon I tried to explain to him that he thought himself wise; and the consequence was that he hated me . . . So I left him, saying to myself, as I went away: Well . . . I am better off than he is, --for he knows nothing, and thinks that he knows: I neither know nor think that I know. In this latter particular, then, I seem to have slightly the advantage of him."[23]

In other words, humility, friend, humility, and I with you.

And with my criticisms of atheism, I do not seek to be offensive, but rather, to recall the words of Socrates (as told by Plato) concerning those that opposed him: "And what is their hatred but a proof that I am speaking the truth."[24] The apostle Paul echoed the same sentiment:

---

[22]Socrates, as quoted by Plato, *Dialogues of Plato*, trans. Benjamin Jowett, Oxford, 1896, as cited by Louis P. Pojman, *Philosophy: The Quest for Truth*, Sixth Edition, New York. Oxford (Oxford University Press, 2006) 13.

[23]Samuel Enoch Stumpf, *Philosophy: History & Problems*, Fourth Edition, New York (McGraw-Hill Publishing Company, 1989) 534.

[24]Samuel Enoch Stumpf, *Philosophy: History & Problems*, 536.

"Have I now become your enemy by telling you the truth?"(Galatians 4:16).

Again, as Socrates faced death, he persevered for truth rather than conform to the accepted wisdom of the day, the Zeitgeist if you will: "Men of Athens, I honour and love you; but I shall obey God rather than you."[25] And this was the same sentiment of the early apostles of Christ who in the face of death, persevered in the truth:"

"But Peter and John replied, 'Judge for yourselves whether it is right in God's sight to obey you rather than God. For we cannot help speaking about what we have seen and heard'" (Acts 4:19-20, see also Acts 5:29).

The Existential cry

And, by the way, if one day you happen to wake up and find yourself in an existential quandary full of loathing and self-doubt and wracked with the pain and isolation of your pitiful meaningless existence, at least you can take a small bit of comfort in knowing that somewhere out there in this crazy mixed-up universe of ours there's still a little place called Albuquerque![26]

---

[25]Samuel Enoch Stumpf, *Philosophy: History & Problems*, 540.
[26]"Weird Al Yankovic, *Albuquerque*, from the album *Running with Scissors*, 1999.

Weird Al Yankovic/Albuquerque

I want to acknowledge my appreciation for the thoughts of the existentialist philosophers concerning the quandary we all face as humans. None of us asked to be born, or were given a choice concerning the circumstances of our lives. We feel the great power of Martin Heidegger's description of "throwness;" the idea that we find ourselves simply thrown into the world, transient, struggling with the meaning of existence, and facing our own death.[27]

Sartre traced this angst to atheism itself:

> "When we speak of forlornness, a term Heidegger was fond of, we mean only that God does not exist and we have to face the consequences of this."[28]

Walters described the naturalist/existentialist position:

> "As naturalists, they more soberly believe the human condition devoid of any overarching, intrinsic meaning . . . Having rejected the traditional religious model, they must find energy and motive for getting through the day and strength to bear the silence of the heavens and the post-mortem annihilation they believe awaits them."[29]

The Doors captured this idea in song:

---

[27]Samuel Enoch Stumpf, *Philosophy: History & Problems*, 497.

[28]Jean-Paul Sartre, *Existentialism and Human Emotions*, New York, Philosophical Library, 1957, pp. 21-23, as quoted by Theodore C. Denise, Nicholas P. White & Sheldon P. Peterfreund, *Great Traditions in Ethics*, Tenth Edition, Belmont CA (Wadsworth Thomson Learning, 2002) 283.

[29]Kerry Walters, *Atheism: A Guide for the Perplexed*, 138-139.

"Riders on the storm. Into this world we're born. Into this world were thrown, like a dog without a bone. An actor out on loan. Riders on the storm."

Martin described the pessimistic outlook of Camus:

"Albert Camus maintained . . . the absurdity of human existence . . . For many people this absurdity is too much to bear; some try to escape by physical suicide and some commit what Camus calls philosophical suicide in which by a leap of faith one assumes, despite the evidence, that the universe is rational and unified. Camus argues that such escapes are dishonest and unauthentic. One must live one's life with the full realization that human existence is absurd, in defiance of the universe, to which one is unreconciled."[30]

So Camus considered a religious leap of faith philosophical suicide. But why should this be so? It seems that Camus has no philosophical place to stand in which to judge as inauthentic those who find meaning in religious faith. On what objective ground or basis can he condemn God belief if the world is absurd to begin with?

But wither do we go? How do we face this existential quandary? Many simply seek to evade the reality; to stay busy enough, or doped up enough, to ignore the burning questions at the deepest levels of our being. Such people will most likely be uninterested in this work. However, it is my fervent hope that we can at least consider the great thoughts of the great thinkers on the question of God's existence.

The reality is that we do exist. We have come into this world without a label and directions attached to us, and

---

[30]Michael Martin, *Atheism: A Philosophical Justification,* Philadelphia PA (Temple University Press, 1990) 17-18

we are trying to make sense of it all. It is our contention that, in fact, there is something like an owner's manual that comes with your car, for the human race, and that is the Bible. It provides us with the answers to our deepest questions: where did we come from?; why are we here?; what should we do with our lives?; and is there an afterlife?

Chapter 2: Varieties of Belief and Unbelief

When it comes to the question of God, we can easily think in terms of *believers and unbelievers*. But as we dig a bit deeper, we find that there is a spectrum of ideas on the subject. On one end, there are those who have been described as the hard or true believers all the way down to hard or true unbelievers or atheists, and everything in between.

Deism

Deism, popular during the enlightenment period, is the idea that God created the world, and largely leaves it to itself. While accepting many traditional religious beliefs and ethical values, it tends to reject miracles (aside from creation) and supernatural revelation. "As Diderot once quipped, a deist is someone who has not lived long enough to become an atheist."[31]

Agnosticism

Then there are those who take the *agnostic* position, a term coined by Huxley for those undecided concerning the existence of God. Steele said of agnosticism:

"'Agnostic' is a word deliberately invented by T. H. Huxley in 1869 to refer to anyone who, like Huxley himself, had no belief in God but was not prepared to deny God's existence. Prior to that date all 'agnostics' had been recognized as atheists . . . To the Victorian ear, 'agnostic' sounded a lot less threatening and more respectable than 'atheist' . . . Recently some people have started using the term 'nontheist' to cover both those who merely fail to

---

[31]Walter Isaacson, *Benjamin Franklin: An American Life,* New York (Simon& Schuster Paperbacks, 2003) 85.

believe in God's existence and those who believe in God's nonexistence."[32]

Agnostics can also be distinguished between a *soft agnosticism* in which the person simply doesn't *yet* know whether God exists (hasn't sufficiently thought through or researched the issue) in contrast to *hard agnosticism* in which the person claims that there is simply insufficient evidence to know decisively whether God exists.

Winfried Corduan explained this difference in slightly different terms:

> "We need to distinguish between *benign* and *malignant* agnosticism. At a certain point in our lives we say honestly that we do not know if there is a God . . . This is *benign agnosticism.* What concerns us here, however, is agnosticism as a dogmatic worldview based on the premise that *we cannot know* if there is a God. This version is malignant agnosticism . . .It is tantamount to saying that we cannot prove atheism to be true, but that we will assume that it is true . . . Thus agnosticism becomes atheism in the guise of epistemological humility."[33]

On the other hand, the skeptic Clarence Darrow was quite willing to take the title:

> "I do not consider it an insult, but rather a compliment to be called an agnostic. I do not pretend to know where many ignorant men are sure—that is all that agnosticism means."[34]

---

[32]David Ramsay Steele, *Atheism Explained: From Folly to Philosophy*, Chicago and La Salle, IL (Open Court Publishing Company, 2008) 17.

[33]Winfried Corduan, *No Doubt About It: The Case for Christianity*, Nashville TN (Broadman & Holman Publishers, 1997) 88-89.

[34]Clarence Darrow, as quoted in *Random House Webster's Quotationary*, Leonard Roy Frank, Editor, New York (Random

Critics of agnosticism

In a stinging attack, Karl Marx said that 'an agnostic is nothing but a gutless atheist.'[35] The atheist David Mills agreed:

> **"Interviewer:** What's the difference between an *atheist* and an *agnostic*? **Mills:** The words atheist and agnostic have totally disparate origins. But the real answer to your question is guts."[36]

Likewise, Robert Frost quipped: "Don't be an agnostic—be something."[37]

Francis Collins said of agnosticism:

> "There are all kinds of agnostics; some arrive at this position after intense analysis of the evidence, but many others simply find it to be a comfortable position that allows them to avoid considering arguments they find discomforting on either side."[38]

In a similar vein, Yeager Hudson described why some embrace agnosticism:

> "Agnosticism is sometimes adopted by persons who do not want to take the trouble to think about their beliefs or to engage in the mental labor required to work out a rationally supported position. Of course, theism or atheism may also be embraced lazily and without thoughtful reflection."[39]

House, 2001) 22.

[35] Karl Marx, as quoted by Norman L. Geisler, *Baker Encyclopedia of Christian Apologetics*, Grand Rapids MI (Baker Books, 1999) 676.

[36] David Mills, *Atheist Universe: The Thinking Person's Answer to Christian Fundamentalism*, Berkeley CA (Ulysses Press, 2006) 26.

[37] Robert Frost, *20,000 Quips & Quotes*, Evan Esar, Editor, New York (Barnes & Noble Books, 1995) 20.

[38] Francis S. Collins, *The Language of God: A Scientist Presents Evidence for Belief*, New York (Free Press, 2006) 16.

The atheist Michael Scriven was also critical of the unreflective agnostic position:

"In practice, an agnostic's position is often the product of an untidy mixture of factors. He may never have happened to come across an argument for either theism or atheism which struck him as compelling; a rough head counting has revealed intelligent people on either side; his nose for social stigmas indicates a slight odor of intellectual deficiency attached to theism by contemporary intellectuals and a suggestions of unnecessary boat rocking or perhaps rabid subversion attached to atheism. This makes the agnostic fence look pretty attractive; so up he climbs, to sit on top. But now we put the challenge to him. Is he incapable of thinking out an answer for himself? If so, he is intellectually inferior to those below; if not, he must descend and demonstrate the failings of the contestants before he is entitled to his perch. Agnosticism as a position is interesting and debatable; agnosticism as the absence of a position is simply a sign of the absence of intellectual activity or capacity."[40]

In the movie the *Life of Pi,* Yann Martel wrote:

"Doubt is useful for a while . . . But we must move on. To choose doubt as a philosophy of life is akin to choosing immobility as a means of transportation."[41]

---

[39]Yeager Hudson, *The Philosophy of Religion,* Mountain View CA (Mayfield Publishing Company, 1991) 163.

[40]Michael Scriven, *God and Reason,* chapter in *Critiques of God: Making the Case Against Belief in God,* Peter A. Angeles, Editor, Amherst New York (Prometheus Books, 1997)110.

[41]Yann Martel, *Life of PI,* as quoted by Sean McDowell & Jonathan Morrow, *Is God Just a Human Invention? And Seventeen Other Questions Raised by the New Atheists,* Grand Rapids MI (Kregel Publications, 2010) 121.

The agnostic's prayer

It is interesting how many agnostics have offered a similar prayer that can perhaps be known as the agnostic's prayer. For instance, Frederick II said: "O God, if there is a God, have pity on my soul, if there is a soul."[42] Or the similar prayer offered by Joseph Ernest Renan: "O Lord, if there is a Lord, save my soul, if I have a soul."[43] Or again, Voltaire who said, "May God, if there is one, save my soul, if I have one."[44]

Menssen and Sullivan made reference to another agnostic prayer:

> "But many inquiring agnostics have already read some Scripture, and, in the manner of the young Charles Ryder in Brideshead Revisited, have mustered the kinds of prayers of which an agnostic is capable ('O God, if there is a God, show me the truth of this gospel, if it is true')."[45]

Types of atheists

Next, then, are the *atheists*. The *soft atheist* doesn't believe in God and finds the evidence for God's existence unconvincing. Then there are the *hard atheists* who not only deny God's existence, but believe that it can be

[42] Frederick II, *Random House Webster's Quotationary*, Leonard Roy Frank, Editor, New York (Random House, 2001) 22.

[43] Joseph Ernest Renan, as quoted in *The Concise Columbia Dictionary of Quotations*, Robert Andrews, Editor, New York (Columbia University Press, 1989) 8.

[44] Voltaire, as quoted by Norman L. Geisler, *Baker Encyclopedia of Christian Apologetics*, 765.

[45] Sandra Menssen & Thomas D. Sullivan, *The Agnostic Inquirer: Revelation from a Philosophical Standpoint*, Grand Rapids MI (William B. Eerdmans Publishing Company, 2007, 9-10.

proven that God doesn't exist, and that such belief is irrational.

Kerry Walters spoke of the "Varieties of Nonbelief"[46] and classified atheist thusly:

> "Overt disbelief or atheism which can be further subdivided into (a) *positive* atheism, an active disbelief in God and (b) *negative* atheism, the absence of belief in God . . . Both positive and negative atheism may be further subdivided into (i) militant and (ii) moderate varieties. Militant atheists . . . tend to think that God-belief is not only erroneous but pernicious . . . Moderate atheists agree that God-belief is unjustifiable, but see nothing inherently pernicious in it."[47]

Julian Baggini further described *militant* atheism:

> "Atheism which is actively hostile to religion I would call militant. To be hostile in this sense requires more than just strong disagreement with religion—it requires something verging on hatred and is characterized by a desire to wipe out all forms of religious belief. Militant atheists tend to make one or both of two claims that moderate atheists do not. The first is that religion is demonstrably false or nonsense, and the second is that it is usually or always harmful."[48]

The new atheists

One expression of the more militant type of atheism is a contemporary movement that has come to be known as "the new atheism" which Roy Varghese described:

---

[46]Kerry Walters, *Atheism: A Guide for the Perplexed*, New York (The Continuum International Publishing Group Inc, 2010) 11.
[47]Kerry Walters, *Atheism,* 12.
[48]Julian Baggini, *Atheism,* New York (Sterling, 2003) 150.

"In the light of this historical progression, the sudden emergence of what has been called the 'new atheism' is of particular interest. The year of the 'new atheism' was 2006 (the phrase was first used by *Wired* magazine in November 2006). From Daniel Dennett's *Breaking the Spell* and Richard Dawkins's *The God Delusion* to Lewis Wolpert's *Six Impossible Things Before Breakfast,* Victor Stenger's *The Comprehensible Cosmos,* and Sam Harris's *The End of Faith* (published in 2004, but the sequel to which, *Letter to a Christian Nation,* came out in 2006), the exponents of a look-back-in-anger, take-no-prisoners type of atheism were out in force . . . The chief target of these books is, without question, organized religion of any kind, time, or place. Paradoxically, the books themselves read like fundamentalist sermons. The authors, for the most part, sound like hellfire-and-brimstone preachers warning us of dire retribution, even of apocalypse, if we do not repent of our wayward beliefs and associated practices. There is no room for ambiguity or subtlety. It's black and white. Either you are with us all the way or one with the enemy. Even eminent thinkers who express some sympathy for the other side are denounced as traitors. The evangelists themselves are courageous souls preaching their message in the face of martyrdom."[49]

Varghese's summed up his assessment of the new atheists:

"It would be fair to say that the 'new atheism' is nothing less than a regression to the logical positivist philosophy that was renounced by even its most ardent proponents."[50]

---

[49]Roy Abraham Varghese, *Preface* p. 16-17 in Antony Flew, *There is a God: How the World's Most Notorious Atheist Changed His Mind,* New York (HarperCollins/HarperOne, 2007)
[50]Roy Abraham Varghese, *Preface* p. 18.

Positive/Negative atheists

David Eller spoke of positive and negative atheists (distinctions he personally rejected):

> "There are two versions or 'degrees' of Atheism, commonly referred to as 'positive' and 'negative' or 'strong' and 'weak' or 'explicit' and 'implicit' . . . The divergence between the two positions in each set is presumably based on whether the Atheist is making a claim or merely refuting a claim . . . Michael Martin, in his *Atheism: A Philosophical Justification,* develops this theme . . . For him, negative Atheists 'are not making any claim to knowledge and the believers are,' and when believers present their reasons and arguments for the existence of God, negative Atheists 'must show that these reasons and arguments are inadequate.'"[51]

The distinction then, seems to be, that a positive atheist makes a positive claim; they can show (or prove) that God does not exist. In contrast, negative atheists merely deny the positive claim of theists that God exists. David Steele referred to those who claim to show that God does not exist (positive atheists) as "disproof atheists"[52] because they have claimed to have *disproven* God's existence.

Implicit/Explicit (or Critical) atheism

George Smith described another distinction among atheists labeling them as implicit and explicit atheism:

> "Atheism may be divided into two broad categories: implicit and explicit. (a) Implicit atheism is the absence of theistic belief without a conscious rejection of it. (b)

---

[51]David Eller, *Natural Atheism*, Cranford New Jersey (American Atheist Press, 2004) 153-154.
[52]David Ramsay Steele, *Atheism Explained,* 17.

Explicit atheism is the absence of theistic belief due to a conscious rejection of it . . . The most significant variety of atheism is explicit atheism of a philosophical nature. This atheism contends that the belief in god is irrational and should therefore be rejected. Since this version of explicit atheism rests on a criticism of theistic beliefs, it is best described as *critical atheism*."[53]

Practical atheists

Then there are the *practical atheists* who though they don't put much thought to speculations about God's existence, nevertheless, *live as though God doesn't exist*, having no place for such concerns in their day to day lives.

Walters gave a similar description:

"Finally, both atheism and agnosticism may be (a) practical, a (frequently uncritical) working assumption of nonbelief that undergirds one's worldview and everyday living; or (b) philosophical, a reflective, intellectually justified nonbelief. Obviously any given nonbeliever's position may be both practical and philosophical."[54]

Likewise, Orlo Strunk, Jr. stated:

"Practical atheism is used here to describe a form of unbelief which is characterized by drift and apathy. It refers to that very large group of people who would never admit to being an atheist but who nevertheless live their individual lives without any meaningful reference to God."[55]

---

[53]George H. Smith, *Atheism: The Case Against God,* Amherst NY (Prometheus Books, 1979, 1989) 13, 17.

[54]Kerry Walters, *Atheism,* 12.

[55]Orlo Strunk, Jr., *The Choice Called Atheism: Confronting the Claims of Modern Unbelief,* Nashville TN (Abingdon Press, 1968)108.

Nominal atheism/anonymous theist

Michael Barnes described what the Roman Catholic theologian Karl Rahner called *nominal atheism:*

> "Nominal atheism. This is the situation of a person who says that all things are part of an ultimate meaninglessness, but who makes this an atheism in name only, Rahner claims, by living deliberately and uncritically, as though life were actually meaningful after all, showing this dedication to values of friendship and family, by courage in the face of bigotry, by endurance in the face of the burden of caring for someone who is alone. If all things are really part of ultimate meaninglessness, such heroic acts of love and courage are at least logically foolish. They will mean nothing in the end, will be swallowed up in the aimless dark eventually. But such atheists live as though they have an implicit faith that being a person in this universe is ultimately meaningful. They act like anonymous theists."[56]

Post-atheism

Alister McGrath called attention to post-atheism:

> "Everywhere there are signs that atheism is losing its appeal . . . The term 'post-atheist' is now widely used to designate the collapse of atheism as a worldview in Eastern Europe and the resurgence of religious belief throughout many of those areas that had once been considered officially atheist."[57]

---

[56]Michael Horace Barnes, *Understanding Religion and Science: Introducing the Debate*, New York (Continuum International Publishing Group, 2010) 101.

[57]Alister McGrath, *The Twilight of Atheism: The Rise and Fall of Disbelief in the Modern World,* New York (Doubleday, 2004) 174.

Crypto-atheism

David Eller defined crypto-atheism as: "Atheists who hide or deny their Atheism."[58] Indeed, Eller is sure that there is a social price to pay for being an atheist in modern America:

> "Some 'freethinkers' or 'agnostics' or 'humanists' prefer those terms to 'Atheist' because of the stigma attached to the latter. I more than understand that stigma of Atheism . . . Theists . . . believe that we are evil, immoral, licentious, unpatriotic, satanic . . . criminal, and other pejorative terms like that."[59]

Lest Eller be unaware, I assure him that Christians are also targets of more than their fair share of "pejorative terms" and persecution.

Is everyone an atheist?

Christopher Hitchens cited Richard Dawkins' idea that everyone is an atheist of some kind:

> "Richard Dawkins may have phrased it most pungently when he argued that everybody is an atheist in saying that there is a god--from Ra to Shiva—in which he does not believe. All that the serious and objective atheist does is to take the next step and to say that there is just one more god to disbelieve in."[60]

David Eller made a similar claim: "All humans are born atheists."[61] Eller suggests that all men are born

---

[58]David Eller, *Natural Atheism*, 15-16.
[59]David Eller, *Natural Atheism*, 15-16.
[60]Christopher Hitchens, *The Portable Atheist: Essential Readings for the Nonbeliever*, Philadelphia PA (De Capo Press, 2007) Introduction 20.
[61]David Eller, *Natural Atheism*, 11.

atheists or what he calls "natural atheists" and that religion is imposed upon children as a part of cultural conditioning.

Born-again and/ or recovered atheists

Eller also used the ironic label of born-again atheists:

"It is presumable that most Atheists are not natural Atheists but 'born-again' Atheists—people who have been through the conversion experience and who have 'deconverted' or 'reconverted' back to their original Atheism . . . because of the experiences that have transpired in the life of the recovered Atheist. Above all, the recovered Atheist is a former Theist."[62]

Eller acknowledged that such "born-again atheists" often have paid an emotional price as a consequence of their *deconversions:*

"Born-again Atheists possess an intimate knowledge of religion from the inside, but the price of that knowledge is often an anger or bitterness toward those who indoctrinated them and the doctrines they were coerced to conform to."[63]

Angry atheists?

The author was once given the opportunity to make an unexpected and impromptu speech at a gathering of atheists in Minnesota. In the midst of my stream of consciousness talk I made the observation that many of the atheists seemed to be angry, negative, and on the attack. What's more, I said, it seemed as if many were angry at the God they claimed didn't exist.

---

[62]David Eller, *Natural Atheism*, 12.
[63]David Eller, *Natural Atheism*, 12.

C. S. Lewis noted this theme:

"Even atheists rebel and express, like Hardy and Housman, their rage against God although (or because) He does not, in their view exist."[64]

James Thrower, likewise, captured this idea as he described the experience of Jean Meslier:

"Such was the renegade priest Jean Meslier, cure of Etrepigny in Champagne, who died in 1729, leaving behind a testament not only to his atheism but to his bitter hatred of religions as the source of all the troubles of mankind and the perpetrator of its cruelest joke. He it was who said that the ills of which beset men would not be cured until 'the last king has been strangled in the entrails of the last priest' . . . In his cooler moments, however, he realized that the monster-God that he railed against could not in fact exist—a fact which depressed him as it would appear later to have saddened and depressed John Stuart Mill and Bertrand Russell, taking the sting out of their rebellious stand. Promethean defiance was not something that accorded with reason."[65]

Robert Morey agreed:

"Is it any wonder then that the modern atheists' champion is Prometheus who said 'I hate all the gods,' who said he would rather suffer death than be the servant of the gods. Prometheus did not deny that the gods existed. His was the rebel cry."[66]

---

[64] C. S. Lewis, *The Problem of Pain: The Intellectual Problem Raised by Human Suffering, Examined with Sympathy and Realism*, New York (Macmillan Publishing Company, 1962) 95.

[65] James Thrower, *Western Atheism: A Short History*, Amherst NY (Prometheus Books, 2000) 100.

[66] Robert A. Morey, *The New Atheism and the Erosion of Freedom*,

Morey further described the anger that is often displayed among atheists:

> "Anyone who reads its literature or debates its leaders finds that modern Anti-theism is fueled by such ignoble motives as bitterness, rage, and hatred. Its spokesman manifest an angry spirit which rages first against God and then . . . . against those who dare believe in Him."[67]

Novelist George Orwell described just such atheists:

> "He was an embittered atheist (the sort of atheist who does not so much disbelieve in God as personally dislikes Him)."[68]

And again, Heywood Broun stated ironically that: "Nobody talks so constantly about God as those who insist that there is no God."[69]

Non-realist theism

C. S. Rodd described a form of theism that is really a form of atheism:

> "Writers like Anthony Freeman are absolutely convinced that living our lives in a good, truthful, and loving way is of supreme value. All the religions, they believe, are human creations—sets of ideas that human beings have devised and ways of life that the saints have practiced. And because they are of supreme value, *they function for us as God*. This is sometimes *called a 'non-realist view of God*, because it does not accept a God who

---

Minneapolis MN (Bethany House Publishers, 1986) 26.

[67]Robert A. Morey, *The New Atheism*, 27.

[68]George Orwell, *Down and Out in Paris and London*, as quoted by *The Macmillan Dictionary of Quotations*, John Daintith, Editor, New York (Macmillan Publishing Company, 1989) 34.

[69]Joseph Ernest Renan, as quoted in *The Concise Columbia Dictionary of Quotations*, Robert Andrews, Editor, New York (Columbia University Press, 1989) 22.

'really exists,' but nevertheless retains the conviction that the virtues which have been associated with religion in the past are of supreme value."[70]

This is a good description of many of the more liberal-leaning churches of Christendom.

Is atheism a "religion"?

Eller raised the perhaps surprising claim that atheism can, at least in practice, be a religion:

> "There are those, for instance, who maintain that Atheism is a belief system too or even a religion . . . Some critics, and even some Atheists, say that Atheism is a religion and/or that Atheists are religious. That depends on your definition of religion. I know people—even intelligent, liberal people—who define religion as anything you feel strongly about."[71]

Eller rejected the claim that atheism is a religion, and strictly speaking, he is correct since there is no divine being worshipped. Nevertheless, religion has often been defined as that which is your highest or ultimate belief, and in that sense, the claim holds some merit, especially for those of a more militant atheistic stance.

Jacques Maritain made the same assertion:

> "Absolute atheism starts in an act of faith in reverse gear and is a full-blown religious commitment. Here we have the first internal inconsistency of contemporary atheism: it proclaims that all religion must necessarily vanish away, and it is itself a religious phenomenon."[72]

---

[70]C.S. Rodd, *Is There a God?* From the *Thinking Things Through* series, no. 9, Peterborough (Epworth Press, 2002) 73-74.

[71]David Eller, *Natural Atheism*, 13-14.

[72]Jacques Maritain, *The Range of Reason*, as quoted in *The Great Quotations*, Compiled by George Seldes, Secaucus NJ (Castle Books, 1978) 467.

Dawkins' spectrum of belief

Richard Dawkins provided a helpful summary of the spectrum of seven types of belief/unbelief concerning God:

"1. Strong theist. 100 per cent probability of God. In the words of C. G. Jung, 'I do not believe, I *know.*' 2. Very high probability but short of 100 per cent. *De facto* theist. 'I cannot know for certain, but I strongly believe in God and live my life on the assumption that he is there.' 3. Higher than 50 per cent but not very high. Technically agnostic but leaning towards theism. 'I am very uncertain, but I am inclined to believe in God.' 4. Lower than 50 per cent. Completely impartial agnostic. 'God's existence and non-existence are exactly equiprobable.' 5. Lower than 50 per cent but not very low. Technically agnostic but leaning toward atheism. 'I don't know whether God exists but I'm inclined to be skeptical.' 6. Very low probability, but short of zero. *De facto* atheist. 'I cannot know for certain but I think God is very improbable, and I live my life on the assumption that he is not there.' 7. Strong atheist. 'I know there is no God, with the same conviction as Jung 'knows' there is one.'"[73]

People change, ideas change

As we close this section on the varieties of belief and unbelief, we should keep in mind that it is not unusual for a person to change their minds about their beliefs. Sometimes preachers reject their faith and become notorious atheists (Dan Barker) and sometimes leading atheist thinkers (Antony Flew) become believers.

Part of being a human is to grow and mature. For some, that may mean dropping childhood or family values in the face of new ideas and new experiences. At

---

[73]Richard Dawkins, *The God Delusion*, New York (Houghton Mifflin Company, 2006) 50-51.

other times, it may mean reconsidering the hard skepticism one had adopted in response to painful experiences in the past.

Such was the personal experience of my own father as he reflected upon the battles he had wrestled with:

> "I think I owe a great deal to God or my higher power as I was one who said I did not believe in God. Well, when you say there is no God, and then you find through a lot of different things that there is, you wonder, will he accept me back? And you find He does, you certainly must be grateful that He is a merciful God, and that He does love all of us."[74]

Part of growing, then, is to be open to the possibility that we have been wrong. It requires a great act of courage to change our ideas, especially in an area so closely impacting our identity as persons. If you are a believer, you owe it to yourself to examine the basis of your beliefs. Do they hold up to examination?

If you have rejected faith in God, you also owe it to yourself, and to all those with whom you will have influence, to examine the basis of your beliefs. Let us strive to have beliefs that have been rigorously tested. In the spirit, of Socrates, let us strive toward the examined life and with Jesus, let us strive toward the way, the truth, and the life (John 14:6).

---

[74]Robert Earl Lagoon, Sr., From a speech given at Hazelton Treatment Center, 1971

Chapter 3: Truth, the Burden of Proof, and the Preponderance of the Evidence

Is absolute proof for God's existence to be expected?

The fact is that the existence of God can neither be logically or philosophically proved nor disproved. The atheist Keith M. Parsons agreed with the Christian theologian Alister McGrath:

> "McGrath is certainly right to assert that neither the theist nor the atheist has conclusive arguments: 'Knockdown and foolproof arguments are simply not available to us.'"[75]

Therefore, we offer the more modest proposal that there are powerful reasons to believe in the existence of God; that the preponderance of the evidence tilts strongly in favor of God belief over atheism. The history of philosophy shows that it is possible to deny virtually anything, no matter how strong the case for it may be.

William C. Davis, a theist, said:

> "Belief in God, like *any* belief, is rationally avoidable, and a determined skeptic will always be able to find a reason—even if somewhat implausible— for persisting in unbelief."[76]

---

[75]Keith M. Parsons, *Atheism: Twilight or Dawn*, chapter in *The Future of Atheism: Alister McGrath & Daniel Dennett in Dialogue*, Robert B. Stewart, Editor, Minneapolis MN (Fortress Press, 2008) 58.

[76] William C. Davis, *Theistic Arguments*, Chapter in *Reasons for the Hope Within*, Michael J. Murray Editor, Grand Rapids MI (William B. Eerdman's Publishing Company, 1999) 21.

Kai Nielsen, an atheist agreed, and stated concerning philosophical discussions:

> "There is nothing that can be established to be absolutely true . . . This is our inescapable situation and we should just learn to live with it and not go on the illusory quest for certainty."[77]

Virtually every proposition imaginable has been subjected to criticism, and therefore, the quest for truth should be about determining among options which has the strongest case.

The atheist Julian Baggini made the same essential point:

> "We tend to think that the mere introduction of grounds for doubt is enough to warrant the suspension of our beliefs. If you can't be sure, don't have an opinion. But this maxim cannot be followed. We cannot be absolutely sure of anything, save perhaps our own existence . . . It does not follow from the fact that we could be wrong that we have no good reasons to think we are right."[78]

One can choose to be a radical skeptic denying whatever he or she chooses. But that has nothing to do with *what, in fact, is true.*

In the same way, while God's existence cannot be proven with absolute certainty, nevertheless, the weight of the evidence is more than sufficient for a man to believe and indeed to act upon it in his life.

Kerry Walters elaborated on the idea:

[77]Kai Nielsen, *Atheism & Philosophy,* Amherst NY (Prometheus Books, 2005) 21, 35.
[78]Julian Baggini, *Atheism,* New York (Sterling, 2003) 37-38

"Strictly speaking, most [proofs of God's existence] aren't proofs at all, if by 'proof' one means an argument which aims to establish its conclusion beyond a shadow of doubt. Instead, most of the arguments aim more modestly to show that belief in God is consistent with reason and everyday experience . . . This point is important to keep in mind, because arguments for God's existence are frequently criticized by opponents for failing to 'prove' their conclusions. But this is an unfair charge. Such arguments should be evaluated in terms of how strong a case they can make rather than held up to an unreasonably rigorous standard of proof."[79]

Antony Flew made the same point:

"Then there is the charge that in philosophy it is never possible to prove to someone that you are right and he or she is wrong. But the missing piece in this argument is the distinction between producing a proof and persuading a person. A person can be persuaded by an abominable argument and remain unconvinced by one that ought to be accepted."[80]

So let it be clear. We do not claim to have absolute and undeniable proof that God exists. Nor do atheists have such proofs for their cause. Bertrand Russell acknowledged this, stating: "I do not pretend to be able to prove there is no God."[81] Even Dawkins agreed that the standard for the debate concerning God's existence was not certainty but probability:

[79]Kerry Walters, *Atheism: A Guide for the Perplexed*, New York (The Continuum International Publishing Group Inc, 2010) 55-56.

[80]Antony Flew, *There is a God: How the World's Most Notorious Atheist Changed His Mind*, New York (HarperCollins/HarperOne, 2007) 41.

[81]Bertrand Russell, as quoted by S. T. Josh, *The Unbelievers: The Evolution of Modern Atheism*, Amherst NY (Prometheus Books, 2011) 157.

"What matters is not whether God is disprovable (he isn't) but whether his existence is *probable.*"[82]

In the end, and again, this is true for atheists as well as believers, there necessarily remains an element of faith. And so, the writer of the book of Hebrews stated: "Now faith is being sure of what we hope for, and certain of what we do not see" (Hebrews 11:1).

The burden of proof

Some atheists have argued that the burden of proof in the debate about God's existence is upon the believer. Baggini stated: "Hence the onus is on the non-atheist, not to demand an explanation from the atheist."[83] Richard Dawkins noted Bertrand Russell's agreement: "Russell's point is that the burden of proof rests with the believers, not the non-believers."[84]

Now, in one sense, I agree. Believers are arguing for belief in something of which there is no direct evidence. You could even say that belief in God is *non-sense* in the sense that God cannot be perceived *by our senses.* No one can make a quick dash to heaven to verify God's existence. Therefore, during our brief sojourn on earth, we must make our judgments about God's existence based upon indirect evidence, logic, reason, and faith.

The atheist Sam Harris stated: "Religion is the one area of our discourse where it is considered noble to

---

[82]Richard Dawkins, *The God Delusion*, 54.
[83]Julian Baggini, *Atheism,* 31-32.
[84]Richard Dawkins, *The God Delusion*, New York (Houghton Mifflin Company, 2006) 53.

pretend to be certain about things no human could possibly be certain about."[85] I agree with Harris that a phony bravado concerning God's existence is unhelpful, but that works both ways!

In that regard, I appreciate Kai Nielsen's candid 'confession' that "even a hard-bitten old atheist like me may sometimes feel the urge to pray that his friend dying in agony need not suffer so."[86] I must confess that when atheists, Kai Nielsen notwithstanding, claim that they never have doubts, I doubt their claims. I suspect that they are either lying to themselves, embarrassed to confess their doubts, or worried they may hurt their cause.

The burden of proof is to all who love truth

Ultimately, therefore, the burden of proof should lie not with the atheist or the believer, but with everyone who loves truth. Both positions should be weighed on their own merits.

I appreciate Kerry Walters' fair assessment:

"So it seems more economical for both the atheist and the theist to cease worrying about which one carries the heaviest burden of proof and to get on with making the best case for their positions that they can. The goal, after all, isn't to score points in a debate, although this is something that apologists on both sides often forget."[87]

The atheist David Steele agreed with this approach:

[85]Sam Harris, *Letter to a Christian Nation*, New York (Alfred A. Knopf, 2006) 67.
[86]Kai Nielsen, *Atheism & Philosophy*, 38.
[87]Kerry Walters, *Atheism: A Guide*, 24.

"Both theists and atheists often assert that, on some particular point, their opponents have 'the burden proof.' I think that making any such claim, in this context is a mistake . . . I can seen no place for it in discussion of a factual question like the existence of God."[88]

Standards of evidence necessary in a courtroom

I take exception to the way Baggini characterized the Christian position:

"Thus Christianity endorsed the principle *that it is good to believe what you have no evidence to believe,* a rather convenient maxim for a belief system for which there is no good evidence."[89]

While the evaluation of the evidence is certainly fair grounds for debate, surely Baggini butchered the Christian's viewpoint by suggesting that Christians are unconcerned about rational arguments and evidence for the faith.

David Steele described the standards of evidence required for both criminal and civil courts in the United States using the legal actions against O. J. Simpson as an example:

"In U.S. courts of law, there are two main conceptions of proof, which we saw being appealed to in the O.J. Simpson trials. Simpson was first tried for murder in a criminal court, where the standard of guilt is 'proof beyond any reasonable doubt.' When he had been acquitted, there was a civil trial, which requires a lesser degree of proof: 'proof on the preponderance of evidence.'"[90]

---

[88]David Ramsay Steele, *Atheism Explained: From Folly to Philosophy*, Chicago and La Salle, IL (Open Court Publishing Company, 2008) 16.

[89]Julian Baggini, *Atheism,* New York (Sterling, 2003) 47.

We are convinced that when weighed objectively by either standard in the manner of a courtroom trial, with evidence for both positions weighed impartially, the God hypothesis wins decisively.

What should an honest inquirer do?

Therefore, honest-hearted people should weigh the arguments for both sides fairly. Kerry Walters believed that discussions about such an important subject as God's existence demands giving it fair hearing:

> "Serious challenges to theism should properly focus on its strongest, most central arguments, not the outlandish claims of fringe extremists that most reasonable people, theist and atheist alike, already reject."[91]

And thus, we proceed, endeavoring to provide fair presentations of atheist positions rather than 'bravely' knocking down straw-men arguments.

Reason and revelation

Christian doctrines are not contrary to reason, but rather offer a rational, systematic, and compelling worldview. Indeed, the Judeo-Christian Scriptures put *us in touch with the highest source of knowledge*, logic and reason available (i.e., God!).

Human reason is as much a gift of God as revelation, and revelation would be of no use without reason. Norman Geisler related the words of Jonathan Edwards: "God wants to reach the heart, but he never bypasses the head along the way."[92]

---

[90]David Steele, *Atheism Explained,* 16.
[91]Kerry Walters, *Atheism: A Guide,* 5.
[92]Jonathan Edwards, as quoted by Norman L. Geisler, *Baker*

Indeed, for this very reason, many of the greatest thinkers of history have been attracted to Christianity, impressed by its comprehensive worldview. C. S. Lewis stated it well: "I believe in Christianity as I believe that the sun has risen, not only because I see it, but because by it I see everything else."[93]

Encyclopedia of Christian Apologetics, Grand Rapids MI (Baker Books, 1999) 237.
[93]C. S. Lewis as quoted by Paul Copan, *True for You But Not for Me: Overcoming Objections to Christian Faith*, Minneapolis MN (Bethany House, 2009 Revised Edition)139-140.

Section Two: Natural Philosophy: Arguments for the Existence of God

"If God did not exist, we should have to invent him. But the

whole of nature cries out to us that God does exist."[94]

Voltaire

We move now to consider some of the classic arguments for the existence of God. Wolff refers to three: "The three proofs are called the *Argument from Design, the Cosmological Proof,* and the *Ontological Proof.*[95]

Before considering the arguments directly, let us consider some of the attacks frequently leveled by skeptics against these classical arguments.

Chapter 4: Even If/Even So Arguments

Let us examine what we can call ***even if or even so*** arguments. That is, even if the theist's argument successfully shows the likelihood of the existence of some supernatural being or beings, **even so,** skeptics protest, it doesn't necessarily prove the existence of the classical God of Christian theism.

For instance, with his criticism of the first cause argument, David Mills used just such an argument:

---

[94]Christoph Delius, Matthias Gatzemeier, Deniz Sertcan & Kathleen Wünscher, *The Story of Philosophy from Antiquity to the Present,* Germany (KÖNEMANN, 2005) 68.

[95]Robert Paul Wolff, *About Philosophy,* Sixth Edition, Upper Saddle River NJ (Prentice Hall, 1995) 393.

"The 'First Cause' argument . . . fails to address *which* god is supposedly proven existent by the argument! In other words, Zeus or Allah has just as much to claim to being the 'First Cause' as does Jehovah or Jesus."[96]

Well, so what! The question of *which* God is the true God is distinct from the question of *whether* there is a God. The first cause argument doesn't need to *identify* which is the true God, but only *that* there is a God.

Michael Martin explained the cosmological argument in preparation for criticizing it:

"In all its forms [the cosmological argument] this is an argument that starts off with certain facts about the world and attempts to infer from them the existence of God . . . In its simplest form the cosmological argument is this: Everything we know has a cause. But there cannot be an infinite regress of causes, so there must be a first cause. This first cause is God."[97]

Martin, then, explained what he thought was the *primary* problem with the cosmological argument so described:

"Perhaps the major problem with this version [which he calls the simple version] of the argument is that **even if** it is successful in demonstrating a first cause, this first cause is not necessarily God. A first cause need not have the properties usually associated with God . . . In itself this problem makes the argument quite useless as support for the view that God exists."[98]

---

[96]David Mills, *Atheist Universe: The Thinking Person's Answer to Christian Fundamentalism*, Berkeley CA (Ulysses Press, 2006) 30-31.

[97]Michael Martin, *Atheism: A Philosophical Justification*, Philadelphia PA (Temple University Press, 1990)96.

[98]Michael Martin, *Atheism*, 97.

Surely, Martin exaggerated by calling the cosmological argument useless, for he has done nothing to refute it. A first cause, we should not forget, must pre-exist and transcend the universe. The fact that someone can imagine other possible candidates for the *identity* of the first cause does not in any way disprove the *existence* of a first cause, or that the first cause may be the biblical God.

Even such a fine philosopher as Paul Edwards used these kinds of arguments. In his discussion of the "causal argument . . . the second of the 'five ways' of Aquinas . . . an uncaused or 'first' cause," Edwards pointed out, "**Even if** this argument were sound it would not establish the existence of God. It would not show that the first cause is all-powerful or all-good or that it is in any sense personal."[99]

Sure, the first cause argument does not prove that the creator of the universe is all powerful. But a being that preceded the universe and was powerful enough to create it is just what the Bible teaches and just what atheists deny.

Sure, the first cause argument does not prove that the creator is good, but how does the possibility of an evil creator god advance the atheist's argument? A bad creator god is still a god, the very thing atheists deny.

Again, Edward's stated:

"Hence, **even if** it is granted that no series of causes can be infinite, the possibility of a plurality of first members has not been ruled out. Nor does the argument (First

---

[99]Paul Edwards, *The Cosmological Argument*, Chapter in *Critiques of God: Making the Case Against Belief in God,* Peter A. Angeles, Editor, Amherst New York (Prometheus Books, 1997) 44-45.

Cause Argument) establish the *present* existence of the first cause. It does not prove this, since experience clearly shows that an effect may exist long after its cause has been destroyed."[100]

In response, we can agree; sure, the first cause argument does not prove that the creator acted alone; it is logically possible that there were accomplices. But again, how does the possibility that there were multiple gods involved in creation advance the atheist cause? Don't atheists deny the existence of any gods?

Again, merely because it is logically *possible* that there were multiple gods involved in creation does not *prove* there were. The Christian claim that the first cause of the universe was the biblical God remains undisturbed by such atheist's arguments.

The cosmological argument has been successful if it supports the existence of a god or gods, and the Christian no more needs to prove that it was only one God, than the atheist needs to go down a list of gods and disprove each one of them.

That is, if an atheist's argument successfully shows that the existence of God is unlikely, he has shown that belief in any god is unreasonable. He doesn't have to go down a list of gods (Yahweh, Allah, Shiva, Vishnu, Zeus etc.) and disprove each one.

Likewise, the Christian, having made a successful argument for a creator does not need to prove that there is only one God. The believer's argument is successful if he has shown the reasonableness of the existence of at least a single God.

---

[100]Paul Edwards, *The Cosmological Argument*, Chapter in *Critiques of God*, 46.

Nor does the first cause argument prove of itself that the creator *continues* to exist. But again, I am not clear how the acknowledgement of a once-upon-a-time supernatural creator of the universe advances the atheist cause? Don't atheists deny the existence of any God at any time?

Again, the first cause argument is perfectly consistent with the biblical claim of an eternally self-existent supernatural being, or God.

The point of the foregoing is to show that in discussions about the cosmological or teleological arguments, the careful reader will have noticed that skeptics from Hume forward have spent a lot of space on these kinds of *even so* arguments, trading four parts ridicule to one part bluster, hoping to awe their readers with clever sophistry, and further hoping they failed to notice the lack of substance in their attacks.

Martin's even so concerning an impersonal first cause

Let us consider further examples. In responding to Aquinas's second way, Martin stated:

> "The same problems that plagued the simple version of the argument plague this more sophisticated version. The first cause, even if established, need not be God."[101]

Indeed, Martin even asked "It is unclear also why a mechanical, nonpersonal cause could not have brought about the universe."[102] Well, it is certainly logically possible, I suppose, that the first cause of the universe

---

[101]Michael Martin, *Atheism,* 99.
[102]Michael Martin, *Atheism,* 104.

was mechanical and impersonal. But the proposal seems to be a desperate attempt at evading the personal God of classical theism.

For to accept Martin's argument would require that *life* has a *non-living source*; that *persons* have *an impersonal source*; and that consciousness has an *unconscious source*.

Again, Martin is welcomed to argue that an unthinking, impersonal, and lifeless thing is possibly the first cause of the universe, if such is even a coherent concept. But such is in no way an argument against the existence of the biblical God.

Michael Scriven's role-linkage multiple-gods argument

Michael Scriven provided a similar argument. He calls it "a combination trick" argument, that seeks to muddy the waters for Christian believers in monotheism. He suggested that it is no more reasonable to believe in one God as creator, sustainer, judge, and lawgiver than it is to believe that there is a separate god for each of these tasks, roles, or attributes. Scriven put it like this:

> "It could be argued that the greatest confidence trick in the history of philosophy is the attempt to make the various arguments for the existence of God support each other by using the same term for the entity whose existence each is supposed to establish. In fact, almost all of them bear on entities of apparently quite different kinds, ranging from a Creator to a moral Lawgiver. The proofs must, therefore, be supplemented with a further proof or set of proofs that shows these apparently different entities to be the same if the combination trick is to work. Otherwise the arguments must be taken separately, in which case they either establish or fail to establish the

existence of a number of remarkable but unrelated entities."[103]

A natural response in light of the law of parsimony, is to suppose that one supernatural being carries out each of the divine functions as in monotheism. But Scriven argued against that conclusion:

> "It can sometimes be argued that considerations of simplicity require one to adopt the hypothesis that only a single entity is involved, when the alternative is to introduce several special entities. But the circumstances in which this is legitimate are quite limited . . . Although there is a greater simplicity in terms of the number of entities involved if we say, for example, that the Creator is the moral Lawgiver, there is a greater complexity in terms of the number of explanations required, since now we must explain why and how one entity could perform these two functions."[104]

As we have already shown, the cosmological argument has been successful if it has shown the *existence of at least one supernatural being,* and one needn't be sidetracked by the question of whether there might be more than one God. One God or many, the cosmological or teleological arguments have done their job.

Scriven, believing in the power of his argument, threw believers a bone to chew:

> "Instead of attempting to establish monotheism, one can, of course, frankly accept the arguments as separate proofs of the existence of separate beings."[105]

---

[103]Michael Scriven, *God and Reason,* chapter in *Critiques of God: Making the Case Against Belief in God,* Peter A. Angeles, Editor, Amherst New York (Prometheus Books, 1997) 111-112
[104]Michael Scriven, *God and Reason,* 112
[105]Michael Scriven, *God and Reason,* 112

But has Scriven really shown that monotheists are inconsistent? Do we have reason to prefer belief in one God over the many?

Indeed, there are solid reasons for believing that all the attributes adhere in one supernatural being. For instance, if a being is omnipotent, then one necessarily has the power to create, and, it follows, that this being also has the authority to prescribe law for His creation.

Is it not like the powers that adhere or pertain to the President of the United States? Upon taking the oath of office, the President becomes the commander in chief of the military, becomes the head of the executive branch, and has veto power over every bill that is passed by congress.

Yes, the designers of the constitution could have assigned separate persons for each of these functions, but they chose to have a strong chief executive, believing that arrangement would be more efficient and effective.

Likewise, there is nothing unusual with the biblical claim that one supernatural being exercises all the attributes ascribed to him by revelation and reason.

Problems with polytheism

Further, there are logical and philosophical arguments that favor monotheism over polytheism. In his article on the cosmological argument, Norman Geisler summed up John Duns Scotus' version of the argument which includes reasons why monotheism is preferred to polytheism, and which I quote in part:

"The First Cause of all producible beings must be one, because a. It is perfect in knowledge, and there cannot be two beings that know everything perfectly, for one would know itself more than the other . . . d. It is infinite in power. If there were two with infinite power, this would mean that there would be two total primary causes of the same effect, and this is impossible, since there cannot be two causes each doing all that causing . . . f. There cannot be two Necessary Beings . . . g. Omnipotent will cannot be in two beings, for then one could render impotent what the other wills omnipotently."[106]

It is interesting, then, that Scriven lamented that his argument was not more well-known: "It is surprising that more attention has not been paid to the linkage arguments, which then become crucial."[107]

I humbly suggest that the reason for the anonymity of his argument is its lack of weight. Monotheism is not some kind of hocus-pocus philosophical trick, but rather is a most philosophically defensible position.

---

[106]Norman L. Geisler, *Baker Encyclopedia of Christian Apologetics*, Grand Rapids MI (Baker Books, 1999) 163.
[107]Michael Scriven, *God and Reason*, 112

Chapter 5: Can God's Existence Be Tested Empirically?

Can God be detected empirically?

The classic arguments for God's existence have not traditionally been empirical in nature (since God is a spirit being i.e., John 4:24). For instance, the ontological argument is an a priori argument based on logic and reasoning alone, apart from any empirical considerations.

Other classic arguments such as the various forms of the *cosmological argument* are arguments by inference. We start from our experience of the world and reason back to a first cause. Beginning with a world filled with motion, with cause and effect, we reason back to an unmoved mover. We see contingent things, and reason back to a necessary Being.

And in the *teleological argument*, we use an argument of analogy. Just as specified complexity *in this world* (i.e. watches, computers) is the result of intelligent creators, so also, the specified complexity in nature as a whole has its source in an intelligent designer!

Again, none of the traditional arguments for God's existence has claimed that God can be *empirically* proved, *since God is by definition a spirit being.* Rather, the Bible has clearly affirmed that the creator is both separate from and transcendent over the universe. As such, He would not be detectable by the instruments of science (microscopes, telescopes, radar, particle colliders etc.).

Victor Stenger's claims for empirically testing God's existence

In light of the foregoing, it is most puzzling to consider the arguments of Victor J. Stenger. Consider his hypothesis:

> "My analysis will be based on the contention that God should be detectable by scientific means simply by virtue of the fact that he is supposed to play such a central role in the operation of the universe and the lives of humans. Existing scientific models contain no place where God is included as an ingredient in order to describe observations."[108]

He further explained his objective:

> "Using the historical association of phenomena that, if observed, cannot be of material origin beyond a reasonable doubt. Since by all accounts God is nonmaterial, his presence would be signaled, beyond a reasonable doubt, by the empirical verification of such phenomena . . . I will show that a number of proposed supernatural or nonmaterial processes are empirically testable using standard scientific methods."[109]

Stenger further explained his thesis:

> "By this criterion, it would seem that the existence of God cannot be empirically refuted because to do so would require making an existential statement applying to the whole universe (plus whatever lies beyond). But, in looking at Popper's example, we see this is not the case for God . . . But God is supposed to be everywhere . . . So when we search for God inside a single box, no matter how small, we

---

[108]Victor J. Stenger, *God the Failed Hypothesis: How Science Shows That God Does Not Exist*, Amherst New York (Prometheus Books, 2007) 13.

[109]Victor J. Stenger, *God the Failed Hypothesis:* 14, 15.

should either find him, thus confirming his existence, or not find him, thus refuting his existence . . . The thesis of this book is that the supernatural hypothesis of God is testable, verifiable, and falsifiable by the established methods of science."[110]

Mr. Stenger is a man of great accomplishment and worthy of respect. But I can't help but to consider his objective as a fool's errand. Sure, we can evaluate indirect arguments for God's existence like the various cosmological explanations.

But it is simply impossible to test the existence of God scientifically. How is that even conceivable? Will someone eventually invent a non-material being detector? Or perhaps a transcendent dimension detector?

Mr. Stenger can check "inside a single box" or "inside every box" in the universe, but he will never detect God, simply for the reason that God is not a part of the universe, but is rather the universe's transcendent creator.

Even the atheist David Steele rejected the kind of notion Stenger argued for:

"This means that God is not physical . . . He cannot be detected by the naked senses or by scientific instruments. No flickering needle on a dial could ever cause some research worker to say 'Hey, we've got some God activity here . . . The existence of God is a hypothesis, but it is not the kind of hypothesis that can be tested by definite observations. It's difficult to imagine someone looking into a microscope or a telescope and exclaiming: 'Wow! This means there is a God after all!'"[111]

---

[110]Victor J. Stenger, *God the Failed Hypothesis,* 27, 29.
[111]David Ramsay Steele, *Atheism Explained: From Folly to Philosophy,* Chicago and La Salle, IL (Open Court Publishing Company, 2008) 5, 16.

Chapter 6: The Ontological Argument

Saint Anselm (1033-1109) was Archbishop of Canterbury. He was the author of the *Ontological Argument* for the existence of God, (although it was Kant that gave the argument its well-known name).[112] Here is his essential argument:

> "We believe you to be something than which nothing greater can be conceived. The question, then, is whether something with this nature exists, since 'the fool has said in his heart that there is no God'[Ps. 14:1, 53:1]. But, surely, when the fool hears the words 'something than which nothing greater can be conceived,' he understands what he hears, and what he understands exists in his understanding—even if he doesn't think that it exists . . . And surely that than which a greater cannot be conceived cannot exist *just* in the understanding. If it were to exist *just* in the understanding, we could conceive it to exist in reality too, in which case it would be greater. Therefore, if that than which a greater cannot be conceived exists just in the understanding, the very thing than which a greater cannot be conceived is something than which a greater *can* be conceived. But surely this cannot be. Without doubt, then, something than which a greater can't be conceived does exist—both in the understanding and in reality."[113]

Unfortunately, I am simply not convinced by Anselm's interesting argument (despite its many able defenders). I am compelled, rather, to agree with those thinkers such

---

[112]Yeager Hudson, *The Philosophy of Religion*, Mountain View CA (Mayfield Publishing Company, 1991) 77.

[113]Saint Anselm, *Proslogion*, Chapter 2, as cited in the *Introduction to Philosophy: Classical and Contemporary Readings,* Fourth Edition, John Perry, Michael Bratman & John Martin Fischer Editors, Oxford (Oxford University Press, 2007) 78.

as Saint Thomas Aquinas who have rejected the ontological argument. I agree with the assessment of the atheist Robert Paul Wolff:

> "Whenever I read the Ontological Argument, I have the same feeling that comes over me when I watch a good magician. Nothing up the sleeve; nothing up the other sleeve; nothing in the hat; presto! A big, fat rabbit. How can Anselm pull God out of an idea?"[114]

Already in Anselm's lifetime there were those who rejected his argument. Such was Gaunilo who wrote his criticism of the Ontological Argument in his work, *Defending the Fool*.[115] Gaunilo made an analogy to Anselm's greatest conceivable being by imagining the greatest island conceivable. If the island did not exist, then it could not be the greatest island conceivable, and therefore it must exist.

William Rowe commented on Anselm's response to Gaunilo's criticism:

> "In his reply to Gaunilo, Anselm insisted that his reasoning applies only to God and cannot be used to establish the existence of things other than God . . . In defense of Anselm against Gaunilo's objections, we should note that the objection supposes that Gaunilo's island is a possible thing . . . Perhaps, then, since Anselm can reject its application to Gaunilo's island on the grounds that the

---

[114]Robert Paul Wolff, *About Philosophy*, Sixth Edition, Upper Saddle River NJ (Prentice Hall, 1995) 407.
[115]Louis P. Pojman provides the texts of Anselm's Ontological Argument from the *Proslogium;* Gaunilo's response to Anselm from *In Behalf of the Fool*; and finally Anselm's rejoinder to Gaunilo's criticism from his Apologetic in Louis P. Pojman, *Philosophy: The Quest for Truth*, Sixth Edition, Oxford (Oxford University Press, 2006) 93-97.

island than which non greater is possible is, like the round square, an impossible thing."[116]

It seems reasonable that Anselm's ontological argument could have application only to God. Nevertheless, it doesn't follow that the argument itself is true. Others have attempted to resurrect, revise, and defend the Ontological argument:

> "Various versions of the argument have been defended by such famous philosophers as Descartes and Leibniz. The twentieth century saw a great revival of interest in the argument, with thinkers such as Charles Hartshorne, Norman Malcolm and Alvin Plantinga defending versions of it."[117]

Indeed, apparently even one as skeptical as Bertrand Russell briefly fell under its sway:

> "While this argument has for brief moments captured very significant thinkers (Bertrand Russell describes how it suddenly hit him that Anselm might be right—for about fifteen minutes)."[118]

I confess that while wrestling with the idea, I have also had momentary flashes of "enlightenment" believing to have been finally persuaded by the argument, only to have reality take me back to my senses shortly thereafter.

---

[116]William Rowe, *An Analysis of the Ontological Argument*, as cited by Louis P. Pojman, *Philosophy: The Quest for Truth,* Sixth Edition, Oxford (Oxford University Press, 2006) 103.

[117]C. Stephen Evans & R. Zachary Manis, *Philosophy of Religion: Thinking About Faith*, Second Edition, Downers Grove IL (InterVarsity Press, 2009) 63.

[118]Carl Sagan, *The God Hypothesis* in Christopher Hitchens, *The Portable Atheist: Essential Readings for the Nonbeliever*, Philadelphia PA (De Capo Press, 2007) 234.

Geisler related that Schopenhauer felt the ontological argument was "a 'charming joke,' a sleight of hand" trick.[119] That is a bit harsh for an argument with such an illustrious career, yet, in my judgment the argument does fail.

Nevertheless, I share with Anselm a faith in the greatest being possibly conceivable. I agree with Blaise Pascal:

> "The fact that I can think of a mountain with a valley doesn't entail that a mountain exists in the world, and similarly, the fact that I can think of God as existing doesn't seem to entail that He exists. For my thought doesn't impose any necessity on things: it may be that I can ascribe existence to God when no God exists, just as I can imagine a winged horse when no such horse exists."[120]

Thankfully, as we shall see, there are strong and persuasive arguments for the existence of God apart from the ontological argument.

Chapter 7: The Teleological Argument (The Argument from Design)

"I cannot imagine how the clockwork of the universe can exist without a clockmaker."[121]

---

[119]Norman L. Geisler, *Baker Encyclopedia of Christian Apologetics*, Grand Rapids MI (Baker Books, 1999) 689.

[120]Blaise Pascal, *Meditations on First Philosophy* in *Introduction to Philosophy: Classical and Contemporary Readings*, Fourth Edition, Edited by John Perry, Michael Bratman & John Martin Fischer, Oxford UK (Oxford University Press, 2007) 187.

[121]Voltaire, *20,000 Quips & Quotes*, Evan Esar, Editor, New York

Voltaire

The *Teleological Argument* has been found persuasive by many great thinkers including American President Thomas Jefferson, who, in an 1823 letter to President Adams stated:

> "On the contrary, I hold (without appeal to revelation) that when we take a view of the universe, in its parts, general or particular, it is impossible for the human mind not to perceive and feel a conviction of design, consummate skill, and indefinite power in every atom of its composition. The movements of the heavenly bodies, so exactly in their course . . . the structure of the earth itself . . . It is impossible I say, for the human mind not to believe that there is in all this, design, cause and effect, up to an ultimate cause, a fabricator of all things from matter and motion, their preserver and regulator . . . So irresistible are these evidences of an intelligent and powerful agent, that, of the infinite numbers of men who have existed through all time, they have believed . . . in the hypothesis of an eternal preexistence of a creator, rather than in that of a self-existent universe."[122]

Reese defined the teleological argument:

> "From 'teleology' . . . one of the three basic arguments for God, taking the purpose, order, or design of the universe as premise for the conclusion that God exists."[123]

George Mavrodes added:

(Barnes & Noble Books, 1995)

[122]Thomas Jefferson, *In God We Trust: The Religious Beliefs and Ideas of the American Founding Fathers*, Norman Cousins, Editor, New York (Harper & Brothers Publishers, 1958) 290.

[123]William L. Reese, *Dictionary of Philosophy and Religion: Eastern and Western Thought*, Atlantic Highlands NJ (Humanities Press, 1980) 570.

"Teleological argument for the existence of God. A world-based line of argument appealing to special features, those aspects of the world which appear to be designed and purposive, analogous to cases of human design."[124]

A key word in Mavrodes' definition is "analogous," since the teleological argument makes the analogy that just as complex structures on earth have intelligent designers and builders, so also the complexity of the universe suggests an intelligent designer and creator. Wolff says, "The technical name for this is an argument from analogy."[125]

The key idea is that intricate design suggests an intelligent designer, what Wallace Matson calls, "The design axiom."[126] Wallace noted that it is often assumed that the teleological argument has been philosophically scrapped to the ash heap of discarded ideas, whereas it is not so:

"Hume's trenchant criticism of the argument, usually considered definitive, was in fact limited in scope . . . The design axiom itself, however, was still left standing, though wobbling."[127]

William Paley and the Argument from Design

Perhaps the best-known version of the teleological argument is that made popular by the English theologian

---

[124]George I Mavrodes, *The Oxford Guide To Philosophy*, Ted Honderich Editor, Oxford (Oxford University Press, 2005) 911.

[125]Robert Paul Wolff, *About Philosophy*, Sixth Edition, Upper Saddle River NJ (Prentice Hall, 1995) 394.

[126]Wallace I. Matson, *The Argument From Design*, chapter in *Critiques of God: Making the Case Against Belief in God*, Peter A. Angeles, Editor, Amherst New York (Prometheus Books, 1997) 60.

[127]Wallace I. Matson, *The Argument From Design*, 68.

William Paley. Geisler and Brooks summarized Paley's argument:

> "William Paley (1743-1805) insisted that if someone found a watch in a field, he would rightly conclude that there had been a watchmaker because of the obvious design. The same must be said of the design found in nature."[128]

Here is the argument in Paley's own words:

> "In crossing a heath, suppose I pitched my foot against a *stone*, and were asked how the stone came to be there; I might possibly answer, that, for anything I knew to the contrary, it had lain there forever . . . But suppose I had found a watch upon the ground, and it should be inquired how the watch happened to be in that place: I should hard think of the answer which I had before given, that, for anything I knew, the watch might have always been there. Yet why should not this answer serve for the watch as well as for the stone? . . . For this reason . . . that, when we come to inspect the watch, we perceive (what we could not discover in the stone) that its several parts are framed and put together for a purpose, e.g., that they are so formed and adjusted as to produce motion, and that motion so regulated as to point out the hour of the day . . . This mechanism being observed . . . the inference, we think, is inevitable; that the watch must have had a maker; that there must have existed, at sometime, and at some place or other, an artificer or artificers, who formed it for the purpose . . . and designed its use."[129]

---

[128]Norman L. Geisler & Ronald M. Brooks, *When Skeptics Ask*, Wheaton IL (Victor Books, 1990) 20.

[129]William Paley, *The Watch and the Human Eye*, as reprinted in *A Modern Introduction to Philosophy: Readings from Classical and Contemporary Sources,* Third Edition, Paul Edwards & Arthur Pap, Editors, New York, (The Free Press, 1973) 419-420.

Of course, not everyone has been convinced by Paley's argument. S.T. Josh suggested that John Stuart Mill had provided a devastating blow to the teleological argument:

> "The best-known proponent of this argument was William Paley, who put forth a celebrated analogy: If one found a watch on a deserted island, one would naturally assume that it had been created by a watchmaker. But Mill destroys this argument in one sentence: 'If I found a watch on an apparently desolate island, I should indeed infer that it had been left there by a human being; but the inference would not be from marks of design, but because I already knew by direct experience that watches are made by men.'"[130]

John Stuart Mill's criticism of the Design Argument

So Mill's argument was that the design inherent in a watch was not decisive in identifying it as the work of a man, an intelligent designer. Rather, it is only by experience that we know watches owe their origin to watchmakers. By this argument, Mill sought to evade the seemingly common-sense argument that when one finds the complexity of a watch, they can infer an intelligent watchmaker. Therefore, it follows, according to Mill, that complexity in nature is not proof of an intelligent designer (or God).

But is this not mere sophistry? Are we to believe that if instead of a watch, that Mill had happened across a lawn mower engine, he would have believed it to be a natural formation? Are we to believe that had Mill stumbled upon say a 747 Jet airplane, he would have

---

[130]S. T. Josh, *The Unbelievers: The Evolution of Modern Atheism*, Amherst NY (Prometheus Books, 2011) 64.

concluded that jumbo Jets just happen randomly and naturally?

S. T. Josh's assessment that Mill had destroyed Paley's argument from design is surely hyperbole. Further, it is noteworthy that John Stuart Mill did not actually reject the teleological argument. Antony Flew stated:

> "The essay "Theism" is chiefly remarkable for the fact that Mill, though rejecting the Christian revelation, and consequently not 'incumbered with the necessity of admitting the omnipotence of the Creator' (p. 186), was still, in spite of Hume and Darwin, sufficiently impressed with the Argument to Design to explore at length the idea of a finite God, allowing 'a large balance of probability in favour of creation by intelligence.'"[131]

Clarence Darrow's criticism of the Design Argument

Clarence Darrow advanced a similar argument against the teleological argument:

> Most men that we know would think that the watch showed a design to accomplish a certain purpose, and therefore must have had a maker. They would reach that conclusion because they are familiar with tools and their use by man. But, suppose the watch had been picked up by a bushman or some other savage or an ape? None of them would draw an inference, for the article would be new to them.[132]

---

[131]Antony Flew, *Divine Omnipotence and Human Freedom*, chapter in *Critiques of God: Making the Case Against Belief in God*, Peter A. Angeles, Editor, Amherst New York (Prometheus Books, 1997) 236.

[132]Clarence Darrow, *The Delusion of Design and Purpose*, as reprinted in *A Modern Introduction to Philosophy: Readings from Classical and Contemporary Sources*, Third Edition, Paul Edwards

Setting aside Darrow's racist language, his argument is not impressive. It is hard to conceive of anyone, even if untouched by modern civilization, concluding, upon finding a watch, that it was a naturally occurring object.

Indeed, the fields of archaeology and paleontology would be useless if they followed such a methodology. They would have to assume any tool-like object found, but not yet identified, was a natural formation. McDowell and Morrow explained:

> "Imagine an archaeologist who discovers an ancient object that looks like an arrowhead or digging tool. She would be fully justified in concluding that it was the product of design, rather than the result of erosion and other natural forces, even if she could not explain the origin or identity of the designer."[133]

Indeed, even such a skeptic as Voltaire was duly impressed with the argument from design: "I shall always be of the opinion that a clock proves a clockmaker, and that the universe proves a God."[134]

The criticisms of the teleological argument by Hume & Martin

The atheist Michael Martin critically assessed the teleological argument:

> "Hume's criticisms of the teleological argument in the *Dialogues* concerning Natural Religion have often been

& Arthur Pap, Editors, New York, (The Free Press, 1973) 446.

[133]Jay W. Richards, *Why Is the Universe Just Right for Life?* chapter in Sean McDowell & Jonathan Morrow, *Is God Just a Human Invention? And Seventeen Other Questions Raised by the New Atheists,* Grand Rapids MI (Kregel Publications, 2010) 99.

[134]Norman L. Geisler, *Baker Encyclopedia of Christian Apologetics,* 765

taken to be decisive. Philo, who presumably is Hume's spokesman, raises many objections to the analogical reasoning used by Cleanthes. He argues that if the analogy were carried to its logical extreme, one would end up with conclusions not acceptable to the theist. For example, machines are usually made by many intelligent beings; hence some form of polytheism rather than monotheism would be warranted by the argument. Also, the beings who create machines have bodies, so God must have a body. If machines have imperfections, one should conclude that God is not perfect."[135]

Natural limits to arguments from analogy

Hume (and Martin) is guilty of violating a principle of interpretation, i.e. that of trying to make a parable walk on all fours. That is, an analogy typically has a central point, and most of the details are incidental background material secondary to the main point.

In discussing biblical parables, a form of analogy, Bernard Ramm stated:

"Determine the one central truth the parable is attempting to teach. This might be called the golden rule of parabolic interpretation for practically all writers on the subject mention it with stress. 'The typical parable presents one single point of comparison,' writes Dodd. 'The details are not intended to have independent significance.' Others have put it this way: Don't make a parable walk on all fours . . . A parable is a truth carried in a vehicle. Therefore there is the inevitable presence of accessories which are necessary for the drapery of the parable, but are not part of the meaning. The danger in parabolic teaching at this point is to interpret as meaningful what is drapery."[136]

---

[135]Michael Martin, *Atheism: A Philosophical Justification,* Philadelphia PA (Temple University Press, 1990) 127.
[136]Bernard Ramm, *Protestant Biblical Interpretation: A Textbook of Hermeneutics,* Third Revised Edition, Grand Rapids MI (Baker

Robert Stein added;

"Ultimately any comparison will break down when pressed . . . Every comparison of two unlike things must sooner or later break down. The fact is that the purpose of an analogy is to convey a basic point of comparison between the picture and the reality to which it corresponds."[137]

The central point of the teleological argument is that evidence of design in nature suggests an intelligent designer for our world. Incidental features of the argument from design should not be pressed beyond this central point of the argument.

And yet this is exactly what Hume does in his unfair use of *the argument ad absurdum* for the teleological argument. And so, Hume argued that since human builders have physical bodies, so also, the teleological argument would suggest (if it is consistent) that God must also have a body, or that since human builders have imperfections, God must also have imperfections.

Sure it is possible that the designer was really a team of designers (or gods); maybe the designer had a physical body, or was an imperfect or weak God. Yet, *a supernatural being (or beings) was the source of the universe. Identifying that supernatural source is secondary to the argument; that there was a supernatural source is the main point.*

And that there was a supernatural source of creation (whether one God or many, whether perfect or imperfect, or whether having some kind of body) is the very thing

Book House, 1970) 283.
[137]Robert H. Stein, *Playing By The Rules: A Basic Guide to Interpreting the Bible*, Grand Rapids MI (Baker Books, 1994) 141.

that atheism denies. As such, Hume's argument simply does nothing to support atheism or to deny theism.

Has evolution dispelled the Teleological Argument?

It is often argued that the theory of evolution has refuted and replaced belief in Paley's argument from design. Although, as a young man, Darwin was quite impressed with Paley and his design argument, he eventually became convinced that his theory of evolution had displaced Paley's argument.

However, as science has advanced since Darwin's time, evidence for the teleological argument is actually gaining rather than losing ground. Peter Whitfield's observations are to the point:

> "The problem of design haunts modern science, but more bafflingly it haunted the natural philosophy of the seventeenth or the eighteenth century, for behind the concept of design lies the problem of purpose. However deeply we probe the structure of matter, the chemistry of life, or the evolution of a galaxy, there is evidence of order, process, and the fulfillment of laws."[138]

Scientists have opened the window on life at the micro-biological and cellular level to reveal incredible complexity. In his 1996 book *Darwin's Black Box*, biochemist Michael Behe described various biochemical processes in the body including the workings of the cilium and the flagellum in the cell as well as the amazing cascade of effects involved in blood clotting.[139]

---

[138]Peter Whitfield, *Landmarks in Western Science: From Prehistory to the Atomic Age*, New York (Routledge, 1999) 244.

[139]Michael J. Behe, *Darwin's Black Box: The Biochemical Challenge to Evolution*, New York (The Free Press, 1996).

Reading Behe's amazing descriptions of the blood clotting process or of the incredible cellular machinery at the microscopic level does not alone prove a divine designer and creator, but they strongly suggest it! I cannot but stand in awe of the great God who has created not only our amazing bodies, but the whole universe in its vast array (Psalm 19:1, Isaiah 44:24).

Design, complexity, and the human eye

Paley himself felt that the example of the human eye was a testimonial to the creation of God and was not explainable by natural processes. He said: "Sturmius held, that the examination of the eye was a cure for atheism."[140] In another place, Paley said:

> "Were there no example in the world of contrivance except that of the eye, it would be alone sufficient to support the conclusion which we draw from it, as to the necessity of an intelligent creator. It could never be got rid of because it could not be accounted for by any other supposition, which did not contradict all the principles we possess of knowledge."[141]

Excursus on the human eye by Michael Behe

A consideration of the process of vision and the workings of the human eye powerfully supports Paley's claim.

As we consider Michael Behe's description of the chemical complexities involved in human vision, let us

---

[140]William Paley, *The Watch and the Human Eye*, 427.
[141]William Paley, *Natural Theology*, Frederick Ferré, (Indianapolis: Bobbs-Merrill, 1963) p. 44, as quoted by William H. Halverson, *A Concise Introduction to Philosophy*, Third Edition, New York (Random House, 1976) 137.

ask not whether evolution is a *possible* explanation for vision, and rather ask the more reasonable question as to how *likely or probable* it is that such complexity is the result of random forces:

"When light first strikes the retina a photon interacts with a molecule called 11-cis-retinal, which rearranges within picoseconds to *trans-retinal* . . . The change in the shape of the retinal molecule forces a change in the shape of the proteins rhodopsin, to which the retinal is tightly bound. The protein's metamorphosis alters its behavior. Now called metarhodopson II, the protein sticks to another protein, called transducin. Before bumping into metarhodopsin II, transducin had tightly bound a small molecule called GDP. But when transducin interacts with metarhodospin II, the GDP falls off, and a molecule called GTP binds to transducin . . . GTP-transducin-metarhodopsin II now binds to a protein called phosphodiesterase, located in the inner membrane of the cell. When attached to metarhodopsin II and its entourage, the phosphodiesterase acquires the chemical ability to 'cut' a molecule called cGMP . . . Initially there are a lot of cGMP molecules in the cell, but the phosphodieterase lowers its concentration, just as a pulled plug lowers the water level in a bathtub.

Another membrane protein that binds cGMP is called an ion channel. It acts as a gateway that regulates the number of sodium ions in a cell.. Normally the ion channel allows sodium flow into the cell, while a separate protein actively pumps them out again. The dual action of the ion channel and pump keeps the level of sodium ions in the cell within a narrow range. When the amount of cGMP is reduced because of cleavage by the phosphodieterase, the ion channel closes, causing the cellular concentration of positively charged sodium ions to be reduced. This causes an imbalance of charge across the cell membrane that, finally, causes a current to be transmitted down the optic nerve to the brain. The result, when interpreted by the brain, is vision.

    If the reactions above were the only ones that operated in the cell, the supply of 11-cis-retinal, cGMP, and sodium ions would quickly be depleted. Something has to turn off the proteins that were turned on and restore the cell to its original state. Several mechanisms do this. First, in the dark the ion channel . . . also lets calcium ions into the cell. The calcium is pumped back out by a different protein so that a constant calcium concentration is maintained. When cGMP levels fall, shutting down the ion channel, calcium ion concentration decreases, too. The phosphodiesterase enzyme, which destroys cGMP, slows down at lower calcium concentration. Second, a protein called guanylate cyclase begins to resythensize cGMP when calcium levels start to fall. Third, while all this is going on, metarhodopsin II is chemically modified by an enzyme called rhodopsin kinase. The modified rhodopsin then binds to a protein known as arrestin, which prevents the rhodopsin from activating more transducin. So the cell contains mechanisms to limit the amplified signal started by a single photon.

    Trans-retinal eventually falls off of rhodopsin and must be reconverted to 11-cis-retinal and again bound by rhodopsin to get back to the starting point for another visual cycle. To accomplish this, *trans*-retinal is first chemically modified by an enzyme to *trans*-retinol—a form containing two more hydrogen atoms. A second enzyme then converts the molecule to 11-cis-retinol. Finally, a third enzyme removes the previously added hydrogen atoms to form 11-cis-retinal, a cycle is complete."[142]

It seems simply incredible that this cascade of effects that produces our amazing vision is the result of random chance.

Steven Rose described another amazing aspect of human vision related to the growing child:

---

[142]Michael Behe, *Darwin's Black Box,* 18-21

"Consider the problem of seeing and of making sense of the world we observe, processes subserved by eye and brain. The retina of the eye is connected via a series of neural staging posts to the visual cortex at the back of the brain. A baby is born with most of these connections in place, but during the first years of life the eye and the brain both grow, at different rates. This means that the connections between the ear and brain have continually to be broken and remade."[143]

Again, it seems incredible that such intricate designs and functions could have resulted from random unguided processes. It screams, rather, for an intelligent designer.

What of apparently bad design?

In light of the amazing complexity of the human body, it might come as a surprise to hear skeptics arguing for poor or bad design (called dystelology)[144] in order to find fault with God's design.

For example, Victor Stenger noted:

"Some evolutionists have tried to counter the Paley claim with what might be called the argument from bad design, pointing out all the ways that a competent engineer could improve upon what nature has given us."[145]

Bertrand Russell held similar sentiments to Stenger:

---

[143]Steven Rose, *Escaping Evolutionary Psychology*, chapter in *Alas, Poor Darwin: Arguments Against Evolutionary Psychology*, Edited by Hilary Rose & Steven Rose, New York (Harmony Books, 2000) 310.

[144]*Signs of Intelligence: Understanding Intelligent Design*, Edited by William A. Demski & James M. Kushiner, Grand Rapids MI (Brazos Press, 2001) 11.

[145]Victor J. Stenger, *God: The Failed Hypothesis, How Science Shows That God Does Not Exist*, Amherst New York (Prometheus Books, 2007) 68-69.

"When you look into this argument from design, it is a most astonishing thing that people can believe that this world, with all the things that are in it, with all its defects, should be the best that omnipotence and omniscience have been able to produce in millions of years. I really cannot believe it."[146]

Likewise, critics point to the evil and suffering in the world and blame God for it. Bertrand Russell again stated:

"Do you think that, if you were granted omnipotence and omniscience and millions of years in which to perfect your world, you could produce nothing better than the Ku Klux Klan or the Fascists?"[147]

We have seen that Darwin believed that his theory of evolution defeated and superseded the teleological argument. It is interesting that his reasons for believing this were primarily based, not on scientific reasons, but rather, because he could not reconcile the evil and suffering in the world with a benevolent God:

"Darwin concluded: 'I cannot see, as plainly as others do, evidence of design & beneficence on all sides of us. There seems to me to be too much misery in the world."[148]

Darwin also said:

---

[146]Bertrand Russell, Why *I Am Not a Theist* in *Introduction to Philosophy: Classical and Contemporary Readings*, Fourth Edition, Edited by John Perry, Michael Bratman & John Martin Fischer, Oxford UK (Oxford University Press, 2007) 88.

[147]Bertrand Russell, as quoted by S. T. Josh, *The Unbelievers: The Evolution of Modern Atheism*, Amherst NY (Prometheus Books, 2011) 158.

[148]Kerry Walters, *Atheism: A Guide for the Perplexed*, New York (The Continuum International Publishing Group Inc, 2010) 86.

"This very old argument from the existence of suffering against the existence of an intelligent First Cause seems to me a strong one."[149]

Suboptimal design?

Setting aside the question of theodicy, and how to reconcile the reality of evil and suffering with the nature of God for later in the book, the question of poor design remains. That is, does nature really exhibit such poor examples of design to cast doubt that it is the creation of God?

Wikipedia described this line of reasoning:

"The argument from poor design, also known as the *dysteleological argument,* is an argument against the existence of a creator God, based on the reasoning that an omnipotent and omnibenevolent God would not create organisms with the perceived suboptimal designs that can be seen in nature . . . The term 'incompetent design', a play on 'intelligent design', has been coined by Donald Wise of the University of Massachusetts Amherst to describe aspects of nature that are currently flawed in design."[150]

David Steele's brash dystelogical assessment

For instance, David Steele ridiculed creationist accounts of origins by claiming that if God designed the human body, He was somewhat of a bungler, getting some things right, and others not so good:

"However, this is to look at only half the evidence relevant to the design hypothesis. We also have to consider

---

[149]Charles Darwin, *Autobiography* in Christopher Hitchens, *The Portable Atheist: Essential Readings for the Nonbeliever,* Philadelphia PA (De Capo Press, 2007) 95.
[150]https://en.wikipedia.org/wiki/Argument_from_poor_design

those many aspects of living organisms which appear, from a design point of view, to be botched or incompetent."[151]

Credit Steele for boldness; but perhaps for a bit of hubris and arrogance as well. He moved on to provide what he considered examples of poor design:

"There are innumerable such examples. One is the fact that human babies naturally have to be born through the bone-enclosed pelvic opening. Untold billions of babies and their mothers have died in childbirth because of this elementary 'design flaw' . . . Any intelligent designer planning the human body from scratch would have installed a birth opening in the lower abdomen, where there is no tight constriction of bones."[152]

I am suspicious that Steele's critical assessment of the human birth system owes more to a lack of scientific knowledge than to any default in the design itself, and I have no doubt that science will eventually make clear that the designs he criticized, are, in fact, optimal to the overall benefit of the human system.

William Demski stated:

"Indeed, there is no such thing as perfect design. Real designers strive for *constrained optimization* . . . Henry Petroski, an engineer and historian at Duke University, aptly remarks in *Invention by Design*: 'All design involves conflicting objectives and hence compromise, and the best designs will always be those that come up with the best compromise.' Constrained optimization is the art of compromise between conflicting objectives."[153]

---

[151]David Ramsay Steele, *Atheism Explained*, 51.
[152]David Ramsay Steele, *Atheism Explained*, 51
[153]William A. Demski, Introduction, *Signs of Intelligence: Understanding Intelligent Design*, Edited by William A. Demski & James M. Kushiner, Grand Rapids MI (Brazos Press, 2001) 9.

Therefore, those who suggest weaknesses in nature's designs should perhaps tread more humbly before casting their aspersions.

Is the human eye poorly designed?

One of the favorite targets of atheists and skeptics for claims of bad design is interestingly enough the human eye. David Steele pressed home his criticism of the idea that God designed the human eye:

> "The human body is an exhibition of engineering disasters. The routing of the optic nerve through the front of the retina, so that there is a 'blind spot' in each eye, and the routing of the male testis around the ureter, when it would be so much simpler and more efficient to take a direct route, are other instances. These sorry failings do not contradict the proposition that many features of the human body display marvelous construction . . . The two aspects exist side by side: dazzling sophistication and crude sloppiness. ID theory has no explanation to offer for the latter. Darwinism tells us to expect both."[154]

The creationist Peter Gurney provided a response to criticisms of the design of the human eye:

> "Although it would appear at first sight that the inverted arrangement of the retina has disadvantages and is inefficient, in reality these objections amount to little. Even evolutionists concede that the inverted retina serves those creatures that possess it, very well; it affords them superb visual acuity. We have reviewed the necessity for this arrangement which turns on the nature of the photoreceptors.
>
> Light at various wavelengths is capable of very damaging effects on biological machinery. The retina, besides being an extremely sophisticated transducer and

---

[154]David Ramsay Steele, *Atheism Explained,* 51-52

image processor, is clearly designed to withstand the toxic and heating effects of light. The eye is well equipped to protect the retina against radiation we normally encounter in everyday life. Besides the almost complete exclusion of ultraviolet radiation by the cornea and the lens together, the retina itself is endowed with a number of additional mechanisms to protect against such damage: The retinal pigment epithelium produces substances which combat the damaging chemical by-products of light radiation. The retinal pigment epithelium plays an essential part sustaining the photoreceptors. This includes recycling and metabolising their products, thereby renewing them in the face of continual wear from light bombardment. The central retina is permeated with xanthophyll pigment which filters and absorbs short-wavelength visible light.

The photoreceptors thus need to be in intimate contact with the retinal pigment epithelium, which is opaque. The retinal pigment epithelium, in turn, needs to be in intimate contact with the choroid (also opaque) both to satisfy its nutritional requirements and to prevent (by means of the heat sink effect of its massive blood flow) overheating of the retina from focused light.

If the human retina were 'wired' the other way around (the verted configuration), as evolutionists such as Dawkins propose, these two opaque layers would have to be interposed in the path of light to the photoreceptors which would leave them in darkness!

Thus, I suggest that the need for protection against light-induced damage, which a verted retina in our natural environment could not provide to the same degree, is a major, if not *the* major reason for the existence of the inverted configuration of the retina."[155]

Jonathan Sarfati, also responded to the critical assessment of the eye's design, particularly to those

---

[155]Peter W. V. Gurney, *Is Our 'Inverted' Retina Really 'Bad Design'?*, The *Journal of Creation*, April 1999, at web address: https://creation.com/is-our-inverted-retina-really-bad-design

made by the evolutionist Kenneth Miller on a special
PBS program:

> "Miller raised the old canard of the backwardly wired
> vertebrate retina, as he has done elsewhere. The [PBS]
> narrator even claimed that the eye's 'nerves interfere with
> images,' and that the so-called 'blind spot' is a serious
> problem . . . It would be nice if anti-creationists actually
> learned something about the eye before making such
> claims . . . In fact, any engineer who designed something
> remotely as good as the eye would probably win the Nobel
> Prize! If Miller and the PBS producers disagree, then I
> challenge them to design a better eye (color perception,
> resolution, coping with range of light intensity, night vision
> as well as day vision, etc.)! And this must be done under
> the constraints of embryonic development . . . Someone
> who does know about eye design is the ophthalmologists
> Dr. George Marshall, who said: 'The idea that the eye is
> wired backward comes from a lack of knowledge of eye
> function and anatomy.' He explained that the nerves could
> not go behind the eye, because that space is reserved for
> the choroid, which provides the rich blood supply needed
> for the very metabolically active retinal pigment
> epithelium (RPE). This is necessary to regenerate the
> photoreceptors, and to absorb excess heat. So it is
> necessary for the nerves to go in front instead. The claim
> on the program that they interfere with the image is
> blatantly false, because the nerves are virtually
> transparent because of their small size and also having
> about the same refractive index as the surrounding
> vitreous humor. In fact, what limits the eye's resolution is
> the diffraction of light waves at the pupil (proportional to
> the wavelength to the pupil's size), so alleged
> improvements of the retina would make no difference . . .
> Some evolutionists claim that the cephalad eye is somehow
> 'right,' i.e., with nerves behind the receptor, and the [PBS]
> program showed photographs of these creatures (e.g.,
> octopus, squid) during this segment. But no one who has
> actually bothered to study these eyes could make such
> claims with integrity. In fact, cephalopods don't see as well

as humans, and the octopus eye structure is totally different and much simpler. It's more like 'a compound eye with a single lense.'"[156]

New research is casting further doubt on the accepted wisdom concerning design flaws in the human eye. For instance, in an article in the *Scientific American Magazine* by Erez Rebak, although written from an evolutionary viewpoint, nevertheless, dispels with the notion of bad design in the human eye, and in particular the so-called problem of the inverted retina:

> "The human eye is optimized to have good colour vision at day and high sensitivity at night. But until recently it seemed as if the cells in the retina were wired the wrong way round, with light travelling through a mass of neurons before it reaches the light-detecting rod and cone cells. New research presented at a meeting of the American Physical Society has uncovered a remarkable vision-enhancing function for this puzzling structure.
>
> About a century ago, the fine structure of the retina was discovered. The retina is the light-sensitive part of the eye, lining the inside of the eyeball. The back of the retina contains cones to sense the colours red, green and blue. Spread among the cones are rods, which are much more light-sensitive than cones, but which are colour-blind.
>
> Before arriving at the cones and rods, light must traverse the full thickness of the retina, with its layers of neurons and cell nuclei. These neurons process the image information and transmit it to the brain, but until recently it has not been clear why these cells lie in front of the cones and rods, not behind them. This is a long-standing puzzle, even more so since the same structure, of neurons before light detectors, exists in all vertebrates, showing evolutionary stability.

---

[156]Jonathan Sarfati, *Refuting Evolution 2: What PBS and the Scientific Community Don't Want You to Know*, Green Forest AZ (Master Books, Inc, 2002) 117, 118, 119, 120.

Researchers in Leipzig found that glial cells, which also span the retinal depth and connect to the cones, have an interesting attribute. These cells are essential for metabolism, but they are also denser than other cells in the retina. In the transparent retina, this higher density (and corresponding refractive index) means that glial cells can guide light, just like fibre-optic cables.

In view of this, my colleague Amichai Labin and I built a model of the retina, and showed that the directional of glial cells helps increase the clarity of human vision. But we also noticed something rather curious: the colours that best passed through the glial cells were green to red, which the eye needs most for daytime vision. The eye usually receives too much blue—and thus has fewer blue-sensitive cones.

Further computer simulations showed that green and red are concentrated five to ten times more by the glial cells, and into their respective cones, than blue light. Instead, excess blue light gets scattered to the surrounding rods.

This surprising result of the simulation now needed an experimental proof. With colleagues at the Technion Medical School, we tested how light crosses guinea pig retinas. Like humans, these animals are active during the day and their retinal structure has been well-characterised, which allowed us to simulate their eyes just as we had done for humans. Then we passed light through their retinas and, at the same time, scanned them with a microscope in three dimensions. This we did for 27 colours in the visible spectrum.

The result was easy to notice: in each layer of the retina we saw that the light was not scattered evenly, but concentrated in a few spots. These spots were continued from layer to layer, thus creating elongated columns of light leading from the entrance of the retina down to the cones at the detection layer. Light was concentrated in these columns up to ten times, compared to the average intensity.

Even more interesting was the fact that the colours that were best guided by the glial cells matched nicely with the colours of the cones. The cones are not as sensitive as the rods, so this additional light allowed them to function better—even under lower light levels. Meanwhile, the bluer light, that was not well-captured in the glial cells, was scattered onto the rods in its vicinity.

These results mean that the retina of the eye has been optimised so that the sizes and densities of glial cells match the colours to which the eye is sensitive (which is in itself an optimisation process suited to our needs). This optimisation is such that colour vision during the day is enhanced, while night-time vision suffers very little. The effect also works best when the pupils are contracted at high illumination, further adding to the clarity of our colour vision."[157]

The foregoing should put to rest arguments claiming poor design in the human eye.

Sin and the fall

Further, when atheists like Bertrand Russell ridicule creationism by wondering if the present world was the best that a divine being could do, they often forget a key piece of the biblical worldview; they fail to account for the destructive effects of mankind's rebellion and fall in the Garden of Eden. Man was cast out of paradise and suffered under the effects of the consequent curse and its corrupting influence evident in every area of our world (Genesis 3:3, 7-19; Romans 8:20-21).

---

[151] Rez Rebak, *The Purpose of Our Eyes' Strange Wiring Is Unveiled: The reverse-wiring of the eyeball has long been a mystery, but new research shows a remarkable structural purpose: increasing and sharpening our color vision*, Scientific American, March 15, 2015, at web address: https://www.scientificamerican.com/article/the-purpose-of-our-eyes-strange-wiring-is-unveiled/

Consider this illustration. A painter is hired to paint a room blue. He does his job and the room looks great. However, later the homeowner decided, against the advice of the painter, to change the color of the trim. Unfortunately, while doing so, he accidentally spilled paint down the wall, leaving a big red mess on the wall.

Would it be fair to criticize the painter for doing a bad job when it was the homeowner that marred the end result. Likewise, it is unfair to criticize God's good creation because it has been marred by man's rebellion.

Fine Tuning and the Anthropic Principle

One form of the teleological argument (the argument from design) that has gained respect is the fine tuning argument.

Scientists have increasingly recognized that the universe appears to have just the right set of physical properties conducive to the development of life, and especially of human life. This recognition has come to be known as the anthropic principle (from the Greek word *anthropos* for man) which seeks to account for why it seems the world was actually designed for our development. Or as physicist Freeman Dyson stated it: "It's like the universe knew we were coming."[158]

Paul Davies brought the question into focus in his 2006 book *The Goldilocks Enigma*.[159] Davies explored various explanations for this anthropic principle, and

---

[158]Freeman Dyson, http://www.rich-hansen.com/universe-knew-coming/

[159]Paul Davies, *The Goldilocks Enigma*, https://en.wikipedia.org/wiki/Anthropic_principle

why the universe appears to have been designed for the formation of life as we know it. *The Goldilocks Enigma* was a perfect metaphor capturing the amazing alignment of scientific facts that are conducive to life; not too hot, not too cold, but just right!

For believers the question is a no-brainer; the world *appears* to have been designed for us *because it was* created for us! Next question.

Supporters of this viewpoint have called this perspective the *fine-tuning argument*, since they believe God has fine-tuned the universe perfectly for life. Wallace Matson alternately called it the "The Probability Argument"[160] since the anthropic principle showed how improbable were the natural occurrence of all the factors leading to life.

Simon Friederich explained how the fine-tuning argument has become a powerful version of the teleological argument:

> "A classic response to the observation that the conditions in our universe seem fine-tuned for life is to infer the existence of a cosmic designer who created life-friendly conditions. If one identifies this designer with some supernatural agent or God, the inference from fine-tuning for life to the existence of a designer becomes a version of the teleological argument. Indeed, many regard the argument from fine-tuning for a designer as the strongest version of the teleological argument that contemporary science affords."[161]

---

[160]Wallace I. Matson, *The Argument From Design*, chapter in *Critiques of God: Making the Case Against Belief in God,* Peter A. Angeles, Editor, Amherst New York (Prometheus Books, 1997) 70.
[161]Simon Friederich, *Fine-Tuning, Stanford Encyclopedia of Philosophy*, August 22, 2017, online at https://plato.stanford.edu/entries/fine-tuning/

Barnes added:

"The strong anthropic principle says that the universe seems to be set up exactly right to eventually produce intelligent life, like humans. A more precisely accurate name for this argument would be to call it 'the argument from fine tuning.' Others have called it the 'goldilocks' argument named after the fairy tale character who rejected things that were too big or too small, too hot or too cold, too soft or too hard, and was satisfied only when she found things that were just right. The universe, says the anthropic principle, seems to have been fine tuned so that things are just right for the long process of cosmic and biological evolution that leads to the emergence of intelligent life like us humans."[162]

Former atheist Antony flew had been unimpressed with traditional formulations of the teleological argument, but was increasingly impressed with the fine-tuning arguments in light of the advances in scientific knowledge:

"Although I was once sharply critical of the argument from design, I have since come to see that, when correctly formulated, this argument constitutes a persuasive case for the existence of God."[163]

More to the point he continued:

"Our Finely Tuned Universe. That vacation scenario is a clumsy, limited parallel to the so-called fine-tuning argument. The recent popularity of this argument has highlighted a new dimension of the laws of nature. 'The

[162]Michael Horace Barnes, *Understanding Religion and Science: Introducing the Debate*, New York (Continuum International Publishing Group, 2010) 171.
[163]Antony Flew, *There is a God: How the World's Most Notorious Atheist Changed His Mind*, New York (HarperCollins/HarperOne, 2007) 95.

more I examine the universe and study the details of its architecture,' writes physicist Freeman Dyson, 'the more evidence I find that the universe in some sense knew we were coming.' In other words, the laws of nature seem to have been crafted so as to move the universe toward the emergence and sustenance of life. This is the anthropic principle, popularized by such thinkers as Martin Rees, John Barrows, and John Leslie."[164]

Examples of fine-tuning

Let us consider some of the evidence advanced in support of the fine-tuning argument. Barnes provided these examples related to our solar system, and specifically the earth:

> "Another set of finely tuned conditions make this particular planet a safe home for life to develop . . . Our planet is marvelously well situated, far enough from the sun not to be crisped, close enough to keep most of its water in a liquid state. Its tilt assures that different parts of the globe receive good doses of warming at different seasons, so the zone for life to develop is large. The moon has enough gravitational drag on the planet so as to keep it from wobbling about. A severe case of wobbles would condemn too many areas to long periods of overheating alternating with long periods of freeze. The giant planets Jupiter and Saturn sweep up enough debris from the solar system that this planet is no longer bombarded constantly be meteors . . . The outer core of the planet, made from iron, generates an electromagnetic field around the earth that protects life from excessive radiation. The list of planetary conditions supportive of life is quite long."[165]

Jay Richards provided further evidence of fine-tuning for life on earth:

---

[164]Antony Flew, *There is a God,* 114.
[165]Michael Horace Barnes, *Understanding Religion and Science,* 173.

"*Life must be in the right type of galaxy.* Of the three types of galaxies, only spiral galaxies (like the Milky Way) can support life. *Life must be in the right location in the galaxy.* We are sitting in just the right place in the Milky Way to avoid harmful radiation. *Life must have the right type of star.* While most stars are too large, too luminous, or too unstable to support life, our sun is just the right size and age . . . *Life must have the right relationship to its host star.* If Earth were slightly closer to or farther from the sun, water would either freeze or evaporate, rendering Earth uninhabitable for complex life. *Life needs surrounding planets for protection.* A habitable planet must have large surrounding bodies (such as Jupiter and Uranus) to protect it from incoming comets. Life requires the right type of moon. If earth did not have a moon of the right size and distance, it would be uninhabitable. The moon stabilizes the earth's tilt, preventing extreme temperatures and thus creating a stable, life-friendly environment."[166]

Hans Küng agreed:

"An extraordinary large number of difficult conditions had to be fulfilled for life to be possible on earth. Such a planet had to have a mean temperature of around 15° Celsius. So it could not be like the glowingly hot Venus (450° Clesius surface temperature), which orbits closer to the Sun, or, farther out, like the ice-cold Mars (70° Clesius mean temperature) where there can be no flowing water. Such a planet should not turn to quickly on its own axis to avoid stormy winds (here

[166]Jay Richards, *Why Is the Universe Just Right for Life?*, chapter in Sean McDowell & Jonathan Morrow, *Is God Just a Human Invention? And Seventeen Other Questions Raised by the New Atheists*, Grand Rapids MI (Kregel Publications, 2010) 97.

the Moon acts like a brake on our earth). At the same time, it should be protected as far as possible from the impact of great lumps of stone (large, heavy Jupiter on the outermost planetary orbit keeps a long way from earth)."[167]

It is certainly possible that such features as the moon acting as a brake to slow the earth's spin and that Jupiter protects the earth from dangerous cosmic debris are merely random results of an undirected and meaningless universe.

But it seems much more likely that they are, in fact, the result of the intelligent design of the Creator.

In an interview with Lee Strobel, Guilliermo Gonzalez mentioned more fascinating evidence in support of the fine-tuning argument:

> "What's really amazing is that total eclipses are possible because the sun is four hundred times larger than the moon, but it's also four hundred times farther away. It's that incredible coincidence that creates a perfect match . . . What intrigued me . . . was that the very time and place where perfect solar eclipses appear in the universe also corresponds to the one time and place where there are observers to see them."[168]

Robin Collins provided further examples of fine-tuning:

> "Calculations indicate that if the strong nuclear force, the force that binds protons and neutrons together in an

[167] Hans Küng, *The Beginning of All Things: Science and Religion,* Grand Rapids MI (William B. Eerdmans Publishing Company, 2005) 134-135.
[168] Guillermo Gonzalez as quoted by Lee Strobel, *The Case for a Creator: A Journalist Investigates Scientific Evidence That Points Toward God,* Grand Rapids MI (Zondervan, 2004) 230.

atom, had been stronger or weaker by as little as five percent, life would be impossible . . .Calculations by Brandon Carter show that if gravity had been stronger or weaker by one part in 10^{40} , then life-sustaining stars like the sun could not exist. This would most likely make life impossible . . . If the neutron were not about 1.001 times the mass of the proton, all protons would have decayed into neutrons or all neutrons would have decayed into protons, and thus life would not be possible . . . If the electromagnetic force were slightly stronger or weaker, life would be impossible."[169]

Puddle theory as an answer to Fine-tuning arguments

In his book, *The Salmon of Doubt*, Douglas Adams provided a very interesting and thought-provoking analogy about a mud puddle that challenges the ideas of fine-tuning and design for the universe:

"Imagine a puddle waking up one morning and thinking, 'This is an interesting world I find myself in, an interesting hole I find myself in, fits me rather neatly, doesn't it? In fact, it fits me staggeringly well, must have been made to have me in it!' This is such a powerful idea that as the sun rises in the sky and the air heats up and as, gradually, the puddle gets smaller and smaller, it's still frantically hanging on to the notion that everything's going to be all right, because this world was meant to have him in it, was built to have him in it; so the moment he disappears catches him rather by surprise. I think this may be something we need to be on the watch out for."[170]

---

[169] Robin Collins, *A Scientific Argument for the Existence of God*, chapter in *Reason for the Hope Within*, Michael J. Murray, Editor, Grand Rapids MI (William B. Eerdmans Publishing Company, 1999) 49.

[170] Douglas Adams, *The Salmon of Doubt: Hitchhiking the Galaxy One Last Time*, Harmony Books, 2002, p. 131. as quoted on Wikipedia at https://en.wikipedia.org/wiki/Fine-tuned_Universe

This parabolic story serves as a warning to avoid narcissistic, we are the center of the universe, thinking. Point well made. However, further reflection shows the flaws in Adams' puddle parable. For since Adams presents us with a thoughtful and reflective puddle, he ought to have had the puddle look over its situation and ask, "Am I the result of natural or designed processes? Are there any signs that I was made this way by an intelligent agency or am I merely the result of chance and natural causes?

If I am puddle, I would be inclined toward belief that I was a result of natural causes. However, if I am a swimming pool, I would be inclined toward the designed inference. I would see my walls constructed of materials that have been shaped and formed by processes that don't occur naturally. I would see the ladder perfectly arranged for the purpose of people to climb on. I would see a filtration system of the complexity and design not found in nature.[171] I would conclude that I was designed by someone for the purpose of swimming.

Alternative universes: Enter the multiverse

The fine-tuning argument is, of course, not popular with those committed to naturalism and atheism, and therefore other alternatives have been advanced to explain the phenomenon. Davies discussion of these alternatives in *The Goldilocks Enigma*[172] included the

---

[171]This is not to say that nature doesn't have effective filtration systems i.e., water running through soil, weatherization etc, but to show the difference between designed and natural systems. Further, even the 'naturally' occurring filtration systems reflect the design of the creator God in the beginning.

[172] Paul Davies, *The Goldilocks Enigma: Why is the Universe Just*

possibility that the design owes its origin to alien beings (isn't God an alien being?); that there are many multitudes of universes or multiverses; and that we just happen to reside in one with apparent design.

Evers explained that:

> "The term 'multiverse' was coined by the American philosopher and psychologists William James in 1895 and refers to the hypothetical set of multiple possible universes (parallel universes/dimensions)."[173]

Michael Martin further explained the concept:

> "Moreover, cosmologists have developed an alternative naturalistic explanatory model in terms of so-called world ensembles. They have conjectured that what we call our universe—our galaxy and the other galaxies—may be one among many alternative universes. The universe as a whole is composed of a vast number of such worlds or universes."[174]

Likewise, John Lennox described the multiverse concept:

> "The only way to avoid the conclusion [of the fine-tuning argument], according to Leslie, is to believe in the so-called 'many worlds' or 'multiverse' hypothesis (popularized in David Deutsch's book *The Fabric of Reality*), which postulates the simultaneous existence of many, possibly infinitely many parallel universes in which (almost) anything which is theoretically possible will ultimately be actualized, so that there is nothing surprising in the existence of a universe like ours."[175]

Right for Life, New York (Simon & Schuster Paperbacks, 2006).

[173]Liz Evers, *It's About Time, From Calendars and Clocks to Moon Cycles and Light Years—A History,* New York (Metro Books, 2015) 191.

[174]Michael Martin, *Atheism: A Philosophical Justification,* Philadelphia PA (Temple University Press, 1990) 133.

Problems with multiverse proposals

Let us consider some of the problems with multiverse proposals. For instance, Gingerich draws attention to the theoretical nature of multiverse claims:

> "While mathematics might show that alternative universes *could* exist, it would be a matter of faith that they actually do exist, with no hope of observational confirmation."[176]

Kerry Walters noted physicist Paul Davies rejection of the concept:

> "It's worth pointing out that physicist Paul Davies rejects the multiverse thesis on the grounds that 'like a blundererbuss, it explains everything and nothing.'"[177]

Flew also made reference to Davies:

> "Both Paul Davies and Richard Swineburne reject the multiverse idea . . . A true scientific explanation, says Davies, is like a single well-aimed bullet. The idea of a multiverse replaces the rationally ordered real world with an infinitely complex charade and makes the whole idea of 'explanation' meaningless. Swineburne is just as strong in his disdain for the multiverse explanation: 'It is crazy to postulate a trillion (causally unconnected) universes to explain the features of one universe, when postulating one entity (God) will do the job."[178]

---

[175]John C. Lennox, *God's Undertaker: Has Science Buried God?*, New Updated Edition, Oxford England (Lion Books, 2009) 74.

[176]Owen Gingerich, *'God's Goof,'and the Universe That Knew We Were Coming*, included in *Science and Religion: Are They Compatible?*, Paul Kurtz, Editor, Amherst New York (Prometheus Books, 2003) 56.

[177]Kerry Walters, *Atheism: A Guide for the Perplexed*, New York (The Continuum International Publishing Group Inc, 2010) 51.

[178]Antony Flew, *There is a God: How the World's Most Notorious*

Evers points out that Davies rejected the multiverse concept as essentially a religious belief:

"Writings in the *New York Times* in 2013, cosmologist Paul Davies slings the worst kind of mud at the hypothesis, comparing it to religion: 'All cosmologists accept that there are some regions of the universe that lie beyond the reach of our telescopes, but somewhere on the slippery slope between that and the idea that there is an infinite number of universes, credibility reaches a limit. As one slips down that slope, more and more must be accepted on faith, and less and less is open to scientific verification. Extreme multiverse explanations are therefore reminiscent of theological discussions. Indeed, invoking an infinite number of unseen universes to explain the unusual features of the one we do see is just as ad hoc as invoking an unseen Creator. The multiverse theory may be dressed up in scientific language, but in essence it requires the same leap of faith.'"[179]

Flew added his perspective:

"As I have mentioned, I did not find the multiverse alternative very helpful. The postulation of multiple universes, I maintained, is a truly desperate alternative. If the existence of one universe requires an explanation, multiple universes require a much bigger explanation: the problem is increased by the factor of whatever the total number of universes is. It seems a little like the case of a schoolboy whose teacher doesn't believe his dog ate his homework, so he replaces the first version with the story that a pack of dogs—too many to count—ate his homework."[180]

Atheist Changed His Mind, New York (HarperCollins/HarperOne, 2007) 118-119.

[179]Liz Evers, *It's About Time, From Calendars and Clocks to Moon Cycles and Light Years—A History*, New York (Metro Books, 2015) 191-192.

[180]Antony Flew, *There is a God*, 137.

Estimating the hypothetical

Further, I find it quite astonishing that even though the concept of mutliverses is entirely hypothetical, absent of any empirical evidence, nevertheless, some have been able to calculate their number at 10,500.[181] William Lane Craig stated: "It turns out that string theory allows around 10^{500} different possible universes governed by present laws of nature."[182] In light of such audacious speculative calculations, we may as well try to estimate how many striped dragons live on the planet Vinoon![183]

Doesn't the word universe include everything already?

I must say I wholeheartedly agree with the common-sense assessment of Vincent Bugliosi about Richard Dawkins' speculations concerning other universes:

> "I thought the dictionary definition of universe was everything that exists, the totality of all things, known and unknown. Hence, there cannot be multiple universes."[184]

---

[181]This number was reported to have been stated by "Cambridge Mathematician" John Barrow in a lecture attended by National Public Radio correspondent Barbara Bradley Hagerty and included in her book *Fingerprints of God: The Search for the Science of Spirituality* (New York, Riverhead, 2009), 269-270, as quoted by Sean McDowell & Jonathan Morrow, *Is God Just a Human Invention? And Seventeen Other Questions Raised by the New Atheists,* Grand Rapids MI (Kregel Publications, 2010) 259.

[182]*The Future of Atheism: Alister McGrath & Daniel Dennett in Dialogue,* Robert B. Stewart, Editor, Minneapolis MN (Fortress Press, 2008) 81.

[183] I am likewise dumbfounded at how Gerald Shroeder knows that there are "10^{56} grams of the entire universe." Gerald Schroeder, *The Science of God: The Convergence of Scientific and Biblical Wisdom,* New York (The Free Press, 1997) 1. Vinoon is fictional on my part.

In another place, Bugliosi continued the thought:

> "I wonder what scientists mean when they say the 'universe is finite' and 'expanding' because of the big bang. The words 'finite' and 'expanding' necessarily mean that at any given point in time there's an end of the universe. But if so, what's at the end of the universe? Certainly not a fence or wall. An invisible line? But if so, what's on the other side?"[185]

Steven Weinberg stated: "By definition the universe is all there is, and there can be nothing outside it."[186]

Gerald Schroeder's answer is that "Space as we know it ends at the edge of the universe (there is no outside to our universe)."[187]

Metaverse to replace universe?

Nevertheless, David Steele offered new terminology to define the totality of all that exists:

> "The word 'universe' is often taken to mean 'everything that exists' . . . People talk of 'parallel universes,' 'alternate universes,' and 'multiple universes.' . . . In order to maintain clarity, it would be useful to mean everything that exists, and I propose the word 'metaverse.' It's part of the definition of 'metaverses' that there can never be more than one metaverse, and there can never be anything outside the metaverse. If there are many universes, they are all by definition parts of the metaverse."[188]

---

[184]Vincent Bugliosi, *Divinity of Doubt,* 56.

[185]Vincent Bugliosi, *Divinity of Doubt,* 294.

[186] Sandra Menssen & Thomas D. Sullivan, *The Agnostic Inquirer: Revelation from a Philosophical Standpoint*, Grand Rapids MI (William B. Eerdmans Publishing Company, 2007, 37.

[187]Gerald L. Schroeder, *Genesis and the Big Bang: The Discovery of Harmony Between Modern Science and the Bible*, New York (Bantam Books 1990) 62.

[188]David Ramsay Steele, *Atheism Explained: From Folly to Philosophy*, Chicago and La Salle, IL (Open Court Publishing

It seems unnecessary to coin a new term, *metaverse,* for the traditional word *universe.* Nevertheless, while I have no trouble with the term itself, I do have a problem with the expansive nature of Steele's definition:

> "If 'metaverse' is defined as 'everything that exists or ever has existed, including God if he exists or ever has existed,' then we have to say that the metaverse cannot possibly have a cause outside of itself."[189]

With a sleight of the philosophical hand, Steele defined God as a part of the universe, and on that basis argued for the impossibility of God as creator. This despite the fact that Christian theology has always maintained that God is a Spirit, independent of and transcendent in relationship to the universe. Therefore, Steele's definition is a misrepresentation of theism and should be rejected.

Multibodies?

Further, how is theorizing multiple universes different from theorizing that each of us may actually have multiple bodies (multibodies)? If the doctor says there is a 90 % chance the disease I have will kill me in the next year, can I find solace in the possibility that in my other hypothetical bodies, I am cancer free!

If the suggestion of multibodies seems incredible, remember that there is as much empirical evidence for the one (multibodies) as there is for the other (mutliverses); none!

And of course, one universe or many, it remains to explain their origin.

Company, 2008) 80.
[189]David Ramsay Steele, *Atheism Explained,* 80-81

Real motive for multiverse proposals

Sarfati commented on the ironic nature of multiverse proposals:

> "It's ironic that many materialists exclude God as an explanation for the complexity of the universe because He cannot be observed by science; but they are happy to postulate the existence of other universes which are also unobservable, even in principle."[190]

Groothius quoted Barr to the same effect:

> "Barr notes that in order to 'abolish one unobservable God,' various multiverse theories require 'an infinite number of unobservable substitutes.'"[191]

Multiverse as a dodge of fine-tuning arguments

It is not coincidental that multiverse proposals have paralleled the growing influence of fine-tuning arguments. John Polkinghorne showed that multiverse proposals are indeed a reaction and a response to the fine-tuning arguments:

> "Disliking the threat of theism, some scientists have sought an alternative explanation of apparent fine-tuning. This is provided by the conjecture of the multiverse . . which supposes that this universe is just one member of a vast portfolio of separate worlds, each with its own different laws and circumstances. If this collection is sufficiently large and varied, it might be that one of these

---

[190]Jonathan Sarfati, *Refuting Compromise: A Biblical and Scientific Refutation of 'Progressive Creationism' (Billions of Years), as Popularized by Astronomer Hugh Ross, Green Forest AZ* (Master Books, 2004) 189.

[191]Barr, *Modern Physics and Ancient Faith*, p. 157 in Douglass Groothuis, *Christian Apologetics: A Comprehensive Case for Biblical Faith*, Downers Grove IL (InterVarsity Press, 2011) 261.

universes is fine-tuned for carbon-life, and that is ours because we are carbon-based life. Our fertile universe is then simply a random winning ticket on some great multiversal lottery . . . In evaluating this proposal, it is important to recognize how speculative much of contemporary fundamental physics has come to be, relying solely on mathematical possibility, without the complementary input of constraining empirical results . . . **For this reason, the multiverse must be classified as a metascientific** approach to the issue of fine-tuning."[192]

John Lennox also described criticism of the multiverse hypothesis by Polkinghorne and Swinburne:

"John Polkinghorne, for instance, himself an eminent quantum theorist, rejects the many-universe interpretation: 'Let us recognize these speculations for what they are. They are not physics, but in the strictest sense, metaphysics. There is no purely scientific reason to believe in an ensemble of universes.'"[193]

Lee Strobel referred to William Lane Craig's similar observations:

"Many physicists subscribe to some sort of multiple universe, or 'multiverse,' theory, although others scoff at the idea, **charging that it's little more than a metaphysical escape hatch to avoid the fine-tuning evidence** for a designer . . . 'It's purely a concept, an idea, without scientific proof,' William Lane Craig, coauthor of *Theism, Atheism, and Big Bang* Cosmology, told me . . . The very fact that skeptics have to come up with such an outlandish theory is because the fine-tuning of the universe points

[192]John Polkinghorne, *God and Physics*, chapter in, William Lane Craig & Chad Meister, Editors, *God is Great, God is Good: Why Believing in God is Reasonable and Responsible,* Downers Grove IL (Inter Varsity Press, 2009) 71.

[193]John C. Lennox, *God's Undertaker: Has Science Buried God?,* New Updated Edition, Oxford England (Lion Books, 2009) 74.

powerfully toward an intelligent designer—and some people will hypothesize anything to avoid reaching that conclusion."[194]

In another place, William Lane Craig stated:

"The Many Worlds hypothesis is essentially an effort on the part of partisans of the chance hypothesis to multiply their probabilistic resources in order to reduce the improbability of the occurrence of fine-tuning. The very fact that they must resort to such a remarkable hypothesis is a sort of backhanded compliment to the design hypothesis in that they recognize that the fine-tuning does cry out for explanation."[195]

Barnes's noted the same weaknesses of the multiverse proposals:

"At this point it is difficult to say whether this is the only universe that has existed. No one has seen or experienced other universes, nor is there even indirect evidence of other universes. So their existence is highly speculative . . . Their main impact so far, is to allow skeptics a way around the SAP [Strong Anthropic Principle] argument by the notion of multiverses."[196]

Is the multiverse concept necessarily tied to naturalistic atheism?

Nevertheless, Lennox provided these words of caution:

[194]Lee Strobel, *The Case for a Creator: A Journalist Investigates Scientific Evidence That Points Toward God*, Grand Rapids MI (Zondervan, 2004) 171.
[195]William Lane Craig, *In Defense of Theistic Arguments*, chapter in *The Future of Atheism: Alister McGrath & Daniel Dennett in Dialogue*, Robert B. Stewart, Editor, Minneapolis MN (Fortress Press, 2008) 82.
[196]Michael Horace Barnes, *Understanding Religion and Science: Introducing the Debate*, New York (Continuum International Publishing Group, 2010) 174-175.

"It should, however, be pointed out that, although Leslie may be correct in suggesting that fine-tuning means that either there is a God or a multiverse, logically, these two options are not mutually exclusive, although they are usually presented as such. After all, parallel universes could be the work of a Creator."[197]

Lennox also described a perhaps surprising implication of the multiverse hypothesis:[198]

"However, if every possible universe exists, then, according to philosopher Alvin Plantinga of Notre Dame University, there must be a universe in which God exists, since his existence is logically possible.

In other words, atheism (or naturalism) is not necessarily the only game in town for multiverse proposals. Lennox showed that such proposals are compatible with theistic interpretations as well."

Finally, the multiverse explanation is in fact, *a God in gaps argument in reverse* since it attempts to explain the known (the universe) by imagined other universes for which there is no evidence. They trade belief in an invisible God for belief in invisible universes. To avoid the very reasonable belief in a single God, they invent multitudes of universes without a shred of evidence, thus revealing their naturalistic biases.

The teleological argument stands

After a rousing criticism of the teleological argument, J.J. C. Smart yet conceded:

"Nevertheless, the argument has a fascination for us that reason cannot easily dispel. Hume, in his twelfth dialogue, and after pulling the argument from design to

---

[197]John C. Lennox, *God's Undertaker*, 75.
[198]John C. Lennox, *God's Undertaker*, 76.

pieces in the previous eleven dialogues, nevertheless speaks as follows: 'A purpose, an intention, a design strikes everywhere the most careless, the most stupid thinker; and no man can be so hardened in absurd systems as at all times to reject it . . . all the sciences almost lead us insensibly to acknowledge a first Author.'"[199]

To conclude the discussion of the argument from design, I want to share a story that Robert Morey included in his book on atheism:

"The noted infidel Robert Ingersoll had decided to visit a new model of the solar system at the New York Planetarium. A scale model of the sun with all the planets moving in orbit around it was suspended from the ceiling. When Ingersoll entered the room and saw the display, he exclaimed, 'This is beautiful! 'Who made it?' The head of the planetarium, a theist, who was escorting Ingersoll, said, 'Why, no one made it. It just suddenly appeared by chance in this room one day.'"[200]

Chapter 8: The Cosmological Argument

The cosmological argument appears in various forms, but all begin with the reality of the world and argue back to the existence of God. William Reese defined the cosmological argument:

"The cosmological argument argues that the cosmos is not self-explanatory, and requires an unconditioned being,

---

[199]J.J. C. Smart, *The Existence of God*, reprinted in *God*, Edited by Timothy A. Robinson, from the Hackett Readings in Philosophy Series, Indianapolis IN (Hackett Publishing Company Inc, 1996) 56.
[200]Robert A. Morey, *The New Atheism and the Erosion of Freedom*, Minneapolis MN (Bethany House Publishers, 1986) 81-22.

God, as its explanation. Typically, the argument proceeds from the condition of motion, causality, or the contingency of the world to the conclusion that an unmoved mover, first cause, and necessary being must exist."[201]

Evans and Manis further defined the cosmological argument:

"Cosmological arguments are, as the name implies, attempts to infer the existence of God from the existence of the cosmos or universe . . . These arguments are sometimes called first-cause arguments because they attempt to infer that God must exist as the first or ultimate cause of the universe."[202]

Perhaps the most famous advocate of the traditional arguments for God's existence was Thomas Aquinas. His *five ways* were summed up by Norman Geisler:

"According to Aquinas, there are five ways we can demonstrate God's existence. We can argue: (1) from motion to an Unmoved Mover; (2) from effects to a First Cause; (3) from contingent being to a Necessary Being; (4) from degrees of perfection to a Most Perfect Being; and (5) from design in nature to a Designer of nature . . . Behind these arguments is the premise that all finite, changing beings need a cause outside themselves."[203]

A thousand years earlier, Aristotle had argued for a different version of the unmoved mover that nonetheless

[201]William L. Reese, *Dictionary of Philosophy and Religion: Eastern and Western Thought*, Atlantic Highlands NJ (Humanities Press, 1980) 108.

[202]C. Stephen Evans & R. Zachary Manis, *Philosophy of Religion: Thinking About Faith*, Second Edition, Downers Grove IL (InterVarsity Press, 2009) 67.

[203]Norman L. Geisler, *Baker Encyclopedia of Christian Apologetics*, Grand Rapids MI (Baker Books, 1999) 725.

inspired Thomas Aquinas in the middle ages. Peter Whitfield explained:

> "The ultimate problem which Aristotle faced was to identify the force which moved the Sun, stars, and planets. This he called the Prime Mover, and seems to have been unable to conceive of it other than a personal deity, which interacts with the spheres not by forcibly impelling them, but by drawing them toward himself with a transcendent power. This theory was to inspire Christian theologians to identify the Prime Mover with God."[204]

The Kalam Cosmological Argument

One of the problems often advanced in criticism of the cosmological argument is based upon the way the argument is stated, or rather misstated. Let us consider a typical example of this with the definition of the cosmological argument offered by the atheist David Eller:

> "The so-called 'cosmological' . . . argument . . .occurs in various forms . . . The best-known version is the 'first cause' argument. It maintains that everything requires a cause for it to be, and so everything (the universe as a whole) requires a cause for it to be. That cause cannot be part of the universe (since a cause must always precede its effect). Finally, there cannot be an infinite succession of causes. Therefore, there must be a first uncaused cause that is outside of or separate from the universe, which we call god(s)."[205]

Overall, Eller's definition is correct. However, in saying "it maintains that everything requires a cause" Eller failed to make an important distinction that is key

---

[204]Peter Whitfield, *Landmarks in Western Science: From Prehistory to the Atomic Age*, New York (Routledge, 1999) 34.

[205]David Eller, *Natural Atheism*, Cranford New Jersey (American Atheist Press, 2004) 25.

to the validity of the cosmological argument, and which is made clear by the Kalam cosmological argument. William Lane Craig explained:

> "As formulated by al-Ghazali, the argument has three simple steps: '*Whatever begins to exist has a cause.* The universe began to exist. Therefore, the universe has a cause.'"[206]

This becomes important when critics ask, "If everything needs a cause, why doesn't God need a cause?" The Kalam cosmological argument anticipates that question and asserts that *it is only those things that have a beginning* that require a cause. *Since God had no beginning, He requires no cause.*

In response to Craig's Kalam cosmological argument, Michael Martin argued:

> "At most, this Kalam argument shows that some personal agent or agents created the universe. Craig cannot validly conclude that a single agent is the creator. On the contrary, for all he shows, there may have been trillions of personal agents involved in the creation."[207]

Martin's argument, rather than undermining the cosmological argument, actually has the opposite effect, in that he concedes the reasonableness of their being a transcendent and preexisting cause of the universe. Quibbling over *the identity* of that first cause, whether it is one or many, is irrelevant to *the fact* of a first cause.

---

[206]William Lane Craig, in Lee Strobel, *The Case for a Creator: A Journalist Investigates Scientific Evidence That Points Toward God,* Grand Rapids MI (Zondervan, 2004) 120.
[207]Michael Martin, *Atheism: A Philosophical Justification,* Philadelphia PA (Temple University Press, 1990) 103.

The argument from motion

Let us consider one form of the cosmological argument, Aquinas' argument from motion:

> "The first and more manifest way is the argument from motion. It is evident from our senses, that in the world some things are in motion. Now whatever is in motion is put in motion by another . . . For motion is nothing else than the reduction of something from potentiality to actuality . . . Therefore, whatever is in motion must be put in motion by another . . . But this cannot go on to infinity, because then there would be no first mover . . . Therefore it is necessary to arrive at a first mover, put in motion by no other; and this everyone understands to be God."[208]

This seems to be a very common-sense argument which probably accounts for its mass appeal, despite the criticisms of it by skeptical philosophers. It has been attacked on the basis of the logical possibility of an infinite regress. Great philosophical arguments have been advanced arguing that an infinite regress is no less possible or plausible than a first cause.

Can there be an infinite regress?

As we have seen, in order to escape the cosmological argument, skeptics have argued for the reasonableness of an infinite regress. For example, Martin stated:

> "Aquinas gives no non-question begging reason why there could not be a nontemporal infinite regress of causes."[209]

---

[208]Thomas Aquinas, *The Five Ways, from the Summa Theologica*, Part 1, as reprinted in *A Modern Introduction to Philosophy: Readings from Classical and Contemporary Sources*, Third Edition, Paul Edwards & Arthur Pap, Editors, New York, (The Free Press, 1973) 408.

This seems to be a case of special pleading; arguing against our normal experience in favor of an infinite regress merely to avoid the powerful implications of the argument from motion.

Of course, one is allowed to believe whatever they wish, but the mere possibility of an infinite regress does not count as a refutation of the first cause argument. An alternate hypothesis alone does not negate another hypothesis unless it is accompanied with arguments that favor the one over the other. But where is the argument that shows an infinite regress more palatable than a first cause for the origin of the universe?

Can the universe itself be the first cause?

Another critical response, by Hume and other philosophers, to the cosmological argument was to argue that the *universe itself* is the first or final cause. For example, Eller asked:

> "Further, if some being can be self-caused or self-grounded, why could not the universe be also? If we are going to imagine something violating every supposed tenet of our experience, why not cut out the middleman and attribute that quality to the universe itself?"[210]

Fair enough. Logic demands that there is either an eternal succession of cause and effect, which seems to defy logic, or that everything can be traced back to an "unmoved mover," (whether it be God or the universe itself) an effect without a cause, which also seems to defy logic.

---

[209]Michael Martin, *Atheism,* 56
[210]David Eller, *Natural Atheism,* 26-27

The inescapable paradox

In other words, we necessarily arrive at a paradox regardless of the choice we make. In that case, the atheist (who believes in an eternal chain of causation, or in an eternal universe) does not have any rational or logical advantage over the believer who believes that God is the final cause.

But science tips the scales in favor of the theist when the implications of the second law of thermodynamics are considered. This is because if the universe is eternal, it should have died a heat death by now. Peacock stated:

> "Increasing entropy is therefore taking the universe towards a final end: if the Second Law makes a beginning essential, it makes an end inevitable."[211]

Henry Morris observed:

> "When all the energy of the cosmos has been degraded to random heat energy, with random motion of molecules and uniform low-level temperature, the universe will have died a 'heat-death.' The fact that the universe is not yet dead is clear evidence that it is not infinitely old."[212]

R. Douglass Geivett elaborated on the same point:

> "Given sufficient time, the universe will eventually run out of energy and reach a state of equilibrium known as 'heat death.' At this stage, all of the universe's useful energy will be gone. If the universe had been in existence for an infinite duration, then it would have already run out of energy. Yet, since there is disequilibrium in the

---

[211]Roy E. Peacock, *A Brief History of Eternity*, Wheaton IL (Crossway Books, 1990) 114.
[212]Henry M. Morris, Editor, *Scientific Creationism*, El Cajon, CA (Master Books, 1974, 1985) 25.

temperature of the universe, it must have a finite past. Therefore, the universe had a beginning."[213]

It seems then, that the most reasonable and rational choice is to accept the conclusion of the cosmological argument that there is a first cause, a beginning less beginner, an unmoved mover, a necessary being as the origin of the contingent world, and this is God.

Problems with alternative explanations to the cosmological argument

The alternative explanations to the cosmological argument offered by skeptics suffer from serious philosophical problems. We have seen that an *eternal universe* is not compatible with the second law of thermodynamics, nor is it consistent with prevailing big-bang cosmology. As we have also seen, arguing for an *eternal regress* of cause and effect runs counter to the second law.

We can illustrate this problem with appeal to a train analogy offered by R. P. Phillips:

> "In a goods train each truck is moved and moves by the action of the one immediately in front of it. If then we suppose the train to be infinite, i.e., that there is no end to it, and so no engine which starts the motion, it is plain that no truck will move. To lengthen it out to infinity will not give it what no member of it possess of itself, viz. the power of drawing the truck behind it. If then we see any truck in motion, we know there must be an end to the series of trucks which gives causality to the whole."[214]

---

[213]R. Douglass Geivett, *How Did the Universe Begin?* Chapter in Sean McDowell & Jonathan Morrow, *Is God Just a Human Invention?*, 75.

[214]R. P. Phillips, *The Principles of Natural Theology*, p. 58, as quoted by Paul Edwards, *A Critique of the Cosmological Argument*,

So those who argue for an eternal regress of cause and effect have the problem of explaining not only how this train ever left the station in the first place, but also how it could still be in motion if it is, in fact, eternal, in violation of the second law of thermodynamics.

Another option open to skeptics desperate for an alternative to the cosmological argument is to argue that the universe just popped into existence, everything from nothing. Eternal effect with zero cause (More on this in Chapter 17). Desperate indeed.

So where does the cosmological argument stand today. Philosopher Paul Edwards provided this assessment:

"The so-called 'cosmological proof' is one of the oldest and most popular arguments for the existence of God. It was forcibly criticized by Hume, Kant, and Mill, but it would be inaccurate to consider the argument dead or even moribund."[215]

---

chapter in Louis P. Pojman, *Philosophy: The Quest for Truth*, Sixth Edition, New York. Oxford (Oxford University Press, 2006) 75.

[215]Paul Edwards, *A Critique of the Cosmological Argument*, chapter in Louis P. Pojman, *Philosophy: The Quest for Truth*, Sixth Edition, New York. Oxford (Oxford University Press, 2006) 73.

Chapter 9: The Argument from Universal Justice

"Though the mills of God grind slowly/Yet they grind exceedingly small; though with patience He stands waiting, with exactness grinds He all.[216]*"*

We now consider the argument from universal justice. The essential idea is that if there is no accounting or reckoning in the afterlife for the lives we have led, injustice will prevail. Stated positively, *that* all will one day face judgment before a holy God will result in universal justice.

For example, Jean Jacques Rousseau stated:

> "Had I no proof of the immortality of the soul than the oppression of the just and the triumph of the wicked in this world, this alone would prevent my having the least doubt of it . . . I should say to myself, we do not cease to exist with this life; everything resumes its order after death."[217]

This becomes a powerful argument for the existence of God, since it is God who makes ultimate justice possible. The fact that all will stand before his holy tribunal ensures that every injustice will be punished and every noble act rewarded.

Walters noted Kant's support of this argument:

---

[216]Henry Wadsworth Longfellow, *Retribution*, as quoted in the *Concise Dictionary of Religious Quotations*, William Neil Editor, Grand Rapids MI (William B. Eerdmans Publishing Company, 1974) 61.

[217]*The Encyclopedia of Religious Quotations*, Frank S. Mead, Editor, Westwood NJ (Fleming H. Revell Company, 1965) 252.

"So if morality is to be salvaged—if the highest good is to be taken seriously as our normative standard—the existence of a beneficent and just God who ultimately guarantees that the righteous will be rewarded with happiness is a necessary postulation. 'It is,' Kant concludes, 'morally necessary to assume the existence of God.'"[218]

Certainly, Adolf Hitler stands out as the epitome of evil in the twentieth century. Under his leadership, the lives of European Jews were at first only disrupted, but eventually destroyed in the most barbaric conditions imaginable.

Now history tells us that as his empire was collapsing around him, Hitler committed suicide in his bunker in Berlin. After all the horrors and atrocities he had committed, was justice done by a suicidal shot to the head? Never would he face even a human tribunal or receive any punishment. From a strictly human stand point, it seems difficult to see how justice was served.

On the other hand, if there is, in fact, a just God ruling the universe, this, then, means that regardless of the fact that Hitler evaded earthly punishment, he will ultimately stand before a perfect, holy, and just God to answer for his actions. That indeed, in the end, justice will prevail in the universe.

The same can be said for every rapist who thought he got away with it, and likewise for every killer who evaded punishment before the law. They will all be judged before the God who knows all the secrets of men.

---

[218]Kerry Walters, *Atheism: A Guide for the Perplexed*, New York (The Continuum International Publishing Group Inc, 2010) 123.

Yes, we know that in our imperfect world, the poor often suffer at the hands of the rich, and the destitute at the hands of their powerful oppressors. Larry Norman asked: "You say all men are equal, all men are brothers, then why are the rich more equal than others."[219]

We know that millions in our world suffer from racism; that millions of innocent babies die in their mother's womb never allowed to breathe the fresh air of life; that wealthy corporations knowingly sell dangerous and deadly products to the public in search of greater profit; that children starve to death while warlords steal the humanitarian relief meant to feed them; that too many women live in fear of being brutalized and murdered by their boyfriends and husbands; and that too many children are terrified of the next cruel beating they will receive at the hands of the very ones charged to protect them.

Yes, we know that so many in our world suffer silently and never find justice in this life. But we can be sure that that there is a God who sees all, and that every person that has ever walked this earth will one day stand before the holy tribunal of the righteous Judge of the universe. And then justice will prevail in the universe.

Soren Kierkegaard stated it starkly:

> "Do you not know that there comes a midnight hour when every one has to throw off his mask? Do you believe that life will always let itself be mocked? Do you think you can slip away a little before midnight in order to avoid this? Or are you not terrified by it?"[220]

---

[219]Larry Norman, *Great American Novel*, Only Visiting This Planet, 1972, Verve

[220]Soren Kierkegaard, *Either/Or* as cited in Robert Bretall, *A*

Atheist's response to the argument from justice

The atheist George Smith criticized the argument from justice thusly:

> "The standard reply to this objection is that God rewards the virtuous and punishes the wicked in an afterlife, so there is an overall balance of justice . . . This approach is so obviously an exercise in theological rationalization that it deserves little comment . . . More importantly, no appeal to an afterlife can actually eradicate the problem of evil. An injustice always remains an injustice, regardless of any subsequent efforts to comfort the victim . . . The Christian may believe that God will punish the perpetrators of evil and compensate the victims of injustice, but this does not explain why a supposedly benevolent and omnipotent being created a world with evildoers and innocent victims in the first place."[221]

We will examine more closely the problem of evil and suffering in another section, but I want to note two things in reaction to Smith. First, his argument seems to undermine the entire basis of the criminal justice system since it also reacts to evil acts *after the fact*, attempting to bring about justice to those who have experienced injustice.

Second, it should be remembered that God created the world without evil, but with the *possibility of evil* contingent upon how man used their God-given free-will.

Morgan showed Bertrand Russell's criticism of the argument from Justice:

Kierkegaard Anthology, New York (The Modern Library/Random House,1946) 99.

[221]George H. Smith, *Atheism: The Case Against God,* Amherst NY (Prometheus Books, 1979, 1989) 84.

"Russell attacked the idea that God is required to remedy injustice in the next life since justice is often thwarted on Earth. He said that if you open a crate of oranges and find the top layer of oranges are bad, that does not mean the bottom oranges will 'redress the balance' by being good."[222]

Russell is welcome to his pessimism, but Christianity is a faith of optimism. The Christian doctrine of original sin asserts that not only the fruit at the top is spoiled, but that the whole crate of oranges is spoiled i.e. we are all sinners. We have all joined Adam and Eve in biting the forbidden fruit.

Yet, God is working all things to the good. He specializes in making lemonade from lemons. As Martin Luther King Jr. put it: "The arc of the moral universe is long, but it bends toward justice."[223]

The whole point of Christianity is that God offers hope and redemption to the world. Man's guilt has a cure in Christ's atonement. God's final tribunal guarantees that the bells of justice will ring forever to the far ends of the universe.

---

[222]Timothy Morgan, *Thank God for Atheists: How the Greatest Skeptics Led Me to Faith*, Eugene OR (Harvest House Publishers, 2015) 94.

[223]Martin Luther King Jr., as quoted by Elaine Pagels, *Revelations: Visions, Prophecy, and Politics in the Book of Revelation*, New York (Viking, 2012) 175.

Section Three: Special Revelation: Miraculous Arguments for the Existence of God

Chapter 10: Miracles

As we continue to examine arguments in favor of the existence of God, let us now consider miracles. Indeed the Bible has reported miracles from Genesis to Revelation, with the penultimate being the resurrection of Jesus Christ. Now, of course, if miracles don't happen, then neither did Christ rise from the dead, and this is precisely the point made by the apostle Paul:

> "If there is no resurrection of the dead, then not even Christ has been raised. And if Christ has not been raised, our preaching is useless and so is your faith. More than that, we are then found to be false witnesses about God, for we have testified about God that he raised Christ from the dead. But he did not raise him if in fact the dead are not raised. For if the dead are not raised, then Christ has not been raised either. And if Christ has not been raised, your faith is futile; you are still in your sins"(1 Corinthians 15:13-17).

It is fair to say that the very foundation of the Bible stands upon the reality of miracles. Geisler referred to Antony Flew's excellent definition of miracles:

> "[Former] Atheist Antony Flew put it well: 'A miracle is something which would never have happened had nature, as it were, been left to its own devices.'"[224]

---

[224]Norman L. Geisler, *Baker Encyclopedia of Christian Apologetics*, Grand Rapids MI (Baker Books, 1999) 450.

Did David Hume philosophically destroy rational arguments for miracles?

Gary Habarmas noted the claims that Hume's criticisms were decisive against the belief in miracles:

> "David Hume destroyed any rational basis for believing in a miracle. At least that's what the New Atheists would like you to think. According to Christopher Hitchens, Hume's book *An Enquiry Concerning Human Understanding* (1748) ended debate on the subject and settled the case against miracles more than two and a half centuries ago."[225]

Since David Hume's attacks on miracles are often considered so decisive, let us consider his arguments. For instance, Hume's definition that, "A miracle is a violation of nature."[226]

It is fair to say that a miracle is in some sense a violation of the normal course of events, wrought by the almighty, or else it wouldn't be a miracle in the first place. Miracles can be thought of as the actions of a supernatural being able to suspend the laws of nature at will. To disprove the possibility of miracles, then, one must first disprove the existence of the miracle-working God.

Miracles are rare by definition

Hume argued:

---

[225]Gary R. Habermas, *Are Miracles Possible?*, chapter in Sean McDowell & Jonathan Morrow, *Is God Just a Human Invention? And Seventeen Other Questions Raised by the New Atheists*, Grand Rapids MI (Kregel Publications, 2010) 47.

[226]David Hume, *An Enquiry Concerning Human Understanding*, Section 10, Indianapolis/Cambridge (Hackett Publishing Company, 1977, 1993) 76.

"Nothing is esteemed a miracle, if it ever happen in the common course of nature. It is no miracle that a man seemingly in good health, should die on a sudden: because such a kind of death, though more unusual than any other, has yet been frequently observed to happen. But it is a miracle, that a dead man should come to life; because that has never been observed, in any age or country."[227]

With this argument, Hume laid down the gauntlet against Christianity, for the claim that a dead man (Jesus Christ) has come to life forms the essential foundation of the Christian faith. We shall consider evidence in support of Christ's resurrection in the next chapter.

Again Hume stated:

"'Upon the whole, then, it appears, that no testimony for any kind of miracle has ever amounted to a probability, much less to a proof . . . It is experience only, which gives authority to human testimony; and it is the same experience, which assures us of the laws of nature."[228]

So Hume argued that miracles are unlikely because they are simply not observed in our regular experience. But again, that is just what we should expect in the case of miracles; that they seldom occur!

Hume, the probability of miracles, and the resurrection of Jesus

Gary Habermas responded to Hume's claims concerning the improbability of miracles:

---

[227]David Hume, *An Enquiry Concerning Human Understanding*, 76-77.
[228]David Hume, *An Enquiry Concerning Human Understanding*, 87.

"Hume's critique of miracles says we should never believe the improbable . . . Following this train of thought, we should never believe that a person has been dealt a royal flush, since the odds against it are 649,740 to 1 . . . The odds against winning a state lottery are usually in the millions to one, yet someone wins. According to Hume, even if you were dealt a royal flush or held a winning lottery ticket, you would not be justified in believing it was true. Similarly, Hume's reasoning would justify denying that a miracle occurred, even if you personally witnessed it! [As was the case with Jesus' disciples]."[229]

Yes, there is powerful evidence for the miracle of the resurrection of Jesus Christ.

William Lane Craig responded:

"Now I would agree with Hume that a *natural* resurrection of Jesus from dead, without any sort of divine intervention, is enormously improbable. But that's not the hypothesis. The hypothesis is God raised Jesus from the dead. That doesn't say anything against the laws of nature, which say dead man don't come back to life *naturally*."[230]

C. S. Lewis rejected Hume's argument as arguing in a circle, assuming what should be proved:

"Now of course we must agree with Hume that if there is absolutely 'uniform experience' against miracles, if in other words they have never happened, why, then they never have. Unfortunately, we know the experience against them to be uniform only if we know all the reports of them are false. And we can know all the reports of them are false only if we know already that miracles have never occurred. In fact, we are arguing in a circle."[231]

[229]Gary R. Habermas, *Are Miracles Possible?*, 48.
[230]William Lane Craig,, Interview with Lee Strobel, *The Case for Faith: A Journalist Investigates the Toughest Objections to Christianity*, Grand Rapids MI (Zondervan, 2000) 88.
[231]C. S. Lewis, *Miracles*, New York (Macmillan, 1947) 105, as quoted

Is Hume's test for miracles reasonable?

Let's now consider perhaps Hume's best-known statement against miracles:

> "That no testimony is sufficient to establish a miracle, unless the testimony be of such a kind, that its falsehood would be more miraculous, than the fact, which it endeavors to establish . . . If the falsehood of his testimony would be more miraculous, than the event he relates; then, and not till then, can he pretend to command my belief or opinion."[232]

But what is this but a begging of the question. Hume takes the chair of Saint Peter and arbitrarily pontificates about miracles, thinly disguising his personal prejudice against miracles as some kind of philosophical truth.

Hume's "factual" objections to miracles

Habermas summed up Hume's 'factual' objections to miracles:

> "Hume gives four 'facts' which he believes discount the rationality of believing in a miracle. First, no historical miracle has been sufficiently attested by honest and reliable men who are of such social standing that they would have a great deal to lose by lying. Second, people crave miraculous stories and will gullibly believe absurd stories, which is evidenced by the sheer number of false tales of miraculous events. Third, miracles only occur among barbarous people. And fourth, miracles occur in all religions and thus cancel each other out, since they espouse contradictory doctrines."[233]

---

by Robert A. Morey, *The New Atheism and the Erosion of Freedom*, Minneapolis MN (Bethany House Publishers, 1986) 78.
[232]David Hume, *An Enquiry Concerning Human Understanding*, 77.
[233]Gary R. Habermas, *Are Miracles Possible?*, 48-49.

Habermas then responded to these arguments:

"As for Hume's first 'in fact' arguments . . . Eleven of the twelve disciples were put to death because of their convictions that Jesus is the risen Lord . . . Jesus' miracles did not occur among a barbarous people, but among the Jews who were a highly educated and sophisticated people . . . The Jews valued education . . . While it is true that other religions have miracle claims, none of the miracles are as powerfully attested as the miracles of Jesus Christ. Unlike the miracles in the Gospels, these other claims tend to be poorly supported in questionable sources far removed from the events."[234]

Certainly Hume raised reasonable points for evaluating claims of the miraculous. It is quite correct to hold miraculous claims to a high standard of evidence. Without doubt, there have been charlatans and deceivers in every age all too happy to dupe the credulous.

Also true is that multiple religions with competing truth claims also report miracles, and they can't all be true, so why believe any? Fair points. But none of this means we must reject all miracles like the resurrection of Jesus Christ any more than we should reject all currency because of counterfeit bills in circulation.

Evans and Manis stated:

"Some of Hume's criticisms seem to presuppose an overly arrogant attitude toward non-western and 'premodern' cultures. In biblical times, for example, contemporary scientific knowledge was obviously lacking, but people knew, just as certainly as people do today, that in the normal course of nature it is not possible for a child to be born of a virgin or for a man to rise from the dead."[235]

---

[234] Gary R. Habermas, *Are Miracles Possible?*, 49-50.
[235] C. Stephen Evans & R. Zachary Manis, *Philosophy of Religion: Thinking About Faith*, Second Edition, Downers Grove IL (Inter

Hume's inconsistency on miracles and induction

Furthermore, Hume was simply inconsistent in his argument on miracles when compared with his arguments against induction. For Hume's philosophy opposed miracles on the basis of the regularity of nature and yet opposed the very same regularity of nature in his arguments against induction.

Michael Martin's argument against theistic belief in miracles

Philosopher Michael Martin attacked traditional belief in miracles *with an even so argument.* That is, even if miracles have occurred, it is not proved that it was the Christian or biblical God that caused it. For instance, Martin asked:

> "Moreover, even if one has good reason to suppose that something is an indirect miracle, there is no good reason to believe that God, rather than some other supernatural force, indirectly brought it about."[236]

Martin made a similar point about miracles in general:

> "Let us suppose that miracles . . . that is, events brought about by the exercise of a supernatural power—do occur. Would this be good evidence for the existence of God? To state my answer briefly, it would not be, since miracles might be the result of the action of other supernatural beings beside God."[237]

Varsity Press, 2009) 132.
[236]Michael Martin, *Atheism: A Philosophical Justification,* Philadelphia PA (Temple University Press, 1990) 208.
[237]Michael Martin, *Atheism: A Philosophical Justification,* 191.

Martin's argument is perplexing to me. As an atheist committed to natural versus supernatural causes, I do not see how explaining an apparent miracle by appealing to "some other supernatural force" instead of the biblical God helps his cause!

Hugh L. McCann on miracles

I very much appreciate Hugh McCann's very thoughtful ideas about miracles. He moves the discussion forward by finding possible common areas of agreement between the theist and the naturalist.

McCann summed up Hume's famous arguments against miracles as having two essential themes:

> "That definition [Hume's definition of a miracle] requires two things: first, that there be a violation of scientific laws; and second, that this violation be a result of God having 'intervened' in the course of nature."[238]

McCann challenged both of Hume's points. Is it true that miracles necessarily are violations of the scientific laws of nature?

The miraculous power of faith on the mind and body

In the example of healing, for instance, McCann calls us to be more open to the reality of seemingly miraculous healings by noting the great likelihood that advances in medicine will show the healing qualities of belief on the mind and the body. Could it be possible that the power of

---

[238]Hugh J. McCann, *Getting Scientific about Religion*, chapter in *The Future of Atheism: Alister McGrath & Daniel Dennett in Dialogue*, Robert B. Stewart, Editor, Minneapolis MN (Fortress Press, 2008) 120.

faith and belief can actually bring about organic changes to physical maladies in the body?

McCann discussed such possibilities:

> "Reports of cases like this [healings] are not at all unusual; if you watch the right television programs you will hear of them with a fair frequency. But the events reported *are* unusual, in that they seem to deviate from the normal course of things . . . Such events, if real, present a challenge to what I have called science proper, in that they appear to defy natural explanation. Now, it is certainly possible that they are not real; a certain percentage of these cases are no doubt fraudulent in some way. But I think it would be foolish to suppose that they all are. Equally, it seems to me mistaken to suppose all such cases are instances of misdiagnosis, or of some other obvious factual error . . . How then should we react to it?"[239]

The question that McCann sought to explore, then, is the power of faith and belief. In the case of apparent physical healings, McCann asked:

> "How are we to know that such a thing has occurred? We do not know what all the scientific laws are, especially when it comes to human healing processes, which are notoriously dependent on the psychological state of patients and perhaps even those around them. There appears, therefore, to be plenty of room for the possibility that in religious settings there are principles at work that are not operative in ordinary circumstances, and which would permit the occurrence of extraordinary events without our feeling that the nature of things had been violated."[240]

McCann's discussion urges caution in assessing whether miracles should be considered violations of

---

[239]Hugh J. McCann, *Getting Scientific about Religion*, 119-120.
[240]Hugh J. McCann, *Getting Scientific about Religion*, 120.

natural laws in the face of our growing scientific knowledge about the bodies' healing properties and the power of faith.

Miracle or just advanced knowledge of the natural

Along the same lines, I would argue that many purported miracles are not really violations of natural laws at all, but are rather possible by God's greater knowledge of what is possible naturally? Many of the medical procedures of today would surely seem miraculous to men brought back to life from past centuries. Likewise, things that now seem to us as miracles may become regular practices with the advance of science.

I would argue that even though such events may not violate any natural laws, yet they deserve to be called miracles since they violated the knowledge base in the cultural-context in which they occurred.

Miracles and God's sustenance of the universe

Hume also defined a miracle as a divine intervention into the normal course of affairs.

McCann questioned that definition in light of traditional Christian theology. Particularly, McCann called attention to the doctrine of God's preservation or (conservation/sustaining) of the universe. Whereas deism presented a God that has created the world, and then leaves it to itself, traditional Christian theology has always maintained God's continued involvement in His creation (Colossians 1:17; Hebrews 1:3).

Benton defined this sustaining activity of God:

"That continual activity of God whereby he maintains in existence the things he created . . . In creation God acted to bring the universe into existence; in conservation God acts to sustain what he has already created . . . According to Scripture, the exercise of that omnipotent energy by which God sustains existence extends over all created things, animate and inanimate."[241]

Kierkegaard affirmed this ongoing work of God:

"To sustain the heavens and the earth by the fiat of his omnipotent word, so that if this word were withdrawn for the fraction of a second the universe would be plunged into chaos."[242]

This continual preservation (*in esse*) pertains to God's active upholding of the universe but does not affect man's freedom of will. In light of the doctrine of preservation McCann asked:

"What does it mean to say that, on a given occasion, God intervenes in the course of nature? It appears to mean that on this occasion [apparent miracle] God plays a stronger hand than usual, that God is directly involved in what takes place rather than standing back from the course of events as God usually does. According to a lot of classical theology, however, this has to be mistaken. Aquinas, to cite just one, believed that God's activity as creator includes not just putting the world in place but sustaining it for its entire existence, so that God is as much responsible for the world surviving another second as God is for its being here at all . . . But if it *is* right, then it is not possible for God to 'intervene' in the course of events,

---

[241]W. W. Benton Jr., *Conservation*, article in the *Evangelical Dictionary of Theology*, Walter A. Elwell, Editor, Grand Rapids MI (Baker Book House, 1984) 268.

[242]Soren Kierkegaard, *Philosophical Fragments* as cited in Robert Bretall, *A Kierkegaard Anthology*, New York (The Modern Library/Random House, 1946) 169.

because God is already as fully involved in the occurrence of everything that goes on as God could possibly be."[243]

Even with the distinction about preservation understood, it must still be faced that there are times in which God acts in a way that is out of the normal pattern. As such, these miraculous events support divine messengers and their messages at key points in His-story.

If God, then miracles

So we end where we began this section on miracles, not wanting to miss the forest for the trees. Geisler reminds us that:

> "The only way to show that miracles are impossible is to disprove the existence of God."[244]

In this sense, most of the arguments against miracles are missing the real point. For if God exists, the possibility of miracles simply follows.

Benjamin Franklin on miracles and wine

I love Benjamin Franklin's amusing take on Jesus' changing of water into wine at the wedding in Cana:

> "We hear of the conversion of water into wine at the marriage in Cana as a miracle. But this conversion is, through the goodness of God, made every day before our eyes. Behold the rain which descends from heaven upon our vineyards; there it enters the roots of the vines, to be changed into wine; a constant proof that God loves us, and

---

[243]Hugh J. McCann, *Getting Scientific about Religion*, 120.
[244]Norman L. Geisler, *Baker Encyclopedia of Christian Apologetics*, Grand Rapids MI (Baker Books, 1999) 450.

loves to see us happy. The miracle in question was performed only to hasten the operation."[245]

---

[245]Benjamin Franklin, Walter Isaacson, *Benjamin Franklin: An American Life*, New York (Simon& Schuster Paperbacks, 2003) 374.

Chapter 11: Miracle of Christ's Resurrection

Perhaps the greatest miracle described in the Bible (outside of creation itself) is the resurrection of Jesus Christ. About this resurrection, Kai Nielsen stated:

"Most Christians, for example, would want to claim as something central to their religion that Christ rose from the dead and that there is a life after the death of our earthly bodies."[246]

Nielsen is quite correct regarding the central place Christ's resurrection holds to Christianity, and to the Christian Gospel, as the apostle Paul argued:

"Now, brothers, I want to remind you of the gospel . . . For what I passed on to you as of first importance: that Christ died for our sins according to the Scriptures, that he was buried, that he was raised on the third day according to the Scriptures" (1 Corinthians 15:1, 3-4).

Yet, despite this importance, Kai Nielsen dismissed even the possibility of its reality: "Given what science teaches us about the world, these things could not happen or have happened."[247] Nielsen certainly has a right to his opinion, but as we shall see, the case for the resurrection stands upon very solid historical ground.

---

[246]Kai Nielsen, *Atheism & Philosophy*, Amherst NY (Prometheus Books, 2005) 102.
[247]Kai Nielsen, *Atheism & Philosophy*, 102.

Claims of Christ's resurrection must meet high standards of evidence

We can begin by noting that the biblical gospels treat the life of Christ, and particularly his resurrection, as facts grounded in history, and not as myths.

Therefore, the investigator should weigh biblical claims about Jesus' resurrection in the same manner as other ancient historical claims. Granted, since the resurrection is a claim for the miraculous, it should, and does, meet very high standards of evidence.

Michael Barnes referenced Hume's high-bar standard or test for miracles:

> "David Hume's answer is the only correct one. A person should proportion belief to the evidence; moreover, extraordinary claims require extraordinary evidence."[248]

We agree that a high-bar standard of evidence is necessary in light of the extraordinary Christian claim that Jesus Christ actually rose bodily from the dead, and such is the case.

Perhaps the leading authority on Christ's resurrection is N. T. Wright who stated:

> "Though admitting it involves accepting a challenge at the level of the worldview itself, the best historical explanation for all these phenomena is that Jesus was indeed bodily raised from the dead."[249]

---

[248]Michael Horace Barnes, *Understanding Religion and Science: Introducing the Debate*, New York (Continuum International Publishing Group, 2010) 18.

[249]Nicholas Thomas Wright, *The Resurrection of the Son of God*, Minneapolis MN (Fortress Press, 2003) 8.

Christ's resurrection in the crosshairs of critics

Since, the Christian faith rises or falls with the resurrection of Christ, it is little wonder it has been so vigorously attacked by atheists and skeptics alike. Indeed, in an entry from his Journals in 1834, Soren Kierkegaard described the stone that sealed Christ tomb thusly:

"Nov. 25. The stone which was rolled before Christ's tomb might appropriately be called the philosopher's stone because its removal gave not only the pharisees but, now for 1800 years, the philosophers so much to think about."[250]

For instance, critics frequently claim that the gospel accounts of the resurrection are proven unreliable by the many contradictions contained in them. Indeed, some of the critics allege that the differences are so severe that it is impossible to reconcile or harmonize them.

For instance, the liberal Episcopal bishop John Shelby Spong stated:

"When we turn to look with scholarly eyes at the resurrection narratives of the New Testament, the anxiety of the fundamentalists rises perceptibly . . . This debate, exciting and ingenious as it is, is not the chief problem biblical literalists have with the resurrection narratives of the New Testament. That problem comes rather with the knowledge that the details of the narratives of the various gospels are simply incapable of being reconciled one with another. Here in the central primary moment of the Christian story there is significant discrepancy in vital details. Literalism is battered when the resurrection narratives are compared."[251]

---

[250]Soren Kierkegaard, *The Journals*, as cited in *A Kierkegaard Anthology*, Robert Bretall Editor, New York (The Modern Library/Random House, 1946) 2

Likewise, Dan Barker also attacked the veracity of the gospel accounts of Jesus' resurrection:

"I HAVE AN EASTER challenge for Christians. My challenge is simply this: tell me what happened on Easter. I am not asking for proof. My straightforward request is merely that Christians tell me exactly what happened on the day that their most important doctrine was born. Believers should eagerly take up this challenge, since without the resurrection, there is no Christianity. Paul wrote, "And if Christ be not risen, then is our preaching vain, and your faith is also vain. Yea, and we are found false witnesses of God; because we have testified of God that he raised up Christ: whom he raised not up, if so be that the dead rise not." (I Corinthians 15:14-15).

The conditions of the challenge are simple and reasonable. In each of the four Gospels, begin at Easter morning and read to the end of the book: Matthew 28, Mark 16, Luke 24, and John 20-21. Also read Acts 1:3-12 and Paul's tiny version of the story in I Corinthians 15:3-8. These 165 verses can be read in a few moments. Then, without omitting a single detail from these separate accounts, write a simple, chronological narrative of the events between the resurrection and the ascension: what happened first, second, and so on; who said what, when; and where these things happened. Since the gospels do not always give precise times of day, it is permissible to make educated guesses. The narrative does not have to pretend to present a perfect picture--it only needs to give at least one plausible account of all the facts. Additional explanation of the narrative may be set apart in parentheses. *The important condition to the challenge, however, is that not one single biblical detail be omitted.* Fair enough?"[252]

[251]John Shelby Spong, *Rescuing the Bible from Fundamentalism: A Bishop Rethinks the Meaning of Scripture*, New York (Harper Collins Publishers, 1991) 217, 218.

[252]Dan Barker, *Losing Faith in Faith: From Preacher to Atheist*, Chapter 24, *Leave No Stone Unturned: An Easter Challenge for*

In response to these claims, we should note several observations. If the early church (or some later editor) was essentially making up the resurrection story, wouldn't they have done a better job of smoothing over the seeming discrepancies?

Further, that there would be seeming discrepancies should not surprise us when we consider the testimony of multiple witnesses to an event today (traffic accident, crime). Indeed, initially, there are often apparent contradictions in eyewitness testimony that are resolved by further investigation.

Norman Geisler pointed out that:

> "When a scientist comes upon an anomaly in nature, he does not give up further scientific exploration. Rather, the unexplained motivates further study . . . The true biblical scholar approaches the Bible with the same presumption that there are answers to thus-far unexplained."[253]

It is my belief that the same is true concerning the gospel testimonies of the resurrection.

Therefore, I take up the challenge of Barker above, and offer the following harmony of the gospel accounts of the resurrection. I do not mean to deny that there may be other possible ways of harmonizing them. Rather, it is a "plausible" harmonization that does not ignore any of the data. I believe that this chronology answers most of the common objections raised by critics.

Christians, First appeared in *Freethought Today,* March 1990, from website address: https://ffrf.org/legacy/books/lfif/?t=stone
[253]Norman L. Geisler, *Baker Encyclopedia of Christian Apologetics,* 75-76.

Order of events related to Christ's resurrection

1. Women left homes early (before sunrise), (John 20:1).
2. Resurrection occurred as dawn is breaking (Mark 16:9).
3. Earthquake occurred (Matthew 28:2).
4. Guards at tomb fled (Matthew 28:4, 11).
5. Women on way to tomb wondered who would move stone (unaware that guards had been placed at tomb the day before) (Mark 16:3).
6. Women arrived at the tomb, finding the stone rolled away and an empty tomb (Luke 24:2-3).
7. Mary Magdalene left the other women at the tomb at the moment when they are all perplexed by the absents of Jesus' body, but before the angelic appearance (Luke 24:3), and left to report the empty tomb to the disciples.
8. After Mary Magdalene's departure, the angels (only Luke mentions the second angel) appeared to the women who remained at the tomb (Mary the mother of James and Joses, Joanna, and Salome), and announced the resurrection of Jesus (Matthew 28:5-6, Mark 16:5, Luke 24:4-8).
9. Following this angelic appearance, these women also headed back into town. (Matthew 28 has a gap that does not include this detail. This visit should not be confused with a later similar visit by the same women in which Jesus appeared to them. Again, Mary Magdalene was not aware of this having departed from the tomb before the other women), (Mark 16:9, Luke 24:9).

10. Finding Peter and John, Mary Magdalene told them about the empty tomb (John 20:2).

11. Mary Magdalene left the disciples and returned to the tomb (inferred from John 20:10-11).

12. Shortly after Mary Magdalene left for the tomb, the other women arrived and told the disciples of the angelic announcement of Jesus resurrection. Mary Magdalene, having just departed before the arrival of other women, had still not heard of the angelic announcement of Jesus' resurrection.

13. Peter and John quickly departed (John 20:3), arriving ahead of Mary Magdalene at the tomb. (Luke's account (24:12) only mentioned Peter by name, not mentioning that John was with him. However, Luke gave the account of the two on the road to Emmaus who remembering the events of the day say, "Then some of our companions (plural) went to the tomb" (Luke 24:24) no doubt reflecting Luke's knowledge that John was with Peter investigating the empty tomb).

14. After they confirmed the empty tomb, Peter and John left, and returned to their homes (John 20:10).

15. Mary Magdalene returned to the tomb (her second visit of the morning), and Jesus appeared to her (this is Jesus' first appearance, John 20:14-17). Following Jesus' appearance to her, Mary Magdalene returned to tell the disciples of Jesus' appearance (John 20:18).

16. Not long after, the other women (Mary the mother of James and Joses, Joanna, and Salome), return to the tomb (their second visit of the morning as

well). Jesus appeared to them as well, his second appearance of the morning (Matthew 28:9-10). (Mary Magdalene MAY have been with the women by this time. If she was, it is the second time she saw Jesus that morning).

17. The Lord appeared to Peter (Luke 24:34).

18. Jesus appeared to two disciples on the road to Emmaus (Luke 24:13-32).

19. Jesus appeared to the 10 disciples (Thomas absent, Judas committed suicide), (Luke 24:36-43, John 20:19-25).

20. Jesus appeared to the disciples (including Thomas) a week later (John 20:26-31).

21. Jesus appeared to seven disciples in Galilee (John 21:1-25).

22. Jesus appeared and gave the great commission to the eleven disciples (Matthew 28:16-20).

23. Jesus appeared to "more than five hundred of the brothers" (1 Corinthians 15:6).

24. Jesus appeared to James (1 Corinthians 15:7).

25. Jesus appeared to the disciples for final teaching and then ascended into heaven (Acts 1:4-9).

Notes on resurrection chronology.

Matthew's account has significant gaps. The first is between 28:4 and 5 (leaving out Mary Magdalene's departure ahead of the other women). The second gap is between 28:8 and 28:9 (leaving out the women's visit into Jerusalem to report to the disciples). Further, Luke's account shows that there must be a gap in Matthew's account between 28:8 and 28:9.

This is because (as Luke recorded in 24:22-24), the women only reported the angelic announcement of Jesus' resurrection to the disciples, but not Jesus' actual appearance to them. It would have made no sense for the women to have reported only the angelic announcement of the resurrection, but not Jesus actual appearance, unless there is in fact a gap in Matthews account, and that Jesus' appearance to the women was later in the morning.

Mark 16:9 is part of the disputed ending of Mark's gospel. Nonetheless, it (Mark's account) is probably correct in reporting that Jesus appeared first to Mary Magdalene, which supports the idea that Mary Magdalene had separated from the other women; otherwise they would have been together for the first appearance.

Mark has a gap between 16:4 and 5, leaving out the first look into the tomb and Mary Magdalene's departure.

Luke 24:22-24 is important in that it shows that the women's first report only involved an angelic announcement of Jesus' resurrection, and not Jesus' appearance which followed later, after the women's second visit to the tomb, of which the two on the road to Emmaus had apparently not yet heard. So there were two visits by the women to the tomb.

Mark 16:10-11 is contained in the disputed text closing Mark's gospel. Nevertheless, this would have been Mary Magdalene's second visit to the disciples, this time announcing the resurrection appearance and not merely the empty tomb. Nor is it implausible that the disciples still had trouble believing the resurrection reports until Jesus appeared to them personally.

Some see a discrepancy as to the time of the women's visit to the tomb and try to pit John 20:1 "Early in the first day of the week, *while it was still dark*, Mary Magdalene went to the tomb" against Mark 16:2 "Very early on the first day of the week, *just after sunrise*, they [the women] were on their way to the tomb." There is absolutely no contradiction. When the women were getting ready and leaving their homes it was the dark just before dawn. By the time they all meet and head to the tomb, dawn is breaking, and the sun is rising.

Some allege a discrepancy as to who went to the tomb. They pit John 20:1 "Mary Magdalene went to the tomb," against Matthew 28:1 "Mary Magdalene and the other Mary went to the tomb," and Mark 16:1 "Mary Magdalene, Mary the mother of James and Salome brought spices," and Luke 24:10 "It was Mary Magdalene, Joanna, Mary the mother of James, and the others with them." The solution is utterly obvious. All the accounts are true and complimentary. There is nothing contradictory of partial reports. By combining the reports, we gain the fullest report of the women who were present resurrection morning.

Some allege a discrepancy as to how many angels were at the empty tomb. Matthew 28:2-5 (see also Mark 16:5) records the announcement of Jesus' resurrection by an angel, whereas, Luke 24:4 records "two men in clothes that gleamed like lightning." Again, the solution is obvious. As has often been pointed out, anywhere you have two angels, you have one. Each author focused upon those details important to their account.

Some allege a discrepancy between Mark's account of an angel (young man) "dressed in a white robe *sitting* on the right side" and Luke's account of "two men in clothes that gleamed like lightning *stood* beside them." Critics claim a contradiction in that Mark has at least one of the "angels" *sitting* whereas Luke has them both *standing.* It is not at all difficult to imagine that the angel was sitting until he stood to make the announcement of the resurrection of Christ.

Some allege a discrepancy between Mark 16:8 which reports that after the angelic announcement the women "said nothing to anyone, because they were afraid" and Luke's report that following the angelic announcement of Christ's resurrection, the women "told all these things to the eleven and to all the others" (Luke 24:9). This is only an apparent contradiction. Both statements are true, the women said nothing to anyone on the way back into town; they didn't stop and tell anyone; they went directly to the disciples and told them. This agrees perfectly with Matthew's account in that the angel commanded the women to "go quickly and tell his disciples: He has risen" (Matthew 28:7).

Some allege that Luke 24:9-10 contradicts the given chronology because it suggests that Mary Magdalene was with the other women when they reported the angelic announcement of Christ's resurrection "to the eleven," whereas the present chronology has Mary Magdalene arriving before, and separate from the other women, and also leaving before the other women arrived to share the angelic announcement with the "eleven and to all the others." However, Luke seems to be summarizing the events at this point. It is true that all the women (including Mary Magdalene) did report what they knew, to the eleven and others, though not necessarily at the same time. Otherwise, Mary Magdalene's behavior at the tomb a little later is incoherent in that she seemed to have no idea of the resurrection (John 20:11-18).

Some allege a contradiction in the gospel accounts that record Jesus' (or the angels) promise that they (the disciples) were to go to Galilee and He (Jesus) would appear to them there (Matthew 28:7, 10, Mark 16:7), whereas in fact he appeared to them first in Judea, and only later in Galilee. It should be noted that Jesus did not say that he would appear to them first in Galilee, or only in Galilee. Jesus did exactly as he promised in that he did appear to them in Galilee and there is no conflict or contradiction. Also, it should be pointed out that the disciples stayed in Jerusalem through the end of the Passover celebration which accounts for the delay in their departure for Galilee for at least a week following resurrection Sunday (John 20:26).

Some allege a contradiction between the apostle Paul's account of the order of Christ's post-resurrection appearances with those found in the Gospels. Critics will say that Paul was wrong in saying that Christ first appeared to the Peter, whereas the gospels report that Jesus appeared first to Mary Magdalene.

It is true that Mark 16: 9 affirms that Jesus appeared first to Mary Magdalene, but it is absolutely false that Paul taught that Jesus appeared first to Peter. Paul's statement in 1 Corinthians 15:5-8 is chronologically accurate but not exhaustive. In other words, the order is correct, but not complete and selective. Paul simply left out Jesus' appearance to Mary Magdalene (as he also left out Jesus' appearance to the other women (Matthew 28:9) and to the two on the road to Emmaus (Luke 24:13-

32). Paul merely selected those appearances he wanted to emphasize.

Theories opposed to the bodily resurrection of Christ

In this section, I will briefly review some of the common attacks on the resurrection of Christ

He wasn't really dead, but swooned. He recovered in the tomb.

The so-called "swoon-theory" was popularized by a seventeenth century critic named Venturini who suggested that Christ didn't really die on the cross, but was placed in the tomb while still alive, and revived in the coolness of the tomb.

Amazing! This theory would have it believed that although Jesus was flagellated to near the point of death, and endured a horrible crucifixion, including a spear through his chest (resulting in a flow of blood), that he yet somehow survived and fooled the highly experienced Roman executioners.

Further, in this extraordinarily weak condition, Jesus was able to remove the large stone that had been rolled into place by the guards (from the inside!), despite the Roman seal affixed to it and the guard standing watch, and somehow made an escape. To believe such a scenario would seem to require more faith than to believe in the resurrection in the first place!

John Ankerberg noted further difficulties with the swoon theory:

"After his crucifixion (which incidentally included a spear thrust into the heart) Jesus was taken down from the cross, wrapped in seventy-five pounds of linen and spices, and placed in a tomb. After three days without food or water, Jesus unwrapped himself (even though his arms had been wrapped against his body . . . moved the one to two-ton stone from the grave entrance and walked some distance on mutilated feet to find his disciples."[254]

Schonfield's Passover Plot (1965)

This theory was popular among some critics of the last generation. The theory suggested that Jesus had a strong sense of being the long anticipated Jewish Messiah. Therefore, he took great measures to ensure that he fulfilled Old Testament prophetic messianic expectations.

The cross was a part of his secret plan. He had intended to drink an elixir (with the help of Joseph of Arimathea) to render Himself unconscious and apparently dead. Timed correctly, His body would be removed from the cross before the sundown beginning Sabbath. The plan would culminate, then, in Jesus' only *apparent* resurrection.

But lo, those involved in this Passover plot had not planned for one tragic event, the executioner's spear through Jesus' heart, leading to his actual death. Nevertheless, the bereaved disciples began to mistakenly believe they had seen the risen Jesus.

This theory goes against everything we know about the kind of character Jesus possessed, and if true, would

---

[254]John Ankerberg in *Resurrected? An Atheist & Theist Dialogue,* Gary R. Habermas & Antony G.N. Flew, Edited by John F. Ankerberg, New York (Rowman & Littlefield Publishers, 2005) 101-102.

render Him one of the biggest impostors of history. Unfortunately for Schonfield, his wildly speculative theory is without a shred of proof in its favor, and is rather the result of an overactive imagination divorced from evidence.

It is impossible to conceive how a mere man (in Schonfield's view) could control so many events, including such necessities as to the place of his birth! John Ankerberg added:

> "This theory makes Christ a fraud and the disciples near-idiots. Moreover, if Christ was dead, how does one account for the many documented Resurrection appearances?"[255]

The disciples stole Jesus' body.

This theory alleged that the disciples stole Jesus' body in order to fool people into believing that He had risen from the dead. Two motives are usually offered to explain the disciples' alleged thievery.

One, that the disciples were psychologically broken by Jesus' death, and couldn't face the fact that He was just another false messiah. Wanting to keep His memory and teachings alive, they stole His body and falsely proclaimed His resurrection.

Related to the first, but with just a twist of sinister, the disciples, desperate to maintain their power in the infant Church, pulled off perhaps the greatest fraud in history.

However, the theory that the disciples stole Jesus' body flies in the face of the facts and common sense. It is

---

[255]John Ankerberg in *Resurrected?*, 102.

simply incredible that all of the disciples kept the secret quiet, and never divulged their plot.

More to the point, Jesus' disciples gave their lives as martyrs. Is it reasonable to believe that they would all die cruel deaths *for what they knew was a lie?* The theory simply doesn't explain how a cowardly band of defeated followers of Christ after the crucifixion, suddenly became the fearless proclaimers of Christ that changed the world in one generation. Christ's actual resurrection best explains that powerful change!

Further, this theory also suffers from the problem of how the disciples were able to steal the body of Christ while the tomb was under a guard. Some point out that the guard wasn't actually placed at the tomb until the day after his crucifixion (Matthew 27:62-66) and suppose that Jesus' body could have been stolen before the guard was placed.

Again, a little thought overcomes this objection. Surely the guard was competent enough to ensure His body was in the tomb before sealing it, as that is the reason they were there. Further, there was great punishment for soldiers who failed to do their duty (notice their fear after the resurrection in Matthew 28:14, and note also the execution of the guards on duty during Peter's miraculous escape from prison in Acts 12:18-19).

The Wrong tomb theory

Although some may find this theory difficult to take seriously, it was proposed in all seriousness by a Harvard New Testament scholar named Kirsopp Lake.

His theory was simple; everyone just went to the wrong tomb! That is, the group of women going out to anoint Christ's body that fateful Sunday morning had just mistaken the wrong tomb for the correct one. After hearing about Christ's missing body and empty tomb, the disciples Peter and John, also went to the wrong tomb.

All the while, there is a guard keeping watch over the actual sealed tomb of Jesus, unaware of all the fuss.

Norman Geisler described the theory:

> "A famous liberal theologian, Kirsopp Lake, presented the theory that the women had gone to the wrong tomb. He suggested that the women went to the tomb early Sunday morning and asked the gardener where Jesus was laid. The gardener then responded 'He is not here,' and the women rushed off to preach the Resurrection before the gardener could turn to point and say, 'He is over there'"[256]

The theory suffers from many obvious weaknesses. It doesn't explain why the guards reported the empty tomb (Matthew 28:11-15), or why Joseph of Arimathea couldn't find his own tomb, or why Kirsopp's alleged gardener didn't correct anyone's misunderstanding, although it was the talk of the town. Nor does it explain why the women went to the wrong tomb despite the fact that they were there when he was placed in the tomb (Matthew 27:61).

Most of all, it doesn't explain why Jesus' highly motivated enemies did not just simply produce Christ's body and destroy Christianity in its infancy.

Why did Christ appear only to believers?

Others have resisted acceptance of the evidence for the resurrection since they assume Christ appeared only

---

[256]Norman Geisler & Ronald Brooks, *When Skeptics Ask* (Victor Books, 1990) p. 126.

to believers, making suspect the veracity of the claims. D. James Kennedy's remarks were to the point:

> "Interestingly, you hear it said sometimes that Jesus never appeared to anybody but believers, but it's not true. He appeared to the guards. They were so terrified by His appearance that they fainted and became as dead men . . . Jesus appeared to James, his brother, who was skeptical. Jesus appeared to Saul, the persecutor. These people were not Christians at the time."[257]

Further, it should not be surprising that Christ's resurrection tended to have a powerful effect upon people, usually changing unbelievers into believers.

The hallucination theory

This theory suggested that the resurrection reports of Christ were merely subjective hallucinations, produced by the intense psychological needs and desires of the disciples.

However, being personal and subjective experiences, hallucinations are not usually shared by multiple people at multiple times, including one event at which the resurrected Jesus appeared to over 500 people: "After that, he appeared to more than five hundred of the brothers at the same time, most of whom are still living" (1 Corinthians 15:6). Paul's note that most of the 500 witnesses were still living meant that his readers could verify the claims of Christ's resurrection for themselves.

The disciples, including doubting Thomas, touched Jesus' resurrected body and even placed their fingers in

---

[257]D. James Kennedy with Jerry Newcombe, *Who Is This Jesus Is He Risen? Examining the Truth About Jesus*, Fort Lauderdale, FL (Coral Ridge Ministries, 2002) 9.

the nail prints of his hands (John 20:20, 27). It seems difficult to accept that the skeptical Thomas only imagined touching Jesus' wounds. Further, Jesus ate with the disciples as well (Luke 24:40-43), even saying to his disciples, "Look at my hands and my feet. It is I myself! Touch me and see: a ghost does not have flesh and bones, as you see I have" (Luke 24:39). Again, it is difficult to believe that a group of eleven men, eating meals with, touching, and having conversations with Jesus, were all merely hallucinating!

We will examine N. T. Wright's critique of the hallucination theory shortly.

Confusion over Jesus' post-resurrection appearances

Some are confused by the apparently different post-resurrection appearances of Jesus.

They note the statement in Mark's Gospel that Jesus appeared in a different form after the resurrection: "Afterward Jesus appeared in a different form *(etera morphe)* to two of them while they were walking in the country" (Mark 16:12).

It is, then, mistakenly claimed that Christ appeared in various unrecognizable forms after his resurrection. The truth, however, is that his appearance was consistent with his appearance as he hung on the cross. The change in his form meant only a change from a carnal/mortal to a glorified/immortal body and did not involve a change in his general appearance.

But why didn't some recognize Jesus after his resurrection?

On the road to Emmaus

Others wonder why the two men on the road to Emmaus didn't recognize Jesus, even though they were walking and talking with Him (Luke 24:13-32). Doesn't this show that Jesus' appearance had changed, and that He was no longer recognizable, even to His disciples? Not at all.

The text itself tells the real reason why His disciples didn't recognize Jesus. It wasn't because of a changed post-resurrection appearance, but rather, as Luke's gospel explains, the disciples "were kept from recognizing him" (Luke 24:16), and later "their eyes were opened and they recognized him" (Luke 24:31). In other words, even after the resurrection, Jesus looked like Jesus! *So much so, that, on this occasion, His disciples had to be kept from recognizing Him.*

Mary Magdalene supposed Jesus to be a gardener

Others point to John's account of Jesus' appearance to Mary Magdalene (John 20:10-18), and wonder why Mary took Him to be a gardener (John 20:15). There are several reasons that explain Mary's mistake.

To begin with, Mary had every reason to believe that Jesus was dead. She saw Him crucified. She saw His lifeless body placed in the tomb. You simply don't expect to see one alive three days after being placed in a tomb.

Also, it was very early in the morning, and not the full light of day. Further, Mary had been crying and had tears in her eyes (John 20:10). Most importantly, the text specifically says that Mary "turned toward Him" (John 20:16) when He said her name, indicating that she had not looked closely at Him till then. Putting these factors together, it is easy to understand how Mary mistook Jesus for a gardener.

N. T. Wright and the historical evidence for the resurrection

There is a long record of Christian apologetics in defense of Christ's resurrection, but I will focus here on the work of Bishop N. T. Wright of Durham, whom it is fair to say, is the foremost defender of the doctrine of Christ's resurrection today.

Wright has done extensive historical research into the cultural setting of the second temple period of Jewish history, and the first century period in which Christ lived. The result of his work is a monumental book entitled: *The Resurrection of the Son of God* in 2003.[258] Wright explained his method:

> "Now, in the book I had great fun drawing a map of Jewish belief in life after death on the larger map of ancient beliefs in life after death in general."[259]

Wright noted how the Christian belief in the bodily resurrection contrasted with ideas of death and the afterlife in surrounding cultures:

---

[258]Nicholas Thomas Wright, *The Resurrection of the Son of God*, Minneapolis (Fortress Press, 2003).

[259]N.T. Wright, Appendix B in Anton Flew, *There is a God: How the World's Most Notorious Atheist Changed His Mind*, New York (Harper One, 2007) 197.

"It is truly remarkable that . . . all the early Christians known to us for the first four or five generations believed in a future bodily resurrection, even though most of them came from the pagan world, where this was regarded as complete and utter rubbish."[260]

Wright also addressed the claims of skeptics that people in the time of Jesus were ignorant and credulous about miraculous claims:

"A modern myth circulating at the moment says that it's only we who have contemporary post-Enlightenment science who have discovered that dead people don't rise. Those people back then, poor things, were unenlightened, so they believed in all these crazy miracles. But that is simply false . . . It's the same with the resurrection of Jesus. People in the ancient world were incredulous when faced with the Christian claim, because they knew perfectly well that when people die they stay dead."[261]

How Christian claims clashed with Jewish expectations and traditions

Wright also showed how radical Christian claims of Jesus' resurrection were, as a first fruit of a future general resurrection, in contrast to Jewish traditional beliefs and expectations:

"First, instead of resurrection being something that was simply going to happen to all God's people at the end, the early Christians said it happened in advance. Now, no first century Jew, as far as we know, believed there would be one person raised ahead of everyone else. So that's a radical innovation."[262]

---

[260]N.T. Wright, Appendix B in Anton Flew, *There is a God,* 198.
[261]N.T. Wright, Appendix B in Anton Flew, *There is a God,* 198.
[262]N.T. Wright, Appendix B in Anton Flew, *There is a God,* 199.

Wright's point is that such innovations are best explained as resulting from the actual events in Christ's life because of their stark contrast to the cultural milieu of second temple Judaism.

A crucified Messiah?

Wright raised another important point:

"They [the early Christians] believed that the Messiah himself had been raised from the dead, which no Second Temple Jew believed because, according to Second Temple Judaism, the Messiah was never going to be killed."[263]

This strikes at the heart of critical attacks on Christ's resurrection since the Jewish expectation during the second temple period was of a conquering Messiah establishing a political kingdom and bringing about a golden age for Israel. Wright elaborated on this idea:

"Nobody expected the Messiah to be raised from the dead, for the simple reason that nobody in Judaism at the time expected a Messiah would die, especially one who would die shamefully and violently."[264]

Further, said Wright:

"The disciples, at the time of Jesus' crucifixion, were completely devastated. Everybody in their world knew that if you were following a prophet or a Messiah or a leader or whatever and that person got executed by the Roman authorities, it meant you had backed the wrong horse. *Since everyone knew that a crucified Messiah was a failed Messiah, the only thing that explains why they said Jesus was the Messiah is that they really did believe He had been bodily raised from the dead.*"[265]

---

[263]N.T. Wright, Appendix B in Anton Flew, *There is a God*, 199.
[264]N. T. Wright, *The Resurrection of Jesus: John Dominic Crossan and N. T. Wright in Dialogue*, 19.

In a debate with John Dominic Crossan, Wright drove home the point by comparing Jesus to other would-be first century messiahs:

> "Supposing, three of four days later [after the death of a Jewish Messianic figure in A.D. 70], some lucky Jew who managed to escape with some friends and be hiding out somewhere saying, 'You know, I think Simon really was the Messiah, You know, we felt God's power at work when he was leading us. I really think he was and is God's Anointed One.' His friends would say, 'You must be crazy. The Romans caught him; they killed him, just like they always do. You know perfectly well what that means. It means that he couldn't possibly be the Messiah, because we all know that when the pagans execute somebody—celebrating their triumph over him—that shows that he couldn't have been the Messiah.' So, without something happening next, all of that stuff goes down the tubes. I think that scene in Luke 24 . . . is spot-on in terms of first century Jewish perceptions: 'We had hoped that he would be the one to redeem Israel,' but the implication is, we know that the fact that they killed him shows that he can't have been. Without something to reverse that, they would say, 'We've just been living in a wonderful dream, but now it's all over and we've woken up.'"[266]

If Jesus had not risen from the dead, there may well have been a movement among his faithful followers, honoring his teachings and example, such as occurred with John the Baptist after his death. But as N.T. Wright so powerfully argued, the explosive spread of Christianity, with the message of a risen messiah, can

---

[265]N.T. Wright in *Who Is This Jesus Is He Risen? Examining the Truth About Jesus*, D. James Kennedy with Jerry Newcombe, 95. Emphasis mine.

[266]N. T. Wright, *The Resurrection of Jesus: John Dominic Crossan and N. T. Wright in Dialogue*, 33-34.

best be explained by the fact that his followers actually believed it happened. Sam Lamerson agreed:

> "I think the best piece of evidence for the Resurrection of Christ is the fact that the Church exists today. There were lots of messiahs that existed in the first century, many of whom were killed by the Roman government. But there's only one Christian Church."[267]

Did the resurrection story develop over time?

Speaking specifically to the gospel accounts of the resurrection, Wright stated:

> "It has been said again and again (and when I was researching the big book I got tired of reading scholars saying this) that (1) Mark was written first, and he's hardly got anything about the resurrection; (2) Matthew comes next, and there's not much more; and then (3) toward the end of the century we get Luke and John, and then and only then do we find stories about Jesus eating broiled fish, cooking breakfast by the shore, inviting Thomas to touch him, and so on.
>   According to the theory, then, there were Christians toward the end of the century who started to believe that Jesus wasn't really human . . . and so Luke and John make up these stories at that stage in order to say, yes, he really was human, the risen Jesus really had bodily form . . . The trouble with that theory . . . is that those narratives . . . have this same Jesus coming and going through locked doors, sometimes being recognized and sometimes not being recognized, appearing and disappearing at will, and finally ascending to heaven. Let me put it like this. If I were making up a narrative in, say, 95 C. E. because I knew that some of my folk were a little insecure on the question of whether Jesus was a really solid human being,

---

[267]Sam Lamerson, in D. James Kennedy with Jerry Newcombe, *Who Is This Jesus Is He Risen? Examining the Truth About Jesus*, Fort Lauderdale, FL (Coral Ridge Ministries, 2002) 96.

I wouldn't put all that material in . . . Anyone writing fictitious accounts of Easter would have made Jesus more clearly recognizable."[268]

The testimony of the women

Along the same lines, Wright noted the unexpected testimony of the women in the gospel accounts of the resurrection:

"[A] fascinating feature of the narratives is the place of the women . . . In the ancient world, Jewish and pagan, women were not credible witnesses in the law court . . . So it's fascinating that in Matthew, Mark, Luke, and John we have Mary Magdalene, the other Marys, and the other women. And Mary Magdalene, of all people (we know she had a very checkered career in the past), is chosen as the prime witness; there she is in all four accounts. As historians we are obliged to comment that if these stories had been made up . . . they would never have had Mary Magdalene in this role . . . *The early Christians would never, never have made this up.* The stories—of the women finding an empty tomb and then meeting the risen Jesus – must be regarded as solidly historical."[269]

Summing things up, Wright stated:

"From all of this I reach certain conclusions. In order to explain the rise of early Christianity, in order to explain the existence of those four resurrection accounts plus bits and pieces of Acts and in Paul, we have to say that the very early church really did believe that Jesus had been bodily raised from the dead. We have no evidence of any very early Christians who believed anything else. But how can we as historians explain that? . . . I discover, as I look for historical explanations, that two particular things must

---

[268]N.T. Wright, Appendix B in Anton Flew, *There is a God,* 203-204, 205.
[269]N.T. Wright, Appendix B in Anton Flew, *There is a God,* 206-207.

have happened: (1) there must have been an empty tomb that was known to be the correct tomb; it couldn't have been a mistake; (2) there must have been appearances of the risen Jesus. Both of these must have occurred."[270]

Wright explained how he arrived at this conclusion:

"Why? Because if there had been an empty tomb and no appearances, everybody would have drawn the obvious conclusion . . . Body snatchers. Tombs were regularly robbed . . . They would never ever have talked about resurrection, if all that had happened was an empty tomb. Equally, you cannot explain the historical data . . . by saying that the disciples must have had some sort of experience they took to be a meeting with Jesus. They knew Jesus had been killed. But they all knew about hallucinations and ghosts and visions."[271]

Hostile witnesses

Further, the soldiers at the tomb, and the Jewish leaders that circulated the story of the stolen body were in effect *hostile witnesses* in support of Christ's resurrection since they testified that Christ's tomb was empty and Christ's body could not be produced. That is, they were essentially admitting that it was the correct tomb and that it was empty.

Wright rejects hallucinations as explanations for resurrection reports

Many critics have simply written off reports of Christ's resurrection appearances as nothing but hallucinations. Wright rejected such claims:

---

[270]N.T. Wright, Appendix B in Anton Flew, *There is a God,* 209-210.
[271]N.T. Wright, Appendix B in Anton Flew, *There is a God,* 210.

"Recently some people have tried to say . . . something like this: 'Ah, well, when those you love die, sometimes you will experience them in the room with you, smiling at you, maybe even talking to you; and then they will disappear again. Maybe that's what happened to these disciples.' . . . This is a well-documented phenomenon as part of the grief process . . . But the crunch is that the early Christians knew about phenomenon like that as well. They knew perfectly well that there were such things as visions, hallucinations, dreams, ghosts, and so on. In other words, if they'd had an experience, however vivid it seemed, of being with Jesus, but if the tomb had not been empty, they would have said, 'My goodness, this was very powerful, and quite consoling in a way; but he hasn't been raised from the dead, of course, because dead people don't get raised . . . and anyway, there is his body in the tomb.'"[272]

In a March 2005 debate with John Dominic Crossan, Wright expanded upon this argument:

"People in the ancient world had visions of people after they died, and that doesn't mean they're alive again—it means they're dead. That's the point. The ancient pagan writers were very clear about that. That's one of the reasons that you have these meals with the dead at the tomb, not to bring them back again, but as a way of making sure that Uncle Joe ain't coming back again . . . This is why Greg Riley is completely wrong in *Resurrection Reconsidered*—you wouldn't then say, well, this is basically the same thing as somebody being alive again. That's precisely what it isn't."[273]

Antony Flew, in a debate with Gary Habermas, also appealed to the idea of hallucinations to explain Christian resurrection claims:

---

[272]N.T. Wright, Appendix B in Anton Flew, *There is a God,* 210-211.
[273]N. T. Wright, *The Resurrection of Jesus: John Dominic Crossan and N. T. Wright in Dialogue*, 35-36.

"My best suggestion is that these were grief-related visions. Apparently, these are fairly common. People who have lost a husband, wife, or close relative and feel distressed about it suddenly have the feeling or seem to see the familiar person around the house and so on. I take it that these were grief-related visions and there was nothing there that anybody else could have seen."[274]

That is, when one has a vision of Grandma shortly after her funeral, they don't go and ask for a refund for her burial plot, and make preparations for her at the nursing home, because they still know (despite the vision) that they're loved one is in fact dead.

On the other hand, Christ's disciples didn't claim to have visions of him, but were actually with him, walking, carrying on conversations, touching him, eating with him, individually and in groups (at one time up to 500 people!), over a period of 40 days. This is not the stuff of illusions and hallucinations. Further, no type of vision explains the empty tomb.

Resurrection vs. cognitive dissonance

Wright also claimed that "I have shown that the idea of resurrection faith being generated by some kind of cognitive dissonance simply doesn't work."[275] The cognitive dissonance theory essentially states that we are uncomfortable when are actions are not in line with our beliefs and emotions, and we are psychologically driven

---

[274]Antony G. N. Flew in *Resurrected? An Atheist & Theist Dialogue*, Gary R. Habermas & Antony G.N. Flew, Edited by John F. Ankerberg, New York (Rowman & Littlefield Publishers, 2005) 8.

[275]275N. T. Wright, *The Resurrection of Jesus: John Dominic Crossan and N. T. Wright in Dialogue*, Edited by Robert B. Stewart, Minneapolis (Fortress Press, 2006) 18.

to resolve the conflict, so that our actions are in line with our beliefs and emotions.

In the case of the apostles, it is suggested that they were so psychologically devastated by Christ's death that it was easier to delude themselves into believing in his resurrection than to face the fact that He was dead. That is, the apostles were so convinced that Jesus was the Messiah, and that he was going to set up a political kingdom, that when he died, they couldn't face this contradiction to their beliefs, and so imagined that he was in fact yet alive.

The cognitive dissonance theory as an explanation for the disciple's belief in Jesus' resurrection suffers from all the same defects just mentioned for the hallucination theory.

Might we rather suggest that it was Christ's enemies who in fact suffered this disorder (cognitive dissonance), being unable to process and accept the powerful evidence of Christ resurrection, and so spread the lie that Christ's disciples stole his body!

The witness of the transformed disciples

In responding to various ancient conspiracy theories which make Jesus' disciples complicit in a resurrection hoax, Pastor D. James Kennedy offered this observation:

> "Connected to the appearances was the transformation of the apostles. One day they were cringing in an upper room for fear of the Jews, and soon after they were boldly upbraiding the Sanhedrin and proclaiming the resurrection of Christ. Consider also their martyrdom. They were crucified, crucified upside down . . . stoned to death . . . Why would they give their lives for what they *knew* to be false?"[276]

The atheist George Smith's false dilemma of faith or fact

George Smith set up a false dilemma by suggesting that one must choose between accepting Christ's resurrection as either historically true or as a matter of faith:

> "Consider the alleged resurrection of Jesus. Either this belief can fulfill the requirement of knowledge or it cannot. Either it is based on evidence, is internally consistent as a belief, and is capable of integration with one's previous knowledge, or it is not. If the belief in the Resurrection can fulfill these standards, it should be accepted as true—but it has then become a proposition of reason and can no longer be accepted on faith. On the other hand, if the belief in the Resurrection cannot meet the requirements of reason, it may be accepted on faith—but it can no longer claim the status of rational."[277]

This is a false dichotomy. It is naturalism begging the question, and reasoning in a circle. We know that miracles can't happen, therefore, Christ could not have been resurrected. But as we have seen, if God exists, miracles can happen. Since Smith has not disproven God's existence, he has not disproven the possibility of Christ's resurrection.

More to the point, rather than the resurrection being either a matter of rational belief or a matter of faith, Christianity has always maintained that the resurrection is both a matter of faith and a matter of fact. In other

[276]D. James Kennedy with Jerry Newcombe, *Who Is This Jesus Is He Risen?*, 8.
[277]George H. Smith, *Atheism: The Case Against God,* Amherst NY (Prometheus Books, 1979, 1989) 123.

words, its factual truth supports the faith of believers in the resurrection.

Dawkins and doubting Thomas

A similar attack was made by Richard Dawkins, who criticized Jesus' apostles (save doubting Thomas) for accepting the resurrection claims without evidence:

> "Thomas demanded evidence . . . The other apostles, whose faith was so strong that they did not need evidence, are held up to us as worthy of imitation."[278]

Dawkins criticism is difficult to understand. How much more evidence did the disciples need? They had personally encountered the risen Jesus. Further, once Thomas encountered Jesus himself, he accepted the resurrection as well; the skeptical Thomas, who had demanded proof, had become fully persuaded by the evidence.

The disciples' record or testimony of their personal experience of Christ's resurrection (New Testament documents) formed a reliable historical record, and as such are to be weighed like other historical records of the period, and it is quite reasonable for Christians to appeal to those records as a basis for their belief in the historicity of Christ's resurrection.

Christ's resurrection and the choice of faith

In this chapter, we have considered only a small portion of the evidence for Christ's resurrection. There

[278]Richard Dawkins, *The Selfish Gene*, (Oxford University Press,1976)198 as quoted by Sean McDowell & Jonathan Morrow, *Is God Just a Human Invention? And Seventeen Other Questions Raised by the New Atheists,* Grand Rapids MI (Kregel Publications, 2010) 21.

are many fine books that have examined the historical evidence in greater detail and have made an impressive case for the resurrection of Jesus Christ.

Yet some still struggle with the seeming impossibility of the concept of a resurrection from the dead. But consider the wisdom of the French scientist and philosopher Blaise Pascal:

> "What reason have atheists for saying that we cannot rise again? Which is the more difficult, to be born, or to rise again? That what has never been, should be, or that what has been, should be again? Is it more difficult to come into being than to return to it?"[279]

---

[279]Blaise Pascal, *Pensées,* 24, as quoted in *The Encyclopedia of Religious Quotations*, Frank S. Mead, Ed. Westwood New Jersey (Fleming H. Revell Company, 1965) 380.

Chapter 12: Miracles of Predictive Prophecy

One of the reasons for accepting the veracity and divine origin of the Judeo-Christian Bible is the prophetic nature of the book(s). That is, within the pages of the Bible, there are prophetic statements purported to have been revealed by God.

These statements have had the effect of speaking truth to the generation that received them (forth telling) or were predictive of future events (foretelling), or both.

That is, some had an immediate application in the time the prophecy was revealed, and a further fulfillment in future history. This is true of many of the messianic prophecies. J. Dwight Pentecost explains the prophetic principle of the law of double-reference:

> "Few laws are more important to observe in the interpretation of prophetic Scriptures than the law of double reference. Two events, widely separated as to the time of their fulfillment, may be brought together into the scope of one prophecy. This was done because the prophet had a message for his own day as well as for a future time."[280]

J. Edwin Hartill explained:

> "Double Reference Principle . . . Definition. It is that peculiarity of the writings of the Holy Spirit, by which a passage applying primarily to a person or event near at hand, is used by Him at a later time as applying to the Person of Christ, or the affairs of His kingdom. Human writers may not have had this in mind, but the Spirit knew."[281]

---

[280]J. Dwight Pentecost, *Things To Come: A Study in Biblical Eschatology*, Grand Rapids MI (Academie Books, 1958) 46.
[281]J. Edwin Hartill, *Biblical Hermeneutics*, Grand Rapids MI (Zondervan Publishing House, 1947) 105.

Messianic prophecies

Consider, for instance, Psalm 22, which had an initial application in the life of Israel's King David, and yet reads like an eyewitness report of Christ's crucifixion one thousand years later:

> "But I am a worm and not a man, scorned by everyone, despised by the people. All who see me mock me; they hurl insults, shaking their heads. 'He trusts in the LORD,' they say, 'let the LORD rescue him. Let him deliver him, since he delights in him'. . . Many bulls surround me; strong bulls of Bashan encircle me. Roaring lions that tear their prey open their mouths wide against me. I am poured out like water, and all my bones are out of joint. My heart has turned to wax; it has melted within me. My mouth is dried up like a potsherd, and my tongue sticks to the roof of my mouth; you lay me in the dust of death. Dogs surround me, a pack of villains encircles me; they pierce my hands and my feet. All my bones are on display; people stare and gloat over me. They divide my clothes among them and cast lots for my garment" (Psalm 22: 6-8, 12-18).

Likewise, the Servant Song of Isaiah 53 portends Christ's crucifixion which occurred seven hundred years later:

> "Who has believed our message and to whom has the arm of the LORD been revealed? He grew up before him like a tender shoot, and like a root out of dry ground. He had no beauty or majesty to attract us to him, nothing in his appearance that we should desire him. He was despised and rejected by mankind, a man of suffering, and familiar with pain. Like one from whom people hide their faces he was despised, and we held him in low esteem.
> Surely he took up our pain and bore our suffering, yet we considered him punished by God, stricken by him, and afflicted. But he was pierced for our transgressions, he was crushed for our iniquities; the punishment that brought us

peace was on him, and by his wounds we are healed. We all, like sheep, have gone astray, each of us has turned to our own way; and the LORD has laid on him the iniquity of us all.

He was oppressed and afflicted, yet he did not open his mouth; he was led like a lamb to the slaughter, and as a sheep before its shearers is silent, so he did not open his mouth. By oppression and judgment he was taken away. Yet who of his generation protested? For he was cut off from the land of the living; for the transgression of my people he was punished. He was assigned a grave with the wicked, and with the rich in his death, though he had done no violence, nor was any deceit in his mouth.

Yet it was the LORD's will to crush him and cause him to suffer, and though the LORD makes his life an offering for sin, he will see his offspring and prolong his days, and the will of the LORD will prosper in his hand. After he has suffered, he will see the light of life and be satisfied by his knowledge my righteous servant will justify many, and he will bear their iniquities. Therefore, I will give him a portion among the great, and he will divide the spoils with the strong, because he poured out his life unto death, and was numbered with the transgressors. For he bore the sin of many, and made intercession for the transgressors" (Isaiah 53).

Comparing these texts with the gospel accounts of Jesus' crucifixion provides striking evidence for God's inspiration of Scripture. Rather than debating whether these passages are absolute proof of supernatural revelation in the Bible, I ask only that the reader keep an open mind and weigh the evidence. Is it not impressive that these two passages (there are many more like them) from the Old Testament written 1000 years (Psalm 22) and 700 years before (Isaiah 53) so accurately portray the circumstances of Christ's crucifixion?

Bugliosi's candid assessment

I appreciate the frank observation made by the otherwise skeptical Bugliosi concerning the striking passage of Isaiah 53 (above):

> "Interestingly, one of the Old Testament's greatest prophets, Isaiah, in Isaiah 53:1-12, predicts a servant of the Lord who 'grew up in the Lord's presence' and who after a trial was led 'as a lamb to the slaughter,' the people not realizing that 'he was dying for their sins,' that he was 'suffering their punishment.' This and other verses in Isaiah . . . describe someone who bears a stunning, eerie resemblance to Jesus of Nazareth . . . *Isaiah 53 has always been, to me, the single most powerful chapter (merely four paragraphs) in the entire Bible that supports Jesus as being the Son of God.*"[282]

More Messianic prophecies

Robert Boyd provided further examples of messianic prophecies. Each example gives a summary title followed by an Old Testament prophecy *concerning Christ* and concluding with its New Testament fulfillment:

Born of a Virgin: Isaiah 7:14a / Matthew 1:22-23; Luke 1:30-33

Born in Bethlehem: Micah 5:2 / Luke 2:11

Adored by great persons: Psalm 72:10 / Matthew 2:1-12

Herod's slaughter of the innocents: Jeremiah 31:15 / Matthew 2:16-18

Holy Family's flight into Egypt: Hosea 11:1 / Matthew 2:13-15

---

[282]Vincent Bugliosi, *Divinity of Doubt: The God Question*, New York (Vanguard Press, 2011) 234.

Preparatory ministry of John the Baptist: Isaiah 40:3 / Matthew 3:3; Luke 1:76

Galilee, place of public ministry: Isaiah 9:1-2 / Matthew 4:12-17

Taking our infirmities: Isaiah 53:4 / Matthew 8:16-17

Purification of the temple: Psalm 69:9 / Luke 19:45-46

Riding into Jerusalem on an ass: Psalm 118:22-23 & Zechariah 9:9 / Mark 11:1-11

Betrayal by a friend: Psalm 41:9/ Matthew 26:47-50; Luke 22:47-48

Sold for thirty pieces of silver: Zechariah 11:13 / Matthew 26:14-16

Disciples forsaking Him: Zechariah 13:7 / Matthew 26:31

Opened not His mouth: Psalm 38:13 & Isaiah 53:7 / Matthew 27:13-14

Smitten and visage marred: Isaiah 50:6 & Zechariah 13:7 / Mark 14:27

Messiah cut off—hands and feet pierced: Isaiah 53:5-6, 10 / John 19:16-18

Crucifixion: Psalm 22:16 / John 20:25-27

Casting lots for His garment: Psalm 22:18 / Matthew 27:35 & John 19:23-24

Stared at upon the cross: Psalm 22:17 / Luke 23:35a, 48

Crucified between two thieves: Isaiah 53:12 / Matthew 27:45 & Mark 15:28

Mocked by the crowd: Psalm 22:7-7; 109:25 / Matthew 27:39-43

Forsaken by God: Psalm 22:1 / Matthew 27:46 & Mark 15:34

Given vinegar to drink: Psalm 69:21 / Matthew 27:48; John 19:28-29

Not a bone broken at Christ's crucifixion: Psalm 34:20 / John 19:31-34

His side pierced: Zechariah 12:10 / John 19:34, 37

His grave with the rich: Isaiah 53:9 / Matthew 27:57-61; John 19:38-42

Jesus prediction of three days in grave: Matthew 12:39-40 / Matthew 27:57-61

The resurrection: Psalm 16:10 / Matthew 28:1-6; John 20:1-12[283]

I do not suggest that these messianic prophecies are something like irrefutable proof of divine origin. A skeptic can always find reasons to protest. But an open-minded observer can see that there is something going on here. That something, I suggest is that a supernatural source is responsible for providing Old Testament prophets, hundreds of years beforehand, insights into the events of Christ's life.

Not everyone is convinced by biblical prophetic claims

The atheist David Eller criticized biblical prophecy:

"At any rate, most 'biblical prophecies' are so vague as to have no real cognitive or predictive value."[284]

---

[283]Adapted, abridged, and modified from original by Robert T. Boyd, *Boyd's Handbook of Practical Apologetics: Scientific Facts, Fulfilled Prophecies, and Archaeological Discoveries That Confirm the Bible*, Grand Rapids MI (Kregel Publications, 1997) 125-127

[284]David Eller, *Natural Atheism*, Cranford New Jersey (American Atheist Press, 2004) 38.

His criticism would be quite on target for the quatrains of alleged prophets like Nostradamus, or the so-called sleeping-prophet Edgar Cayce, or for the daily newspaper horoscopes, but this is hardly a fair assessment of biblical prophecy, as the foregoing have shown.

Olivet Discourse and A.D. 70

Near the end of his public ministry Jesus was teaching in the temple. While leaving the temple, Jesus' disciples were taken with the magnificence of the buildings.

Jesus gathered with his disciples on the Mount of Olives. Looking west across the Kidron Valley, they had a great view of the temple that was even then being completed (having been begun by King Herod in 9 B. C.). In response to His disciples' comments about the temple, Jesus began what has become known as the Olivet Discourse:

> "Some of his disciples were remarking about how the temple was adorned with beautiful stones and with gifts dedicated to God" (Luke 21:5).

Jesus' response must have surely startled His disciples, for He predicted the absolute destruction of the temple, something utterly inconceivable at that time:

> "'Do you see all these things?' he asked. 'Truly I tell you, not one stone here will be left on another; every one will be thrown down'" (Matthew 24:2).

This was no trivial prediction on Jesus' part since these stones were substantial:

"According to Josephus (*Antiquities*, 15.11.3), these 'massive stones' were white and some them were 37 feet (11.3 m) high and 18 feet (5.5) wide."[285]

The disciples naturally wanted to know how and when these predicted events would occur:

"'Teacher,' they asked, 'when will these things happen? And what will be the sign that they are about to take place?'"(Luke 21:7).

Jesus' answer provided a description of the coming destruction:

"When you see Jerusalem being surrounded by armies, you will know that its desolation is near. Then let those who are in Judea flee to the mountains, let those in the city get out, and let those in the country not enter the city. For this is the time of punishment in fulfillment of all that has been written. How dreadful it will be in those days for pregnant women and nursing mothers! There will be great distress in the land and wrath against this people. They will fall by the sword and will be taken as prisoners to all the nations. Jerusalem will be trampled on by the Gentiles until the times of the Gentiles are fulfilled" (Luke 21:20-24).

Jesus' amazing prediction was fulfilled precisely in A. D. 70 when the Romans, under the future emperor Titus, destroyed the city and its temple. Everett Ferguson provided historical context for the Jewish revolt against Rome:

"The seizure of seventeen talents from the temple treasury by the governor Florus, coming after a string of

---

[285] *NIV Archaeological Study Bible: An Illustrated Walk Through Biblical History and Culture*, Grand Rapids MI (Zondervan, 2005) 1652.

incidents in an atmosphere of seething unrest, precipitated the revolt of A. D. 66. The legate of Syria advanced on Jerusalem to put down the disturbance, but he was put to flight, and zealot leaders were convinced the hour of deliverance had come . . . Nero appointed Vespasian to put down the revolt. By the end of 67 Galilee was subdued. Its command had been held by Josephus, who has left a very detailed account of the progress of the war (*The Jewish War*) . . . The year A.D. 69 was the year of the "four emperors" in Roman history. Out of the civil war Vespasian emerged victorious. In the meantime Vespasian had left his son Titus to lay siege to Jerusalem. The siege was pressed in earnest in A. D. 70. . . . On the ninth day of the fifth month (August 5), the anniversary of the destruction of the first temple by the Babylonians, the sanctuary was set on fire by the invaders. A month later the whole city was in Titus' hands."[286]

VanderKam added:

"In 70 CE Titus laid siege to Jerusalem with his four legions and several other contingents of troops . . . Titus and his forces systematically took each of Jerusalem' three walls by smashing them with their battering rams. In this time of extreme peril, says Josephus, the fighting between Jewish groups in the city finally gave way to unity of purpose. As resistance continued, Titus ordered that a stone wall be raised around Jerusalem to prevent import of supplies to an already starving population. Once the Roman forces made their way into the city, the temple compound became the site of intense fighting. Josephus (who was in the Roman camp) says that in a Roman council of war, a decision was made to spare the temple itself. Nevertheless, in the course of the conflict the building was burned."[287]

---

[286]Everett Ferguson, *Backgrounds of Early Christianity*, Grand Rapids MI (William B. Eerdmans Publishing Company, 335-336
[287]James C. VanderKam, *An Introduction to Early Judaism*, Grand Rapids MI (William B. Eerdmans Publishing Company, 2001) 44.

It should not escape notice that the Romans had decided to spare the temple, contrary to Jesus' prophecy of destruction. In the course of events, however, Jesus' prediction proved true while the Roman plan disintegrated.

So complete was the destruction that Jesus' prediction that "not one stone here will be left on another' was fulfilled in every detail:

> "This prophecy was fulfilled literally in A. D. 70, when the Romans under Titus completely destroyed Jerusalem and the temple buildings. Stones were even pried apart to collect the gold leaf that melted from the roof when the temple was set on fire. Excavations in 1968 uncovered large numbers of these stones, toppled from the walls by the invaders."[288]

In the fourth century, the Church historian Eusebius described the destruction of Jerusalem and its temple, and Jesus' prediction of it:

> "These things happened in the second year of Vespasian's reign, in exact accordance with the prophetic predictions of our Lord and Savior Jesus Christ, who by divine power had foreseen them as though already present, and wept and mourned over them, as we learn from the holy evangelists, who have set down His very words. On one occasion He said, as if to Jerusalem herself:
>
> > *"If only, even you, had known today the way of your peace! But now it is hidden from your sight. For a time will come upon you when your enemies will throw up an earthwork round you and encircle you and hem you in on every side, and bring to the ground both you and your*

---

[288] *NIV Archaeological Study Bible: An Illustrated Walk Through Biblical History and Culture*, Grand Rapids MI (Zondervan, 2005) 1605

children" . . . And again: *"When you see Jerusalem encircled by armies, then you may be sure that her desolation is near."*

Anyone who compared our savior's words with the rest of the historian's account of the whole war could not fail to be astonished, and to acknowledge as divine and utterly marvelous the foreknowledge revealed by our savior's prediction."[289]

Critics question Christ's Prophecy

It should be no surprise that skeptics have leveled their attacks against Christ's amazing prophecy. In typical fashion, liberal critics, unable to accept miracles, simply late date the gospels, suggesting that Christ's prediction was nothing but a later fabrication.

Such after the fact "predictions" are called *Vaticinium ex eventu* by scholars. While it offers skeptics a simple alternative explanation for Christ's apparent prophetic knowledge (they were made up after the fact), it simply does not square with the historical facts.

Paul L. Maier shows a glaring weakness of the liberal evasion of Christ's prophecy concerning the destruction of Jerusalem:

> "Many liberal scholars suggest that the Gospels were written after the destruction of Jerusalem. Why: Because Jesus makes such an accurate prediction on the way to the Cross that indeed, Jerusalem would be destroyed. That is called prophecy after the fact, shall we say . . . Now Matthew, as you know, delights in prophecy/fulfillment,

---

[289]Eusebius, *The History of the Church From Christ to Constantine,* Translated with an introduction by G. A. Williamson, New York (Dorset Press, 1965) 117-118 (Book 3.7) Scripture citations Eusebius quoted are Luke 19:42-44 and Luke 21:20 which I italicized in contrast to Eusebius' words for clarity.

prophecy fulfillment—those couplets. So often Matthew
says, 'This was accomplished by Jesus that it might be
fulfilled what the prophet said,' and so on. Can you
imagine that if the book of Matthew had been written after
the fall of Jerusalem, wild horses couldn't have prevented
Matthew from saying, 'And Jesus' prediction was fulfilled
when Jerusalem was destroyed.' He doesn't say that."[290]

The Christian flight to Pella

Another historical weakness of the critics' explanation
is that shortly before the destruction of Jerusalem, in
light of Christ's prediction of the coming destruction of
Jerusalem, Christians migrated *en masse* to Pella. This
was in stark contrast to the migration of most Jews who
were fleeing *to* Jerusalem for safety. Gary DeMar
explained:

"During the Jewish and Idumean revolts against Rome
(A. D. 66-70), Pella, a rock fortress, hidden in the hill
country approximately sixty miles northeast of Jerusalem,
became a refuge for many Christians."[291]

DeMar quoted the statement of William Whiston in
accord with this fact:

"Affording the Jewish Christians in the city an
opportunity to calling to mind the prediction and caution
given them by Christ about thirty-three years and a half
before . . . By complying with which those Jewish
Christians fled to the mountains of Perea, and escaped
destruction."[292]

[290]Paul L. Maier in D. James Kennedy with Jerry Newcombe, *Who Is This Jesus Is He Risen?* 60-61.
[291]Gary DeMar, *Last Days Madness: Obsession of the Modern Church,* Atlanta GA (American Vision, Inc. 1994) 96.
[292]William Whiston, note b in Josephus, *Wars of the Jews,* 2:19:6, 631-32, as quoted by Gary DeMar, *Last Days Madness: Obsession*

DeMar summed it upped:

"Forty years earlier Jesus had given the warning to flee to the mountains when the holy city was seen encompassed by armies. Those who believed the prophecy and acted upon it escaped with their lives."[293]

The highly respected historian Philip Shaff described the flight to Pella:

"The Christians of Jerusalem, remembering the Lord's admonition, forsook the doomed city in good time and fled to the town of Pella in the Decapolis, beyond the Jordan, in the north of Perea, where king Herod Aprippa II, before whom Paul once stood, opened to them safe asylum."[294]

We know of the Christian flight to Pella from two sources. The first is that of the early church historian Eusebius:

"Furthermore, the members of the Jerusalem church, by means of an oracle given by revelation to acceptable persons there, were ordered to leave the City before the war began and settle in a town in Perea called Pella. To Pella those who believed in Christ migrated from Jerusalem."[295]

---

of the Modern Church, Atlanta GA (American Vision, Inc. 1994) 96-97.

[293]Gary DeMar, Last Days Madness: Obsession of the Modern Church, Atlanta GA (American Vision, Inc. 1994) 97.

[294]Philip Schaff, History of the Christian Church, Volume 1, Apostolic Christianity A. D. 1-100, Grand Rapids MI (WM. B. Eerdmans Publishing Company, 1910) 402.

[295]Eusebius, The History of the Church From Christ to Constantine, Translated with an introduction by G. A. Williamson, New York (Dorset Press, 1965) 111 (Book 3.5, 3)

In addition to Christ's prophecy, Eusebius mentioned a later revelation to the Church warning them to flee Jerusalem before its destruction.

The second source for the Christian flight to Pella was the fourth-century apologist Epiphanius:

"From there it took its beginning after the exodus from Jerusalem when all the disciples went to live in Pella because Christ had told them to leave Jerusalem and to go away since it would undergo a siege. Because of this advice they lived in Perea after having moved to that place, as I said."[296]

In another place, Epiphanius provided further details:

"So Aquila, while he was in Jerusalem, also saw the disciples of the disciples of the apostles flourishing in the faith and working great signs, healings, and other miracles. For they were such as had come back from the city of Pella to Jerusalem and were living there and teaching. For when the city was about to be taken and destroyed by the Romans, it was revealed in advance to all the disciples by an angel of God that they should remove from the city, as it was going to be completely destroyed. They sojourned as emigrants in Pella, the city above mentioned in Transjordania. And this city is said to be of the Decapolis."[297]

Epiphanius confirmed that the Christians that had fled to Pella before its destruction in A.D. 70, returned to Jerusalem after the consummation of the Jewish War. In addition to Christ's prophecy, Epiphanius confirmed the

[296]Epiphanius, *Panarion*, *29,7,7-8* as cited in Wikipedia article *The Flight to Pella at: https://en.wikipedia.org/wiki/Flight_to_Pella*
[297]Epiphanius, *On Weights and Measures*, 15 as cited in Wikipedia article *The Flight to Pella at: https://en.wikipedia.org/wiki/Flight_to_Pella*

further revelation given to the church shortly before the destruction of Jerusalem.

The Warning of Jesus of Ananus

Dr. Clyde Billington described a further prophetic pronouncement of another Jewish prophet named Jesus leading up to the destruction of Jerusalem:

> "At the Passover Feast in 70 A. D., there was also in attendance a strange Jew named Jesus the son of Ananus. He had first appeared in Jerusalem in 62 AD.—four years before the war began—and he had for the last 7 years wandered about the city only saying one thing: 'Woe, woe to the city of Jerusalem, to the people, and to the holy temple.'"[298]

Billington further described how Jesus son of Ananus' message changed slightly before the final destruction of Jerusalem:

> "At the very start of the Roman siege of Jerusalem, Jesus the son of Ananus suddenly made a slight change in the message which he had been repeating for seven years. Now he said: 'Woe, woe again to the city of Jerusalem, and to the people, and to the temple, and woe to me also.' As soon as he said the added phrase 'woe to me also' a stone from a Roman catapult came flying over the wall and struck him and killed him instantly."[299]

Into this highly-charged atmosphere, with multiple prophecies of doom filling the air, and the memory of Christ's own announcement of coming destruction, it is

---

[298]Clyde Billington, *New Testament Archaeology, Articles and Supplementary Readings, The Destruction of Jerusalem and the Temple in 70 A.D.,* Part IV, p. 241
[299]Clyde Billington, *New Testament Archaeology,* 242.

not surprising that the Christians fled the holy city for the safety of Pella.

The best explanation of all the facts is that Jesus Christ actually predicted the Roman 70 A. D. destruction of Jerusalem and its temple nearly a generation before it occurred.

Skeptics attempt to discredit Christ's prediction by late dating the biblical gospels. But there is not a shred of evidence that proves a post A. D. 70 composition of the synoptic gospels, and there are many able New Testament scholars that defend a pre-70 A. D. date.

Likewise, those who call into question the historical reliability of the reports of the Christian's flight to Pella seem motivated more by their anti-supernatural bias than by any defects in the historical reports themselves. Indeed, many able historians defend the accuracy of the accounts by Eusebius and Epiphanius.[300]

---

[300]See for example: P.H.R. Van Houwelingen, *Fleeing Forward: The Departure of Christians from Jerusalem to Pella,* Westminster Theological Journal, 65, 2003, 181-200 at web address: https://web.archive.org/web/20150403123403/http://oud.tukampen. nl/uploads/documents/124.pdf and Jonathan Bourgel, *The Jewish-Christian's Move from Jerusalem as a Pragmatic Approach*, at web address: https://www.academia.edu/4909339/THE_JEWISH_CHRISTIANS_ MOVE_FROM_JERUSALEM_AS_A_PRAGMATIC_CHOICE

Chapter 13: Twelve: The Argument from Experience

Another argument often put forward by believers is sometimes called the argument from experience. Although it is subjective in nature, the Christian testifies to the positive impact faith in Christ has made for his or her life. Sharing their faith with others seems as natural to the Christian as a doctor sharing medicine to sick patients.

Those who hear such testimony are wise to consider it carefully. The changed lives reported by believers should be weighed with an open mind. Indeed, for those who have experienced it, faith is a guiding force in their lives, providing clarity, meaning, and inward peace that was previously absent.

D. E. Trueblood described the deep religious convictions of Blaise Pascal:

> "The celebrated French mathematician, Blaise Pascal, used the word 'Fire' in capital letters, as the central feature of the record of his life-shaking experience. This record, which Pascal's servant found sewed into the scholar's coat, at the time of his death . . . The word 'Fire' was most emphasized, probably in the effort to show that what he perceived has about it the same indubitable quality that we find in the flame, which warms, lights, and even burns."[301]

In the same spirit, are the words of the martyred missionary Jim Elliot who cried out to God:

---

[301]D. E. Trueblood, *The Evidential Value of Religious Experience*, as reprinted in *A Modern Introduction to Philosophy: Readings from Classical and Contemporary Sources,* Third Edition, Paul Edwards & Arthur Pap, Editors, New York, (The Free Press, 1973) 438.

"God, I pray Thee, light these idle sticks of my life and may I burn for Thee. Consume my life, my God, for it is Thine. I seek not a long life, but a full one, like you, Lord Jesus."[302]

Perhaps Elliot had been inspired by the words of the biblical prophet Jeremiah:

"His word is in my heart like a fire, a fire shut up in my bones. I am weary of holding it in; indeed, I cannot" (Jeremiah 20:9).

These inspirational words testify to the change that comes upon those who find a faith in Jesus Christ. We see His hand in the events of our lives, finding comfort in that still small voice of God's guidance. We are equally convinced that God speaks through His word the Bible, and accordingly, make every effort to order our lives by its principles.

---

[302] Jim Elliot, at following web address: http://justinchilders.blogspot.com/2006/06/some-of-my-favorite-jim-elliot-quotes.html

Section Four: Science and Faith

Chapter 14: Harmonizing Faith and Science

The Joy of discovery

We live in an interesting world and in a fascinating universe. Our knowledge is of course limited. As much as we have learned, there is much more to learn. We may sometimes feel that we live in an advanced society, at least relative to the past, but our ancestors will probably be amused by our 'advanced technology.'

But this state of limited knowledge should not discourage us. Rather, we live in exciting times. No doubt, this drive to know, to understand, is itself a gift of God. Surely this is what the great polish astronomer Johannes Kepler meant when he cried out: "O God, I am thinking thy thoughts after thee."[303] Francis Collins, who directed the Human Genome Project made a similar observation:

> "I experience a sense of awe at the realization that humanity now knows something only God knew before. It is a deeply moving sensation that helps me appreciate the spiritual side of life."[304]

The astronomer Robert Jastrow concluded his book *God and the Astronomers* with a similar thought:

---

[303]Johannes Kepler, as cited in *The Encyclopedia of Religious Quotations*, Frank S. Mead, Editor, Westwood NJ (Fleming H. Revell Company, 1965) 176.

[304]Francis Collins, as quoted by Dorothy Nelkin, *Less Selfish Than Sacred?: Genes and the Religious Impulse in Evolutionary Psychology,* chapter in, *Alas, Poor Darwin: Arguments Against Evolutionary Psychology*, Edited by Hilary Rose & Steven Rose, New York (Harmony Books, 2000) 27-28.

"For the scientist who has lived by his faith in the power of reason, the story ends like a bad dream. He has scaled the mountains of ignorance; he is about to conquer the highest peak; as he pulls himself over the final rock, he is greeted by a band of theologians who have been sitting there for centuries."[305]

Science and faith: Conflicting and competing models of truth

It is often claimed that a conflict exists between science and religious faith, and one must choose between one or the other. Worse yet, it is often suggested that the choice is really between rational science and irrational faith. Is that a fair assessment?

Not at all. The Bible does not distinguish between religious and scientific truths. They are all God truths. This means that as our scientific knowledge advances, the apparent conflict with religious faith recedes.

That the world is reflective of the orderly mind of God was a key to the birth of modern science. And so Fackenheim stated:

"To the Protestant mind, schooled in the Bible, nature is not divine, but the *work* of God; and God created it for human use. It was this belief—still according to Whitehead—that made modern experimental science possible. Hence one might well conclude that in some ways modern science is closer in spirit to Biblical faith than its pre-modern predecessor."[306]

---

[305]Robert Jastrow, *God and the Astronomers*, New York (Warner Books, Inc, 1978, 1980) 105-106.

[306]Emil L. Fackenheim, *On the Eclipse of God* as reprinted in *A Modern Introduction to Philosophy: Readings from Classical and Contemporary Sources,* Third Edition, Paul Edwards & Arthur Pap, Editors, New York, (The Free Press, 1973) 526.

The two-book doctrine: Science and faith as complimentary and confluent

Wesley Allan showed that the early founders of the modern scientific method such as Francis Bacon believed that science and faith were not in conflict, but complimentary:

> "Bacon's rhetoric thus propounded the *two books doctrine*, the Bible was one of God's revelations, the Book of God's Word, but nature was a second revelation, the Book of God's works. This doctrine placed the study of God's works in nature as an act of worship conjoined with the study of God's Word, the Scriptures."[307]

In this spirit, pursuing science was an act of worship leading to a greater knowledge of God and His creation, a world of order waiting to be discovered. John Lennox also highlighted Francis Bacon's approach of integrating science and faith:

> "It was this conviction that led Francis Bacon (1561-1626), regarded by many as the father of modern science, to teach that God has provided us with two books—the book of Nature and the Bible."[308]

Sidney Hook showed that this was the view of Thomas Aquinas as well:

[307]Wesley D. Allen, *Modern Science: Charting A Course for the Future,* chapter in *Science: Christian Perspectives for the New Millennium,* Editors Scott B. Luley, Paul Copan & Stan W. Wallace, Addison TX (Christian Leadership Ministries, 2003) 238.
[308]John C. Lennox, *God's Undertaker: Has Science Buried God?,* New Updated Edition, Oxford England (Lion Books, 2009) 21.

"Aquinas, however, also assumed that although the truths of revelation are not the same as the truths of reason, the two must nevertheless be logically compatible."[309]

This complimentary approach to science and faith has been very successful as Allen argued:

"The conviction that all phenomena of nature should follow a master plan because God has designed the universe according to his perfect character was a central motivation of Copernicus, Kepler, and Newton. Despite common misperceptions, the conflict between some of these scientific luminaries and the established church was not rooted in basic Christian theology itself, but rather in the widespread influence that Aristotelian philosophy had gained in the church in the middle ages. Galileo is noted for his statement that the book of nature is written by the hand of God in the language of mathematics. This theme is echoed in the words of Kepler: 'The chief aim of all investigations of the external world should be to discover the rational order and harmony which has been imposed on it by God and which He revealed to us in the language of mathematics.'"[310]

Barnes referred to Stark's similar claims:

"If indeed the method of science is universally effective, then a fascinating historical question is why the scientific method developed fully first in Europe rather than springing up in cultures around the world . . . The sociologist Rodney Stark, among others . . . proposes that monotheism helped. The God of Western religions has long

---

[309]Sidney Hook, *Modern Knowledge and the Concept of God*, chapter in *Critiques of God: Making the Case Against Belief in God*, Peter A. Angeles, Editor, Amherst New York (Prometheus Books, 1997) 26.

[310]Wesley D. Allen, *Modern Science: Charting A Course for the Future*, chapter in *Science: Christian Perspectives for the New Millennium*, Editors Scott B. Luley, Paul Copan & Stan W. Wallace, Addison TX (Christian Leadership Ministries, 2003) 240.

been described as the one who planned or designed the universe with perfect intelligence. Belief in this, Stark argues, led people to expect the universe to be rationally comprehensible and therefore able to be studied rationally."[311]

Stark responded to the naturalist argument that the church held back the advance of science in the West:

"Encouraged by the Scholastics and embodied in the great medieval universities founded by the church, faith in the power of reason infused Western culture, stimulating the pursuit of science . . . The West is said to have surged ahead precisely as it *overcame* religious barriers to progress, especially those impeding science. Nonsense. The success of the West, including the rise of science, rested entirely on religious foundations, and the people who brought it about were devout Christians."[312]

Again, Stark stated:

"Not only were science and religion compatible, they were inseparable—the rise of science was achieved by deeply religious Christian scholars."[313]

Stephen Barr added details illustrating the positive effects Christianity had upon the rise of modern science:

"One of the great contributions of the Bible, which helped clear the ground for the later emergence of science, was to desacralize and depersonalize the natural world . . . No more were the Sun or stars or oceans or forests the haunts of ghosts or gods, nor were

---

[311]Michael Horace Barnes, *Understanding Religion and Science: Introducing the Debate*, New York (Continuum International Publishing Group, 2010) 70.

[312] Rodney Stark, *The Victory of Reason: How Christianity Led to Freedom, Capitalism, and Western Success*, New York (Random House, 2005) Introduction X-XI.

[313] Rodney Stark, *The Victory of Reason,* 12.

they endowed with supernatural powers. They were mere things, creations of the one God."[314]

The Galileo affair

But what of the oft-repeated claim that the church has been the enemy of science, most notably in the so-called Galileo Affair? Did not the Church attack and persecute Galileo for his stand in defense of the helio-centric nature of our solar system?

Marcelo Gleiser explained:

"Although Galileo is commonly represented as one of the greatest martyrs in the fight for freedom of expression, and the church as the intolerant villain, the truth is more complex."[315]

Timothy Moy provided some important historical context to this question:

"Over the past few decades, historians of science have been reexamining the 'Galileo Affair'—Galileo's trial by the Roman Catholic Church in 1633 . . . Almost all historians agree that it was *not* primarily because Galileo believed in Copernican heliocentrism . . . By this point, many—perhaps most—church officials had already concluded that Copernicus's system was the most accurate."[316]

Peacock expanded upon the true factors that led to Galileo's conflict with the church:

---

[314] Stephen M. Barr, *Modern Physics and Ancient Faith*, Notre Dame IN (University of Notre Dame Press, 2003) 5.

[315] Marcelo Gleiser, *The Dancing Universe: From Creation Myths to the Big Bang*, Hanover New Hampshire (Dartmouth College Press, 1997, 2005) 98.

[316] Timothy Moy, *The Galileo Affair*, in *Science and Religion: Are They Compatible?*, Paul Kurtz, Editor, Amherst New York (Prometheus Books, 2003) 139.

"He [Galileo] didn't suffer fools gladly and while he attracted admirers, he also created many enemies and displayed an acerbic nature toward those who opposed him. These were his own university colleagues . . . What of his [Galileo's] opponents? They were initially the university professors, loosely formed into an opposition, the *Liga,* centered in Florence."[317]

Indeed, the controversy expanded to involve the church, but its roots are far from the simplistic picture often offered that suggest a cleavage between science and faith.

Moy added:

"Unfortunately, Galileo's trouble with the Church later became a popular archetype for the historical relationship between science and religion. Nothing could be farther from the truth. For most of the medieval and Renaissance periods, and even stretching into the eighteenth-century Enlightenment, the primary supporter of research and teaching in the sciences was the Roman Catholic Church. In fact, one historian of science, John Heilbron, has recently published a book entitled *The Sun in the Church* that documents how the Church, in the aftermath of the Galileo affair, continued to promote research into evidence for heliocentrism, even to the point of turning entire cathedrals into giant pinhole cameras to measure the apparent diameter in the solar disk at various times of the year."[318]

Vern Bullough agreed that the Church has had a positive influence on modern intellectual growth:

"The early Christian Church in the West had a strong intellectual tradition. In fact, one of the reasons it appealed

[317]Roy E. Peacock, *A Brief History of Eternity,* Wheaton IL (Crossway Books, 1990) 140, 142.
[318]Timothy Moy, *The Galileo Affair,* 143.

to intellectuals is that it incorporated much of classical learning into its theology."[319]

It should be remembered that the idea that the earth was the center of the solar system (and the universe) did not come from the Bible, but from the Ptolemaic system. Yeager Hudson explained:

"We can see this process at work in the Christian tradition during the Middle Ages when the Ptolemaic theories of astronomy were taken over and blended with biblical ideas to generate a Christian cosmology . . . Ptolemy, an astronomer who lived during the second century of the Common Era, depicted the earth as the center of the universe, with the moon, the planets, the sun, and the stars all revolving around the earth. The central place of importance this theory gave to man's habitat made it very attractive to Christian theologians, who incorporated it so fully into their doctrines that they soon forgot they had borrowed it from the secular science of the day. When scientific astronomy developed in the fourteenth and fifteenth centuries, a battle in the Christian tradition began between the defenders of the now orthodox doctrine that embraced Ptolemaic astronomy and such astronomers as Copernicus (1473-1543), Kepler (1571-1630), and Galileo (1564-1642), who taught that the earth is not the center of the universe."[320]

Again, *the battle for the heliocentric model was being fought by devout Christian believers* (Copernicus, Kepler et al) who were striving to remove the secular Ptolemaic influence from both sound science and theology.

---

[319]Vern Bullough, *Science and Religion in Historical Perspective*, in Timothy Moy, *The Galileo Affair*, in *Science and Religion: Are They Compatible?*, Paul Kurtz, Editor, Amherst New York (Prometheus Books, 2003) 131

[320]Yeager Hudson, *The Philosophy of Religion*, Mountain View CA (Mayfield Publishing Company, 1991) 145-146.

As the controversy over Galileo's support of heliocentrism heated up, even then, he had support in high place in the Roman Catholic Church:

"Even after Galileo's support for the Copernican system was made public, he received several letters from high Church officials expressing their admiration for his work, including one from Cardinal Maffeo Barberini, soon to become Pope Urban VIII."[321]

Gleiser added:

"In 1623 Cardinal Maffeo Barbarini, who seven years earlier had played an important role in smoothing things out for Galileo, became Pope Urban VIII. This was the opportunity Galileo was waiting for to launch a renewed attack on the Earth-centered universe of the Church. He dedicated *Il Saggiatore* to Urban and was received by him for six long audiences during the spring of 1624. The Pope's admiration for Galileo was sincere. In 1620 he had written a poem to Galileo titled *'Adualtio Perniciosa'* . . . During Galileo's visit he gave him a silver and gold medal, a pension for his son, and a glowing letter to the Tuscan court in which he wrote of all the virtues 'of this great man, whose fame shines in the heavens, and goes on earth far and wide.'"

---

[321] Marcelo Gleiser, *The Dancing Universe: From Creation Myths to the Big Bang*, Hanover New Hampshire (Dartmouth College Press, 1997, 2005) 105.

Indeed, Galileo had the Church's support to write his book on heliocentrism, provided that it was offered as a hypothesis:

"In May 1630, Galileo want to Rome to make sure he could proceed with the publication of the manuscript. The Pope received him for a long audience and confirmed that he had no objection to presenting the merits of the Copernican model, as long as it was treated as a hypothesis."[322]

Many powerful people in the Church advised Galileo to take a more tactful approach to the controversy. Yet he ignored that advice, choosing a more reckless and confrontational course, to his own detriment;

"According to Francesco Niccolini, then Tuscan ambassador in Rome, the Pope was furious with Galileo . . . He felt outwitted, deceived, and betrayed by someone he held very dear."[323]

Eventually, Galileo succumbed to Church pressure and recanted. He was sentenced to house arrest for the remainder of his life.

---

[322] Marcelo Gleiser, *The Dancing Universe: From Creation Myths to the Big Bang*, Hanover New Hampshire (Dartmouth College Press, 1997, 2005) 114.

[323] Marcelo Gleiser, *The Dancing Universe: From Creation Myths to the Big Bang*, Hanover New Hampshire (Dartmouth College Press, 1997, 2005)115-116.

Nevertheless, Sean McDowell pointed out that the "persecution" that Galileo actually endured was relatively benign:

"After his trial before the Inquisition, he [Galileo] was placed under the care of the archbishop of Siena, who housed him in his beautiful palace for five months, Galileo was then released to his home in Florence where he received a church pension for the rest of his life."[324]

Gleiser added the interesting historical detail that:

Galileo died in 1642, the year Isaac Newton was born. All but three of his bones rest in the Church of Santa Croce, next to the remains of Michelangelo and Machiavelli. The missing ones, those of the middle finger of his right hand, are displayed under a glass dome in the Museum for the History of Science in Florence.[325]

Catholic philosopher Stephen Barr reacted to the argument that the Christian church has been an enemy of scientific progress:

"The fact is that the attitude of the Church has overwhelmingly been one of friendliness to

---

[324] Sean McDowell, *Are Christianity and Science at Odds?*, Chapter in *True Reason: Confronting the Irrationality of the New Atheism,* Tom Gilson & Carson Weitnauer, Editors, Grand Rapids MI (Kregel Publications, 2012) 194.

[325] Marcelo Gleiser, *The Dancing Universe: From Creation Myths to the Big Bang,* Hanover New Hampshire (Dartmouth College Press, 1997, 2005) 119.

scientific inquiry. Long before Galileo, and continuing to the present day, one can find examples in every century, not merely of church patronage of science, but of important scientific figures who were themselves monks, priest, and even bishops."[326]

Is the scientific field bias free?

David Eller argued that whereas the creation science and intelligent design movements are biased pseudo-science, secular science has no agenda or bias: "Science knows no loyalty to tradition, authority, prejudice, or personal preference."[327]

Eller certainly expresses a noble ideal which should be the goal of all scientists. Unfortunately, however, scientists are as prone to yield to their own presuppositions and biases as those in any other human endeavor.

Philip Johnson stated:

> "On the one hand, modernists say that science is impartial fact-finding, the objective and unprejudiced weighing of evidence. Science in that sense relies on careful observations, calculations, and above all, repeatable experiments. That kind of objective science is what makes technology possible . . . On the other hand, modernists also indentify science with naturalistic philosophy. In that case science is not free of prejudice. On

[326] Stephen M. Barr, *Modern Physics and Ancient Faith*, Notre Dame IN (University of Notre Dame Press, 2003) 8-9. Barr proceeded to provide a very impressive and informative list of accomplished scientists who were also committed Christian believers.
[327] David Eller, *Natural Atheism*, Cranford New Jersey (American Atheist Press, 2004) 189.

the contrary, it is *defined* by a prejudice. The prejudice is that all phenomena can ultimately be explained in terms of purely natural causes."[328]

Robert A. Morey captured the spirit of the age:

"The situation abruptly changed after Hegel (1770-1831). Atheists became anti-theists as they were not actively 'against' God, seeking to wage war on God and on those who believed in Him. Thus the pure atheism of nonbelief gave way to a crusade of anti-theism. No longer did they simply not believe in God. They now hated God and wished to destroy all faith . . . Hegel and those that followed him, such as Feuerbach, Nietzsche, Marx, etc., believe that God had to be pushed aside in order for man to be free to be his own God."[329]

It is difficult to take seriously the denials of a naturalistic bias present in much modern science. John Lennox passed along the warning of Thomas Kuhn concerning the danger of such an approach:

"Thomas Kuhn warned of paradigms that produced a box-like structure so rigid that things that did not fit into it were often simply overlooked. If something has simply got to be true, then conflicting evidence can easily be ignored or superficially dismissed as irrelevant. To avoid this danger, Richard Feynman emphasized that one should always be careful to record all the evidence against one's theories . . . since the easiest person to fool is oneself."[330]

Amir Aczel stated:

[328]Phillip E. Johnson, *The Wedge of Truth: Splitting the Foundations of Naturalism*, Downers Grove IL (InterVarsity Press, 2000) 14.
[329]Robert A. Morey, *The New Atheism and the Erosion of Freedom*, Minneapolis MN (Bethany House Publishers, 1986) 25-26.
[330]John C. Lennox, *God's Undertaker,* 99.

"The problem with the science in the books and lectures of the New Atheists is that it is not pure science—the objective pursuit of knowledge about the universe. Rather, it is 'science with a purpose': the purpose of disproving the existence of God . . . They bend and distort science to further their own agendas in a way that is not too different from what scientists in the pay of a pharmaceutical company might be doing in writing a favorable report about a questionable drug the company makes."[331]

The two magesteriums and a double-truth universe: Science and faith as separate worlds of truth

Another approach proposed for the intersection of faith and science is to keep them in separate realms, never the twain should meet.

This is the view popularized by the scientist Stephen Jay Gould with his idea of the two magesteriums of science and religion. One is simply to keep religious beliefs compartmentalized in one part of the brain and scientific truths in another. That is, science describes facts while religion provides purpose and meaning. This allows people, suggested Gould, to retain faith in the Bible for finding meaning in their lives, without being stumbled by its alleged scientific mistakes.

Gould's idea was not new. Richard Tarnas commented on how scientific gains being made during the enlightenment were challenging long-held religious beliefs leading to a bifurcation among intellectuals:

"Thus arose the psychological necessity of a double-truth universe. Reason and faith came to be seen as

---

[331]Amir D. Aczel, *Why Science Does Not Disprove God*, New York (HarperCollins Publishers, 2014)18.

pertaining to different realms, with Christian philosophers and scientists, and the larger educated Christian public, perceiving no genuine integration between the scientific reality and the religious reality . . . Attempts to bridge the two generally failed to preserve the character of one or the other."[332]

This was an attempt at a compromise position seeking to end conflicts between faith and science. But as Tarnas stated, the harmonization was usually at the expense "of one or the other." The Bible was often simply reinterpreted in a less than faithful or literal matter, eliminating the miraculous, resulting in the stripped-down version represented by liberal Christianity.

Kerry Walters noted the irony that a leading scientist, Stephen Jay Gould, was a leading advocate of this approach at a rapprochement between science and faith:

"Ironically, the most influential defender of a separate-but-equal understanding of naturalism and supernaturalism is an atheist: the late paleontologist Stephen Jay Gould. He calls his thesis NOMA: Non-Overlapping Magisteria. (Magisterum, of course, is Latin for 'authority.') According to Gould, the naturalist claims of science and the supernaturalist claims of religion are based upon two different kinds of authority, both equally legitimate. Trouble arises when one authority encroaches or overlaps onto the other. But when kept in their separate spheres, difficulties disappear . . . the distinction between the two is still fairly clear: science asks, 'what is the universe made of (fact) and why does it work this way (theory),' while religion focuses on 'questions of moral meaning and value.'"[333]

---

[332]Richard Tarnas, *The Passion of the Western Mind: Understanding the Idea That Have Shaped Our World View*, New York (Ballantine Books, 1991) 302.

Rose and Rose made reference to a statement put forward by an organization of scientists:

"According to a statement by the American Association for the Advancement of Science (AAAS), the differences between science and religion have to do with the kind of questions asked: 'Science is about causes, religion about meaning. Science deals with how things happen in nature, religion with why there is anything rather than nothing. Science answers specific questions about the workings of nature, religion addresses the ultimate grounds of nature."[334]

This statement is partially true, but mostly false. True, religion deals with ultimate questions, but so does science. True, science deals with causes, but so does religion. It is impossible to conceive how the two domains avoid intersection. The road to true science and the road to true religion will necessarily lead to the same destination.

Further, Lennox showed the subordinate role religion is usually expected to play when the two magisterium's intersect:

"In other words, science and religion can peacefully co-exist as long as religion does not invade the realm of science . . . the bottom line is science deals with reality, religion does not."[335]

---

[333]Kerry Walters, *Atheism: A Guide for the Perplexed*, New York (The Continuum International Publishing Group Inc, 2010) 42-43.

[334]Dorothy Nelkin, *Less Selfish Than Sacred?: Genes and the Religious Impulse in Evolutionary Psychology*, chapter in, *Alas, Poor Darwin: Arguments Against Evolutionary Psychology*, Edited by Hilary Rose & Steven Rose, New York (Harmony Books, 2000) 18.

[335]John C. Lennox, *God's Undertaker*, 40.

But such compartmentalizing cannot have intellectual integrity. Truth is truth. And all truth must have a confluence.

I recall a situation in which one of my children was being taught evolution in school and the teacher was openly ridiculing those who believed in a literal interpretation of Genesis. I attempted to open a dialogue with the science teachers at the school. What was ironic was that I was the one that wanted to talk about the scientific evidence concerning evolution while the science teachers were attempting to show how to maintain belief in Genesis through non-literal interpretations.

The science teachers were simply following the two magisteriums model, taking science at face value while reinterpreting the Bible as so much mythology, though with some nice inspirational stories and ideals.

But the Bible makes many statements concerning science and history that cannot simply be brushed aside or reinterpreted. It is either correct in what it affirms or it is not. Bible believing Christians maintain that science and faith can and must be consistent with the facts of the real world.

Did God create the world or didn't He. Was Adam the first human being, or did man evolve from some kind of pre-human hominid? Did Moses lead the Israelites across the parted seas, or was that a myth? Did Jesus really rise from the dead?

These are essential questions to the Christian faith. To provide a synthesis between science and faith that guts the Christian faith of these literal truths is to commit a fatal compromise. These truths are as vital to Christianity as the heart and brain are to the body.

It is possible, and in fact, intellectually satisfying, to believe in both hard scientific facts and the literal interpretation of the Bible, as many of the greatest scientists of history have proven.

The God of the Gaps arguments

Atheists often accuse believers of using "God of the gaps" arguments. That is, whenever there is an issue in which science does not yet have an answer, the theist prematurely concludes that such is proof for the existence of God. However, if believers would simply withhold judgment, science would eventually be able to explain the apparent gap in scientific knowledge without appeal to a supernatural being.

We can go back to the eighteenth century for the roots of the god in the gaps argument:

> "Baron d' Holbach wrote, in a France where social and intellectual tensions were becoming intolerable, 'Theology is but the ignorance of natural causes reduced to a system,' and again 'When man ascribes to 'the gods' the production of some phenomenon . . . does he in fact do anything more than substitute for the darkness of his own mind, a sound to which he has been accustomed to listen with reverential awe? Among the group centered around Diderot and the *Encyclopedie,* d' Holbach (1723-1789) was perhaps the most strident atheist. To him . . . God was merely a label for man's ignorance of nature's secrets."[336]

Richard Dawkins further explained what is meant by the god in the gaps:

> "Searching for examples of irreducible complexity is a fundamentally unscientific way to proceed: a special case of

---

[336]Peter Whitfield, *Landmarks in Western Science: From Prehistory to the Atomic Age*, New York (Routledge, 1999) 180.

arguing from present ignorance. It appeals to the same faulty logic as 'the God of the Gaps' strategy condemned by the theologian Dietrich Bonheoffer. Creationists eagerly seek a gap in present-day knowledge or understanding. If an apparent gap is found, it is assumed that God, by default, must fill it."[337]

For example, atheists point to the teleological argument as a God of the gaps argument. That is, Christians believed that apparent design in nature was proof of God's creative activity since science had no way to account for the complex structures found in nature. However, we now know (the argument goes) that evolution can account for these structures, removing the gap that theist had tried to fill with God belief.

We have seen, however, that the teleological argument remains quite forceful, and this, ironically, is due to *increasing scientific knowledge* i.e., the fine tuning argument etc.

God of the gaps works both ways

While past mistakes should certainly be cause for caution, nevertheless, it needs to be pointed out that the God of the gaps argument can cut both ways.

For there have been arguments advanced by skeptics to disprove the existence of the creator God that were also based on faulty scientific assumptions. In effect, they had made what we could call "no God in the gaps arguments."

Hugh Ross stated:

---

[337]Richard Dawkins, *The God Delusion*, New York (Houghton Mifflin Company, 2006) 125.

"In the twentieth century we see the reverse of the God of the gaps. Non-theists, confronted with problems for which ample research leads to no natural explanations and instead points to the supernatural, utterly reject the possibility of the supernatural and insists on a natural explanation even if it means resorting to absurdity."[338]

Creationist Walter Bradley made a similar point when he criticized evolutionists for chalking up to chance what they cannot explain scientifically (Yes, maybe the evolution of life is quite unlikely, but if we just give it enough time, won't it eventually happen!). And so Bradley stated: "Chance is nothing more than the god of the gaps of the atheist."[339]

Biochemist Michael Behe, responding to evolutionary critics of the arguments in his book, *Darwin's Black Box* stated:

"'You know, Darwinists always accuse folks in the Intelligent Design Movement of making an argument from ignorance. Well, that's a pure argument from ignorance! They're saying, 'We have no idea how this [irreducible complexity] could have happened, but let's assume evolution somehow did it,' You've heard of the God-of-the-gaps'—inserting God when you don't have another explanation? Well, this is 'evolution-of-the-gaps.' Some scientists merely insert evolution when they don't understand something.'"[340]

[338]Hugh Ross, *The Creator and the Cosmos: How the Greatest Scientific Discoveries of the Century Reveal God*, Colorado Springs CO (Navpress, 1993) 66.

[339]Walter L. Bradley, *Does Recent Scientific Evidence Support An Intelligently Designed Universe?*, Chapter in *Science: Christian Perspectives for the New Millennium*, Scott B. Luley, Paul Copan & Stan W. Wallace Editors (CLM & RZIM Publisher, 2003) 201.

[340]Michael Behe, as quoted by Lee Strobel, *The Case for a Creator: A Journalist Investigates Scientific Evidence That Points Toward God*, Grand Rapids MI (Zondervan, 2004) 256.

Antony Flew expressed similar concerns later in his life:

> "And in this, it seems to me, lies the peculiar danger, the endemic evil, of dogmatic atheism. Take such utterances as 'We should not ask for an explanation of how it is that the world exists; it is here and that is all' or 'Since we cannot accept a transcendent source of life, we choose to believe the impossible: that life arose spontaneously by chance from matter' or 'The laws of physics are 'lawless laws' that arise from the void—end of discussion.' They look at first sight like rational arguments that have a special authority because they have a no-nonsense air about them. Of course, this is no more sign that they are either rational or arguments."[341]

The God of the gaps, no God in the gaps, and vestigial organs

Evolutionary claims concerning vestigial organs are an example of such God of the gaps argument in reverse (no god in the gaps). A hundred years ago, skeptics ridiculed creationists by suggesting that many unexplained body features were really vestigial organs, supposed useless remnants from bygone evolutionary history. But as science progressed, virtually every claimed vestigial remnant has now been shown to have a purpose.

In other words, in the gap of scientific knowledge, skeptics tried to prove there was no creator God, and that evolution was the only reasonable explanation for

---

[341]Antony Flew, *There is a God: How the World's Most Notorious Atheist Changed His Mind*, New York (HarperCollins/HarperOne, 2007) 86-87.

vestigial organs. But, alas, the scientific evidence itself has destroyed their arguments.

These mistakes of the past should give pause to anyone using language like "Junk DNA," for I have little doubt that the so-called junk DNA will be found to have a valuable purpose.

Finally, vestigial organs, even if merely useless remnants, would not be a proof of evolution since it would only show a loss of function or information, and not an increase in design or specificity as evolution supposes.

Chapter 15: The Paradoxical Universe

Given the stark reality of our own existence, and of the universe we dwell in, we are faced with very perplexing questions. Reason offers help.

We can assume that either the universe is eternal or it had a beginning. This much seems sure. If the universe had a beginning, then it seems there are only a few possibilities to explain its origin.

Either it just somehow popped into existence, or it was created by some powerful force or being that pre-existed it.

The other obvious option is that the universe itself is in some way eternal.

So the bottom line is that when we consider the existence of the universe, we necessarily arrive at a paradox. For we either have an eternal universe without a cause, a universe that just popped into existence without a cause, or a universe created by an eternal uncaused supernatural being. One of these choices is not only a possibility, but is a logical necessity.

Model theories of the origin of the universe

We have noted that arguments concerning the origin of the universe (cosmogony) can be divided into two classes: those that affirm an eternal universe and those in which the universe had a beginning. This is helpful in general, yet, there are many variations and combinations of these views that make strict divisions difficult.

Eternal universe models

The view most consistent with an eternal universe is the **steady-state** model. Some posit a form of the big-bang model in which the material that exploded in the **big-bang** was eternal. There is also the **oscillating** model which is consistent with either an eternal universe or with a universe with a beginning. We will consider it under the eternal models of the universe in our discussion. Variations on the oscillating model include the **big-crunch** and the **big-bounce** which continue to have advocates.

Models of the universe with a beginning

Among those theories that propose a beginning for the universe, the prevailing model remains the **Big Bang** theory. Also increasingly popular are theories in which the universe somehow just popped into existence in some sort of grand cosmic **quantum fluctuation**.

Of course, the biblical view is of a creation of the universe *ex nihilo* by the power of the Almighty God. Heber D. Curtis said, "The more I know of astronomy, the more I believe in God."[342]The famed astronomer Johannes Kepler cried out: "O God, I am thinking thy thoughts after thee."[343]

Paul Sutter, an astrophysicist at Ohio State University explained how Kepler's religious views impacted his preference for heliocentrism over geocentrism:

> "Kepler penned a work in defense of the Copernican model, but not on physical or mathematical grounds— Kepler's argument was religious. He said that since the *Son* of God was at the center of the Christian faith, the *sun*

[342] *The Encyclopedia of Religious Quotations*, Frank S. Mead, Editor, Westwood NJ (Fleming H. Revell Company, 1965) 170.
[343] *The Encyclopedia of Religious Quotations*, 176.

ought to be at the center of the universe. Ergo, heliocentrism."[344]

So let us proceed exploring the origin of our universe aware of the paradoxes that accompany the journey.

"Time may change me,

but I can't change time"[345]

David Bowie

[344]Paul Sutter, *Going Bananas: The Real Story of Kepler, Copernicus and the Church*, 2017 at web address: www.space.com/35772-copernicus-vs-catholic-church-real-story-.html.
[345] David Bowie, *Changes*, Hunky Dory, RCA Records, 1971

Chapter 16: Eternal Universe Models

We first consider models that argue for an eternal universe. Supporters find an eternal universe more comprehensible and compelling than theories proposing a beginning of the universe. Perhaps reasoning that it is easier to argue for an eternal universe than to offer an explanation of how the universe began without a creator to create it.

Big-bang from eternally pre-existing stuff

For instance, David Mills combines belief in the big-bang theory with an eternal universe. In regard to what it was that exploded in the big-bang, Mills suggested that it was some sort of eternal stuff:

> "Regardless of its form, however, the universe—which is the sum of all mass-energy—could not, according to the mass energy conservation law, come into existence *ex nihilo* in the way demanded by creationism. According to this well-confirmed scientific principle, our universe of mass-energy was never created, and cannot be annihilated . . . Our universe of mass-energy, in one form or another, always existed."[346]

Mills apparently believed that God could not create the universe because he would have been bound by the very laws He created and was therefore restricted by "the mass energy conservation law" from creating the universe.

---

[346]David Mills, *Atheist Universe: The Thinking Person's Answer to Christian Fundamentalism*, Berkeley CA (Ulysses Press, 2006) 74, 76.

In response, we note that since God existed prior to and apart from the universe (transcendence), He was not bound by such laws.

Indeed, many naturalist' cosmogonies argue for essentially the same thing, claiming that the current laws were not applicable during the earliest stages of the big-bang. How much more should it be clear that a supernatural being would not be bound by natural laws?

Examining eternal universe models

David Eller makes a typical argument in favor of an eternal universe:

> "If some being can be self-caused or self-grounded, why could not the universe be also? If we are going to imagine something violating every supposed tenet of our experience, why not cut out the middleman and attribute that quality to the universe itself?"[347]

Fair enough. Let's examine these claims.

The Steady-State Model

One example of an eternal universe model is known as the steady-state model first proposed by astronomer Fred Hoyle. Pojman briefly described the steady-state model:

> "The steady state model holds that the universe never had a beginning, but has always existed in the same state. As the galaxies mutually recede, new matter comes into existence in the voids left by the retreating galaxies, so that the overall state of the universe remains the same."[348]

---

[347]David Eller, *Natural Atheism*, Cranford New Jersey (American Atheist Press, 2004) 26-27.
[348]Louis P. Pojman, *Philosophy: The Quest for Truth*, Sixth Edition,

Pojman's evaluation of the steady-state model is not flattering:

> "Ever since this model was first proposed in 1948, it has never been very convincing. According to S. L. Jaki, this theory never secured 'a single piece of experimental verification.' It always seemed to be trying to explain away the facts rather than explain them. According to Jaki, the proponents of this model were actually motivated by 'openly anti-theological, or rather anti-Christian motivations' . . . According to Ivan King, 'The steady-state theory has now been laid to rest.'"[349]

Implications of first law of thermodynamics on steady-state theory

One of the reasons the steady-state theory has fallen on bad times is the implications of the first and second laws of thermodynamics. Beginning with the first law, also called the law of conservation, Fred Hereen showed how it impacted negatively on the steady-state theory:

> "Also called the law of conservation of mass and energy, this law states that matter and energy can be neither created nor destroyed . . . neither mass nor energy can appear from nothing . . . Concerning the first law of thermodynamics, Isaac Asimov wrote, 'This law is considered the most powerful and most fundamental generalization about the universe that scientists have ever been able to make.' Thus the steady-state theory's demand for a continual creation of new matter violates the first law of thermodynamics."[350]

New York. Oxford (Oxford University Press, 2006) 61-62

[349]Louis P. Pojman, *Philosophy: The Quest for Truth*, 62.

[350]Fred Heeren, *Show Me God: What the Message from Space is Telling Us About God*, Revised Edition, Wheeling IL (Day Star Publications, 1997) 128-129

William Lane Craig added his assessment of the
steady-state theory:

> "'A good example is the Steady State theory proposed in
> 1948,' he replied. 'It said that the universe was expanding
> all right but claimed that as galaxies retreat from each
> other, new matter comes into being out of nothing and fills
> the void. *So in contradiction to the First Law of
> Thermodynamics, which says that matter is neither being
> created or destroyed, the universe is supposedly being
> constantly replenished with new stuff.*"[351]

Implications of the second law of thermodynamics on the steady-state theory

But it gets worse for advocates of the Steady-State
theory, and other eternal universe models, since such
theories also run contrary to the second law of
thermodynamics. Stanley W. Angrist explained:

> "An interesting implication of the concept of entropy
> and of the second law of thermodynamics is the indication
> that 'time is a one-way street.' That is time moves in one
> direction only; toward the future . . . Like time, it is a one-
> way variable that marks the universe as being older today
> than it was yesterday. As the British astronomer Sir
> Arthur S. Eddington once said, entropy is 'Time's Arrow.'"[352]

"Time's arrow," the second law of thermodynamics,
shows, then, that the universe had both a beginning and
is moving toward an end. In that sense, the universe can
be thought of as a pre-wound clock ticking down until all

---

[351]William Lane Craig, as quoted by Lee Strobel, *The Case for a
Creator: A Journalist Investigates Scientific Evidence That Points
Toward God*, Grand Rapids MI (Zondervan, 2004) 138.

[352]Stanley W. Angrist, *Entropy* in *The New Book of Popular Science*,
Deluxe Library Edition, Volume 3, Danbury CT (Grolier
International, 1994) 219.

its energy is spent and the clock stops. In the same way, we know the universe had a beginning (when the clock was wound up) and is winding down toward an end.

Paul Davies stated:

> "Today, few cosmologists doubt that the universe, at least as we know it, did have an origin at a finite moment in the past. The alternative—that the universe has always existed in one form or another—runs into a rather basic paradox. The sun and stars cannot keep burning forever: sooner or later they will run out of fuel and die."[353]

Fred Heeren further explained the implications of the second law of thermodynamics for our universe:

> "Thus we know that the universe cannot be eternal; it could not have been dissipating forever. If it had been eternally dissipating, it would have run down long ago"[354]

Jonathan Sarfati added:

> "1st law: The **total** amount of mass-energy in the universe is **constant**. 2nd law: The amount of energy **available for work** is running out, or *entropy* is increasing to a maximum. If the total amount of mass-energy is limited, and the amount of usable energy is decreasing, then the universe cannot have existed forever; otherwise, it would already have exhausted all usable energy—the 'heat death' of the universe. For example, all radioactive atoms would have decayed, every part of the universe would be the same temperature, and no further work would be

[353]Paul Davies, *The Big Bang—and Before*, a paper presented at the Thomas Aquinas College Lecture Serios, Santa Paula, CA, March 2002, quoted by Copan and Craig, *Creation Out of Nothing*, pp. 243-244, as further quoted by Douglass Groothuis, *Christian Apologetics: A Comprehensive Case for Biblical Faith*, Downers Grove IL (InterVarsity Press, 2011) 227.
[354]Fred Heeren, *Show Me God,* 129

possible. So the obvious corollary is that the universe began a finite time ago with a lot of usable energy, and is now running down."[355]

J.P. Moreland stated the matter clearly:

"Applied to the universe as a whole, the Second Law states that everyday the universe becomes more and more disorganized. In other words, it is burning up. It will eventually die a cold death. The main implication of this is, as one physicist [Paul Davies] put it, 'The universe did not always exist.'"[356]

Eternal universe advocates respond to problems raised by the second law

Carl Sagan thought he had an answer to those who pointed out the implications of a beginning demanded by the second law:

"It's by no means clear, by the way, that the Second Law of Thermodynamics applies to the universe as a whole, because it is an experimental law, and we don't have the experience with the universe as a whole."[357]

Sagan was desperately hoping that there are exceptions to the fundamental scientific laws on thermodynamics that could provide an

---

[355]Jonathan Sarfati, *Refuting Compromise: A Biblical and Scientific Refutation of 'Progressive Creationism'(Billions of Years), as Popularized by Astronomer Hugh Ross, Green Forest AZ* (Master Books, 2004) 181.

[356]J. P. Moreland, & Kai Nielsen, *Does God Exist?: The Debate Between Theists & Atheists*, Amherst NY (Prometheus Books, 1993) 38.

[357]Carl Sagan, *The God Hypothesis* in Christopher Hitchens, *The Portable Atheist: Essential Readings for the Nonbeliever*, Philadelphia PA (De Capo Press, 2007) 232.

atheistic/naturalistic loophole to save an eternal universe hypothesis and keep the Creator God out of the universe.

Is God subject to the second law?

Sagan continued his criticisms thusly:

> "It's always struck me as curious that those who wish to apply the Second Law of Thermodynamics to theological issues do not ask whether God is subject to the Second Law. Because if God were subject to the Second Law of Thermodynamics, then God could have only a finite lifetime."[358]

Atheist George Smith made essentially the same categorical mistake as Sagan:

> "Is the Second Law of Thermodynamics an inexorable law of nature? Yes, according to Robbins, because it 'has never been contradicted.' Never? Then what prevented his eternal, personal, and transcendent god from suffering a gruesome heat-death? If the Second Law is not applicable to god, it is not inexorable. If this is so, on what grounds can the theist assert that the Second Law applies to the entire universe and cannot, under any circumstances be contradicted?"[359]

It is disappointing that Sagan and Smith are content to set up straw-men to knock down, rather than seriously responding to the implications of the second law for their systems.

---

[358]Carl Sagan, *The God Hypothesis* in Christopher Hitchens, *The Portable Atheist: Essential Readings for the Nonbeliever*, Philadelphia PA (De Capo Press, 2007) 232.
[359]George H. Smith, *Atheism: The Case Against God,* Amherst NY (Prometheus Books, 1979, 1989) 254-255.

They seem unaware of the biblical teaching that God transcends the universe He created just as the artist transcends his art. For instance, Millard Erickson stated:

"The other aspect of the relationship of God to the world is his transcendence. By this we mean that God is separate from and independent of nature and humanity."[360]

Sagan and Smith sought to evade the severe implications the first and second law hold for eternal universe models with the red herring argument that God should have been subject to the same laws, and in so doing ignored the transcendent nature of God advocated by Christian theology.

Gerald Schroeder makes this important point:

"Now if the law of entropy, which is always true on Earth, is cosmically applicable (and recall that all leading physicists assume the laws of physics that we observe on Earth are applicable throughout the universe; without this assumption there is no basis for any calculations of cosmology)."[361]

That is, for those such as Sagan or Smith whom question whether the law of entropy (the 2nd law of thermodynamics) applies to the universe as a whole (and not just here on earth), Schroeder shows the desperate nature of their evasion. By singling out one law for doubt, they are in fact evading the implications of modern cosmological science.

---

[360]Millard J. Erickson, *Christian Theology*, Second Edition, Grand Rapids MI (Baker Books, 1998) 338.
[361]Gerald L. Schroeder, *Genesis and the Big Bang: The Discovery of Harmony Between Modern Science and the Bible*, New York (Bantam Books 1990) 80.

The Oscillation Model (cyclic models)

The Oscillation model is a variation of big bang cosmology that posits a future contraction of the universe after the current expansion has reached its apex (the big crunch) or even a series of expansions and contractions (thus the word oscillation). Most advocates believe that this is an eternally ongoing process.

The same problems exist for the oscillation model that have plagued the steady-state model. Roy Peacock explained the problems raised for the oscillation model by the second law of thermodynamics by comparing it to a bouncing ball on a gym floor:

> "Potential and kinetic energy are repeatedly exchanged as the ball bounces . . . Entropy takes its toll and available energy progressively reduces until the ball no longer bounces. The picture of a universe following a series of cycles of expansion and contraction gives a similar pattern. Entropy takes its toll again and the process runs down, each cycle being at a higher temperature with the increase of entropy . . . the process in the universe is constrained to have an end and a beginning."[362]

Pojman provided a concise summary of the difficulties of the oscillation model:

> "According to this model, the universe is sort of like a spring, expanding and contracting from eternity. This model became a sort of 'great white hope' for atheistic scientists, who terribly wanted it to be true so as to avoid an absolute beginning of the universe. You may have seen Carl Sagan, for example, in his popular *Cosmos* program

---

[362]Roy E. Peacock, *A Brief History Of Eternity*, Wheaton IL (Crossway Books, 1990) 89. For more problems with the Oscillation theory, see Hugh Ross, *The Fingerprint of God*, Orange CA (Promise Publishing Company, 1991) pp. 97-105.

on public television propounding this model and reading from the Hindu scriptures about cyclical Brahman years in order to illustrate the oscillating universe. There are, however, at least two very well-known difficulties with the oscillating model, which Sagan did not mention. First, the oscillating model is physically impossible . . . the fact remains that it is only a theoretical possibility, not a real possibility . . . Second, the observational evidence is contrary to the oscillating model . . . The oscillating model, therefore, is seriously flawed. It contradicts both the known laws of physics and the current observational evidence."[363]

William Lane Craig took Daniel Dennett to task for his advocacy of the oscillating universe model:

"Dennett also floats the old idea of an eternally oscillating universe in order to secure an infinite past . . . he [is] apparently unaware of the manifold problems that led to the demise of such models in the late 1970s . . . Moreover, since the thermodynamic properties of oscillating models require that the oscillations increase over time, such a model cannot be extended into the infinite past."[364]

Big bounce

A theory currently gaining traction is a form or revival of the oscillating universe theory called the big bounce which supporters claim is in accordance with the most recent developments in cosmology and physics. Clara Moskowitz described it:

[363]Louis P. Pojman, *Philosophy: The Quest for Truth*, 62.
[364]*The Future of Atheism: Alister McGrath & Daniel Dennett in Dialogue*, Robert B. Stewart, Editor, Minneapolis MN (Fortress Press, 2008) 83.

"An underdog idea posits that the birth of this universe was not actually the beginning—that an earlier version of spacetime had existed and contracted toward a "big crunch," then flipped and started expanding into what we see today."[365]

Recently, *Time* reported that Stephen Hawking spoke for a group of scientists critical of the big bounce theory and in defense of standard big bang cosmology:

"Stephen Hawking and 32 fellow scientists have written a critical letter in response to an article published in *Scientific American* that details an alternative theory on how the universe began. Hawking and his colleagues firmly believe in the widely-accepted theory of inflation, which describes how the universe rapidly expanded following the Big Bang. But three physicists, Anna Ijjas, Paul J. Steinhardt, Abraham Loeb, argued in the article that another theory, the "Big Bounce," was more likely an explanation for the universe's origins.

Hawking and his peers did not entertain the idea. 'By claiming that inflationary cosmology lies outside the scientific method, IS&L [the authors of the earlier article] are dismissing the research of not only all the authors of this letter but also that of a substantial contingent of the scientific community,' they wrote' to *Scientific American.* 'Moreover, as the work of several major, international collaborations has made clear, inflation is not only testable, but it has been subjected to a significant number of tests and so far has passed every one,' the letter added."[366]

---

[365]Clara Moskowitz, *Did the Universe Boot Up With a Big Bounce?*, Scientific American, August 3, 2016 at web address: https://www.scientificamerican.com/article/did-the-universe-boot-up-with-a-big-bounce/

[366]Aric Jenkins, *Stephen Hawking and Fellow Scientists Dismiss 'Big Bounce' Theory in Letter*, May 13, 2017, at web address: http://time.com/4778304/stephen-hawking-scientific-american-

Geisler explained that the big-bounce model suffers from the same problems as its oscillation model predecessor did:

"According to the well-established second law of thermodynamics, each succeeding rebound would have less explosive energy than the previous until eventually the universe would not rebound again. Like a bouncing ball, it would finally peter out, showing that it is not eternal."[367]

The foregoing shows the weakness of eternal universe models and points in the direction of models of a universe with a beginning. William Lane Craig stated:

"Indeed, the history of twentieth-century cosmology can be viewed as one failed attempt after another to avert the absolute beginning predicted by the Standard Model."[368]

Philosopher John Locke's rejection of an eternal universe

John Locke rejected the possibility that something (the universe) could have its origin in nothing:

"There is no truth more evident, than that something must be from eternity. I never yet heard of any one so unreasonable, or that could suppose so manifest a contradiction, as a time wherein there was perfectly nothing. This being of all absurdities the greatest, to imagine that pure nothing, the perfect negation and

---

letter-big-bounce/
[367]Norman L. Geisler, *Baker Encyclopedia of Christian Apologetics*, 103, Also p. 400.
[368]William Lane Craig, *In Defense of Theistic Arguments*, chapter in *The Future of Atheism: Alister McGrath & Daniel Dennett in Dialogue*, Robert B. Stewart, Editor, Minneapolis MN (Fortress Press, 2008) 75.

absence of all beings, should ever produce any real existence."[369]

Stumpf further described John Locke's skepticism about any account of the universe apart from a creator:

"Thus 'man knows, by an intuitive certainty, that bare nothing can no more produce any real being than it can be equal to two right angles.' From this starting point Locke argued that since there are in fact existing things that begin and end in time, and since a 'nonentity cannot produce any real being, it is an evident demonstration, that from eternity there has been something.' Reasoning in a similar way, he concludes that this eternal Being is 'most knowing' and 'most powerful' and that 'it is plain to me we have a more certain knowledge of the existence of God, than of anything our senses have not immediately discovered to us.'"[370]

In conclusion, Groothius noted the irony of scientists that argue for an eternal universe:

"It seems arbitrary and ad hoc to search for explanations for anything and everything in the universe (as science does) but not to seek an explanation for the universe as a whole."[371]

---

[369]Paul Edwards, *A Modern Introduction to Philosophy: Readings from Classical and Contemporary Sources,* Third Edition, Paul Edwards & Arthur Pap, Editors, New York, (The Free Press, 1973) 379.

[370]John Locke, as quoted by Samuel Enoch Stumpf, *Philosophy: History & Problems*, Fourth Edition, New York (McGraw-Hill Publishing Company, 1989) 270.

[371]Douglass Groothuis, *Christian Apologetics: A Comprehensive Case for Biblical Faith*, Downers Grove IL (InterVarsity Press, 2011) 212-213.

Chapter 17: Models of a Universe with a Beginning

Big Bang Theory

"Nothin' from nothin' leaves nothin'[372]

Certainly, the prevailing theory for the origin of the universe over the last generation has been the big-bang theory, the name given it by the astrophysicist Fred Hoyle.[373]

Hans Küng explained that:

"It was a theologian . . . an astrophysicist at the university of Louvain, Abbé Georges Lemaître (1894-1966) . . . Who within the framework of the general theory of relativity in 1927 developed the model of an expanding universe and was the first to put forward the hypothesis of the 'primeval atom' or the 'Big Bang.'"[374]

The big-bang theory was initially resisted by many simply because it seemed to confirm the biblical idea of a creation and beginning for the universe.

---

[372]*Nothing for Nothing*, Billy Preston & Bruce Fisher, © Universal Music Publishing Group

[373]Fazale R. Rana, *How Did Life Begin?*, chapter in Sean McDowell & Jonathan Morrow, *Is God Just a Human Invention? And Seventeen Other Questions Raised by the New Atheists,* Grand Rapids MI (Kregel Publications, 2010) 87. It is ironic that although Hoyle coined the term "Big-bang" he himself developed and supported the steady-state model.

[374] Hans Küng, *The Beginning of All Things: Science and Religion,* Grand Rapids MI (William B. Eerdmans Publishing Company, 2005) 9.

Source of Big-bang singularity?

However, *even* if one accepts the big bang hypotheses, one has still the problem of explaining the *origin* of the universe. While the big bang model argues that roughly 14 billion years ago, all the matter and energy that make up our present universe were at that time formed as a dense singularity that somehow exploded, it does not explain where this matter and energy came from in the first place.

Something from nothing?

How can **something** come from **nothing?** The ancient Roman writer and philosopher Lucretius stated, "I have shown above that nothing can be created from nothing."[375] Likewise, Epicurus said: "Nothing is created out of that which does not exist."[376]

Francois-Marie Voltaire argued for the existence of God since something cannot come from nothing:

> "He is a necessary being, inasmuch as the machine could not exist, but for him . . . He is eternal, for He cannot have sprung from non-entity, which being nothing can produce nothing."[377]

---

[375]Lucretius, as quoted by Samuel Enoch Stumpf, *Philosophy: History & Problems*, Fourth Edition, New York (McGraw-Hill Publishing Company, 1989) 815.

[376]Epicurus, *The Pleasant Life*, as quoted by Theodore C. Denise, Nicholas P. White & Sheldon P. Peterfreund, *Great Traditions in Ethics*, Tenth Edition, Belmont CA (Wadsworth Thomson Learning, 2002) 38.

[377]Francois-Marie Voltaire, as quoted by Norman L. Geisler, *Baker Encyclopedia of Christian Apologetics*, Grand Rapids MI (Baker Books, 1999) 765.

What exploded in the Big Bang?

In discussions about the universe, the elephant in the room is to ask for an explanation of the big bang. What is the origin of the singularity that exploded in the big bang, and what caused it to explode?

The skeptic author and attorney Vincent Bugliosi asked a very telling question about the big bang theory, and the origin of the supposed singularity:

> "When I went to the library to take out a few books on the big bang theory . . . to search for one thing and one thing only: *What* was it that exploded into the universe? Remarkably, one 400-page book on the big bang actually managed in the author's terrible incompetence, to avoid mentioning the issue. None of them paid more than a very passing reference to it. But from books and articles, here is what a few of the writers say. One said it was 'subatomic particles' that exploded in a zillionth of a second into the universe. Another said it was 'packets of energy.' Another defined the energy as 'negative energy in the form of radiation and exotic fields.' Another said it was 'a primeval atom.' Yet another said it was 'a swirling dust of mathematical points.' I have no idea what any of these things are. But I do know that whatever they are, they are *something*, and this is the big problem. It would seem that no one can actually believe that the big bang exploded out of nothing, completely empty space, which would be an impossibility. It had to have exploded out of *something*. And no matter how small or subatomic that something is, the question is, *Who put that something there?* If it wasn't the creator, then how did it come into existence?"[378]

In a similar vein, Yeager Hudson argued:

---

[378]Vincent Bugliosi, *Divinity of Doubt: The God Question*, New York (Vanguard Press, 2011) 89-90.

"The Big Bang theory, and the other cosmologies astronomers have explored during the twentieth century, all leave unanswered the question of where the matter/energy of which the universe consists ultimately came from. If the universe as we know it began when the concentrated material of the world exploded and began the expansion that we can still observe, the question remains where the material came from, how it came to be concentrated at a single point, and why it exploded."[379]

Likewise Varghese stated:

"Absolute nothingness means no laws, no vacuums, no fields, no energy, no structures, no physical or mental entities of any kind—and no 'symmetries.' It has no properties or potentialities. Absolute nothingness cannot produce something given endless time—in fact, there can be no time in absolute nothingness."[380]

William Lane Craig continued the theme:

"You see, the idea that things can come into being uncaused out of nothing is worse than magic. At least when a magician pulls a rabbit out of a hat, there's the magician and the hat! But in Atheism, the universe just pops into being out of nothing, with no explanation at all . . . We certainly have empirical evidence for the truth of the premise. This is a premise that is constantly confirmed and never falsified. We never see things coming into being uncaused out of nothing. Nobody worries that while he's away at work, say, a horse might pop into being, uncaused, out of nothing, in his living room."[381]

---

[379]Yeager Hudson, *The Philosophy of Religion*, Mountain View CA (Mayfield Publishing Company, 1991) 150.

[380]Roy Abraham Varghese, Appendix in Antony Flew, *There is a God: How the World's Most Notorious Atheist Changed His Mind*, New York (HarperCollins/HarperOne, 2007) 170.

[381]William Lane Craig, as quoted by Lee Strobel, *The Case for a Creator: A Journalist Investigates Scientific Evidence That Points Toward God*, Grand Rapids MI (Zondervan, 2004) 121.

For all those Missouri skeptics who want to believe only what they can see, it is most ironic that they turn to theories that explain the origin of the universe out of nothing, and without even a God to make it happen.

Is the Big Bang a Miracle?

Hans Küng asked a penetrating question about the Big-Bang theory and then quoted Easterbrook's agreement:

"Is that really asking too much of human reason? One can look at it the other way around. How much 'faith' does the standard cosmological model ask of human reason? Did the billions of galaxies come into being from a tiny unit after the big bang? Isn't that a kind of 'scientific belief in a miracle?' At all events, that is what the American scientific journalists Greg Easterbrook thinks:

For 'sheer incredibility, nothing in theology or metaphysics could touch the Big Bang. If this description of the genesis of the cosmos came from the Bible or the Qur'an instead of the Massachusetts Institute for Technology it would certainly be treated as an exaggerated myth.'"[382]

Creation *Ex Nihilo*

It is ironic, I say, because although skeptics have long maligned the biblical concept of creation out of nothing,

---

[382] Hans Küng, *The Beginning of All Things: Science and Religion,* Grand Rapids MI (William B. Eerdmans Publishing Company, 2005) 45.

creatio ex nihilo, as an incoherent concept, yet, increasingly, atheists are now embracing the idea.

For instance, Sidney Hook found the concept of creation *ex Nihilo* incoherent:

> "When we speak of God as 'creating' the world, there is no difficulty with the notion of plan or purpose. But there is a grave difficulty with the notions of the instrument and subject matter. For God is supposed to have created the world out of nothing—*ex nihilo*. Now in our experience nothing is or can be created out of nothing. There is always some subject matter, some instrument. How, then, is creation *ex nihilo* to be understood? . . . These makeshift attempts to demystify the mystery of *creatio ex nihilo* either call our attention to something which is unusual in speech or action but which is otherwise intelligible, or generate mysteries as dark as the one they would illumine. The concept of a transcendent God, who creates the world *ex nihilo*, in time or out of time, can no more be clearly thought than the concept of the last number in a series in which every number has a successor."[383]

Yet, in the face of the strong evidence that the universe had a beginning, and seeking to avoid the obvious conclusion that God created it, atheists are increasingly resorting to creation out of nothing by nothing theories.

And so atheist Victor Stenger argued:

> "Prominent physicists and cosmologists have published, in reputable scientific journals, a number of other scenarios by which the universe could have come about 'from nothing.'"[384]

---

[383]Sidney Hook, *Modern Knowledge and the Concept of God*, chapter in *Critiques of God: Making the Case Against Belief in God,* Peter A. Angeles, Editor, Amherst New York (Prometheus Books, 1997) 27, 29.

The difference, however, and it is profound, is that whereas Bible believers appeal to a supernatural being as the source for the creation from nothing, atheistic supporters of creatio ex nihilo have no source whatsoever; everything from nothing!

I suggest that it is more rational to believe in a God who created the world from nothing than to believe that the world came into existence from nothing and by nothing.

The universe as a quantum fluctuation

An increasingly popular explanation for the origin of the universe is that it just happened to pop into existence in some kind of random quantum fluctuation.

For instance, David Mills argued:

> "New discoveries in quantum theory, as well as research done by Stephen Hawking and his colleagues, have demonstrated that matter can and does arise quite spontaneously from the vacuum fluctuation energy of 'empty' space."[385]

When we hear arguments suggesting that quantum fluctuations can explain (at least theoretically) how the universe could have just popped into existence from nothing, we should be aware that a verbal sleight of hand trick may be at play. The old expression "if it sounds too good to be true, it probably is" serves as a caution here. Likewise, the expression "there's no free lunch" also applies.

---

[384]Victor J. Stenger, *God: The Failed Hypothesis, How Science Shows That God Does Not Exist*, Amherst New York (Prometheus Books, 2007) 126.

[385]David Mills, *Atheist Universe: The Thinking Person's Answer to Christian Fundamentalism*, Berkeley CA (Ulysses Press, 2006) 31.

Let us keep in mind the tongue in cheek cautionary warning made by physicists Richard Feynman: "I think I can safely say that nobody understands quantum mechanics."[386]

In other words, let us keep it fixed in our minds that many of these cosmological theories are at bottom, sheer speculation. Yes, brilliant and sophisticated speculations, but speculations just the same.

Further, supporters of the quantum fluctuation origins model of the universe admit that even in quantum vacuums, **something rather than nothing pre-exists**. In other words, the theory explains a possible, though quite unlikely way, in which the universe came to exist in its present form, but it doesn't explain the origin of the energy needed to fluctuate in the first place.

William Lane Craig explained problems with the various quantum fluctuation theories:

> "These subatomic particles the article talks about are called 'virtual particles.' They are theoretical entities, and it's not even clear that they actually exist . . . These particles, if they are real, do not come out of nothing. The quantum vacuum is not what most people envision when they think of a vacuum—that is, absolutely nothing. On the contrary, it's a sea of fluctuating energy, an arena of violent activity that has a rich physical structure and can be described by physical laws. These particles are thought to originate by fluctuations of the energy in the vacuum. So it's not an example of something coming into being out of nothing, or something coming into being without a cause. The quantum vacuum and the energy locked up in the vacuum are the cause of these particles. And then we have to ask, well, what is the origin of the whole quantum

---

[386]Vincent Bugliosi, *Divinity of Doubt: The God Question*, New York (Vanguard Press, 2011) 90.

vacuum itself? Where does *it* come from . . . You've simply pushed back the issue of creation."[387]

Amir Aczel explained the house of cards that underlies quantum models, in this case by Lawrence Krauss:

"A prime example that characterizes this new trend in 'scientific atheism' is the book *A Universe from Nothing: Why There Is Something Rather than Nothing* (2012), by Lawrence M. Krauss, which has become a best seller. According to the author, a physicist . . . the universe came 'out of nothing'—out of the sheer 'laws of physics.' . . . Then Krauss employs quantum theory to conclude that the total energy in the universe is identically zero, and that hence the cosmos arose 'out of nothingness.' Just how he knows that the total energy is exactly zero when the universe is known to contain large amounts of 'dark matter' and 'dark energy,' about which we know close to nothing, Krauss doesn't explain. He also doesn't reveal how the laws of physics themselves emerged. He says that 'quantum mechanics tells us that there must be a universe.' We will see, in fact, that quantum theory tells us no such thing."[388]

Aczel elaborated on the point:

"Lawrence Krauss's book . . . claims that the universe came about out of sheer nothingness, with nothing preexisting. For proof, Krauss relies on a paper written by the physicist Alexander Vilenkin . . . 'Quantum Origin of the Universe,' presenting a discussion of theoretical physics . . . to attempt to trace the very origin of our universe. In the last page of his article, Vilenkin notes the following: 'Most of the problems discussed in this paper belong to **'metaphysical cosmology,' which is the branch of**

---

[387]William Lane Craig, as quoted by Lee Strobel, *The Case for a Creator,* 123.

[388]Amir D. Aczel, *Why Science Does Not Disprove God,* New York (HarperCollins Publishers, 2014) 16-17.

cosmology totally decoupled from observations.' . . . But Vilenkin's nothingness is not absolute nothingness. He requires many things for his universe to come about: quantum foam, Einstein's gravitational field, the Higgs field, quantum tunneling, and other physical entities and laws. Therefore, to claim, as Krauss does in his book, that thus a universe can be created out of sheer nothingness is deceptive . . . A 'universe out of nothing' in the sense of Lawrence M. Krauss is still a figment of the imagination and has no basis in any objective reality."[389]

Martin Gardner added his opinion:

"It is fashionable now to conjecture that the Big Bang was caused by a random quantum fluctuation in a vacuum devoid of space and time. But of course such a vacuum is a far cry from nothing . . . There is no escape from the superultimate questions: 'Why is there something rather than nothing, and why is the something structured the way it is?'"[390]

Dennett and Craig interchange on beginning of universe

Daniel Dennett accepted the position that the universe had a beginning out of nothing, sort of:

"What does need its origin explained is the concrete Universe itself, and as Hume's Philo long ago asked: Why not stop at the material world? It . . . does perform a version of the ultimate bootstrapping trick; it creates itself *ex nihilo*. Or at any rate out of something that is well-nigh indistinguishable from nothing at all."[391]

---

[389]Amir D. Aczel, *Why Science Does Not Disprove God*, New York (HarperCollins Publishers, 2014)128, 131, 136.

[390]Martin Gardner, *Science and the Unknowable*, in *Science and Religion: Are They Compatible?*, Paul Kurtz, Editor, Amherst New York (Prometheus Books, 2003) 327.

[391]Daniel Dennett, *Breaking the Spell: Religion as a Natural*

Dennett wants to have his cake and eat it too, having the world created out of absolutely nothing and yet, or perhaps, a little something. William Lane Craig rightfully exposed the shallowness of Dennett's idea:

> "Here Dennett spoils his radical idea by waffling at the end: maybe the universe did not create itself out of nothing but at least out of something 'well-nigh indistinguishable from nothing.' This caveat evinces a lack of appreciation of the metaphysical chasm between being and nothingness. There is no third thing between being and nonbeing; if anything at all exists, however, ethereal, it is something and therefore not nothing. So what could this be? Dennett doesn't tell us."[392]

It is not clear how something can create itself. The Christian claim that God created the world out of nothing, *ex nihilo*, has been roundly criticized by philosophers. But at least the believer's model includes a supernatural agent doing the creating. Dennett has nothing (or something "well-nigh indistinguishable from nothing") creating out of nothing.

Hans Küng shows the very speculative nature of quantum fluctuations as an explanation for the origin of the universe:

Phenomenon (New York: Viking, 2006), 242, as quoted by William Lane Craig, *In Defense of Theistic Arguments*, Chapter in *The Future of Atheism: Alister McGrath & Daniel Dennett in Dialogue*, Robert B. Stewart, Editor, Minneapolis MN (Fortress Press, 2008) 75.

[392]William Lane Craig, *In Defense of Theistic Arguments*, Chapter in *The Future of Atheism: Alister McGrath & Daniel Dennett in Dialogue*, Robert B. Stewart, Editor, Minneapolis MN (Fortress Press, 2008)75-76.

"This applies even to some distinguished physicists when asked where the universe ultimately comes from. Thus Gert Binnig, who won the Nobel Prize for physics in 1986 . . . explains:

'Perhaps the whole thing came into being like this: by the reproduction of something (I don't know what) a vacuum was created or space. With this space the properties of space also came into being, e.g. its symmetries. And by the reproduction of these properties some forms of energy came into being, how, I cannot say.'"[393]

Again, Hans Küng takes such accounts to task for both what they are (wild speculation unsupported by empirical data) and how they are presented (striking overconfidence and hubris):

"At all events, it is surprising how in the question of the initial conditions of the cosmos cosmologists labor to overturn elementary philosophical statements such as *ex nihilo nihil fit,* 'nothing comes out of nothing.' Here some in all earnestness seek to avoid the problem of origins by creating a universe that functions as its own mother, 'It created itself' (Richard Gott and Lin-Xin Li). 'How nice,' one might explain. Faced with the self-confidence with which such theories are presented, I am reminded of the remark attributed to the Russian Nobel Prize winner for

---

[393] Hans Küng, *The Beginning of All Things: Science and Religion,* Grand Rapids MI (William B. Eerdmans Publishing Company, 2005) 56.

physics, Lev Lanau (1908-68): 'Cosmologists often err, but they never doubt.'"[394]

---

[394] Hans Küng, *The Beginning of All Things: Science and Religion,* Grand Rapids MI (William B. Eerdmans Publishing Company, 2005) 71.

Chapter 18: Then who made God?

We have seen that the arguments for God's existence are compelling indeed. The skeptic's natural objection is to ask "Well, then who created God?" or "How, then, did God come into existence?"

But such is just the point; by definition God had no beginning. Again, this is no more irrational than the claims of those who believe in an eternal and uncaused universe.

Let us consider the arguments of famed philosopher Bertrand Russell along these lines:

> "One day, at the age of eighteen, I read John Stuart Mill's Autobiography, and I there found this sentence:
> 'My father taught me that the question 'Who made me?' cannot be answered, since it immediately suggests the further question 'Who made God?' That simple sentence showed me, as I still think, the fallacy in the argument of the First Cause. If everything must have a cause, then God must have a cause. If there can be anything without a cause, it may just as well be the world as God."[395]

Creationist Jonathan Sarfati described the Kalam cosmological argument which provides an answer to the dilemma young John Stuart Mill (and later Bertrand Russell) faced:

> "It goes back to the church theologian Bonaventure (1221-1274), and was also advocated by medieval Arabic philosophers. The word *kalam* is the Arabic word for 'speech,' but its broader semantic range includes 'philosophical theism' or 'natural theology.' The *kalam*

---

[395]Bertrand Russell, *Why I Am Not A Christian and other essays on religion and related subjects*, New York (A Touchstone Book, 1957) 6-7.

argument's most prominent modern defender is the philosopher and apologist Dr. William Lane Craig. The logical argument is formulated as follows: 1. Everything **which has a beginning** has a cause. 2. The universe has a beginning. 3. ∴ the universe has a cause . . . The universe requires a cause because it had a beginning . . . God, unlike the universe, had no beginning, so doesn't need a cause."[396]

The logical advantage, then, must be with theism since belief in God is consistent with logic, reason, and modern science. On the other hand, belief in an eternal universe is inconsistent with fundamental laws of science (i.e., the first and second laws of thermodynamics).

---

[396]Jonathan Sarfati, *Refuting Compromise: A Biblical and Scientific Refutation of 'Progressive Creationism'(Billions of Years),* as *Popularized by Astronomer Hugh Ross, Green Forest AZ* (Master Books, 2004) 179.

Chapter 19: The Origin of Life

How to explain the origin of biological life?

"We have been discussing the origin of the universe at the cosmic level. At this point, we will zoom in to a more earthly question. Life! That is, how did life arise on earth from lifeless chemicals in the first place? Antony Flew asked, 'How did life as a phenomenon originate from nonlife.'"[397]

Victor Stenger acknowledged this 'gap' in scientific understanding:

"Evolution removes the need to introduce God at any step in the process of the development of life from the simplest earlier forms. It does not explain the origin of life, so this gap remains."[398]

The simpler explanation, in accord with Ockham's principle, is that God created life on earth (or wherever it exists). But the prevailing theory of scientists today is that life arose on earth through an unguided random natural process.

Keep in mind that scientists, with the most advanced labs and technology available, have been trying unsuccessfully to replicate life for decades. Nevertheless, we are asked to believe that life 'just happened,' when one day lightning struck some pre-biotic soup in a fateful pond, somewhere in early earth history.[399]

---

[397]Antony Flew, *There is a God: How the World's Most Notorious Atheist Changed His Mind*, New York (HarperCollins/HarperOne, 2007) 91.

[398]Victor J. Stenger, *God: The Failed Hypothesis, How Science Shows That God Does Not Exist*, Amherst New York (Prometheus Books, 2007) 52.

[399]Or perhaps in a hot deep-sea vent.

If the day does come that modern science develops the ability to create life from inanimate matter, it will only prove how unlikely it was that life arose spontaneously, given the intense scientific efforts that were required to achieve that result.

The problem of biogenesis, spontaneous generation, and pre-biotic-soup

It is most remarkable that scientists accept the theory that life originally arose spontaneously despite the fact that such a theory violates a fundamental law of science. For instance, consider this public school textbook definition of the law of biogenesis:

> "Have you ever walked out after a thunderstorm and found earthworms all over the sidewalk? . . . It is no wonder that people used to think the earthworm had fallen from the sky when it rained. It was a logical conclusion based on repeated experience. But was it true? Jan Baptist van Helmont wrote a recipe for making mice by placing grain in a corner and covering it with rags. For much of history, people believed that living things came from non-living matter, an idea called the theory of spontaneous generation. People also believed that maggots came from decaying meat. In 1668, Francesco Redi, an Italian doctor, performed one of the first controlled experiments in science. He showed that maggots hatch from eggs that flies had laid on the meat, and not from meat itself . . . It was not until the mid-1800s that Louis Pasteur, a French chemist, showed conclusively that living things do not come from nonliving materials . . . The work of Redi, Spallanzani, Pasteur, and others provided enough evidence finally to disprove the theory of spontaneous generation. It was replaced with biogenesis, the theory that living things come only from other living things."[400]

---

[400]Lucy Daniel, Edward Paul Ortleb & Alton Biggs, *Merrill Life*

And so, life comes from life, period. That's the law of biogenesis.

A certain paradox, however, exists in the *Merrill Life Science* textbook (and many like it). On the one hand, it provided excellent information explaining how scientists determined spontaneous generation is false. On the other hand, it appealed to the very same spontaneous generation it had just debunked to explain the origin of life on earth. Is this some form of scientific schizophrenia?

The *Merrill Live Science* textbook authors asked the right question: "If living things can come only from other living things, how then did life on Earth begin?"[401] But their answer must surely be considered a work of art in sophistry.

They described the theory of Alexander Oparin that in the early Earth various gases combined in and:

> "fell into hot seas. Over a period of time, the chemical compounds in the seas formed new and more complex compounds. Eventually, the complex compounds were able to copy themselves and make use of other chemicals for energy and food."[402]

Next the authors described how:

> "Stanley L. Miller set up an experiment using the chemicals suggested in Oparin's hypothesis. Electrical sparks were sent through the mixture of chemicals. At the end of a week, new substances, similar to amino acids that

Science, New York (Glencoe Division of Macmillan/McGraw-Hill School Publishing Company, 1994) 10-11.

[401]Lucy Daniel, Edward Paul Ortleb & Alton Biggs, *Merrill Life Science*, 11.

[402]Lucy Daniel, Edward Paul Ortleb & Alton Biggs, *Merrill Life Science*, 11.

are found in all living things, had formed. This showed
that substances present in living things could come from
nonliving materials in the environment."[403]

The "substances, similar to amino acids" that
developed are still not alive, but are merely "substances
present in living things." Well, water itself fits that
description.

So, while the *Merrill Life Science* textbook *suggested*
that the experiment proved chemicals to life theories, the
reality is far from demonstrated or proved. We are still
left waiting for the explanation of how--the magic-
moment of transformation--life arose from non-living
chemicals.

The *Merrill Life Science* authors conclude: "Evidence
suggests that life was formed from nonliving matter
sometime between 4.6 billion and 3.5 billion years ago."[404]

The dissonance is breathtaking! The authors very
clearly stated that: "living things come only from other
living things" and then proceed to the conclusion that
"life was formed from nonliving matter."

The whole theory of life arising in some pond during
an electrical storm has more the feel of a fairy tale than
of hard science. Atheist's cling to such theories as a child
might cling to Santa Clause or the Easter Bunny,
choosing to accept a theory that violates a fundamental
law of science (i.e. the law of biogenesis), rather than
accepting the more reasonable conclusion that life owes
its origins to a creator God.

---

[403]Lucy Daniel, Edward Paul Ortleb & Alton Biggs, *Merrill Life Science*, 12.

[404]Lucy Daniel, Edward Paul Ortleb & Alton Biggs, *Merrill Life Science*, 12.

Antony Flew showed how desperation has caused scientists to accept such irrational ideas:

> "So how do we account for the origin of life? The Nobel Prize-winning physiologist George Wald once famously argued that 'We choose to believe the impossible: that life arose spontaneously by chance.'"[405]

Jonathan Wells explained that it remains an intractable problem today:

> "A biochemist can mix all the chemical building blocks of life in a test tube and still not produce a living cell."[406]

In light of the seemingly insurmountable obstacles facing those who posit the spontaneous generation of life, Chuck Edwards noted the irony of Richard Dawkins explanation of the same:

> "How does Dawkins account for the origin of life? Dawkin's explanation is an 'initial stroke of luck'! (I'm not kidding, those are his actual words.)."[407]

---

[405]Antony Flew, *There is a God: How the World's Most Notorious Atheist Changed His Mind*, New York (HarperCollins/HarperOne, 2007) 131.

[406]Jonathan Wells, *Icons of Evolution: Science or Myth? Why Much of What We Teach About Evolution is Wrong*, Washington D.C. (Regnery Publishing, Inc., 2000) 23.

[407] Tom Gilson, *Richard Dawkin's Illusions*, chapter in *True Reason: Confronting the Irrationality of the New Atheism,* Tom Gilson & Carson Weitnauer, Editors, Grand Rapids MI (Kregel Publications, 2012) 50. Dawkin's quote is from *The God Delusion*, 140.

Chapter 20: How Did the Original Primordial Life Replicate?

For the sake of argument, let's concede the very unlikely possibility that one day a miracle occurred in earth's ancient pre-biotic soup. Lightning struck setting in motion the first life out of lifeless chemicals. This raises another difficult question; How did that new life survive, and even replicate?

The 2004 book, *Origins of Life* by Fazale Rana and Hugh Ross, examined extensively the difficulties involved with the naturalistic theories for the origin of life, and specifically the prebiotic soup theories for the origin of life on earth. In this excerpt, they described *the synergy problem:*

> "The problem for the origin of life extends beyond trying to account for the simultaneous occurrence of over 250 different proteins. It also demands the appearance of DNA, RNA, and complex carbohydrates to form the cell wall, plus the lipids to form the cell's membrane. All these molecules must come together at once and operate in an orchestrated fashion for life to be possible. Herein lies the dilemma: The cell wall and membrane cannot be constructed without proteins, RNA, and DNA and the molecules cannot achieve stability without the cell wall and membrane. There can be no proteins without DNA and RNA, and there can be no DNA and RNA without proteins."[408]

Dr. Stephen Meyer of the *Discovery Institute* discussed the same issue:

---

[408]Fazale Rana & Hugh Ross, *Origins of Life: Biblical and Evolutionary Models Face Off,* Colorado Springs CO (Navpress, 2004) 165.

"In other words, you've got to have a self-replicating organism for Darwinian evolution to take place, but you can't have a self-replicating organism until you have the information necessary in DNA, which is what you're trying to explain in the first place."[409]

Which seems more reasonable; to believe that all the complexity in the universe, in the human body, and even in the smallest cell, have resulted from completely random processes or that it was designed by an infinitely wise creator?

Antony Flew noted this lack of explanation among evolutionary scientists for the origin of replication in cells:

"The origin of self-reproduction is a second key problem. Distinguished philosopher John Haldane notes that origin-of-life theories 'do not provide a sufficient explanation, since they presuppose the existence at an early stage of self-reproduction, and it has not been shown that this can arise by natural means from a material base.'"[410]

Flew also made reference to Paul Davies' criticisms of evolutionary scientist's failure to account for the origin of self-replicating cells:

"Paul Davies highlights the same problem. He observes that most theories of biogenesis have concentrated on the chemistry of life, but 'life' is more than just complex chemical reactions. The cell is also an information storing, processing and replicating system. We need to explain the origin of this information, and the way in which the

---

[409]Stephen C. Meyer, as quoted by Lee Strobel, *The Case for a Creator: A Journalist Investigates Scientific Evidence That Points Toward God,* Grand Rapids MI (Zondervan, 2004) 286.
[410]Antony Flew, *There is a God,* 125.

information processing machinery came to exist' . . . The problem of how meaningful or semantic information can emerge spontaneously from a collection of mindless molecules subject to blind and purposeless forces presents a deep conceptual challenge."[411]

Further, Flew referenced the thoughts of Antonio Lazcano:

"Antonio Lazcano, the president of the International Society for the Study of the Origin of Life, reports: 'One feature of life, though remains certain: Life could not have evolved without a genetic mechanism—one able to store, replicate, and transmit to its progeny information that can change with time . . . Precisely how the first genetic machinery evolved also persists as an unresolved issue.'"[412]

Aczel added:

"We don't know how the first living organisms came about, before they evolved into higher creatures. And we don't know the process that led to the emergence of eukaryotic cells—a huge advance over the earlier, simple single-celled organisms. (Eukaryotic cells are those that have complex structures inside such as mitochondria, are protected by a membrane, and contain their genetic material in a nucleus) . . . We have no idea how such sophisticated cells became a reality."[413]

DNA and proteins: The chicken or egg problem

Fazale Rana explained the problem for the supposed evolution of life at the beginning stages:

---

[411]Antony Flew, *There is a God,* 128-129.

[412]Antony Flew, *There is a God: How the World's Most Notorious Atheist Changed His Mind,* New York (HarperCollins/HarperOne, 2007) 130.

[413]Amir D. Aczel, *Why Science Does Not Disprove God,* New York (HarperCollins Publishers, 2014) 209-210.

"The relationship between protein and DNA has been a persistent paradox for origin-of-life researchers. Here's why: the genetic information in DNA is required for the construction of proteins, but the information of DNA can only be processed with the help of proteins. In other words, DNA requires proteins, yet proteins require DNA. How could two mutually dependent systems emerge separately? This chicken-and-egg problem has confounded scientists for decades . . . Any valid theory for how life began must be able to explain information's origin. Yet this is precisely what the RNA-first model *cannot* explain. The RNA-first model either presupposes or ignores the origin of information. Here's the bottom line: scientists have no idea how the information in primitive forms of RNA could have formed spontaneously on the early earth . . . There are no plausible scenarios for how RNA could have evolved into modern cells. These are a few of the reasons why Scripps biochemist Gerald Joyce concludes, 'You have to build straw man upon straw man to get to the point where RNA is a viable first biomolecule.'"[414]

---

[414]Fazale R. Rana, *How Did Life Begin?* chapter in Sean McDowell & Jonathan Morrow, *Is God Just a Human Invention? And Seventeen Other Questions Raised by the New Atheists,* Grand Rapids MI (Kregel Publications, 2010) 88, 88, 89.

Chapter 21: Creation or Evolution

The false caricature of Creationism

Some object to students being exposed to creationism out of concern about religion being brought into the public school classroom.

Fair enough. But what objection could there be to exposing students to the *scientific* problems with evolutionary theories? In the true scientific spirit, shouldn't there be a balanced approach to teaching about evolution, teaching both the scientific support for and criticisms of evolutionary theories?

Instead, students are exposed to phony caricatures in which creationism is ridiculed as so much superstition and ignorance. Students remain unaware of the widespread support for creationism among scientists at the highest academic levels, and the scientific reasons for their rejection of the evolutionary model.

The parable of the turtle

Sometimes, the stereotypical view of creation science is ridiculed by being compared to mythical folk stories from India in the parable of the turtle. For instance, the philosopher John Locke told this version:

> "He would not be in a much better case than the Indian before mentioned who, saying that the world was supported by a great elephant, was asked what the elephant rested on; to which his answer was—a great tortoise: but being again pressed to know what gave support to the broad-backed tortoise, replied—something, he knew not what."[415]

---

[415]John Locke, *An Essay Concerning Human Understanding*,

Eller tells the more common version of the story:

"There is a famous anthropological story, attributed to various cultures, about a religious belief that the world rests, for example, on a turtle's back. The curious anthropologist asks, 'What does the turtle stand on?' The informant answers, 'On the back of a larger turtle.' When the anthropologist asks what that turtle stands on, the informant responds, 'It's turtles all the way down.'"[416]

But such ridicule betrays the true scientific credentials of creationism and the intelligent design movements. Not only were many of the greatest scientists of history creationists (Kepler, Newton, Bacon, etc.), but so are a substantial portion of professional and academic scientists today.[417]

Evolution and Creationism in the science classroom

The American public needs to understand that creationism is solidly based upon modern science. I am convinced that most Americans do not really understand what creationists actually believe and have not taken the time to seriously study their claims. Rather, they have simply accepted the stereotypical images popularized in the media; ignorant fundamentalist Bible-thumpers living with their intellectual heads buried in the sand.

Chapter 23, 2 as reprinted in *Classics of Western Philosophy*, Steven M. Cahn, Editor, Indianapolis IN (Hackett Publishing Company, 1977) 510.

[416]David Eller, *Natural Atheism*, Cranford New Jersey (American Atheist Press, 2004) 26.

[417]Consider the list of creationist and Intelligent Design scientists available at Ration-Wiki at: https://rationalwiki.org/wiki/Lists_of_creationist_scientists

Creation scientists have been criticized for not publishing in peer-reviewed professional scientific journals. This charge would be funny were it not so tragic, since there has been a concerted effort to exclude scientists who openly hold to creationism from these very publications.

Scientists with outstanding academic credentials and professional accomplishments have been censored from professional journals and fired from teaching positions simply for holding creationist's views. This in direct opposition to the spirit of free academic inquiry and the scientific ideal of following the evidence wherever it leads.

Further, supporters of evolution have been guilty of slanting research and suppressing evidence that would undermine their evolutionary commitments. In other words, they have allowed their naturalistic philosophical biases to override their scientific integrity.

Despite the stranglehold and monopoly that evolutionary theory holds in academia and in the popular media, it is amazing how strong creationist beliefs remain amongst the general public. Perhaps, this shows that the real state of scientific evidence is not so tilted in favor of evolution as its supporters have hitherto supposed!

Gerald Shroeder made this assessment of the current state of affairs:

"Despite all the Bible—science confrontations, despite the battles over high-school textbooks and controversies about government codes on how and when to teach evolution, the fact is science and religion are both thriving."[418]

My question for skeptics is this; if Christianity, or even religion in general, is so detrimental to the scientific enterprise, why is science thriving in America, which many consider among the most religious nations on the planet?

Competing scientific models

The real state of affairs in origins science is that we have two basic models; the evolutionary and creation models. They are both reasonable models. They both have powerful explanatory powers.

Let me illustrate this with a thought experiment in which a group of students are shown a table with a moist surface and on which small amounts of water have run over the edges and unto the floor. They were asked to explain how the situation had come about.

Most of the students assumed the simple explanation that water had been applied to the table surface with some running over the edge. Others, however, speculated that ice had been placed upon the table and was left to melt, leaving the same result.

Both explanations or theories are perfectly reasonable and consistent with the evidence. Yet only one is true. This is an example of *the principle of undetermination of theory by data* as explained by W. Christopher Stewart:

---

[418] Gerald Schroeder, *The Science of God: The Convergence of Scientific and Biblical Wisdom,* New York (The Free Press, 1997) 2.

"For any given body of observational data, there
are always an indefinite number of theories of
hypotheses capable of explaining the data. (This is
known as the 'undetermination of theory by data.')."[419]

This, I suggest, is the situation with the creation-
evolution debate. Both offer reasonable scientific
explanations of the relevant data. However, of course,
they can't both be true. It is my contention that in the
creation-evolution debate, creationism is the preferred
scientific explanation offering a better explanation of the
data, and of course is a simpler explanation since it does
not suffer from all the scientific difficulties associated
with evolution, as we shall shortly consider.

The Creation Model

Let us consider the basic creation model. It begins
with the assumption (based upon strong arguments) that
the universe, and particularly, our world, is a creation of
God, as described in the Genesis account of the Bible.

This includes the creation of the basic kinds in the
animal kingdom. It should be clear that each of the kinds
was created with a full complement of genetic material
(frontloaded), allowing for a maximum of diversity within
the kinds over time. All that now exists has resulted from
either a reshuffling or loss of the original genetic
materials of creation.

Further, at the heart of creationism is the Bible's
account for the origin of evil, sin, and death as a result of

---

[419] W. Christopher Stewart, *Religion and Science*, chapter *in Reason
for the Hope Within,* Michael Murray Editor, Grand Rapids MI
(William B. Eerdmans Publishing Company, 1999) 337.

man's rebellion against God in the Garden of Eden. This loss of paradise came with a price, and accounts for the origin of mutations and their impact on the unfolding genetic history of life on earth.

Further, there is nothing objectionable with the concept of natural selection to creationists, per se. It is common-sense that those organism best suited to their environment will have the greatest survivability. What creationist do object to is the idea that natural selection is a creative force that actually causes genetic changes in creatures. For that, there is no evidence. Natural selection can have a sifting effect, eliminating those not suited for a certain environment, but it does not create anything new in the gene pool.

Creationists also deny that mutations are a creative force. They can reshuffle existing features and genetic information, but they cannot produce new information, features, or specificity, and are almost always destructive to organisms and their ability to replicate.

The Evolutionary Model

The naturalist' account offers no explanation for either the origin of life, nor for how the first cells developed the ability to replicate and reproduce, nor how prokaryotic cells somehow evolved into eukaryotic cells.[420]

---

[420]Lynn Margulis advanced the interesting theory of endosymbiosis in her1967 paper, *On the Origin of Mitosing Cells*, which proposed the theory that mitochondrion (tiny power plants) in eukaryotic cells developed out of a symbiotic relationship that resulted when one prokaryotic cell devoured another. Despite the multitude of problems with the theory (how did this first accident develop the ability to replicate?), it has gained acceptance among some evolutionists (what other explanation have they?)

Despite these problems, evolutionary theory explained that organisms that responded and adapted (including through mutations) to their environment had the greatest chance of survival (natural selection), and over millions and billions of years, the accumulation of these changes (adaptations) has produced the current state of the world.

Charles Taylor called this idea *dark genesis*:

> But the sense of kinship was greatly strengthened by what I've been calling our dark genesis, the idea that our humanity emerged out of an animal life which we share with other living things.[421]

Now both are reasonable models, but creationists are convinced that the scientific evidence favors the creationist model.

Devolution

Further, I am an advocate of the idea of *devolution*. It is essentially the opposite of the evolutionary model. It affirms that rather than beginning with a single simple organism for life which increases in complexity and diversity through time (anagenesis and cladogenesis), devolution argues that God created all the basic forms of life at the beginning. All the complexity and genetic possibilities were contained in these original forerunners from the start.

Gerald Shroeder calls this frontloading model the "latent library."[422] Schroeder explained this latent library idea:

---

[421]Charles Taylor, *A Secular Age*, Cambridge MA (The Belknap Press of Harvard University Press, 2007) 344.

"According to the 'latent library' theory, all this information is quietly present in the genome, waiting for the cue to be expressed . . . The concept of a latent library posits a mechanism very different form the classical theory of evolution wherein random mutations provide the changes in morphology."[423]

While I disagree with the broad parameters of Schroeder's views on evolution, the idea that rather than life beginning from the very simplest forms of life and then ever-advancing toward greater complexity and diversity, the *scientific* record actually supports an opposite approach in which all the genetic diversity was present from the beginning (front-loaded) in the basic created kinds, and from there advanced to the diversity we find today, but within limits of the basic created kinds.

That is, various factors and forces acted to bring the great diversity of life present today. These factors certainly included natural selection, the simple reality that those creatures that are most fit for the changing environment will have the greatest chance of survival, for themselves and their offspring.

Devolution and variation

Let's consider some of these forces that have driven the variety of life in our world.

Jonathan Sarfati explained:

---

[422] Gerald Schroeder, *The Science of God: The Convergence of Scientific and Biblical Wisdom,* New York (The Free Press, 1997) 90.

[423] Gerald Schroeder, *The Science of God, 90-91.*

"A large population as a whole is less likely to lose established genes because there are usually many copies of the genes of both parents . . . But in a small, isolated population, there is a good chance that information can be lost by random sampling. This is called *genetic drift* . . . In an extreme case, where a single pregnant animal or a single pair is isolated, e.g., by being blown or washed onto a desert island, it may lack a number of genes of the original population. So when its descendants fill the island, this new population would be different from the old one, with less information. This is called the *founder effect*. Loss of information through mutations, natural selection, and genetic drift can sometimes result in different populations losing such different information that they will no longer interbreed . . . Thus a new 'species' is formed."[424]

Creatures that shared a common ancestor (one of the original types) can eventually branch off into similar but unique types similar to the process known as cladogenesis. This is not evolution, but devolution, since it results in a loss of genetic information rather than through an increase in complexity (as would be expected in evolutionary models).

Jonathan Sarfati described this process of devolution:

"An important aspect of the creationist model is often overlooked, but it is essential for a proper understanding of the issues. This aspect is the deterioration of a once-perfect creation . . . From this premise of perfection followed by deterioration, it follows that mutations, as would be expected from copying errors, destroyed some of the original genetic information . . . Many allegedly imperfect structures can also be interpreted as a deterioration of once-perfect structures."[425]

[424]Jonathan Sarfati, *Refuting Evolution: A Response to the National Academy of Sciences' Teaching Abut Evolution and the Nature of Science*, Green Forest AR (Master Books, 1999) 36-37.
[425]Jonathan Sarfati, *Refuting Evolution*, 33-34.

Antony Flew supported this idea by pointing out evolution's inability to provide a mechanism for new specificity and design:

> "In my book *Darwinian Evolution*, I pointed out that natural selection does not positively produce anything."[426]

That is, natural selection can only choose from what is, it does not create new features (novelty).[427] The problem for evolutionary theory is that neither natural selection nor mutations "positively produce anything," anything new that is.

What we learn from breeding

We can see evidence of this account of creation through the science of breeding (husbandry). In the same way that breeders can bring about purposeful diversity, God made possible through natural processes such as the bottleneck, genetic drift, and the founder's effects.

Pandas and People explained:

> "Dogs are bred to develop widely differing offspring, not by adding genetic material to the gene pool, but by selecting smaller sets of genes from the larger and richer store of genetic material."[428]

Pandas and People argued, then, that much of the variety of life in the world was caused, not by an *increase*

---

[426]Antony Flew, *There is a God: How the World's Most Notorious Atheist Changed His Mind*, New York (HarperCollins/HarperOne, 2007) 78.

[427]Gabriel Dover, *Anti-Dawkins*, chapter in, *Alas, Poor Darwin: Arguments Against Evolutionary Psychology*, Edited by Hilary Rose & Steven Rose, New York (Harmony Books, 2000) 71.

[428]*Of Pandas and People: The Central Questions of Biological Origins*, Second Edition, Percival Davis & Dean H. Kenyon, Editors, Dallas TX (Haughton Publishing Company, 1999) 10.

in information or specificity, but rather through the *loss or rearrangement* of existing genetic material in the gene pool:

> "Most variations are produced by recombination of existing genes. The tremendous differences that divide a Pekingese, a Poodle, and a Greyhound illustrate the range of variation that may exist within the gene pool of any interbreeding population. These variations are produced when dog breeders isolate particular genes governing size, curly hair, or speed, within a single breed. The genes can be combined and recombined in a vast number of different ways. Most changes in the living world are produced in this way—not by the introduction of anything new into the gene pool, but by simple recombination of existing genes."[429]

Breeding trade-offs

As with the old saying, there is no free lunch, so there are trade-offs that result in the breeding process:

> "Intensive breeding may produce interesting and useful varieties, but it tends to deplete the adaptive gene pool of the lineage, leading to increased susceptibility to disease or environmental change. It also tends to concentrate defective traits through inbreeding, and the farther the morphology is shifted from species norm (average), the more it produces developmental discordance, stress, and decreased fertility."[430]

The downward trend in health the further from the species norm is a result of the natural limits of evolution or adaption. Further, the variations in the dog kind are not the result of increased, but decreased or reshuffled genetic information. Jonathan Sarfati explained:

---

[429] *Of Pandas and People,* 11.
[430] *Of Pandas and People,* 11.

"However, all the breeders do is select from the information *already present*. For example, Chihuahuas were bred by selecting the smallest dogs to breed from over many generations. But this process eliminates the genes for large size. The opposite process would have bred Great Danes from the same ancestral dog population, by eliminating the genes for small size. So the breeding has *sorted out* the information mixture into separate lines. All the breeds have less information than the original dog/wolf kind. Many breeds are also the victims of hereditary conditions due to mutations, for example the 'squashed' snout of the bulldog and pug. But their loss of genetic information and their inherited defects mean that purebred dogs are less 'fit' in the wild than mongrels, and veterinarians can confirm that purebreds suffer from more diseases."[431]

Pandas and People stated:

"As any dog owner knows, breeds retain their distinctive characteristics only when they are prevented from interbreeding . . . For if he does, he, too, will own mongrels . . . In nature as well, distinctions are maintained . . . a group may split off from its parent population and become isolated. Eventually, it may no longer interbreed with members of the parent population. This is termed reproductive isolation."[432]

The foregoing makes clear that what many consider evidence for evolution is no such thing. Variation is achieved by reproductive isolation; by a smaller population getting separated from the larger population, and the resulting loss of genetic information.

Sarfati made this interesting, but important, observation:

[431]Jonathan Sarfati, *Refuting Evolution*, 43.
[432]*Of Pandas and People*, 16.

"But if Great Danes and Chihuahuas were only known from the fossil record, they would probably have been classified as different species or even different genera . . . Creationists regard the breeds of dogs as showing that God programmed much variability into the original dog/wolf created kind."[433]

And, of course, what is true of the dog (canine) kind, is also true of all the other kinds as well, accounting for the great diversity in the world. We must understand that this is not as the result of Darwinian evolution since it does not result from an increase in genetic information and specificity.

Sarfati elaborated on these ideas concerning dogs:

"Note that: [One] They are now *adapted* to their environment. [Two] They are now more *specialized* than their ancestors . . . [Three] This has occurred through *natural selection.* [Four] There have been *no new genes* added. [Five] In fact, genes have been lost from the population—i.e., there has been *a loss of genetic information* . . . [Six] Now the population is less able to adapt to future environmental changes."[434]

The loss of genetic information can result in further divisions or types, not again, as a result of evolution, but of devolution.

Evolutionary change or limited change?

Though, at the beginning, the basic kinds had a full genetic load and the fullest ability to adapt, yet, creationists believe that there are limits to how far these changes can occur. Sarfati explained:

---

[433]Jonathan Sarfati, *Refuting Evolution,* 43-44.
[434]Jonathan Sarfati, *Refuting Evolution,* 35-36.

"To put it another way, breeders can produce sweeter corn or fatter cattle, but they have not turned corn into another kind of plant or cattle into another kind of animal."[435]

As with breeding, so in nature, there are natural limits, (what Darwin called "the immutability of species)"[436] to evolution in accord with the biblical record.

Pandas and People showed that mutations cannot produce new structures:

"There is no evidence mutations create new structures. They merely alter existing ones. Mutations have produced for example, crumpled, oversized, and undersized wings [in fruit flies]. They have produced double sets of wings. But they have not created a new kind of wing. Nor have they transformed the fruit fly into a new kind insect. Experiments have simply produced variations of fruit flies."[437]

It is important to understand that creationist do not deny small variations or changes (sometimes called micro-evolution or adaption) within species (i.e. Darwin's Finches).

Ironically, these small changes (that creationists accept) are often used to prove Darwinian or macro-evolution. But what supporters of evolution need to prove is not small variations at the micro level, but instead large or macro changes from one kind to another.

Hunter pointed out:

---

[435] *Of Pandas and People,* 11.
[436] Phillip E. Johnson, *Darwin on Trial,* Downers Grove IL (InterVarsity Press, 1991) 47.
[437] *Of Pandas and People,* 11-12.

"Darwin's book was entitled *The Origin of Species*, but he never did actually explain how species originate—the process of speciation . . . One of the thorny obstacle's regarding speciation is the fact that a population's capacity to change seems limited. Instead of small changes accumulating and resulting in large changes, the small changes appear to be bounded. Darwin was well-aware of this problem. He bred pigeons and made it his business to understand state-of-the-art animal husbandry and breeding. And the state of the art, then and now, is a story of change within limits."[438]

At the bottom, the difference between creationism and evolution is the question of how macroevolutionary changes could occur. Sure, natural selection can favor organisms with features most suitable for their environment. *But the question is how those features became available in the first place.* It is at this point that we must remember that *new features require new information.* A mutation can occur only upon what already exists. *But the question is how new complex features could develop in the first place?*

John Lennox explained:

"This refers to large-scale innovation, the coming into existence of new organs, structures, body-plans, of qualitatively new genetic material; for example, the evolution of multicellular from single-celled structure. Macroevolution thus involves a marked increase in complexity. This distinction between micro and macroevolution is the subject of considerable dispute since the gradualist thesis is that macroevolution is to be accounted for simply by extrapolating the processes that drive microevolution over time."[439]

[438]Cornelius G. Hunter, *Darwin's God: Evolution and the Problem of Evil*, Grand Rapids MI (Brazos Press, 2001) 53-54.
[439]John C. Lennox, *God's Undertaker: Has Science Buried God?*, New

In other words, what nature actually shows is devolution rather than evolution. Lennox asked from whence, then, does the creative power arise?:

"In the neo-Darwinian world the motive factor of morphological change is natural selection, which can account for the modification and loss of parts [devolution]. But selection has no innovative capacity; it eliminates or maintains what exists. The generative and ordering aspects of morphological evolution are thus absent from evolutionary theory."[440]

Lennox further described the idea that there are natural limits to the extent of evolutionary change:

"One eminent biologist whose research convinced him that there was a limit to what mutation and natural selection could do and so led him to reject neo-Darwinism was Piere Grassé of the Sorbonne in Paris, who was President of the Académie Francaise and editor of the definitive 28 volume work *Traité de Zoologie* . . . In his book Grassé observed that fruit flies remain fruit flies in spite of the thousands of generations that have been bred and all the mutations that have been induced in them. In fact, the capacity for variation in the gene pool seems to run out quite early on in the process, **a phenomenon called genetic homeostasis.** There appears to be a barrier beyond which selective breeding will not pass because of the onset of sterility or exhaustion of genetic variability. If there are limits even to the amount of variation the most skilled breeders can achieve, the clear implication is that *natural* selection is likely to achieve very much less. It is not surprising that he argued that microevolution could not bear the weight that is often put upon it."[441]

Updated Edition, Oxford England (Lion Books, 2009) 102.
[440]John C. Lennox, *God's Undertaker,* 105.
[441]John C. Lennox, *God's Undertaker,* 109-110.

The compromise model of Theistic Evolution

Strictly speaking, whether evolution is true or false is irrelevant to the question of God's existence. Many religious believers accept the theory of evolution, and believe that God both created and guided the process.

Nevertheless, it is my personal conviction that the theory of evolution is bad science, bad philosophy, and bad religion. It has been promoted by those who seek to evade supernatural explanations for the origin of the universe, and more specifically, the origin of life.

It is also my conviction that most of the believers that accept theistic evolution have never seriously considered the scientific weaknesses of the evolutionary model, perhaps out of a fear of being ridiculed, or having their faith ridiculed. The result is that they have a compromised faith, having needlessly rejected essential biblical truths concerning origins.

Therefore, I defend here the biblical account of a supernatural creation as literally described in the book of Genesis and reject naturalistic accounts of origins promoted to defend the faith of atheism (faitheism).

Chapter 22: Problems for Evolutionary Theory

It is not my intention to provide a full critique of evolutionary theory. Others are much more qualified and able than I for such an effort. I will simply share a brief overview of some of the problems inherent in the evolutionary view and how these are sufficient to show that one can be a serious thinker, and yet remain unconvinced of the validity of evolution. *Yes, one can be an intellectually fulfilled theist!*

The fossil record

Let's begin with the fossil record. Given the widespread acceptance of evolution, you would think that the fossil record is an unbroken chain of transitions, one creature slowly evolving into another. Philip Johnson suggested that the record shows otherwise:

> "But what if the necessary links are missing not only from the world of the present, but from the fossil record of the past as well? Darwin acknowledged that his theory implied that 'the number of intermediate and transitional links, between all living and extinct species, must have been inconceivably great.' One might therefore suppose that geologists would be continually uncovering fossil evidence of transitional forms. This, however, was not the case. What geologists did discover was species, and groups of species, which appeared suddenly rather than at the end of a chain of evolutionary links. Darwin conceded that the state of the fossil evidence was 'the most obvious and gravest objection which can be urged against my theory'"[442]

Gerald Shroeder characterized the fossil records thusly:

---

[442]Phillip E. Johnson, *Darwin on Trial*, Downers Grove IL (InterVarsity Press, 1991) 46-47.

"In the entire fossil record, with its millions of specimens, no mid-way transitional fossil has been found at the basic level of phylum or class, no trace of an animal that was half the predecessor and half the successor."[443]

The fossil record and falsifiability?

It is helpful to consider this situation in light of Karl Popper's falsification theory. Anthony O'Hear described Popper's ideas concerning falsifiability:

"Popper always took a skeptical Humean stand on induction, as a result of which he claimed it is impossible to verify or even to confirm a universal scientific theory with any positive degree of probability. What we can do, though, is to disprove a universal theory. While no number of observations in conformity with the hypothesis . . . can show that the hypothesis is true . . . only one observation . . . will refute the hypothesis. Falsification can get a grip where positive proof is ever beyond us; the demarcation between science and non-science lies in the manner in which scientific theories make testable predictions and are given up when they fail their tests."[444]

Robert Paul Wolff added:

"But now Popper takes a dramatic and unexpected turn. The aim of science isn't really to *confirm* general theories at all, he says. The real aim of science is to advance our understanding of the world by putting forward theories that can be *disconfirmed* . . . So, Popper suggests, we should turn things around, and see the scientist as

---

[443] Gerald Schroeder, *The Science of God: The Convergence of Scientific and Biblical Wisdom,* New York (The Free Press, 1997) 95. Shroeder followed this statement of the only possible exception he was aware i.e. that of the archaeopteryx, which Shroeder rejects as a truly transitional fossil.

[444] Anthony O'Hear, *The Oxford Guide to Philosophy*, Ted Honderich, Editor, Oxford (Oxford University Press, 2005) 739.

endlessly putting forward hypothesis—theories to be tested—in the hope that the evidence will refute them, and thereby tell us something we did not already know."[445]

We can ask if Darwinian evolution has made any predictions concerning the fossil record that could be scientifically falsified? The answer is clearly yes. Although Darwin was convinced that paleontologists would eventually confirm his belief in a multitude of transitional creatures in the fossil record, that has simply not been the case.

Norman Geisler referenced the well-known quote in which Stephen Jay Gould conceded the weakness of the fossil record in supporting the evolutionary account:

> "Harvard paleontologist Stephen Jay Gould admitted that 'the extreme rarity of transitional forms in the fossil record persists as the trade secret of paleontology. The evolutionary trees that adorn our textbooks have data only at the tips and nodes of their branches; the rest is inference, however reasonable, not the evidence of the fossils."[446]

Darwin himself conceded that the fossil record of his day did not support his theory of evolution. But he was confident that this was due merely to the incomplete fossil record available during his lifetime.[447] Nevertheless, Darwin predicted that as the work of paleontology advanced, it would clearly show the gradual evolution of creatures from one kind to another. This was Darwin's evolutionary hypothesis.

---

[445]Robert Paul Wolff, *About Philosophy*, Sixth Edition, Upper Saddle River NJ (Prentice Hall, 1995) 288.

[446]Norman L. Geisler, *Baker Encyclopedia of Christian Apologetics*, Grand Rapids MI (Baker Books, 1999) 184.

[447]Phillip E. Johnson, *Darwin on Trial*, 46-47.

160 years have come and gone. How has Darwin's hypothesis faired against the evidence? Despite popular assumptions, it has not fared well as Philipp Johnson explained:

"Darwin's theory predicted not merely that fossil transitionals would be found; it implied that a truly complete fossil record would be mostly transitional, and that what we think of as fixed species would be revealed as mere arbitrary viewpoints in a process of continual change . . . The fossil record today on the whole looks very much as it did in 1859, despite the fact that an enormous amount of fossil hunting has gone on."[448]

Johnson referred to the prominent evolutionary scientist Stephen Jay Gould's assessment of the fossil record:

"The history of most fossil species includes two features particularly inconsistent with gradualism: 1. Stasis. Most species exhibit no directional change during their tenure on earth. They appear in the fossil record looking pretty much the same as when they disappear. Morphological change is usually limited and directionless. 2. Sudden appearance. In any local area, a species does not arise gradually by the steady transformation of its ancestors; it appears all at once and 'fully formed.'"[449]

---

[448]Phillip E. Johnson, *Darwin on Trial*, 48, 50.
[449]Stephen Jay Gould, as quoted by Phillip E. Johnson, *Darwin On Trial*, Downers Grove IL (InterVarsity Press, 1991) 50. It should be noted that Gould's honest assessment of the fossil record caused him, along with Niles Eldridge to propose *punctuated equilibrium*, the idea that important evolutionary changes occur quickly (in geologic time) and on the edges of populations, and so leave little fossil evidence. As such, the theory does not hold up well to Popper's falsifiability test, since the evidence supposed to support it *is the lack of evidence for evolution..*

In other words, Darwin's evolutionary hypothesis has failed Popper's test; it has been falsified by the fossil record. The only place that the fossil record has supported the evolutionary hypothesis is in the wishes of evolutionary scientists and in the imaginations of textbook artists.

Let it not slip by unnoticed that the *creationists* of Darwin's day predicted that the ongoing fossil record would have the very nature that Gould described, saltation and stasis; creatures would appear suddenly, fully formed, and would remain in that form through their time in the fossil record. The creationist model therefore, has passed Popper's test in that its prediction has not been falsified by the fossil record as has Darwin's model.

Darwin's strongest and weakest

It is interesting that what Darwin believed was the "gravest objection" that could be "urged against my theory" remains the weakest link today. What is more interesting is that what Darwin thought was the strongest evidence for his evolutionary theory is now known to be completely fraudulent. DeRosa explained:

> "Haeckel is an extremely controversial figure. A trained German physician and devout evolutionist, he used fake data in his embryo research to prove evolution. Haeckel falsified drawings of various vertebrate embryos (chick, hog, calf, rabbit, etc.) in an attempt to show they are all almost identical in the earliest stage of development . . . Haeckel called this a 'biogenetic law' and adopted the phrase 'ontogeny recapitulates

phylogeny' to describe how the stages of evolution are, he claimed, repeated during the development of the embryo. This 'law' of Haeckel's has been largely rejected by all sides in the evolution debate."[450]

While the recapitulation theory that Haeckel popularized and championed has now been discredited, unfortunately for Darwin, he believed it powerfully proved his evolutionary theory. DeRosa further explained:

"Jonathan Wells, author of *Icons of Evolution*, notes that the alleged similarity between embryos at the outset of life was to Darwin convincing evidence for his theory. Darwin believed that 'community in embryonic structure reveals community of descent' . . . This embryo similarity was, for Darwin, 'by far the strongest single class of facts in favor of' his theory. But, of course, the Haeckel illustrations on which Darwin reached that conclusion were faked."[451]

Let it not be overlooked that the recapitulation theory, though now rejected, was put forth as fact for decades by evolutionists and indeed, was used to ridicule creationism.

For instance, the recapitulation theory was used to "prove" evolution at the famous Scopes-Monkey Trial in 1925 along with other now widely discredited "scientific facts" as Answers in Genesis explained:

[450] Tom DeRosa, *Evolution's Fatal Fruit: How Darwin's Tree of Life Brought Death to Millions*, Fort Lauderdale FL (Coral Ridge Ministries, 2006) 118.
[451] Tom DeRosa, *Evolution's Fatal Fruit,* 118-119

"In the record of the Scopes Trial, human evolution was falsely supported with examples like Piltdown Man, vestigial organs, embryonic recapitulation, and human development. Many of these examples have been shown to be fraudulent or untenable."[452]

How could consciousness evolve?

From a naturalistic perspective, explaining the origin of consciousness has been a major challenge. That is, how did a pile of chemicals come to achieve self-awareness? How did a collection of physical materials arrive at a state of consciousness? And so J. P. Moreland asked "How mind or consciousness could have arisen in a world of only matter."[453]

Roy Varghese noted the failure of the so-called new atheists to even seriously address this perplexing question:

"In the first place, they refuse to engage the real issues involved in the question of God's existence . . . They fail to address the issue of the origins of the rationality embedded in the fabric of the universe, of life understood as autonomous agency, and of consciousness, conceptual thought, and the self. Dawkins talks of the origins of life and consciousness as 'one-off' events triggered by an 'initial stroke of luck.' Wolpert writes: 'I have purposely [!] avoided any discussion of consciousness, which still remains mostly poorly understood.' About the origin of consciousness, Dennett, a die-hard physicalist, once wrote, 'and then a miracle happens.'"[454]

[452] Answers in Genesis, *The Scopes Trial Settled the Question of Evolution,* November 3, 2018, https://answersingenesis.org/scopes-trial/scopes-trial-settled-question-of-evolution/

[453] J. P. Moreland, & Kai Nielsen, *Does God Exist?: The Debate Between Theists & Atheists,* Amherst NY (Prometheus Books, 1993) 36.

Richard Dawkins was candid about the problem:

"There are aspects of human subjective consciousness that are deeply mysterious. Neither Steve Pinker nor I can explain human subjective consciousness—what philosophers call qualia. In *How the Mind Works*, Steve elegantly sets out the problem of subjective consciousness, and asks where it comes from and what's the explanation. Then he's honest enough to say, 'Beats the heck out me.' That is an honest thing to say, and I echo it. We don't know. We don't understand it."[455]

Varghese explained:

"But the atheist position is that, at some point in the history of the universe, the impossible and inconceivable took place. Undifferentiated matter (here we include energy) at some point, became 'alive,' then conscious, then conceptually proficient, then an 'I.'"[456]

Varghese added:

"First of all, neurons show no resemblance to our conscious life. Second and more important, their physical properties do not in any way give reason to believe that they can or will produce consciousness. Consciousness is correlated with certain regions of the brain, but when the same systems of neurons are present in the brain stem there is no 'production' of consciousness. As a matter of fact, as physicist Gerald Shroeder points out, there is no

---

[454]Roy Abraham Varghese, *Preface,* p. 17. In Antony Flew, *There is a God: How the World's Most Notorious Atheist Changed His Mind,* New York (HarperCollins/HarperOne, 2007)

[455]Richard Dawkins & Steve Pinker, *Is Science Killing the Soul?,* http://www.edge.org/3rd_culture/dawkins_pinker/debate_p4.html, as quoted by *The Future of Atheism: Alister McGrath & Daniel Dennett in Dialogue,* Robert B. Stewart, Editor, Minneapolis MN (Fortress Press, 2008) 13.

[456]Roy Abraham Varghese, Appendix A in Antony Flew, *There is a God,* 163.

essential difference in the ultimate physical constituents of a heap of sand and the brain of Einstein."[457]

Julian Baggini conceded:

"For example, many would agree that we do not have a rational explanation for how consciousness can be produced in the brain, but there are rational reasons to suppose consciousness exists because we are all conscious beings. In this sense it is rational to believe in the existence of what cannot be explained."[458]

Baggini was certainly correct to argue belief in consciousness is rational since it obviously exists. But what he doesn't explain is just how consciousness can come into existence in the first place.

Carl Sagan likewise admitted the difficulty of explaining the origin of consciousness:

"And, indeed, we do not know the details in any but the very broadest brush about the evolution of consciousness."[459]

J. P. Moreland's criticism was to the point:

"Labeling these features 'emergent phenomena' is just a placeholder for the problem, not a solution (e.g. consciousness simply emerges when matter reaches a suitable form of complexity). How, for example, could it be that they emerged in the first place? . . . It is hard to see how finite consciousness could result from the rearrangement of brute matter; it is easier to see how a conscious being could produce finite consciousness . . . In general, physic-chemical reactions do not generate

[457]Roy Abraham Varghese, Appendix A in Antony Flew, *There is a God,* 174.

[458]Julian Baggini, *Atheism,* New York (Sterling, 2003) 116.

[459]Carl Sagan, *The God Hypothesis* in Christopher Hitchens, *The Portable Atheist: Essential Readings for the Nonbeliever,* Philadelphia PA (De Capo Press, 2007) 234.

consciousness. Some say they do in the brain, yet brains seem similar to other parts of organisms' bodies (e.g., both are collections of cells totally describable in physical terms). How can like causes produce radically different effects? The appearance of mind is utterly unpredictable and inexplicable. This radical discontinuity seems like a rupture in the natural world."[460]

Paul Copan added:

"For instance, Ned Block acknowledges that we have 'no conception'—'zilch'—that enables us to explain subjective experience or to *begin* to account for conscious life; 'Researchers are stumped.'"[461]

Copan pressed the point:

"Jaegwon Kim wonders how 'a series of physical events, little particles jostling against one another, electric current rushing to and fro' could blossom into 'conscious experience.' Why should *any* experience emerge when these neurons fire?"[462]

Barr criticized the approach of naturalistic attempts to explain consciousness:

"The philosopher David Chalmers, in his book *The Conscious Mind,* summarizes the various materialist

[460]J. P. Moreland, *The Image of God and the Failure of Scientific Atheism*, chapter in William Lane Craig & Chad Meister, editors, *God is Great, God is Good: Why believing in God is Reasonable and Responsible*, Downers Grove IL (Inter Varsity Books, 2009) 37-39.

[461]Paul Copan, *God, Naturalism, and the Foundations of Morality*, chapter in *The Future of Atheism: Alister McGrath & Daniel Dennett in Dialogue*, Robert B. Stewart, Editor, Minneapolis MN (Fortress Press, 2008) 147. Ned Block's quote comes from *Consciousness*, in *A Companion to the Philosophy of Mind*, ed. Samuel Guttenplan, (Oxford: Blackwell, 1994), 211

[462]Paul Copan, *God, Naturalism, and the Foundations of Morality*, chapter in *The Future of Atheism,* 147. Jaegwon Kim's quote is from *Philosophy of Mind* (Boulder: Westview, 1996), 8.

approaches to the problem. One is what he calls 'don't-have-a-clue materialism, which he defines as the following view: 'I don't have a clue about consciousness. It seems utterly mysterious to me. But it must be physical, as materialism must be true.' Such a view, he finds, 'is held widely, but rarely in print.'"[463]

Of course, creationists have no such problem, understanding that consciousness and intelligence are a gift from our conscious and intelligent Creator. Lennox showed how the creationist model for the origin of consciousness is more rational than the atheistic and naturalistic explanation, by showing the nonsensical and backward nature of the evolutionary model:

"Instead of the universe's matter being a product of mind, the minds in the universe are a product of matter."[464]

Robert Morey summarized key philosophical problems with a naturalist perceptive:

"They would [naturalistic materialists] have us accept: a. Everything ultimately came from nothing. b. Order came from chaos. c. Harmony came from discord d. Life came from non-life. e. Reason came from irrationality. f. Personality came from non-personality. g. Morality came from amorality. Believing the above claims of the materialist takes far greater faith than believing that a personal, infinite, rational God created this universe!"[465]

---

[463] Stephen M. Barr, *Modern Physics and Ancient Faith*, Notre Dame IN (University of Notre Dame Press, 2003) 16.

[464] John C. Lennox, *God's Undertaker*, 80.

[465] Robert A. Morey, *The New Atheism and the Erosion of Freedom*, Minneapolis MN (Bethany House Publishers, 1986) 98.

Fraud and suppression

Another concern of creationists has been the distortion of scientific evidence in order to promote evolution and suppress creationism. Since the time of Darwin, evolutionists have been guilty of fraud, deception, and suppression in an attempt to advance Darwinian evolution.

For example, Phillip Johnson stated:

"Suppose that paleontologists became so committed to the new way of thinking that fossil studies were published only if they supported the theory and were discarded as failures if they showed an absence of evolutionary change. As we shall see, that is what happened. Darwinism apparently passed the fossil test, but only because it was not allowed to fail."[466]

Groothius agreed:

"Moreover, scientist qua scientists are not exempted from unfair biases and prejudices. Although scientists claim to follow the evidence wherever it leads, they are just as susceptible to dogmatism, propaganda, egotism, and authoritarianism as any religious believer supporting a religious cause."[467]

Further, examples of fraud in the name of evolution abound. We could start with drawings of embryos by Ernst Haeckel that were offered in science textbooks for decades to prove evolution, even though they were known to be fraudulent.[468]

---

[466]Phillip E. Johnson, *Darwin on Trial*, 48.

[467]Douglass Groothuis, *Christian Apologetics: A Comprehensive Case for Biblical Faith*, Downers Grove IL (InterVarsity Press, 2011) 304.

[468]Jonathan Wells, *Icons of Evolution: Science of Myth? Why Much of*

The example of Archaeoraptor and fraud

In an interview with Lee Strobel, Jonathan Wells blew the whistle on fraud being perpetrated to support evolutionary theory:

> "Paleontologists, however, have been on a frenzy to try to locate an actual reptilian ancestor for birds. Driven by an all-consuming commitment to evolutionary theory, their zeal has resulted in some recent embarrassments for science. Wells was more than willing to regale me with some examples. 'A few years ago, the National Geographic Society announced that a fossil had been purchased at an Arizona show that turned out to be 'the missing link between terrestrial dinosaurs and birds that could actually fly,' he said. 'It certainly looked that way. They called it *Archaeoraptor*, and it had the tail of a dinosaur and the forelimbs of a bird. *National Geographic* magazine published an article in 1999 that said there's now evidence that feathered dinosaurs were ancestors of the first bird.' 'That sounds pretty convincing 'I said.
> 'Well, the problem was that it was a fake!' Wells said.' A Chinese paleontologist proved that someone had glued a dinosaur tail to a primitive bird. He created it to resemble just what the scientist had been looking for. There was a firestorm of criticism—the curator of birds at the Smithsonian charged that the Society had become aligned with 'zealous scientist' who were 'highly biased proselytizers of the faith that birds evolved from dinosaurs.'
> Then Wells made a blanket statement that struck me at the time as being too cynical. 'Fakes are coming out of these fossil beds all the time,' he said, 'because the fossil dealers know there's big money in it.'"[469]

What We Teach About Evolution is Wrong, Washington D.C (Regnery Publishing, Inc, 2000) 81-109.
[469]Jonathan Wells, from an interview in Lee Strobel, *The Case for a Creator: A Journalist Investigates Scientific Evidence That Points Toward God*, Grand Rapids MI (Zondervan, 2004)70.

Lee Strobel then provided a quote from the widely respected ornithologist Alan Feduccia that supported Well's claims about fraud:

> "Ornithologist Alan Feduccia, an evolutionary biologist at the University at North Carolina at Chapel Hill [in an interview in *Discover* magazine said] Archaeoraptor is just the tip of the iceberg. There are scores of fake fossils out there, and they have cast a dark shadow over the whole field. When you go to these fossil shows, it's difficult to tell which ones are faked and which ones are not. I have heard there is a fake-fossil factory in Northeast China, in Liaoning Province, near the deposits where many of these recent alleged feathered dinosaurs were found. Asked what would motivate such fraud, Feduccia replied: 'Money. The Chinese fossil trade has become big business. These fossil forgeries have been sold on the black market for years now, for huge sums of money."[470]

Eventually, in a letter written by Lewis M. Simmons at the invitation of the editors of the *National Geographic* Magazine, the fraud was conceded:

> "It's a tale of misguided secrecy and misplaced confidence, of rampant egos clashing, self-aggrandizement, wishful thinking, naïve assumptions, human error, stubbornness, manipulation, backbiting, lying, corruption, and, most of all, abysmal communications."[471]

---

[470]Alan Feducia, *Discover* magazine interview as quoted by Lee Strobel, *The Case for a Creator: A Journalist Investigates Scientific Evidence That Points Toward God,* Grand Rapids MI (Zondervan, 2004)70-71.

[471]Lewis M. Simmons, *Archaeoraptor Fossil Trail, National Geographic*, Vol. 198, No. 4, October 2000, p. 128, as quoted by Walt Brown*, In the Beginning: Compelling Evidence for Creation and the Flood,* Phoenix AZ (Center for Scientific Creation, 2008) 340.

Chapter 23: Creationist Response to Supposed Proofs for Evolution

Does the rapid adaption of diseases prove evolution?

It has filtered into the popular culture that evolution has been proven by recent studies in the spread of diseases like HIV. But before such conclusions are prematurely accepted, we should read the fine print.

The example of antibodies

For instance, consider the case of antibodies (immunoglobulin's) in the human body. Our blood (particularly certain types of white blood cells) contains proteins that can recognize foreign and destructive invaders (antigens) and produce antibodies to fight and destroy them.

The wonderful thing about them is their versatility. Rather than having to have literally hundreds of specific cells able to fight off each of the hundreds of diseases we may encounter, antibodies react to any actual invaders building a unique defense for that disease. They are like super-cool cellular spies that infiltrate the enemy and steal their secret codes. With the secret blueprints in hand, our bodies create weapons specifically destructive to the invaders. This means that the body will be much stronger in repulsing that disease if it is ever encountered again.

This is testimony to the wonderful design of our creator.

HIV, viruses, and evolution

The same is true in the case of viruses like HIV. William Demski responded to the oft repeated claim that the HIV virus and bacterial resistance prove evolution:

"In one sense, Harris and Dawkins are right. HIV and bacterial resistance provide great examples of natural selection in action. But here is the pivotal question: can we extrapolate minor adaptations within the HIV virus and bacteria (*microevolution*) to account for the diversification of life (*macroevolution*)? Recent evidence points to the exact opposite of what the New Atheists claim . . . As a virus, HIV has far less genetic information than a typical cell. HIV can mutate extraordinarily fast and is thus a great test case for the limits of the creative powers of natural selection. With millions of infections worldwide, the HIV virus has undergone countless mutations. It is therefore uniquely positioned to help determine whether natural selection is viable, as Darwin surmised. So, what have these mutations shown? According to biochemist Michael Behe, author of *The Edge of Evolution*, 'very little . . . on a functional biochemical level the virus has been a complete stick-in-the-mud.'

HIV has not gone through the radical changes we should expect . . . HIV functions exactly the same as when it was discovered fifty years ago. Although minor changes have allowed it to resist certain drugs, no fundamentally new structures or biological information have emerged. This is also true for malaria, E. Coli, and all other microorganisms that scientists have studied over the past century. Claiming that HIV or bacterial mutations provide evidence for macroevolution is a leap of faith far beyond available evidence."[472]

---

[472]William A Demski, *Is Darwinian Evolution the Only Game in Town*, Sean McDowell & Jonathan Morrow, *Is God Just a Human Invention? And Seventeen Other Questions Raised by the New Atheists,* Grand Rapids MI (Kregel Publications, 2010) 61-62.

While certain cells have the ability to react and respond to their environment, this does not show that they have changed in their essential nature. From the beginning they had this ability to adapt as part of their defensive systems. Gerald Schroeder explained this idea with the example of houseflies and DDT resistance:

> "The rapid adaptation of the housefly to DDT is not the result of chance mutations of their genetic material producing just in the nick of time, the needed resistance to the chemical. In the pre-DDT world, the resistance was already present, but few flies expressed the genetic trait. When the introduction of DDT into the flies' environment demanded this trait, those progeny in which it was expressed became the more numerous strain. The resistance of hundreds of insect species to chemicals that were toxic to their ancestral generations is noisome testimony to this ability for change to occur within a morphotype."[473]

A biological weapon analogy

Suppose that police were able to acquire a machine that could laser-scan any keyhole and make a perfect key for it. If they knew the location of a terrorist's cell, they could quickly make a key, gain access, and nullify the threat.

For the sake of argument, if all members of that terrorist group used the same lock, that key, once obtained, would aid in the destruction of all similar future threats. This is essentially how antibodies work.

---

[473]Gerald L. Schroeder, *Genesis and the Big Bang: The Discovery of Harmony Between Modern Science and the Bible*, New York (Bantam Books 1990) 137.

They discover the biological invader's secret information in order to create counter-weapons to destroy them.

Key questions

When faced with claims of macroevolution, there are important questions to be considered. For instance, does the proposed example show an increase in specified information; whole new designs not previously seen? Or is the change merely the result of a loss or reshuffling of information? In the case of the biochemical arms-races being reported in the media, they do not prove Darwinian evolution.

Peppered Moths (*Biston Betularia*)

David Mills appealed to the oft-repeated argument of England's Peppered Moths to support evolution:

> "Let's look at one more quick example of modern evolution at work. In the early 1800's, light-colored lichens covered many of the trees in the English countryside. The peppered moth was a light-colored insect that blended in unnoticeably with the lichens. Predators had great difficulty distinguishing the peppered moth from its background environment, so the moths easily survived and reproduced. Then the Industrial Revolution came to the English countryside. Coal-burning factories turned the lichens a sooty black. The light-colored peppered moth became clearly visible. Most of them were eaten. But because of genetic variation and mutation, a few peppered moths displayed a slightly darker color. These darker moths were better able to blend in with the sooty lichens, and so lived to produce other darker-colored moths. In little over a hundred years, successive generations of peppered moths evolved from almost completely white to completely black."[474]

One can easily understand from Mills' description how his readers (not to mention impressionable students) would be impressed, if not amazed, at this seeming example of evolution in action. And yet, the whole argument is a house of cards without any foundation in fact. Jonathan Wells explained:

> "Most introductory biology textbooks now illustrate this classical story of natural selection with photographs of the two varieties of peppered moth resting on light- and dark-colored tree trunks. What the textbooks don't explain, however, is that biologists have known since the 1980s that the classical story has some serious flaws. The most serious is that peppered moths in the wild don't even rest on tree trunks. The textbook photographs, it turned out, have been staged . . . The peppered moth, *Biston betularia*, comes in various shades of gray. One hundred and fifty years ago, most peppered moths were 'typical' forms, which have predominantly light gray scales with a few black scales scattered among them (hence the name, 'peppered') . . . The only thing that happened was a change in the proportion of two varieties of a pre-existing species of moth."[475]

There is no objection to describing the experiences of these peppered moths as an example of natural selection. However, to describe it as evolution, or more precisely macroevolution, is grossly misleading. No genetic changes or mutations have occurred. There were only, as Wells explained, variations in the populations of the two

[474]David Mills, *Atheist Universe: The Thinking Person's Answer to Christian Fundamentalism*, Berkeley CA (Ulysses Press, 2006) 110.
[475]Jonathan Wells, *Icons of Evolution: Science of Myth? Why Much of What We Teach About Evolution is Wrong,* Washington DC (Regnery Publishing, Inc, 2000) 138, 140, 143-144.

previously existing types, with both types remaining to
this day.

Darwin's finches

Darwin's finches are another supposed example of
evolution that is no such thing. Jonathan Sarfati quoted
the statement about Darwin's finches in the National
Academy of Sciences' (NAS) book *Teaching about
Evolution*:

> "A particularly interesting example of contemporary
> evolution involves the 13 species of finches studied by
> Darwin on the Galápagos Islands, now known as Darwin's
> finches . . . Drought diminishes supplies of easily cracked
> nuts but permits the survival of plants that produce larger,
> tougher nuts. Droughts thus favor birds with strong, wide
> beaks that can break these tougher seeds, producing
> populations of birds with these traits."[476]

Sarfati replied to the National Academy of Science
argument concerning finch variation:

> "However, again, an original population of finches had
> a wide variety of beak sizes. When a drought occurs, the
> birds with insufficiently strong and wide beaks can't crack
> the nuts, so they are eliminated . . .Again, no new
> information has arisen."[477]

So again, natural selection yes, but evolution, no! All
along, the variability of beak types and sizes has been
contained in the genetic pool of the finches. No new

---

[476] *Teaching About Evolution and the Nature of Science*, p. 19, The
National Academy of Sciences, 1998, as quoted by Jonathan
Sarfati, *Refuting Evolution: A Response to the National Academy
of Sciences' Teaching Abut Evolution and the Nature of Science*,
Green Forest AR (Master Books, 1999) 42.
[477] Jonathan Sarfati, *Refuting Evolution:* 42.

genetic information or features has been shown by these natural variations.

The horse sequence

Another frequently cited example of evolution is the horse sequence often pictured in school textbooks. For instance, the *Merrill Life Science* textbook says:

> "Figure 6-1 shows how the horse has changed over time. The evolution of the horse. Notice the change from several toes to a single hoof."[478]

Jonathan Sarfati responded:

> "The horse sequence is another popular evidence of a fairly complete series of transitional fossils . . . however . . . Even informed evolutionists regard horse evolution as a bush rather than a sequence . . . the so-called Eohippus is properly called *Hyracotherium,* and has little that could connect it with horses at all. The other animals in the 'sequence' actually show hardly any more variation between them than that *within* horses today. One non-horse and many varieties of the true horse kind does not a sequence make."[479]

Scott Huse agreed:

> "Horse Non-sense. The fossil horse series is one of the most commonly cited evidences in support of evolution. It is, however, plagued with numerous major difficulties and discrepancies. It has been constructed on the basis of evolutionary presuppositions rather than on scientific fact."[480]

---

[478]Lucy Daniel, Edward Paul Ortleb & Alton Biggs, *Merrill Life Science*, New York (Glencoe Division of Macmillan/McGraw-Hill School Publishing Company, 1994) 130.

[479]Jonathan Sarfati with Mike Matthews, *Refuting Evolution* 2, Green Forest AR (Answers in Genesis, 2002) 132-133.

[480]Scott M. Huse, *The Collapse of Evolution*, Grand Rapids MI (

Huse explained some of the problems with the theory, which I quote only in part:

"One of the most highly praised and well-known examples of 'proof' for organic evolution is the famous fossil horse series . . . the horse series is plagued with many serious problems . . . The sequence from small many-toed forms to large one-toed forms is completely absent in the fossil record. Eohippus, the earliest member of the horse evolution series, is completely unconnected by any sort of link to its presumed ancestors, the condylarths . . . The teeth of the animals found are either grazing or browsing types. There are no transitional types of teeth . . . Two modern-day horses (*Equus nevadenis* and *Equus occidentalis*) have been found in the same fossil stratum as Eohippus! This fact is fatal to the concept of horse evolution since horses were already horses before their supposed evolution."[481]

Finally, Huse quoted famed scientist (paleontologist) George Gaylord Simpson's assessment of the horse series:

"The uniform continuous transformation of Hyracotherium into Equus, so dear to the hearts of generations of textbook writers, never happened in nature."[482]

Shroeder pointed out that:

"Thomas Huxley (1825-1895), known as Darwin's bulldog . . . promoted a falsified fossil record that purportedly proved the smooth evolution of the modern horse."[483]

Baker Book House,1983) 105.
[481]Scott M. Huse, *The Collapse of Evolution*, 104, 106.
[482]George Gaylord Simpson, *Life of the Past*, Yale University Press, New Haven CT, 1953, p. 119 as cited by Scott M. Huse, The Collapse of Evolution, Grand Rapids MI (Baker Book House,1983) 106

Cornelius Hunter noted that from a strictly scientific perspective: "It would be just as reasonable to model the horse sequence simply as different species."[484]

What about Archaeopteryx?

Phillip Johnson explained the impact of archaeopteryx on the acceptance of evolutionary theory:

> "The discovery of archaeopteryx—an ancient bird with some strikingly reptilian features—was enough fossil confirmation in itself to satisfy many . . . *Archaeopteryx* ('old wing'), a fossil bird . . . was discovered soon after publication of *The Origin of Species*, and thus helped enormously to establish the credibility of Darwinism and to discredit skeptics like Agassiz . . . It is on the whole bird-like, with wings, feathers, and wishbone, but it has claws on its wings and teeth in its mouth. No modern bird has teeth, although some ancient ones did, and there is a modern bird, the hoatzin, which has claws. *Archaeopteryx* is an impressive mosaic. The question is whether it is proof of a reptile (dinosaur) to bird transition, or whether it is just one of those odd variants, like the contemporary duck-billed platypus, that have features resembling those of another class but are not transitional intermediates in the Darwinian sense."[485]

What about alleged human evolution?

Scott Huse described the basic creationist' interpretation of the fossil record regarding alleged human evolution:

---

[483]Gerald Schroeder, *The Science of God: The Convergence of Scientific and Biblical Wisdom,* New York (The Free Press, 1997) 9.

[484]Cornelius G. Hunter, *Darwin's God: Evolution and the Problem of Evil,* Grand Rapids MI (Brazos Press, 2001) 111.

[485]Phillip E. Johnson, *Darwin on Trial,* Downers Grove IL (InterVarsity Press, 1991) 49, 78.

"Creationists argue that the fossils cited by evolutionists do not represent stages of human evolution at all, but rather are derived from apes, men, or neither. They are not from animals intermediate between men and apes. There are many impressive museum exhibits throughout the world that claim to demonstrate human evolution. Although these exhibits are based upon extremely fragmentary evidences, they are nevertheless presented as well-established fact."[486]

Marvin Lubenow's assessment is informative:

"Another major line of evidence used to support the concept of human evolution is the fossil record. We have all seen pictures of the impressive sequence allegedly leading to modern humans . . . What is not generally known is that this sequence, impressive as it seems, is a very artificial and arbitrary arrangement because (1) some fossils are selectively excluded if they do not fit well into the evolutionary scheme; (2) some human fossils are arbitrarily downgraded to make them appear to be evolutionary ancestors when they are in fact true humans; and (3) some nonhuman fossils are upgraded to make them appear to be human ancestors."[487]

Geisler summed up some of the evidence:

"Further, some of the bones once widely touted as transitional species are now known not to have been, even by evolutionists. Piltdown Man, a basic form in science texts and museums for years, turned out to be a fraud. Nebraska Man was a reconstruction from one tooth, which turned out to be that of an extinct pig. Yet Nebraska Man was used as evidence in the Scopes Trial (1925) to support teaching evolution in public schools. The fossil evidence for Peking Man vanished. Some question its validity, based on

---

[486]Scott M. Huse, *The Collapse of Evolution*, 96-97.
[487]Marvin L. Lubenow, *Bones of Contention: A Creationist Assessment of Human Fossils*, Grand Rapids MI (Baker Book House, 1992) 21.

studies before the pieces of the bone disappeared. . . . Even some evolutionists believe Australopithecine was an orangutan. Not one primate fossil find to date that has been subjected to objective scientific scrutiny is a strong candidate for the human family tree."[488]

Vestigial organs

Allow me to show how evolutionists have been guilty of the very God of the gaps types of arguments that they accuse creationists of using. Claims concerning vestigial organs are a regular feature of books espousing evolution. These are supposed to be useless physical features, leftovers from evolutionary history.

Groothius explained:

"Supposedly the human body contains organs or structural remnants inherited from our animal predecessors that now serve no purpose. *The Structure of Man* (1895) by Ernst Wiedersheim listed eighty-six vestigial organs, but recent research has brought this into question . . . Losing a function is not the same as evolving entirely new functions (or new species from previous species). It rather indicates a degenerative form of evolution."[489]

In other word, alleged vestigial organs would only show devolution not evolution; the loss of function, not the emergence of new genetic information or function. And so Geisler added:

---

[488]Norman L. Geisler, *Baker Encyclopedia of Christian Apologetics*, Grand Rapids MI (Baker Books, 1999) 490.

[489]Douglass Groothuis, *Christian Apologetics: A Comprehensive Case for Biblical Faith*, Downers Grove IL (InterVarsity Press, 2011) 295-296.

"One might even say that an organ that has lost its function would not demonstrate that we are evolving, but devolving—losing some organs and abilities. This is the opposite of evolution."[490]

Vestigial organs do have a purpose

Evolutionist have filled incomplete scientific knowledge of the human body with their false evolutionary theories. But, the facts are against the theory of vestigial organs as science is increasingly showing.

A prime example has been the human appendix which was for a long time thought to be a useless remnant of evolution. Now, however, it is increasingly clear that the appendix is quite useful in helping fight disease. Jonathan Sarfati explained how science has shown purpose and function in many previously classified vestigial organs including the appendix:

"Evolutionists often argue that such things as flightless birds' small wings, pigs' toes, male nipples, legless lizards, the rabbit's digestive system, the human appendix, and hip bones and teeth in whales are useless and have no function. They claim these features are 'left-overs of evolution' and evidence for evolution. The 'vestigial' organ argument for evolution is an old chestnut, but it is not valid. First, it is impossible to prove that an organ is useless. The function may simply be unknown and its use may be discovered in the future. This has happened with more than 100 formerly alleged useless vestigial organs in humans, that are now known to be essential . . . It is now known that the human appendix contains lymphatic tissue and helps control bacteria entering the intestines. It

---

[490]Norman L. Geisler, *Baker Encyclopedia of Christian Apologetics*, 227.

functions in a similar way to the tonsils at the upper end of the alimentary canal, which are known to fight infections. Tonsils also were once thought to be useless organs."[491]

Cornelius Hunter added:

"In 1895 Ernst Wiedersheim published a list of eighty-six organs in the human body that he supposed to be vestigial. The vast majority of items on Wiedersheim's list are now known to be functioning organs . . . In 1981 zoologist S. R. Scadding analyzed Wiedersheim's claims and had difficulty finding a single item that was not functional, although some are so only in a minor way. He concluded that the so-called vestigial organs provide no evidence for evolutionary theory."[492]

Homologies: Common ancestors or common designer?

Homologies are similar features with similar functions in diverse creatures. These are claimed as proof of evolution. But it is better to ask if the homologous features are the result of common ancestry or of a common designer?

Hunter spoke to the argument that similarity among species proves evolution:

"The genetic code and the DNA molecule are often cited as homologies that provide strong evidence for evolution . . . [and] as evidence against the doctrine of divine creation. For example, Ridley claims that whereas the genetic code is preserved across species, it would not be if the species had been created independently. Apparently Ridley believes that if there is a Creator, then he is obliged to use different genetic codes for the different species . . . It seems

---

[491]Jonathan Sarfati, *Refuting Evolution 2*, 209-210.
[492]Cornelius G. Hunter, *Darwin's God,* 32.

for Ridley the notion of a 'common architect' does not support divine creation."[493]

Jonathan Wells countered such arguments:

"But biologists have known for a hundred years that homologous structures are often not produced by similar developmental pathways. And they have known for thirty years that they are often not produced by similar genes, either. So there is no empirically demonstrated mechanism to establish that homologies are due to common ancestry rather than common design."[494]

David Menton explained:

"Homology is an underlying similarity between different kinds of animals recognized by both evolutionists and creationists. All terrestrial vertebrates, for example, share a widespread similarity (homology) of body parts. Evolutionists insist that this similarity is the result of evolution from a common ancestor. Creationists, on the other hand, argue that this similarity reflects the theme of a common Creator and the need to meet similar biological requirements."[495]

The origin of Evolution

It is interesting to learn that Darwin's theory of evolution was not a novel scientific idea, but was rather a product of its time. Indeed, it owes as much to the social

---

[493]Cornelius G. Hunter, *Darwin's God,* 44-45.

[494]Jonathan Wells, *Survival of the Fakest, The American Spectator,* December 2000/ January 2001, p. 22 as quoted by Walt Brown, *In the Beginning: Compelling Evidence for Creation and the Flood,* Phoenix AZ (Center for Scientific Creation, 2008) 59.

[495]David N. Menton, *Vestigial Organs—Evidence for Evolution?,* chapter in *The New Answers Book 3,* Ken Ham General Editor, Green Forest AR (Master Books, 2009) 233.

sciences as to hard natural science. Hilary Rose explained:

> "It was Darwin's encounter later in the same month with Thomas Malthus's *Essay on the Principle of Population,* originally published in 1798, which was to prove decisive for *The Origin of Species.* Malthus's bleak message that the growth of human populations inexorably outstripped the available food supply was immensely read. Its thesis of the iron necessity of laissez-faire capitalism spoke directly both to the troubles of the times and to Darwin of a solution to his theoretical troubles . . .
>
> Central to understanding how this shared culture worked is the way in which Darwin uses the Malthusian theory of competition within human populations over scarce resources, and then more slowly explores and extends its utility in a biological context . . .
>
> Much to the irritation of the biologists' reading of *The Origin* as a hugely innovative and purely scientific text, the social historians see Darwin's theorizing as part and parcel of his times—the innovation lies in transferring a social theory into biological discourse."[496]

Rose proceeded to show how Darwin's theory adapted Malthus struggle of humans for scarce supplies into a racial struggle of human races for superiority:

> "Thus while Malthus divides his population between the innately Deserving Rich and the equately innately Underserving Lower and Middling Classes, Darwin's populations are racialized . . . A racialized version of Malthus offered him the solution; the 'races' are in conflict for scarce resources and the best adapted will survive . . . For Darwin this best fitted 'race' was naturally the British."[497]

---

[496]Hilary Rose, *Colonizing the Social Sciences,* chapter in *Alas, Poor Darwin: Arguments Against Evolutionary Psychology,* Edited by Hilary Rose & Steven Rose, New York (Harmony Books, 2000) 129, 130, 131.

If, as Rose has shown, Darwin was influenced in great measure by the social sciences, and Malthus in particular; evolutionary thought has been intensely trying to repay the favor by affecting the thought of virtually every other field of thought (think of Dennett's metaphor of evolution as the universal acid).

But museums prove evolution

Isn't it true that science museums are filled with evidence proving evolution to any reasonable mind? Consider this anecdotal response from scientist Gerald Schroeder:

"The magnificent Natural History Museum in London devotes an entire wing to demonstrating the fact of evolution. They show how pink daisies can evolve into blue daisies, how gray moths change into black moths, how over a mere few thousand years, a wide variety of cichlid fish species evolved in Lake Victoria. It is all impressive. Impressive, until you walk out and reflect upon that which they were able to document. Daisies remained daisies, moths remained moths, and cichlid fish remained cichlid fish. These changes are referred to as micro-evolution. In this exhibit, the museum's staff did not demonstrate a single unequivocal case in which life underwent a major gradual morphological change."[498]

---

[497]Hilary Rose, *Colonizing the Social Sciences*, 130-131.

[498] Gerald Schroeder, *The Science of God: The Convergence of Scientific and Biblical Wisdom,* New York (The Free Press, 1997) 31.

Section Five: Atheist's Arguments Against the Existence of God

Chapter 24: Is God Talk Coherent?

God as a mystery

Discussions in the debate between belief and unbelief will sometimes result in attacks on Christians for using words like "mystery," "mysteries," and "miracles" when contemplating the deep things of God.

Such language has been attacked as an alleged get out of jail free-card when beliefs defy a rational explanation. Kai Nielsen's comments are representative of such atheists' attacks: "Instead of being candid about their total incomprehension, believers use the evasive language of mystery."[499]

But are such attacks fair? How could there not be some area of mystery when finite beings are attempting to comprehend an infinite God and the majesties of His creation? The prophet Isaiah captured this idea:

> "As the heavens are higher than the earth, so are my ways higher than your ways and my thoughts than your thoughts" (Isaiah 55:9).

Paul Edwards was more even-handed on the issue when he showed that such talk about mysteries and miracles are not the exclusive property of believers:

---

[499]Kai Nielsen, *Atheism & Philosophy*, Amherst NY (Prometheus Books, 2005) 61.

"Those who insist that the super-ultimate why-question is meaningful do not usually deny that it very radically differs from *all* other meaningful why-questions. To mark the difference they occasionally refer to it by such labels as 'mystery' or 'miracle.' Thus Koestenbaum remarks that 'questions of this sort do not lead to answers but to a state of mind that appreciates the miracle of existence,' they call attention to 'the greatest of all mysteries.' Heidegger writes that the question 'is incommensurable with any other' . . . Calling the super-ultimate why-question a 'mystery' or a 'miracle' or 'incommensurable' or 'extraordinary' does not in any way remove the difficulty; it is just one way of acknowledging that there is one."[500]

Edwards added:

"The scientist Julian Huxley . . . also speaks of the 'basic and universal mystery—the mystery of existence in general . . . why does the world exist?'"[501]

Walters stated:

"The astronomer Carl Sagan . . . was perfectly comfortable with recognizing and embracing mystery. 'Our contemplations of the cosmos stir us,' he writes. 'There's a tingling in the spine, a catch in the voice, a faint sensation as if a distant memory of falling from a great height. We know that we are approaching the grandest of mysteries."[502]

The idea of mystery, then, is not the exclusive property of believers alone. Any review of scientific writings on cosmology and cosmogony abound in similar terminology. And why not? What is the problem with

[500]Paul Edwards, Why? *A Modern Introduction to Philosophy: Readings from Classical and Contemporary Sources,* Third Edition, Paul Edwards & Arthur Pap, Editors, New York, (The Free Press, 1973) 806.
[501]Paul Edward, *Why?,* 804.
[502]Kerry Walters, *Atheism,* 163.

admitting that there is much that is beyond our present comprehension, and perhaps will always be this side of eternity?

Defending the meaningfulness of "God talk"

Let us not consider another more frequently leveled attack on theism; the idea that the very notion of "God" (as a word or idea) is incomprehensible or incoherent.

It is important to note that there is often a difference between what professional philosophers mean by such claims versus how they are sometimes expressed at the popular level. Less informed atheists sometimes overstate their case to suggest that any so-called God-talk is meaningless. Kai Nielsen corrected this false claim:

> "The concept of God is not so utterly incoherent as to vitiate religious belief . . . In arguing that the concept of God is incoherent, I am not claiming that 'God' is utterly meaningless . . . Thus it is plainly a mistake to say that God-talk is meaningless."[503]

Nevertheless, some atheists still attempt to claim that all discussions about God are meaningless. To them, we ask, if statements about God are meaningless, how is it possible that atheists can fill books hundreds of pages long discussing the ostensibly meaningless concept? Again, if God talk is so incoherent, how is that most of the people who have ever lived have found "God" to be an essential and meaningful aspect of their lives?

---

[503]Kai Nielsen, *Atheism & Philosophy*, 119-120, 121

Skeptical attacks on the meaningfulness of "God Talk"

Timothy Robinson addressed the claim that 'God talk' is incoherent:

"Disproofs of God's existence, like the proofs of it, can be divided into *a priori* and *a posteriori* arguments. The *a priori* argument in this instance claims that it is not possible for God to exist because the traditional philosophical conception of God is incoherent. What this means is either that some of the attributes ascribed to God contradict one another, or that one of these attributes is self-contradictory . . . The believer's response is that . . . it is possible to define the traditional attributes in other ways that are not self-contradictory and do not conflict with one another, and these coherent definitions capture everything that one is required to believe about God. I am going to assume here that all the arguments which claim that the concept of God is incoherent can be dealt with in that manner—that there are ways of understanding God's attributes that do violence neither to the laws of logic nor to religious tradition."[504]

Despite Mr. Robinson's defense of the reasonableness of 'God talk,' there has been much ink spilled by skeptics trying to prove otherwise. This can be traced back at least as far as the Scottish philosopher David Hume. Kerry Walters explained:

"David Hume famously prepared the way for the claim that religious discourse is meaningless in his *An Enquiry Concerning Human Understanding* when he expressly singled it out as nonsense: 'If we take in our hand any volume of divinity or school metaphysics, for instance; let

---

[504]Timothy A. Robinson, *God,* from the Hackett Readings in Philosophy series, Indianapolis IN (Hackett Publishing Company, Inc, 1996) Introduction, xix.

us ask. Does it contain any abstract reasoning concerning quantity or number? No. Does it contain any experimental reasoning concerning matter of fact and existence? No. Commit it then to the flames: for it can contain nothing but sophistry and illusion' (Hume 1955, p. 173). For Hume, only those propositions or statements which express either the relations between ideas ('abstract reasoning') or facts ('experimental reasoning') make any sense . . . Propositions that fail to meet Hume's two criteria have no truth value, but instead are illusory, or meaningless."[505]

Hume's fork

This was later to be called Hume's fork since it separated knowledge into two types; those known by reason to be necessarily true (i.e. mathematical equations etc.), and those that can be proven or disproven empirically. Donald Palmer explained:

"Hume's philosophy began with a revival of Leibniz's analytic/synthetic distinction, or in Hume's words, a distinction between 'relations of ideas' and 'matters of fact' . . . What Hume was claiming was that there are basically only three categories of analysis. Given any proposition whatsoever, that proposition is either ANALYTIC, SYNTHETIC, or NONSENSE."[506]

Palmer further explained how Hume's position related to the question of God's existence:

"Now, with Hume's method in hand, if we turn to some of the traditional philosophical topics, like GOD, WORLD, and SELF, we arrive at some pretty startling conclusions . . . Hume believed it was impossible to trace the idea of God

---

[505]Kerry Walters, *Atheism,* 82.

[506]Donald Palmer, *Looking at Philosophy: The Unbearable Heaviness of Philosophy Made Lighter,* Second Edition, Mountain View CA (Mayfield Publishing Company, 1994) 180-181, 182.

back to sense data. He said, 'Our ideas reach no further than our experience. We have no experience of divine attributes and operations. I need not conclude my syllogism. You can draw the inference yourself.' So, although Hume didn't actually say so, his method seems to imply that the idea of God is vacuous and that statements about God are literally nonsense."[507]

But as with all such criteria, it is important to ask how the test applied to itself.

That is, how does Hume's fork fare under its own criterion? Alan Rhoda considered this question:

"But what about Hume's Fork itself? It too is an object of "human reason or enquiry." Accordingly, it too must either be a relation of ideas or a matter of fact. Which is it? It does not seem to be a relation of ideas, since its denial does not obviously entail a contradiction. Nor does it seem to be a matter of fact, since Hume presents the Fork as though it were an *a priori* truth knowable independently of experience. Hume's Fork is, therefore, a *prima facie* counterexample to itself. Given the importance of the Fork in Hume's thought, this suggests that there's something amiss at the very foundations of Hume's philosophy."[508]

Rhoda made clear that although Hume's Fork may be helpful in clarifying language, it cannot be pressed too far, at least for skeptics, since while taking it as a binding rule may well dispense with God talk, yet, at the same time it dispenses with itself!

In our next chapter, we shall see the fruition of Hume's ideas about the meaningfulness of 'God talk" among the movement known as Logical Positivism.

---

[507]Donald Palmer, *Looking at Philosophy,* 185-186.
[508]Alan Rhoda, *What's Wrong With Hume's Fork*, February 3, 2006, at web address: http://www.alanrhoda.net/blog/2006/02/whats-wrong-with-humes-fork.html

Chapter 25: Logical Positivism and the Verifiability Criterion

Concerning the existence of God, there have been philosophers who have tried to end the debate before it even starts by claiming that theological and metaphysical propositions are simply non-sense.

Michael Martin quoted the oft-repeated quip of Bradlaugh:

> "For example, Charles Bradlaugh, a well-known nineteenth-century atheistic orator and writer, argued: 'The Atheist does not say 'there is no God,' but he says: 'I know not what you mean by God; I am without the idea of God; the word 'God' is to me a sound conveying no clear or distinct affirmation.'"[509]

The irony, of course, is that Bradlaugh's statement was quoted approvingly by Michael Martin in his 500 page book discussing this "God" that has "no clear or distinct affirmation."

The Logical Positivist movement

Roy Varghese explained the logical positivist's program:

> "A little background information will be of value here. Logical positivism, as some might remember, was the philosophy introduced by a European group called the Vienna Circle in the early 1920s and popularized by A. J. Ayer in the English-speaking world with his 1936 work *Language, Truth, and Logic*. According to the logical positivists, the only meaningful statements were those capable of being verified through sense experience or true

---

[509]Michael Martin, *Atheism: A Philosophical Justification*, Philadelphia PA (Temple University Press, 1990) 41.

simply by virtue of their form and meaning of the words used . . . At the heart of logical positivism was the verification principle, the claim that the meaning of a proposition consists in its verification. The result was that the only meaningful statements were those used in science, logic, or mathematics. Statements in metaphysics, religion, aesthetics, and ethics were literally meaningless, because they could not be verified by empirical methods. They were neither valid nor invalid. Ayer said that it was just as absurd to be an atheist as to be theist, since the statement 'God exists' simply has no meaning."[510]

Kerry Walters showed how the logical positivists were carrying on in the tradition of Hume's Fork:

"Inspired by Hume, proponents of the twentieth-century philosophical school known as logical positivism proposed a theory of meaning based on verifiability. According to this model, statements may possess formal meaning, factual meaning, and cognitive meaning. A necessary and sufficient condition for formal meaning is that the statement be either analytic or self-contradictory (this corresponds to Hume's first standard).

A necessary and sufficient condition for factual meaning is that the statement can be at least in principle empirically verified or falsified (Hume's second standard). Any statement which meets either of these two meaning standards thereby possesses cognitive meaning, is either true or false, and deserves to be taken seriously. Any other statement is neither true nor false but nonsensical and good only for the flames."[511]

---

[510]Roy Abraham Varghese, *Preface,* p. 12 of Antony Flew, *There is a God: How the World's Most Notorious Atheist Changed His Mind,* New York (HarperCollins/HarperOne, 2007)

[511]Kerry Walters, *Atheism: A Guide for the Perplexed,* New York (The Continuum International Publishing Group Inc, 2010) 82-83.

Not surprisingly, God talk did not fare any better under the logical positivist's verifiability criterion than it did under Hume's fork as Kerry Walters explained:

> "Now propositions about God—such as 'God exists'—fail to exhibit either formal or factual meaning, and therefore lack cognitive meaning as well. They're neither analytic . . . or tautologous nor self-contradictory. So there's no way to establish their truth or falsity on purely formal grounds. Additionally, there is no way to verify or falsify the proposition by appealing to experience, because users of the word 'God' mean by it a transcendent—that is nonempirical—being. Consequently, God discourse is meaningless. Strictly speaking, one can neither assert nor deny the existence of God, because all such claims are gibberish."[512]

So there it is all nice and tidy. The verbal murder of God. That is, the logical positivists didn't have to waste time making rational arguments concerning the existence of God; they just defined any such talk as nonsense.

The fading logical positivist movement

In contrast to its early heady days, the logical positivist's and their criterion of meaning have fallen out of favor amongst most philosophers, although its ideas are still esteemed in some circles. Because some atheists still appeal to the arguments of the logical positivists as decisive against belief in God, we shall take the opportunity to respond.

One atheist philosopher that has sympathies toward the verifiability criterion is Kai Nielsen. Here, Nielsen

---

[512]Kerry Walters, *Atheism,* 83.

discussed the views of the logical positivist leader A. J. Ayer:

> "In the twentieth century with certain analytic philosophers the question has come to the fore about whether these key religious utterances have any truth-value at all. A. J. Ayer defending the modern variety of empiricism called 'logical empiricism' argued in his *Language, Truth, and Logic* (London, 1935) that such key religious utterances are devoid of cognitive reasoning . . . In a well known passage Ayer comments that it is very important not to confuse his view with agnosticism or atheism, for as he puts it:
> 'And our view that all utterances about the nature of God are nonsensical, so far from being identical with, or even lending any support to, either of these familiar contentions [theism or atheism], is actually incompatible with them. For if the assertion that there is a god is nonsensical, then the atheist's assertion that there is no god is equally nonsensical'
> The central point Ayer is making is that such religious utterances do not assert anything and thus they can neither be doubted, believed, nor even asserted to be false. With such considerations pushed to the front, the key question becomes whether such religious utterances have any informative content at all."[513]

The logical positivists seemed to have wanted their cake and eat it too. What I mean is that on the one hand, they were claiming some sort of neutrality on the God question. Their criterion of meaning doesn't technically address the reality of God's existence. Yet, to say about something (like God) that it is nonsense *is* to say

---

[513]Kai Nielsen, *Atheism & Philosophy*, Amherst NY (Prometheus Books, 2005) 107.

something about it, which is hardly neutral. No wonder some atheists still appeal to the logical positivist's ideas.

Indeed, Warnock suggested that rather than being truly neutral, the logical positivists did have an agenda:

> "But first, it has to be remembered that most advocates of the so-called Verification Principle were by no means disinterested. They were not merely concerned to analyze and to clarify the concept of meaning, but also to 'eliminate metaphysics.'"[514]

So much for a dispassionate search for the truth!

Does the verifiability criterion pass its own test of meaningfulness?

As with Hume's fork, we shall see that the Achilles' heel of the logical positivist's verifiability criterion is that it does not pass its own test of meaningfulness. N. T. Wright explained:

> "Think, for instance, of the standard reply to the logical positivists' principle that we can only count as 'knowledge' that which could in principle be falsified; *how might that principle itself be falsified?*"[515]

Weaknesses of the verification criterion

Warnock explained the problems that led to the downfall of the verifiability criterion as a live option among scholars:

---

[514]G. J. Warnock, *Verification and the Use of Language* reprinted in *A Modern Introduction to Philosophy: Readings from Classical and Contemporary Sources,* Third Edition, Paul Edwards & Arthur Pap, Editors, New York, (The Free Press, 1973) 781.

[515]Nicholas Thomas Wright, *The Resurrection of the Son of God,* Minneapolis MN (Fortress Press, 2003) 22.

"What, then, are we to do with all those meaningful sentences which have no concern whatever with truth or falsity? Cleary there is an enormous number of such sentences. There are imperative sentences, used (mainly) to ask questions. There are sentences used as prayers; to make promises; to give verdicts; to express decisions; to pass moral judgments; or to make proposals. It is nonsensical to ask of a question, an order, a prayer, or a proposal, whether it is true of false."[516]

Ewing added his criticisms of the logical positivist's verifiability criterion:

"Now I should have thought the first duty of any advocate of a verification theory of meaning would be to inquire how his theory itself was to be verified . . . How could we verify the statement that all meaningful statements are verifiable? The first difficulty is that it is a universal proposition and therefore can never be conclusively established merely be experience. The statement that all meaningful statements are verifiable is therefore not itself verifiable. *It follows that if it is true it is meaningless.* But a sentence cannot possibly be both true and meaningless. Therefore the sentence in question cannot be true, but must be either meaningless or false."[517]

The emperor's verifiability criterion has no clothes on!

It seems amazing, then, that the brilliant philosophers and linguists that formed the infamous Vienna Circle, and formulated the ideas of the logical

---

[516]G. J. Warnock, *Verification and the Use of Language* , 782.

[517]A. C. Ewing, *Meaninglessness* reprinted in *A Modern Introduction to Philosophy: Readings from Classical and Contemporary Sources,* Third Edition, Paul Edwards & Arthur Pap, Editors, New York, (The Free Press, 1973) 771-772.

positivist's movement, could have had such a blind spot about the inherent weakness of their own program.

In fact, A. J. Ayer showed that Ludwig Wittgenstein himself was aware of the problem:

> "To adopt this standpoint is to follow the example of Wittgenstein, who at the end of his *Tractatus Logico-Philosophicus* asserts that the propositions contained in it are nonsensical. They are means for enabling the sympathetic reader to 'see the world rightly.' Having profited by them he must discard them. He must throw away the ladder after he has climbed up on it . . . But if you admit that your propositions are nonsensical, what ground have you given anybody for accepting the conclusions that you deduce from them. If we admit that the proposition in which we attempt to formulate our criterion of significance is nonsensical, does not our whole demonstration of the impossibility of metaphysics collapse?"[518]

So Wittgenstein, fully aware of the underlying philosophical problem with logical positivism, basically said "never mind."[519]

Such philosophical sophistry reminds me of Arthur Pap's comment that "Nowhere is the temptation to talk nonsense parading as profundity as great as in philosophy."[520] Kai Nielsen agreed: "He remembers with

[518]A. J. Ayer, *Demonstration of the Impossibility of Metaphysics* reprinted in *A Modern Introduction to Philosophy: Readings from Classical and Contemporary Sources,* Third Edition, Paul Edwards & Arthur Pap, Editors, New York, (The Free Press, 1973) 768.
[519]This reaction reminds me of the skit on the Saturday Night Live program with Emily Littela (played by Gilda Radner), giving commentary on the news segment, ranting and raving about a subject, only to have it pointed out that she had heard wrong (i.e. "What's all this talk about natural racehorses?" when the real subject was natural resources!). Her reaction, when corrected, was always "never mind." Essentially, this is what Wittgenstein did in his book *Tractatus Logico-Philosophicus.*

a sense of its appropriateness Hobbes's remark that there is nothing so absurd that some philosopher has not said it."[521]

At any rate, Ayer raised a typical criticism of the logical positivist verifiability criterion, that the criterion fails its own test and is thus meaningless. But Ayer valiantly tried to revive the corpse.

Can the verifiability criterion be rescued?

Ayer attempted saving the verifiability criterion by finding an independent method of confirmation for the results of the criterion. Ayer explained his proposition:

> "There are some prima facie propositions which by universal agreement are given as significant and some expressions which are agreed to be meaningless. Trusting our criterion if it accepts the former class and rejects the latter, we apply it to such doubtful cases as that of the propositions of metaphysics, and if they fail to satisfy it we pronounce them nonsensical . . . We should lose faith in our criterion when we found that it also admitted the significance of expressions which were universally agreed to be meaningless."[522]

Ayer attempted to save the criterion by comparing the findings of the criterion with commonly accepted wisdom, the latter adding support to the former. But public opinion cannot come to the rescue of bad logic or poorly reasoned philosophical arguments.

---

[520]Arthur Pap, *A Modern Introduction to Philosophy: Readings from Classical and Contemporary Sources,* Third Edition, Paul Edwards & Arthur Pap, Editors, New York, (The Free Press, 1973) 755.

[521]Kai Nielsen, *Atheism & Philosophy*, Amherst NY (Prometheus Books, 2005) 252.

[522]A. J. Ayer, *Demonstration of the Impossibility of Metaphysics,* 768-769.

A higher standard and begging the question

I am willing to grant the difficulty of asking someone to believe in God (or in other metaphysical propositions) because of the fact that it (the God Hypothesis) is empirically unverifiable in nature. Indeed, there are many metaphysical claims that I am skeptical of as well. I agree, therefore, that metaphysical claims like "God exists," demand strong rational support.

Nonetheless, even the atheist George Smith, no friend of theism, conceded the death of the logical positivist's arguments against the coherence of the concept of God:

> "The meaning of 'god' . . . has been a center of controversy in modern philosophical thought. A. J. Ayer, in his famous *Language, Truth, and Logic* (published in 1935), argued that 'to say that 'God exists' is to make a metaphysical utterance which cannot be either true or false. And . . . no sentence which purports to describe the nature of a transcendent god can possess any literal significance.' *The principle on which Ayer based his rejection of theology is now considered to be defunct.*"[523]

John Hick's eschatological verification

One interesting response to the logical positivist' meaningfulness criterion was John Hick's argument that belief in God actually meets the verifiability criterion since it can in principle be proven in the future:

> "Hick has devoted much effort to rebut the challenges of philosophers who maintain that belief in God is one or other of these things—meaningless, self-contradictory,

---

[523]George H. Smith, *Atheism: The Case Against God,* Amherst NY (Prometheus Books, 1979, 1989) 30.

false or improbable. Thus he has argued . . . accepting the Verifiability Principle, Hick insists that statements asserting the existence of God are in principle—not indeed by observations in this life, but by 'eschatological' observations, i.e., observations carried out in a life after death."[524]

Kerry Walters summed up the consensus reaction to Hick's argument among philosophers:

"Most famously (and bizarrely, in the eyes of many), John Hick argued that religious claims are 'eschatologically' verifiable—that is, their truth or falsity are verifiable or falsifiable after death."[525]

Martin clarified Hick's position:

"One of the most interesting attempts to meet the verificationist' challenge is an argument from John Hick. Hick argues that although no observation in this life could confirm the statement 'God exists' (G) more than its negation, one could imagine postmortem observations that would. This Hick calls *eschatological verification*."[526]

The important distinction, from a philosophical perspective, is that although the actual verification could occur only after death, for the sake of argument, the verification is imaginable in this life. Interestingly enough, says Hick, religious belief cannot be disconfirmed since if it turns out to be wrong, there will be nobody there to disconfirm it:

---

[524]Paul Edwards, *A Modern Introduction to Philosophy: Readings from Classical and Contemporary Sources,* Third Edition, Paul Edwards & Arthur Pap, Editors, New York, (The Free Press, 1973) 392.
[525]Kerry Walters, *Atheism,* 83.
[526]Michael Martin, *Atheism,* 66.

"Although Hick argues that Christian theism can be confirmed by postmortem experience, he maintains that it cannot be disconfirmed. He says that Christian theism may be false but '*that* it is false can never be a fact which anyone has experientially verified."[527]

Hick's philosophical argument is correct as far as it goes. Nevertheless, whether faith in God is meaningful is something we want to address on this side of eternity. According to the Bible (1 Thessalonians 4:13-18), however, at least one generation will be able to get their eschatological verification on planet earth when Jesus Christ returns to rule and reign at His second coming.

[527]Michael Martin, *Atheism,* 66-67.

Chapter 26: Falsification, a Gardener, a Unicorn, & Poy

The atheistic falsifiability challenge

Atheists challenge believers by asking them what it would take to falsify their beliefs. That is, what fact or event would prove theism wrong (falsify it)? The suggestion is that believers are so blindly committed to their beliefs that nothing, no matter how convincing, would lead them to abandon their belief in God. This seems to be a strange argument since people abandon Christian faith, and indeed all religious faith, all the time.

Perhaps the only definitive way to falsify the existence of God would be to go to heaven and see who is home?[528] Indeed, one would have to be omniscient (all-knowing) to know with certainty whether God exists. That is, you would have to be God in order verify or falsify God's existence!

Nevertheless, Kai Nielsen challenged believers and unbelievers alike to consider what would have to happen to shake their belief or non-belief in God:

> "Try this little experiment for yourselves: if you think of yourselves as believers, what *conceivable* turn of observable events would make you say you were mistaken or probably mistaken in holding that belief; and if you

---

[528]Apparently, Sartre has already checked since he unequivocally proclaimed "There is nothing in heaven." Jean Paul-Sartre, *The Humanism of Existentialism*, as included in *Existentialism: Basic Writings*, Second Edition, Charles Guignon & Derk Pereboom Editors, Indianapolis/Cambridge (Hackett Publishing Company, Inc., 2001) 293.

think of yourself as an atheist or as an agnostic try this experiment on yourself: what *conceivable* turn of observable events, if only you were to observe them, would make you say you were mistaken or probably mistaken in denying or doubting that it is true or probably true that there is a God? If the God you believe in, deny, or doubt, is anything like the nonanthropomorphic God I have just characterized, I predict you will not be able to answer that question. But if this is so, and I think it is, then your alleged God-statements 'There is a God' or 'God created the world' are devoid of factual significance."[529]

As Nielsen explained, the argument works both ways. For while theism, strictly speaking, is not falsifiable, neither is atheism. So if theism is consequently judged as being "devoid of factual significance," then consistency demands that atheism also be judged as equally "devoid of factual significance"!

Paul Edwards referred to the similar challenge of Antony Flew:

"According to Flew—and this is a view shared by quite a few other contemporary philosophers—a statement is not really intelligible, it has no factual content if it is compatible with any conceivable state of affairs."[530]

Indeed, Flew made this challenge during a 1948 debate as described by Louis Pojman:

"In this 1948 Oxford University Symposium, [Antony] Flew challenges theists to state the conditions under which they would give up their faith, for, he contends, unless one can state what would falsify one's belief, one does not have

[529]Kai Nielsen, *Atheism & Philosophy*, 155. He makes the same argument on page 76
[530]Paul Edwards, *A Modern Introduction to Philosophy*, 397. Of course, this was before Flew changed his position and accepted the existence of God.

a meaningful belief. If nothing could count against the belief, it does not make a serious assertion, for serious truth claims must be ready to undergo rational scrutiny."[531]

More recently, Flew turned this argument around to all his former atheist colleagues:

"I therefore put to my former fellow-atheists the simple central question: 'What would have to occur to constitute for you a reason to at least consider the existence of a superior mind?'"[532]

Invisible garden parable

While still a leading atheist, Antony Flew used the parable of an invisible gardener to illustrate how God-belief was not falsifiable, and was therefore, meaningless:

"Let us begin with a parable. It is a parable developed from a tale told by John Wisdom in his haunting and revelatory article 'Gods.' Once upon a time two explorers came upon a clearing in the jungle. In the clearing were growing many flowers and many weeds. One explorer says, 'Some gardener must tend this plot.' The other disagrees, 'There is no gardener.' So they pitch their tents and set a watch. No gardener is ever seen. 'But perhaps he is an invisible gardener.' So they set up a barbed-wire fence. They electrify it. They patrol it with bloodhounds. (For they remember how H. G. Wells' *The Invisible Man* could be both smelt and touched though he could not be seen.) But no shrieks ever suggested that some intruder has received a shock. No movements of the wire ever betray an invisible climber. The bloodhounds never give cry. Yet still the Believer is not convinced. 'But there is a gardener,

[531]Louis P. Pojman, *Philosophy: The Quest for Truth*, Sixth Edition, New York. Oxford (Oxford University Press, 2006) 143-144.
[532]Antony Flew, *There is a God: How the World's Most Notorious Atheist Changed His Mind*, New York (HarperCollins/HarperOne, 2007) 88.

invisible, intangible, insensible to electric shocks, a gardener who has no scent and makes no sound, a gardener whom comes secretly to look after the garden which he loves.' At last the Sceptic despairs. 'But what remains of your original assertion? Just how does what you call an invisible, intangible, eternally elusive gardener differ from an imaginary gardener or even from no gardener at all?"[533]

Morgan described a similar illustration by Bertrand Russell:

"Bertrand Russell's parable of the celestial teapot . . . For those unfamiliar with it, Russell's parable compares the premise of God to the premise of a Chinese teapot revolving around the sun in an elliptical orbit somewhere between the Earth and Mars. It is too small to be detected by our most powerful telescopes, yet those who believe in its presence consider it an 'intolerable presumption on the part of human reason to doubt it' . . . It is no easier to disprove God than to disprove Russell's celestial teapot."[534]

The invisible unicorn at the skeptic's summer camp

One further story illustrates this same essential atheistic argument about falsifiability and faith.

There was a summer camp in Minnesota (and other locations) set up by skeptics for their children as an alternative to religious-based summer camps. Dawkins described one of the activities of these camps:

"A philosophical favourite is the invisible, intangible, inaudible unicorn, disproof of which is attempted yearly by

---

[533]Louis P. Pojman, *Philosophy,* 144.
[534]Timothy Morgan, *Thank God for Atheists: How the Greatest Skeptics Led Me to Faith,* Eugene OR (Harvest House Publishers, 2015) 205.

the children at Camp Quest . . . Camp Quest . . . is run by secular humanists, and the children are encouraged to think skeptically for themselves."[535]

I suspect that this exercise was inspired by Antony Flew's gardener parable. The children were to go into the woods to find an "invisible, intangible, inaudible unicorn." Obviously, they would quickly realize that such a creature could not be found (even if it existed).

The goal was that the children would see how ridiculous and superstitious it was to believe in an invisible creature roaming the woods, and by extension how ridiculous it is to believe in an invisible God.

But the problem with the exercise is that it is not a fair comparison. For while there is absolutely no evidence for the existence of the invisible unicorn (or the invisible gardener, or the celestial teapot), *there is* compelling and weighty evidence in support of the existence of God.

Antony Flew's conversion to belief in the invisible gardener

Indeed, the author of the invisible gardener parable, Antony Flew, one of the twentieth centuries' leading atheist voices, became persuaded that the evidence *does* support belief in God. He described his conversion to theism in his book *There is a God: How the World's Most Notorious Atheist Changed His Mind.* "In brief, as the title says, I now believe there is a God!"[536]

Kerry Walters explained:

---

[535]Richard Dawkins, *The God Delusion*, New York (Houghton Mifflin Company, 2006) 53.
[536]Antony Flew, *There is a God*, 1.

"British philosopher Antony Flew, one of the most perceptive atheists of the late twentieth century, underwent an intellectual conversion in 2004. Believing that honest thinkers must always 'follow the argument where it leads,' Flew moved from an overt denial of God's existence to a rather cerebral version of deism. The move was prompted by his conclusion that the existence and complexity of the universe as well as the origin of life are inexplicable in the absence of a divine Creator. Flew is clear that the God he now believes in isn't theistic, and that he in no way can be called a Christian. Instead, his deity is an intelligent but impersonal First Cause."[537]

It is understandable that Flew's rejection of atheism caused great consternation among atheists. You can almost hear the trauma in Walter's begrudging description. He tried to soften the blow by pointing out that Flew had not converted to a full-blown Christian theism (whew!), yet deism *is* nonetheless a type of theism, and that's that.

Walters further explained some of the specific issues that were instrumental in Flew's conversion from atheism to God-belief:

"Flew writes that there are three questions which he found increasingly inescapable—why does nature obey laws? How did conscious purposeful life arise from matter? Why is there anything at all instead of nothing?—and that the more he thought about them, the more persuaded he became that they could only be answered by postulating an intelligent designer."[538]

Walters then described the reaction of atheists to Flew's conversion to theism:

---

[537]Kerry Walters, *Atheism,* 32.
[538]Kerry Walters, *Atheism,* 40.

"Predictably, Flew's conversion has dismayed his erstwhile fellow atheists. Responses have ranged from reasoned rebuttals to rather hysterical charges that Flew is in his dotage. In response, Flew defends himself by posing a somewhat barbed challenge to his former fellow atheists: 'What would have to occur or to have occurred to constitute for you a reason to at least consider the existence of a superior mind?'"[539]

Flew's challenge to his former atheistic comrades is instructive. I very much appreciate the honest assessment of Kerry Walters by conceding that atheists, no less than theists, have a problem with what would count to falsify their beliefs:

"An Atheist operating from a naturalistic worldview probably can't in all honesty imagine what Flew wants him to—that is, a reason to take God-belief seriously—because his worldview doesn't allow for even the possibility of such a thing . . . Even if God Almighty were to appear before him and announce Himself, the atheist would probably chalk the experience up to a psychotic episode."[540]

Kai Nielsen and the 'god' Poy

Kai Nielsen offered an extended metaphor supposed to illustrate the fallacy of God belief:

"Suppose I ask you to believe in Poy, an utterly nonsensical term, a made-up word of mine. But I can't tell you what Poy is. You can't in that circumstance, no matter how much you want to, believe in Poy or have faith in Poy. To do that, you would have to have some understanding of what Poy is. Now what I'm trying to argue is when you really think through to what God is supposed to be, you will see that you have no more understanding of God,

---

[539]Kerry Walters, *Atheism,* 32.
[540]Kerry Walters, *Atheism,* 33-34.

except as a familiarity in the language, than you have an understanding of Poy. There's no way of conceptually identifying God that isn't equally problematic."[541]

As much as I appreciate Kai Nielsen's effort, I do not think his analogy of Poy represents the true situation that theists, and particularly Christians, are in.

That is, there are simply no reasons for believing in the existence of Poy (sorry if that offends any Poyians!). The case for the existence of God, on the other hand, has much to commend it. The classic arguments for the existence of God are powerful indeed, and have been persuasive for most of the people who have ever lived.

The existence of the universe itself cries out for a creator. We can know much about such a God. For instance, that He is an ancient and likely eternal being, that He is powerful if not omnipotent; and that He is very intelligent if not omniscient.

Further, Christians contend that this creator God has actually communicated to man; this revelation is the Judeo-Christian Bible, and as such greatly informs us of our Creator. If Kai Nielsen ever comes across a revelation from Poy which is supported by great public miracles, do please let us know!

Van Doren's challenge to supernatural revelation of God

Like Nielsen, Atheist Carl Van Doren was critical of the idea of the Bible as revelation from God and asked:

---

[541]J. P. Moreland, & Kai Nielsen, *Does God Exist?: The Debate Between Theists & Atheists*, Amherst NY (Prometheus Books, 1993) 54.

"Suppose a god did exist, and suppose he did communicate his will to any of his creatures. What man among them could comprehend that language? What man could take the dictation? And what man could overwhelmingly persuade his fellows that he had been selected and that they must accept him as authentic?"[542]

I confess that these kinds of questions from atheists baffle me. Does not Van Doren understand that Christians believe that God is almighty in power? If God can create the universe, and man in it, certainly it is a small thing for Him to effectively communicate with His creatures. Likewise, it remains but a small thing for God to authenticate the message of His servants through signs, miracles, and wonders.

When God called Moses to be his spokesman and to lead the Israelites, Moses asked the Lord: "What if they do not believe me or listen to me and say, 'The Lord did not appear to you?"(Exodus 4:1). The Lord responded by giving Moses the ability to do three powerful miracles (Exodus 4:2-9). "'This, said the Lord, 'is so that they may believe that the Lord . . . has appeared to you'" (Exodus 4:5).

[542]Carl Van Doren, *Why I Am Unbeliever* in Christopher Hitchens, *The Portable Atheist: Essential Readings for the Nonbeliever*, Philadelphia PA (De Capo Press, 2007) 140.

Chapter 27: Are God's Attributes Contradictory?

It is typical to hear theism attacked as being incoherent. Often, it is asserted that the traditional attributes ascribed to God are either contradictory or incoherent in themselves.

For instance, some have argued that the idea of a being (God) existing without a physical body is nonsensical. The concept of a spiritual being is viewed as an oxymoron. Antony Flew showed that such attacks have receded in response to recent scholarship among theologians and philosophers:

> "In *God and Philosophy* and later publications, I argued that the concept of God was not coherent because it presupposed the idea of an incorporeal omnipresent Spirit. My rationale was fairly straightforward. As we understand it in ordinary meanings and corresponding usage, a person is a creature with flesh and blood. In this respect, the expression 'person without a body' seemed nonsensical . . . Although formidable, this critique has been credibly addressed by theists. Since the 1980s and 1990s, there has been a renaissance of theism among analytic philosophers. Many of these thinkers have done extensive studies on the attributes traditionally attributed to God . . . Two thinkers, Thomas Tracy and Brian Leftow, have systematically responded to the challenge of defending the coherence of the idea of an 'incorporeal omnipresent Spirit.' While Tracy addresses the question of how a bodiless agent can be identified, Leftow attempts to show both why a divine being must be outside space and time and how a bodiless being can act in the universe."[543]

---

[543]Antony Flew, *There is a God: How the World's Most Notorious Atheist Changed His Mind*, New York (HarperCollins/HarperOne, 2007) 148-149.

Coherence of God's attributes and the stone paradox

Almost everyone has heard the riddle that seeks to cast doubt on the existence of God. Kerry Walters explained:

> "A simple way of illustrating the second strategy of a divine impossibility argument—showing that in exercising an attribute God contradicts the attribute—is to recall a question that most first year philosophy students encounter: Can God make a rock too heavy for God to pick up? On the surface, the question seems silly. But it gestures at a more serious puzzle: can God perform an act which entails God's limitation?"[544]

Victor Stenger called this the Paradox of Omnipotence:

1. "Either God can create a stone that he cannot lift, or he cannot create a stone that he cannot lift.
2. If God can create a stone that he cannot lift, then he is not omnipotent.
3. If God cannot create a stone that he cannot lift, then he is not omnipotent.
4. Therefore, God is not omnipotent."[545]

---

[544]Kerry Walters, *Atheism: A Guide for the Perplexed*, New York (The Continuum International Publishing Group Inc, 2010) 79-80.

[545]Michael Martin & Ricki Monnier, eds, *The Impossibility of God*, Amherst New York (Prometheus Books, 2003) 49-60 as cited by Victor J. Stenger, *God the Failed Hypothesis: How Science Shows That God Does Not Exist*, Amherst New York (Prometheus Books, 2007) 33.

Theistic response to the stone paradox

There are several points to offer in a theistic response to this seeming paradox. Douglass Groothius showed the weakness of this challenge:

> "The famous 'paradox of the stone' claims that the divine attribute of omnipotence is self-contradictory. This objection is usually posed as a question: Can God make a stone so heavy that God cannot lift it? (A similar, nontheological question is, "What happens when the irresistible force meets the immovable object?) . . . This dilemma is fueled by confusion concerning omnipotence and logic. Omnipotence cannot mean the ability to do anything, irrespective of logical coherence. As Aquinas put it, God's power only pertains to actualizing logically possible states of affairs; it does not apply to actualizing logically impossible conditions. God cannot make a square circle, simply because the very idea is contradictory and thus cannot possibly be initiated. Likewise, for God to create something he could not lift would be a contradiction, and contradictions cannot possibly attain."[546]

In his fictional work, John Perry had his character Cohen make the same point:

> "When we say that God is omnipotent, we mean God can perform any act or task that makes sense. We don't mean that God can make something that is both round and square, or can make two and two add up to five, or anything like that."[547]

So, to say that God is omnipotent does not mean to say that He can do anything, but only those things that

---

[546]Douglass Groothuis, *Christian Apologetics: A Comprehensive Case for Biblical Faith*, Downers Grove IL (InterVarsity Press, 2011) 197.

[547]John Perry, *Dialogue on Good, Evil, and the Existence of God*, 146.

are possible. There are in fact several things that God
cannot do; He cannot sin; He cannot cease to exist; He
cannot make a square circle—but these do not suggest a
limit to His power. Augustine understood this 1600 years
ago:

> "Neither is His power diminished when we say that He
> cannot die or fall into error, for this is in such a way
> impossible to Him, that if it were possible for Him, He
> would be of less power. But assuredly He is rightly called
> omnipotent, though He can neither die nor fall into error . .
> . Wherefore, He cannot do some things for the very reason
> that He is omnipotent."[548]

Some skeptics have referred to Matthew 19:26: "Jesus
looked at them and said, 'With man this is impossible,
but with God all things are possible.'" They then ask, if
all things are possible for Jesus, then can he make a
stone so big He can't lift it?

Norman Geisler answered such questions:

> "This is based on a misconception. When the Bible
> declares that God can do what is impossible, it does not
> refer to what is actually impossible but to what is *humanly*
> impossible."[549]

Also, since God is omnipotent, it would have to be an
infinite rock to challenge His infinite power. But what is
an infinite rock? Such a thing is both inconceivable and
incomprehensible. Surely it is folly to attempt an answer
to a riddle whose premise is incomprehensible.

[548]Saint Augustine, as quoted by Theodore C. Denise, Nicholas P.
White & Sheldon P. Peterfreund, *Great Traditions in Ethics*, Tenth
Edition, Belmont CA (Wadsworth Thomson Learning, 2002) 65.
[549]Norman L. Geisler, *Baker Encyclopedia of Christian Apologetics*,
Grand Rapids MI (Baker Books, 1999) 428.

Finally, arguing that God talk is meaningless based upon the stone paradox is as ridiculous as suggesting *that the laws of physics are meaningless based upon the paradox of what happens when the irresistible force meets the immovable object.*

Is a non-material personal being incoherent?

In his book, *God: The Failed Hypothesis*, Victor Stenger related several formal arguments against traditional theism, a collection he reproduced from Martin and Monnier, that purported to show that God-talk is incoherent, of which we consider one:

> "1. If God exists, then he is nonphysical.
> 2. If God exists, then he is a person (or a personal being).
> 3. A person (or personal being) needs to be physical.
> 4. Hence, it is impossible for God to exist."[550]

The argument looks very impressive, all laid out as it is. But it all hinges on one false proposition: that a person must exist in a physical form. But why? It merely begs the question, assuming what it should prove. It seeks to eliminate a whole class of supernatural beings (God, angels) as illogical, but fails to make the case as to why this should be so.

Further, if God existed prior to the creation of the physical universe, it must have been as a non-physical person. The idea of a non-physical person may be outside

---

[550]Michael Martin & Ricki Monnier, eds, *The Impossibility of God,* Amherst New York (Prometheus Books, 2003) 49-60 as cited by Victor J. Stenger, *God the Failed Hypothesis: How Science Shows That God Does Not Exist,* Amherst New York (Prometheus Books, 2007) 33.

of our normal experience, but it is certainly a coherent philosophical concept.

Section Six: The Origin of Ethics and Morality

Jean-Paul Sartre laid the cards on the table concerning ethics in the absence of God:

> "The existentialist, on the contrary, thinks it very distressing that God does not exist, because all possibility of finding values in a heaven of ideas disappears along with Him . . . Dostoevsky said, 'If God didn't exist, everything is permissible.' That is the very starting point of existentialism. Indeed, everything is permissible if God does not exist, and as a result man is forlorn, because neither within him nor without does he find anything to cling to."[551]

Let us explore, then, the foundation of values, morals, and ethics, and how such questions can be answered in relation to the question of God's existence.

Chapter 28: The Divine Command Theory

The Christian position is clear. Morals and ethics are derived from God, and known through either special revelation (the Bible, prophets, apostles) or through natural revelation (God-given reason and conscience).

Perhaps the clearest example of Christian ethical theories is the *Divine Command Theory* although other theories have their advocates.

Atheist David Eller made, perhaps, an unwitting concession to this viewpoint:

---

[551]Jean-Paul Sartre, *An Existential Ethic*, as quoted by Samuel Enoch Stumpf, *Philosophy: History & Problems*, Fourth Edition, New York (McGraw-Hill Publishing Company, 1989) 728.

"Morality can never be said to be 'true.' Morality must, thus, be relative; the only way it could be absolute (the same for everyone everywhere in every time) would be through the successful imposition of one particular set of morals or values on everyone else, most likely by force."[552]

Eller acknowledged the virtual impossibility of a universally applicable and objective system of ethics without it being imposed by some outside force. And that is just what Christians believe; ethics are derived from the universal sovereign.

Although Eller presented the idea in perhaps sinister overtones, biblical ethical commands flow from a benevolent God for His creatures own good (the train on the tracks runs the smoothest).

Criticism of the Divine Command Theory: Men make ethical judgments independent of God including believers

Kai Nielsen challenged the coherence of the divine command theory in which ethics are derived from God:

"It is indeed true that, for the believer at least, it's being *God* who commands it, who wills it, that makes all the difference. This is so because believers assume that God is good. But now, it should be asked, *how* does the believer *know,* or indeed *does* he know, that God is good, except by what is in the end his own quite fallible moral judgment that God is good? Must he not appeal to his own considered judgments, his own moral sense here? Is there any escaping that? . . . We can see from the very structure of this argumentation that we must use our own moral insight to decide whether God's acts are good . . . Fallible

[552]David Eller, *Natural Atheism*, Cranford New Jersey (American Atheist Press, 2004) 102.

or not, our own moral understanding is logically prior to our religious understanding."[553]

Nielsen elaborated on this argument:

"For the sake of argument assume that Jesus is the perfect genuine revelation, still it is we finite creatures who saw in Jesus' behavior perfection and goodness. Using our own finite moral powers, we recognized that Jesus was this moral exemplar pointing to the infinite perfection of God; beyond that we also recognized that the parables of the Bible were so noble and inspiring that the Bible ought to be taken as our model on moral matters. *But these things show, as clearly as can be, that in making these moral assessments we already have a moral criterion, quite independent of the Bible, God, and Jesus, in virtue of which we make these moral judgments.*"[554]

So for Nielsen, the fact that we are able to judge that God is good shows that we have in ourselves (independent of God) the ability to know right and wrong, and to make ethical judgments:

"Such linguistic evidence clearly shows that good is a concept which can be understood quite independently of any reference to the deity, that morality without religion, without theism is quite possible . . . This clearly show that our understanding of morality and knowledge of goodness are independent of any knowledge that we may or may not have of the divine."[555]

---

[553]Kai Nielsen, *Atheism & Philosophy*, Amherst NY (Prometheus Books, 2005) 214-215.

[554]Kai Nielsen, *Atheism & Philosophy*, 151. Nielsen makes the same argument in *Ethics Without God*, in a chapter entitled *Morality and the Will of God* in *Critiques of God: Making the Case Against Belief in God*, Peter A. Angeles, Editor, Amherst New York (Prometheus Books, 1997) 246.

[555]Kai Nielsen, *Ethics Without God*, as a chapter entitled *Morality and the Will of God* in *Critiques of God: Making the Case Against Belief in God*, Peter A. Angeles, Editor, Amherst New York

The implication of Nielsen's argument is clear; man, of himself, is able to make moral choices and so God-belief is superfluous to morality.

Man's moral capacity as an innate gift or God

While it is acknowledged that we are able to make moral judgments, we should remember that this is affected (or clouded) by man's sinful nature. More importantly, this ethical sense in man is by borrowed capital from God, for it is God who has made us thus. I think this is what Pojman was driving at with a question he posed as the moderator of a debate between Moreland and Nielsen:

> "The question is essentially, is one of the reasons secular people are moral is because God made the world the way it is to put a kind of moral inclination into people?"[556]

Christians affirm that it is, indeed, God who has given man his reasoning abilities and the guidance of the conscience. The implication is that even our moral judgments (including our judgment that God is good) are ultimately dependent upon God.

Paul Copan showed that this moral sense applies to believers and unbelievers alike:

> "Because *all* humans have been made in God's image (Gen. 1:26-27, 9:3; James 3:9) and are thus intrinsically valuable (endowed with dignity, conscience, rights, duties, and the basic capacity to recognize right and wrong), it is

---

(Prometheus Books, 1997) 248.

[556]J. P. Moreland, & Kai Nielsen, *Does God Exist?: The Debate Between Theists & Atheists*, Amherst NY (Prometheus Books, 1993) 132.

no surprise that nontheists of all stripes know the same sorts of moral truths as believers."[557]

Further, despite our culture's growing rejection of the Christian values that have formed the foundation of our Western culture, nevertheless, these continue to have a residual effect upon our present standards, whether they are acknowledged or not, in the same way that a man's influence continues to be felt in the lives of his children.

And so Groothius stated:

"The moral traditions of the west, shaped significantly by Christianity, revolt against this kind of devaluation of human beings. Yet when secular moral systems cling to this notion of equality, they illicitly depend on stolen capital from Christian theism."[558]

The apostle Paul spoke of this moral endowment in all men:

"Indeed, when Gentiles who do not have the law, do by nature things required by the law, they are a law for themselves, even though they do not have the law, since they show that the requirements of the law are written on their hearts, their consciences also bearing witness" (Romans 2:14-15).

"Hurrying faster than a bad conscience after a sinner!"[559]

---

[557]Paul Copan, God, *Naturalism, and the Foundations of Morality*, chapter in *The Future of Atheism: Alister McGrath & Daniel Dennett in Dialogue*, Robert B. Stewart, Editor, Minneapolis MN (Fortress Press, 2008) 146.

[558]Douglass Groothuis, *Christian Apologetics: A Comprehensive Case for Biblical Faith*, Downers Grove IL (InterVarsity Press, 2011) 360.

[559]Soren Kierkegaard, *Either/Or* as cited in Robert Bretall, *A*

Soren Kierkegaard

The conscience

In reference to the conscience, it is a challenge for atheists to explain its origin in an evolutionary or naturalistic scheme? From a theistic perspective, the answer is simple; the conscience was placed in mankind by their Creator, standard equipment if you will.

The point of the foregoing is to show that, contrary to Nielsen's assertion that man's ethical sense is independent of God, it is, in fact, wholly dependent upon God. In order for Nielsen's argument to succeed, he would have had to have shown, not that man can *recognize* goodness, but that *he can establish or determine the good apart from an appeal to God.*

Blue and green beads

Let's illustrate this idea. Suppose we are asked to sort out a pile of beads on a table. We are to put the blue beads in one pile and the green in the other. Well to make this assessment, we must first know what "blue" is and what "green" is. That is, we must first understand the nature of the colors blue and green before we can accomplish the task.

In this respect, Nielsen is correct (by way of analogy). We must be able to understand the concept of good (and what is not good) before we can make moral judgments.

Now, when I discern the color of the beads, I am only recognizing their independent qualities. I do not *make*

Kierkegaard Anthology, New York (The Modern Library/Random House,1946) 42 them blue or green; I merely *recognize* what they, in fact, are. Likewise, when one has recognized what (or who) is good, he has not *determined* what is good, but has merely recognized what was, in fact, good.

Just as we have an innate ability to distinguish between colors (long before we learn the words "green" and "blue") as part of the apparatus of God's creation, so also, God's gift of reason and conscience help us distinguish between good and evil.

The fact that we can recognize good from evil does not support Nielsen's argument that ethics can be established apart from God. It remains true that without God, there is simply no universally applicable basis or foundation for morality?

The Bible, on the other hand, shows that while man has an ethical sense, he also struggles with the sin nature and a preponderance to selfishness. Ignoring that inner voice of guidance eventually results in a hardened conscience.

Ethics as properly basic

Another closely related argument is that morals are simply properly basic, and hence, need no further source or authority. The idea is that we simply have an intuitive knowledge of ethical standards, independent of the Divine.

Our newspaper headlines, however, seem to belie this claim. Many simply reject what most consider basic moral values. They ask themselves, "Why should I do what others expect of me? Nobody has the right to tell me what to do. I will do what I want."

The atheist can offer no response to such questions since they reject any authoritative moral standards.

Criticism of the Divine Command Theory: Reward and punishment are a poor basis for morality?

Some claim that the divine command theory is a weak basis for morality since it depends upon fear and punishment. Walter's explained:

> "Many atheists reject religious ethics on the grounds that any moral system which encourages agents to be good solely for the sake of reward (heaven) or to refrain from doing evil solely to escape punishment (hell) is unworthy of the name . . . Philosopher Colin McGinn claims that 'to do good only for the sake of reward is corrupting' . . . and humanist Jim Herrick dismisses religious ethics on the ground that it tends to offer 'a carrot and stick approach to morality.'"[560]

These criticisms may seem to have some initial validity, but a bit of reflection alleviates the concerns raised. For instance, is not life filled with similar examples of so-called 'carrot and stick' rewards systems? Do not employers reward their employees with paychecks, bonuses, raises, and promotions for good work? Likewise, do not employers reserve the right to fire or otherwise punish employees for poor performance?

---

[560]Kerry Walters, *Atheism: A Guide for the Perplexed*, New York (The Continuum International Publishing Group Inc, 2010) 125.

Do not schools reward students that work hard with good grades while at the same time giving bad grades to those who don't do their work? Indeed, students who get into trouble can be expelled, held back a grade, or not graduate at all.

And what of families? Do not parents reward their children for good behavior (allowances etc.) and punish them for bad behavior (time outs, grounding, loss of privileges)? Is it fair to suggest that such families are using corrupt standards? Such a notion seems ridiculous on its face.

Further, although fear of punishment may partly motivate children to obey their parents, it seems almost too obvious to point out that the major motivation of a child's behavior is their place as members of a family, and more specifically, the love that members of a family have for each other.

Most children, at least implicitly, know that their parents love them, and have their best interest at heart; that the parental rules are for their good. As such, the primary motive for obeying is their mutual love, and only secondarily the fear of possible punishment.

The Bible teaches the same principle for the relationship between believers and God. Christians are members of God's family. God loves us. All his moral standards are intended for our good. Indeed, we find that when we ignore God's standards, we are only hurting ourselves and others. Christians are thankful for God's love and are motivated by our love to obey His standards.

The apostle Paul commended the Christians at Thessalonica because of "your labor prompted by love"(1

Thessalonians 1:3). The apostle John said, "We love because he first loved us"(1 John 4:19).

"But to live outside the law, you must be honest"[561]

Bob Dylan

Christian freedom and the law of love

The New Testament presents a new kind of moral law called the law of love, or the law of Christ. Charles Ryrie explained:

> "Now the Mosaic Law was done away with in its entirety as a code. It has been replaced with the law of Christ."[562]

Under the Mosaic law, obedience to God's moral law was a requirement for covenant blessings. Under the New Covenant, covenant blessings are already assured on the basis of Christ's perfect sacrifice. Therefore, under the law of Christ, moral obedience for the believer is motivated by our love for Christ; and out of thanksgiving for all that He has done for us.

Peter Ditzel of *Word of His Grace Ministries* put it this way:

> "Romans 8:2 shows what is really at work: 'For the law of the Spirit of life in Christ Jesus made me free from the law of sin and of death' (Romans 8:2). We are free from the law because the law of the Spirit of life in Christ Jesus has liberated us from it. But, you may say, that's exchanging being under one law for being under another, isn't it? No.

---

[561]Bob Dylan, *Absolutely Sweet Marie*, Audiam, Inc,
[562]Charles C. Ryrie, *Basic Theology*, Wheaton IL (Victor Books, 1987) 305.

Notice: 'For what the law couldn't do, in that it was weak through the flesh, God did, sending his own Son in the likeness of sinful flesh and for sin, he condemned sin in the flesh; that the ordinance of the law might be fulfilled in us, who walk not after the flesh, but after the Spirit' (Romans 8:3-4). God didn't take us from being under one law and put us *under* another. He took us from being under law by having Jesus Christ fulfill the law in us who walk according to the Spirit. This is what Paul means by 'the law of the Spirit of life in Christ Jesus' in verse 2. It is not a law that we are *under*, but a law that we are *in* because we are *in* Christ Jesus, and it is a law that is in us, because Jesus Christ is in us."[563]

Geisler reminded us of the great words of Saint Augustine: "This is reminiscent of the Augustine maxim: 'Love God and do what you will.'"[564] The foregoing shows that Christians are primarily motivated by love of God. Christ has already paid the price for our sins and we are on our way to glory. We are not earning our way to heaven through works and merit. Christ has already done that work for us. We now walk by or in God's grace and our good works overflow out of thankful hearts.

This is not to deny that God corrects His children like any good father (Hebrews 12). But such punishment is remedial in nature and ultimately for our own good.

---

[563]Peter Ditzel, *Are Christians Ever Under Law?*, Word of His Grace Ministries, web address: http://www.wordofhisgrace.org/wp/under-law-of-christ/

[564]Norman L. Geisler, *Baker Encyclopedia of Christian Apologetics*, Grand Rapids MI (Baker Books, 1999) 406.

Chapter 29: The Euthyphro Challenge

There is a well-known challenge to theism made famous by Plato in his work *Euthyphro* known appropriately as the "Euthyphro dilemma." Yeager Hudson explained:

> "Plato's dialogue *The Euthyphro* is a discussion between Socrates and the arrogant young man Euthyphro, who claims to be very knowledgeable about the meaning of 'virtue.' Virtue, he tells Socrates, is what is pleasing to the gods. But Socrates sees an important ambiguity in the claim and proceeds to bring it to light by asking this question: Is virtue pleasing to the gods because it is good, or is it good because it is pleasing to the gods?"[565]

The Euthyphro dilemma seeks to undermine belief in God by putting the theistic believer in a conundrum over the relationship between God and the good (and evil). Antony Flew explained the force of the argument:

> "Perhaps the most powerful of all skeptical arguments, this has appealed especially to the clearest and skeptical minds, striking straight and decisively to the heart of the matter. It was, for instance, central to J. S. Mill's rejection of Christianity."[566]

The Euthyphro dilemma stated

Here are some presentations of the dilemma, the first by Peter King:

---

[565]Yeager Hudson, *The Philosophy of Religion*, Mountain View CA (Mayfield Publishing Company, 1991) 231.

[566]Antony Flew, *Divine Omnipotence and Human Freedom*, chapter in *Critiques of God: Making the Case Against Belief in God,* Peter A. Angeles, Editor, Amherst New York (Prometheus Books, 1997) 227-228.

"What, for example, is the relationship link between morality and God (or the gods)? In his dialogue *Euthyphro,* Plato poses a problem to the believer that has been debated by philosophers and theologians ever since—a problem known as the Euthyphro Dilemma: are pious things pious because the gods love them, or do the god's love them because they're pious? The same dilemma can be raised for morality, in terms of monotheism: are moral actions good because god commands them, or does god command them because they're good?

Neither horn of this dilemma is very attractive to the believer. If God's commands create morality, (this is known as Divine Command Theory), then he could have commanded very differently—for example, that murder is good and charity evil—and our moral values would have been reversed; if on the other hand, god commanded that murder is evil because it is evil, then morality is independent of god's will, so he hasn't created everything (and is subject to morality just like the rest of us)."[567]

Atheist Julian Baggini explained it this way:

"To put it another way, the only thing that can show that a lawgiver is moral is that his or her laws conform to a moral standard which is independent of the moral lawgiver. So if the lawgiver is God, God's laws will only be moral if they conform to moral principles which are independent of God.

Plato made this point extremely clearly [sic] in a dialogue called *Euthyphro*, after which the following dilemma was named. Plato's protagonist Socrates posed the question, do the gods choose what is good because it is good, or is the good good because the gods choose it?

---

[567]Peter J. King, *100 Philosophers: A Guide to the World's Greatest Thinkers*, New York (Quarto Inc, 2004) 6-7.

If the first option is true, that shows that the good is independent of the gods (or in a monotheistic faith, God). Good just is good and that is precisely why a good God will always choose it. But if the second option is true, then that makes the very idea of what is good arbitrary. If it is God's choosing something alone that makes it good, then what is there to stop God choosing torture, for instance, and thus making it good?

This is of course absurd, but the reason why it is absurd is that we believe that torture is wrong and *that is why* God would never choose it. To recognize this, however, is to recognize that we do not need God to determine right and wrong. Torture is not wrong just because God does not choose it. To my mind, the Euthyphro dilemma is a very powerful argument against the idea that God is required for morality."[568]

How should Christians respond?

How then should a Christian respond to the Euthyphro dilemma? Let us begin by noting that rather than being a true dilemma, it is instead a false dichotomy. There is a perfectly reasonable solution that leaves the believer impaled on neither horn of the alleged dilemma.

When God created the universe, His creation reflected His perfect goodness (Genesis 1:31). The moral qualities that He revealed to mankind were likewise a reflection of this goodness, flowing from the divine nature.

Because God can act only according to His divine holy nature (He cannot sin or do wrong), nothing but righteous qualities could flow from Him as commands for His creatures. This goodness wasn't something external

---

[568]Julian Baggini, *Atheism: A Brief Insight*, New York / London (Sterling Publishing Company, 2003) 54-56

to or independent of God that He had to choose from as if He went shopping at the ethical systems superstore.

Rather, His ethical commands are merely an extension of His very being. Therefore, the Euthyphro dilemma is of no consequence. There was no "good" that existed independent of God, that God had to choose of necessity, nor did He choose the good arbitrarily out of a menagerie of possible characteristics. Instead, the good that was essential to the character of God was expressed in the universe He created. It simply could have been no other way.

And so William Lane Craig argued:

> "Hence, God's commandments are not arbitrary but necessarily flow from his own nature. They are necessary expressions of the way God is."[569]

Geisler explained that this theistic response to the Euthyphro dilemma is known in philosophy as *essentialism*:

> "Essentialism as it related to moral principles and God's will is the view that ethical principles are rooted ultimately in the unchangeable divine essence, not simply in God's changeable will. It is opposed to divine *voluntarism* which asserts that something is good because God wills it . . . Theists . . . believe that God wills things in accordance with his own unchangeable good nature. This is called divine essentialism."[570]

---

[569]William Lane Craig, *Why I Believe God Exists*, a chapter in Norman L. Geisler and Paul K. Hoffman, *Why I Am a Christian: Leading Thinkers Explain Why They Believe,* Grand Rapids MI (Baker Books, 2001) 78.

[570]Norman L. Geisler, *Baker Encyclopedia of Christian Apologetics*, Grand Rapids MI (Baker Books, 1999) 216.

And so Groothius summed up the Christian reaction to the Euthyphro challenge:

> "This dilemma is in fact a chimera since the theist can escape between the horns uninjured. The Euthyphro argument trades on a straw man (or straw god) that creates a false dilemma. Bible Theism . . . claims God as the source of all goodness on the basis of both God's character and God's will. God's moral will is based on God's changeless nature . . . Just as God does not create himself, so he does create moral values, which are eternally constituent of his being."[571]

Baggini's revised version of the Euthyphro Dilemma

However, Baggini refused to give up so easy. He attempted to restate or revise the Euthyphro dilemma in a manner that countered the theistic essentialist argument:

> "Some think the way out of the dilemma is to say that God just is good, so the question the dilemma poses is ill-formed. If God and good are the same thing then we cannot ask whether God chooses good because it is good—the very question separates what must come together.
> But the Euthyphro dilemma can be restated in another way to challenge this reply. We can ask: *is God good because to be good just is to be whatever God is; or is God good because God has all the properties of goodness?* If we choose the former answer we again find that goodness is arbitrary, since it would be whatever God happened to be, even if God were a sadist. So we must choose the second option: God is good because he has all the properties of goodness. But this means the properties of goodness can be

[571]Douglass Groothuis, *Christian Apologetics: A Comprehensive Case for Biblical Faith*, Downers Grove IL (InterVarsity Press, 2011) 356.

specified independently of God and so the idea of goodness does not in any way depend upon the existence of God.

Hence there is no reason why a denial of God's existence would necessarily entail a denial of the existence of goodness."[572]

Baggini's revision does not advance the argument

Baggini reversed the order of the argument. Rather than asking what makes good good (in relation to God), he asks what makes God good (in relation to the good). But Baggini's restatement of the argument is not really an advance on the original statement of the Euthyphro dilemma.

Indeed, the results of Baggini's restatement remain the same; goodness is arbitrary since it depends upon what God is (so if God's character were different, what is considered good would be different) **or** God is good because He is made good by the quality of goodness He possesses (in other words, God is made good by a quality of goodness that is independent of God). Baggini simply insists that the relationship between God and goodness is either arbitrary on the one hand or that goodness is independent of God on the other.

He has proven neither as we have already shown. The relationship between God is neither arbitrary (since God's moral ideals could only reflect his holy nature) nor is goodness something independent of God since nothing but God existed at the creation.

---

[572]Julian Baggini, *Atheism*, 56-57.

Turning the tables on the Euthyphro dilemma

But let us take this to the next step by restating the Euthyphro Dilemma ourselves, but in a different direction than did Baggini. Let us ask our atheist friends whether the good they have chosen to live by (assuming they have moral standards) is good because they chose it or did they choose it because it is good?

That is, did they make the good good by choosing it or did they choose it because it was of itself good? Now, if our atheist friend answers that their choosing the good made it good, then it is they rather that are being arbitrary, for surely they could have made other choices (as our world shows) such as living a life filled with things like torture, murder, theft, and the like.

On the other hand, if they chose the good because it was good, then this means that this goodness is independent of them, and is a binding moral obligation or duty. This suggests that there are absolute ethical and moral standards applicable to all.

If so, it raises some interesting questions. For instance, what are these standards? How can we find them? Who or what determined these standards? Of course, it is just at this point that Christianity claims God comes in since He is the author of universally applicable moral standards.

Another consequence of this second option is the denial of all forms of relativism since rather than each person choosing their own moral standards, they are duty bound to submit to the good.

Chapter 30: In Search of Ethics in an Atheistic World

W. C. Fields, was once caught reading the Bible. When asked

what he was doing, his response was equal to the occasion. He

said, 'Just checking for loopholes, my dear; just checking for

loopholes.'[573]

Another problem for proponents of atheism is how to account for the nearly universal feeling that such things as right and wrong exist in the first place. It seems apparent that if there is no God, there can be no basis for universally applicable and objective moral standards, what philosopher Bernard Williams called an "Archimedean point."[574]

Imagine with me if you will, that the Starship Enterprise has been given a new assignment. Kirk, Spock, and the rest of the crew have been sent to boldly go forth throughout the universe in search of a sure foundation for ethics and morality. Being unable to appeal to God as the source for ethics, it seems the mission is destined for failure.

---

[573]J. P. Moreland, & Kai Nielsen, *Does God Exist?: The Debate Between Theists & Atheists*, Amherst NY (Prometheus Books, 1993) 34.

[574]Bernard Williams, *Ethics and the Limits of Philosophy*, Cambridge, Harvard University Press, 1985, pp. 28-29, as quoted by Theodore C. Denise, Nicholas P. White & Sheldon P. Peterfreund, *Great Traditions in Ethics*, Tenth Edition, Belmont CA (Wadsworth Thomson Learning, 2002) 358.

Finding an Archimedean point for ethics without God

S. T. Joshi asked us to: "Recall the words spoken by Ivan Karamazov in Feodor Dostoyevsky's *The Brothers Karamazov*: "If there is no God, then everything is permitted."[575]

President John Adams agreed that ethics are necessarily derived from God. To the French philosopher Condorcet's claim that the ideals of the "'natural equality of mankind' were the foundation of all morality" he responded:

> "There is no such thing without a supposition of a God. There is not right or wrong in the universe without the supposition of a moral government and an intellectual and moral governor."[576]

Atheists can have good morals, but cannot provide an authoritative source for them

It is important to clear up a common misunderstanding. *We do not deny that atheists can have moral standards or live moral lives.* Rather, we argue that there is simply no objective basis or universally binding source of ethics apart from God.

The result of atheism can only be some form of relativism. An ethical jungle, where: "each man does

---

[575]Feodor Dostoyevsky, *The Brothers Karamazov*, as quoted by Garrett J. DeWeese & J. P. Moreland, *Philosophy Made Slightly Less Difficult: A Beginner's Guide to Life's Big Questions*, Downers Grove IL (InterVarsity-Press, 2005) 98.

[576]John Adams, as quoted by John Eidsmoe, *Christianity and the Constitution: The Faith of Our Founding Fathers*, Grand Rapids MI (Baker Books, 1987, 1995) 281.

what is right in his own eyes" (Judges 21:25), resulting in moral anarchy.

In the absence of God, and God's law, wherefore is the source of morality? We all have an instinctual belief that there are in fact, objective standards of right and wrong. Kant stated:

> "Two things fill the mind with ever new and increasing admiration and awe, the oftener and more steadily we reflect on them: the starry heavens above and the moral law within."[577]

Although Kant criticized the traditional arguments for the existence of God, he was convinced that morality demanded the existence of God, and this no doubt provided the basis for Nietzsche's jibe that Kant was "a sneaky Christian to the end."[578]

Baggini admits that finding a source of atheistic ethics is difficult: "When it comes to saying what the source of morality is, however, there are no easy answers."[579]

It seems to escape most skeptics that by rejecting God, they reject any kind of objective foundation for judging good from evil. They are like a man who has climbed a tree to cut off a branch, forgetting that they are sitting on the branch being sawn. Yes, they might get the

---

[577]Immanuel Kant, as quoted by Antony Flew, *A Dictionary of Philosophy*, Revised Second Edition, New York (Gramercy Books, 1979, 1999) 192.

[578]Friedrich Nietzsche, *Twilight of the Idols*, as quoted in *Existentialism Basic Writings*, Second Edition, Charles Guignon &Derk Pereboom, Editors, Indianapolis/ Cambridge (Hackett Publishing Company, Inc, 2001) 180.

[579]Julian Baggini, *Atheism,* New York (Sterling, 2003) 63.

branch down (God belief), but they (objective morality) will fall with it. Kerry Walters summed up this point:

> "The very possibility of morality still depends on the existence of a God who gives universal, objective, and absolute moral laws that establish our ethical responsibilities. The very fact that atheists are capable of criticizing religion on ethical grounds indicates that they have some notion of objective right and wrong."[580]

That is, the very fact that skeptics criticize Christians for claiming there are absolute values means that they also appeal to some universally binding law which serves as a basis for their criticism. Norman Geisler stated: "Atheists can believe in morality, but they cannot justify this belief."[581]

C. S. Lewis and the universally compelling idea of right and wrong

Perhaps no one captured this idea better than C.S. Lewis who referred to it as the *law of human nature:*

> "Now what interests me about all these remarks is that the man who makes them is not merely saying that the other man's behavior does not please him. He is appealing to some kind of standard of behaviour which he expects the other man to know about. And the other man very seldom replies: 'To hell with your standard.' Nearly always he tries to make out that what he has been doing does not really go against the standard, or that if it does there is some special excuse . . . It looks, in fact, very much as if both parties had in mind some kind of Law or Rule or fair play or decent behaviour or morality or whatever you like to call it, about

---

[580]Kerry Walters, *Atheism: A Guide for the Perplexed*, New York (The Continuum International Publishing Group Inc, 2010) 122.
[581]Norman L. Geisler, *Baker Encyclopedia of Christian Apologetics*, Grand Rapids MI (Baker Books, 1999) 58.

which they really agreed . . . This law was called the Law of Nature because people thought that every one knew it by nature and did not need to be taught it."[582]

Lewis further illustrated the point:

"Whenever you find a man who says he does not believe in a real Right and Wrong, you will find the same man going back on this a moment later. He may break his promise to you, but if you try breaking one to him, he will be complaining 'It's not fair' before you can say Jack Robinson."[583]

Lewis summed up the consequences of this idea with a profound and succinct description of the human condition:

"These, then, are the two points I wanted to make. First, that human beings, all over the earth, have this curious idea that they ought to behave in a certain way, and cannot really get rid of it. Secondly, that they do not in fact behave in that way. They know the Law of Nature; they break it. These two facts are the foundation of all clear thinking about ourselves and the universe we live in."[584]

The Axiological Argument for the existence of God

The formal name for Lewis' *law of nature* is the *axiological argument.*

"Now we're going to examine this issue of moral absolutes by taking a hard look at an argument for the existence of God known as the "Axiological" Argument. "Axio" means the "study of values" and the Axiological

[582]Clive Staple Lewis, *Mere Christianity*, New York (A Touchstone Book/ Simon & Schuster, 1952, 1996) 17-18.
[583]Clive Staple Lewis, *Mere Christianity*, 19.
[584]Clive Staple Lewis, *Mere Christianity*, 21.

Argument uses the presence of values or 'mores' to prove the existence of God. It's a simple argument:

(1) There is an Objective (Absolute) Moral Law (2) Every Law Has a Law Giver (3) Therefore, there is an Objective (Absolute) Law Giver (4) The Objective (Absolute) Law Giver is God

Like other arguments, if the foundation of the argument is true, the conclusion of the argument is also true. In this case, if there is an absolute Moral Law, then there has to be an Absolute Moral Law Giver. If we can prove there are moral absolutes, the argument is over."[585]

The argument from our moral sense (axiological argument) is compelling indeed.

---

[585] *Evidence for God from Morality: The Axiological Argument*, Hannover International Bible Church, Hannover Germany, from website   address: http://www.hannoveribc.com/clientimages/25727/apologetics/eviden cefrommorality.pdf

Chapter 31: Ethical Models

Having considered the Divine Command theory, let us consider other ethical models in the marketplace of ethics considering how they compare with the Divine command theory.

Utilitarianism

Jeremy Bentham and John Stuart Mill popularized Utilitarianism, which seeks the greatest good for the greatest amount. That is, moral standards are determined by the results of our actions, the consequences, hence it is also known as Consequentialism.

Those actions which bring pleasure are desirable or good, whereas those actions that result in pain are accordingly undesirable or bad.

One weighs an ethical question using the utilitarian calculus, attempting to predict the pleasure or pain resulting from each of their options, and choosing the one that leads to the most pleasure and the least pain.

Though this may seem to be hedonistic, it needn't be so. Advocates of Utilitarianism distinguish between types of pleasure, giving priority to the more cultivated or intellectual pleasures over those of the flesh. They also distinguish between short and long term impacts, taking into account the long term pain that can result from short term pleasures (and vice-verse).

Further, the Utilitarian system must also consider the cost/benefit not only for the individual, but for the whole of society as well since as Donne said, "No one is an island entire to itself."[586]

Finally, because Utilitarianism is concerned with the results or consequences of actions they are in contrast to *Deontological* ethics which are concerned about the right or wrong of *the act itself* (i.e., the Ten Commandments) regardless of the consequences.

Problems of Utilitarianism

One of the chief problems of Utilitarianism is that it fails to take into account the reality and impact of sinful human nature. The biblical prophet put it this way: The heart is deceitful above all things and beyond cure. Who can understand it?"(Jeremiah 17:9; compare with Romans 3:23).

The novelty song from the animated children's special *How the Grinch Stole Christmas* that described the Grinch can just as well describe the soul of unregenerate mankind as well:

> "Your soul is an appalling dump heap overflowing with the most disgraceful assortment of rubbish imaginable mangled up in tangled up knots! You're a foul one, Mr. Grinch, You're a nasty wasty skunk, Your heart is full of unwashed socks, your soul is full of gunk, Mr. Grinch. The three words that best describe you are as follows, and I quote, "Stink, stank, stunk"!"[587]

---

[586] John Donne, Meditation XVII, *Devotions Upon Emergent Occasions,* at web address: https://web.cs.dal.ca/~johnston/poetry/island.html

[587]Theodor "Dr. Seuss" Geisel, *The Grinch Theme Song*, from the program *How the Grinch Stole Christmas*, 1966, Retrieved from the following website: http://www.41051.com/xmaslyrics/grinch.html,

Please suffer me one more animated example that illustrates the dark side of human nature. This time, from one of my childhood heroes, Huckleberry Hound. In this scene, Huck chases a fox trying to steal chickens from his henhouse. The narrator then says:

> "You really can't blame farmer Huckleberry for feeling that way about the prowling fox. This foxy fiend is a shrewd, sly, conniving, cunning, predatory, mean, cruel critter. This barnyard burglar would swipe a dozen chickens at one time. Let's face it. This guy is a sneaky, low-down, worthless, no-good, cowardly, creepy, ornery, good for nothing chicken stealing varmint."

I love the reaction of the fox, who after enduring this descriptive onslaught, said, perhaps speaking for us all:

> "Well Gee-whiz. Nobody's perfect!"[588]

Unfortunately, these amusing descriptions hit too close to home as a metaphor for the human condition, and spell trouble for a Utilitarian ethic since the one evaluating the anticipated results of his or her actions invariably does so through a self-centered and even self-deceptive lense.

In this respect, it is like putting the fox in charge of the henhouse! Therefore, a strict utilitarian ethic, though well-intentioned, is simply naïve. J.J.C. Smart captured this idea:

> "He knows that in particular cases where his own interests are involved his calculations are likely to be biased in his own favour. Suppose that he is unhappily

---

[588] *Cock-a-Doodle Huck,* The Huckleberry Hound Show, Hanna Barbera, 1958. Watch the episode online at: https://www.imdb.com/title/tt1495268/

married and is deciding whether to get divorced. He will in all probability greatly exaggerate his own unhappiness (and possibly his wife's) and greatly underestimate the harm done to his children by the break up of the family."[589]

What is really needed is not an ethic at the mercy of sinful self-interest, but an ethic external to an authoritative over sinful mankind.

The only possible candidate for such an authoritative and universally applicable ethic is one given by God. Indeed, I would argue that *the Christian gospel is the only real hope for bringing the greatest happiness to the greatest many.* Christ died for all that all may be reconciled to God (Romans 5:8-11; 1 Corinthians 15:3-4). This is the path that will bring the greatest blessings not only in this life, but forevermore.

However, it is interesting that John Stuart Mills intended that Utilitarianism be conducted in the spirit of the golden rule:

> "In the golden rule of Jesus of Nazareth, we read the complete spirit of the ethics of utility. To do as one would be done by, and to love one's neighbor as oneself, constitute the ideal perfection of utilitarian morality."[590]

In principle, it is possible to consider Utilitarianism consistent with biblical principles provided that our self-centeredness was kept in clear view, and with the further

---

[589]J.J.C. Smart, *Extreme and Restricted Utilitarianism* in *Introduction to Philosophy: Classical and Contemporary Readings*, Fourth Edition, Edited by John Perry, Michael Bratman & John Martin Fischer, Oxford UK (Oxford University Press, 2007) 513-514.

[590]John Stewart Mills, *Utilitarianism*, London, Longman's, Green, 1897, Chapter 2, pp. 24-25, as quoted by Theodore C. Denise, Nicholas P. White & Sheldon P. Peterfreund, *Great Traditions in Ethics*, Tenth Edition, Belmont CA (Wadsworth Thomson Learning, 2002) 165.

understanding that the Christian gospel as the true goal in seeking to bring the greatest good to the greatest many.

Unfortunately, this is not the path taken by most advocates of Utilitarianism.

Deontological-Kantian Ethics

The philosopher Immanuel Kant is known for his Deontological system of ethics, which featured the categorical imperative, the importance of duty, and treating others as ends rather than means.

For instance, an advocate of a Deontological ethic would consider all lies wrong, even if the lie might save someone's life (more on this later). The idea is to fulfill your duty to do the right regardless of the consequences. Deontological ethics enjoys advocates among Christian believers.

The Categorical Imperative

Kant summed up his ethical system in what he called a categorical imperative in which he implores each person to contemplate what the world would be like if everyman practiced what they themselves practiced:

> "There is therefore only a single categorical imperative and it is this: 'Act only on that maxim through which you can at the same time will that it should become a universal law.'"[591]

---

[591]Immanuel Kant, *Groundwork of the Metaphysic of Morals* in *Introduction to Philosophy: Classical and Contemporary Readings*, Fourth Edition, John Perry, Michael Bratman & John Martin Fischer, Editors, Oxford (Oxford University Press, 2007) 542.

Here is another of Kant's formulations of the categorical imperative (he had several slightly different forms or wordings of the categorical imperative):

> "The universal imperative of duty may also run as follows: 'Act as if the maxim of your action were to become through your will a UNIVERSAL LAW of NATURE.'"[592]

Onora O'Neill showed the difficulty of precisely defining Kant's imperative:

> "One of the things that makes Kant's moral theory hard to understand is that he gives a number of different versions of the principle that he calls the Supreme Principle of Morality, and these different versions don't look at all like one another."[593]

Nevertheless, Kant's ethics have a clear theme.

The Practical Imperative: Treating others as ends and not as means

In addition to the categorical imperative, Kant had a further principle, which he called the *practical imperative,* to complete his ethical system, the importance of loving rather than using people for selfish purposes:

> "The practical imperative will therefore be as follows: Act in such a way that you always treat humanity, whether in your own person or in the person of any other, never simply as a means, but always at the same time as an end."[594]

---

[592]Immanuel Kant, *Groundwork of the Metaphysic of Morals,* 543.

[593]Onora O'Neill, *Kantian Approaches to Some Famine Problems* in *Introduction to Philosophy: Classical and Contemporary Readings,* Fourth Edition, John Perry, Michael Bratman & John Martin Fischer, Editors, Oxford (Oxford University Press, 2007) 553.

That is, by treating each person as an end themselves, we seek their highest good. We do not use them for selfish gain.

Putting Kant's ethics to use

Let us consider how Kant applied his categorical imperative to the issue of lying:

> "Then I presently become aware that, while I can will the lie, I can by no means will that lying should be a universal law. For with such a law there would be no promises at all, since it would be in vain to allege my intention in regard to my future actions to those who would not believe this allegation, or if they overhastily did so, would pay me back in my own coin."[595]

In other words, if one considers telling a lie to avoid an uncomfortable situation, they should first ask themselves if they want to live in a world where everyone lies in a similar situation. It seems that Kant's system of ethics owes much to the cultural influence of Christianity and the ideals of Jesus Christ.

While Kant rejected the traditional arguments for the existence of God, nevertheless, it was the demand for an authoritative ground of ethics that formed the basis of Kant's argument *for* the existence of God.

Stumpf summed up Kant's position:

---

[594]Immanuel Kant, *Groundwork of the Metaphysic of Morals,* 545.

[595]Immanuel Kant, *Fundamental Principles of the Metaphysics of Morals*, in *Critique of Practical Reason and Other works on the Theory of Ethics,* as cited by Samuel Enoch Stumpf, *Philosophy: History & Problems,* Fourth Edition, New York (McGraw-Hill Publishing Company, 1989) 683.

"The moral universe also compels us to postulate the existence of God as the grounds for the necessary connection between virtue and happiness . . . we must postulate 'the existence of a cause of the whole of nature which is distinct from nature and which contains the ground of this connection, namely, of the exact harmony of happiness with morality,' and thus 'it is morally necessary to assume the existence of God.'"[596]

Copan elaborated:

"Kant actually posits God, freedom, and immortality in order to make sense of morality; his is not a secular ethical system but one that requires God's existence."[597]

Kant's system of ethics, then, is saturated with biblical themes and is used to argue for the belief in God. Indeed, the categorical imperative and the practical imperative are merely restatements of the golden rule and the teachings of Jesus. Kant's system of ethics is an ethics of duty, of doing the right thing regardless of the consequences. Doing right, of course, has its own rewards, most especially because God rewards the good. Kantian Duty ethics are merely one form of the Divine Command theory as many philosophers have recognized, and as such are popular among many believers.

But what about lying?
My opinion about lying is that it is normally wrong (almost always), but that an exception can be made when a greater good will result from the lie.

---

[596]Samuel Enoch Stumpf, *Philosophy: History & Problems*, 319.
[597]Paul Copan, God, *Naturalism, and the Foundations of Morality*, chapter in *The Future of Atheism: Alister McGrath & Daniel Dennett in Dialogue*, Robert B. Stewart, Editor, Minneapolis MN (Fortress Press, 2008) 150-151.

This becomes a case of competing interests similar to the situation of competing rights in jurisprudence (The right to free speech, *yelling fire in a crowded theater*, can be curtailed by the safety rights of the other moviegoers who could be injured in a panicked stampede).

Likewise, the duty to tell the truth can be set aside for the greater good of saving lives. I believe that those who lied to the Nazi's to save the lives of innocent Jews during the Holocaust (there are many examples on record) were right to temporarily set aside the normal biblical principle against lying for the more important biblical principle of preserving and protecting innocent life.

The Bible itself shows such with the example of Rahab lying to protect the lives of the Jewish spies (Joshua 2:1-21). And indeed, she is commended in the Bible for her subterfuge in protecting God's servants (James 2:25).

This principle, however, should not be pressed too far as the old expression "hard cases make bad law" shows.

Natural Law

Yeager Hudson described the origins and basic ideas of natural law:

> "It comes as a great surprise to some to learn that during much of the history of the West, even in the Christian tradition, the divine command theory has not been the standard or accepted position. Among the ancient Greeks, as we have said, morality was believed to be grounded in human rationality and had nothing to do with religion or the gods . . . The Romans also seem to be the originators of the concept of natural law, not only as a term

to describe the regularities in the operation of the material world but also to name the principles recognized by human reason as valid for the regulation of human moral and political life.

These principles have nothing to do with the gods or religion, but are written, as it were, into the very structure of reality itself and are discoverable by any humans who take the trouble to reason carefully. This, according to the Romans, is the reason that fundamental moral and social values are so similar from one culture to another despite their great differences in details . . . There is an objective natural law from which morality can be inferred by any rational person, whether a religious believer or not. At least in principle, everyone who reasons carefully enough and succeeds in transcending the biases of his or her culture should arrive at the same set of fundamental moral principles binding for all."[598]

How should a Christian respond to the argument that natural law is an objective basis for morality, apart from any concern with the gods, as Hudson described?

Proponents of natural law should remember the important place the gods have actually played in Greek and Roman thought, and how much more in Christian thought.

If we ask, what is the source of these moral laws, and how they came to be within the very fabric of existence, the only answer can be the gods (or the biblical God). Again, who is it that made man a rational being and placed a conscience in his soul, if not God.

So, while natural law can explain the great similarities in morality across cultures (do not murder, do not lie, etc.,) it cannot explain the ultimate origin of

---

[598]Yeager Hudson, *The Philosophy of Religion*, Mountain View CA (Mayfield Publishing Company, 1991) 239-240, 241

ethics as derived from God(s). Thomas Aquinas said of natural law:

> "Hence the Psalmist [Psalm 4:6] thus implies that the light of natural reason, whereby we discern what is good and what is evil, which is the function of the natural law, is nothing else than an imprint on us of the divine light. It is therefore evident that the natural law is nothing else than the rational creature's participation of the eternal law."[599]

Further, for those who reject the existence of the god's, or the biblical God, what is it that compels or binds anyone to these natural laws? What prevents one from arbitrarily choosing any set of moral values he desires? If no gods, whom does the atheist feel accountable to but to himself?

Questions to consider for non-theistically grounded ethical systems

For any system of ethics not grounded in the Divine, several questions may be asked.

What is the source of the ethical approach? How can one *know* it is true? What is the authority behind it? That is, if there is not a God that stands behind it, why should anyone accept it or comply with it? Isn't it just an opinion? And how can its advocates avoid the charge that they are merely imposing their morals upon everyone else?

---

[599]Thomas Aquinas, *Summa Theologica*, as quoted by Theodore C. Denise, Nicholas P. White & Sheldon P. Peterfreund, *Great Traditions in Ethics*, Tenth Edition, Belmont CA (Wadsworth Thomson Learning, 2002) 82.

Chapter 32: Forms of Relativism

Cold-Hearted orb that rules the Night

Removes the colours from our sight

Red is grey and yellow white?

But we decide which is right and which is an illusion[600]

We have examined various ethical models that have in common the belief that there are objective moral standards (Moral Absolutism) to be found and followed. Most recognize God as the ultimate source of ethics or that they can be found through the use of human reason, itself a gift of God.

But what of those who reject the existence of God? How can they arrive at ethical or moral standards? All ethical models that deny objective moral standards fall under the general category of relativism and/or moral skepticism since they deny the very possibility of absolutist ethics.

Moral Skepticism

There are, then, some naturalists who just concede the impossibility of a universally applicable ethical system. For instance, J. L. Mackie began a work on ethics with this unambiguous assertion:

---

[600]Graham Edge, *Late Lament* from the song *Nights in White Satin* by The Moody Blues, © T.R.O. INC.

"There are no objective values. This is a bald statement of the thesis of this chapter . . . Since it is with moral values that I am primarily concerned, the view I am adopting may be called moral skepticism . . . another name often used, as an alternative to 'moral skepticism,' for the view I am discussing is 'subjectivism' . . . What I have called moral skepticism is a negative doctrine, not a positive one; it says what there isn't, not what there is. It says that there do not exist entities or relations of a certain kind, objective values or requirements, which many people have believed to exist."[601]

Give Mackie credit for clarity and frankness. Likewise, Nicholas Sturgeon stated:

"This provides an argument for moral skepticism because one obviously possible explanation for our difficulty in settling moral disagreements is that they are really unsettleable, that there is no way of justifying one rather than another competing view on these issues; and a possible further explanation for the unsettleability of moral disagreements, in turn, is moral nihilism, the view that on these issues there just is no fact of the matter, that the impossibility of discovering and establishing moral truths is due to there not being any."[602]

It seems unavoidable that any attempt to find an objective and universally binding ethic is doomed apart from an appeal to God as the lawgiver.

Atheist David Eller agreed with Mackie and Sturgeon, arguing that moral statements are illusory, and merely

[601]J. L. Mackie, *The Subjectivity of Values* in *Introduction to Philosophy: Classical and Contemporary Readings*, Fourth Edition, John Perry, Michael Bratman & John Martin Fischer, Editors, Oxford (Oxford University Press, 2007) 749-750.

[602]Nicholas L. Sturgeon, *Moral Explanations* in *Introduction to Philosophy: Classical and Contemporary Readings*, Fourth Edition, John Perry, Michael Bratman & John Martin Fischer, Editors, Oxford (Oxford University Press, 2007) 765.

personal expressions of feelings (Emotivism) and nothing more:

> "Cultural relativism makes sense and is crucial to grasp because some things—such as values, norms, morals, beliefs, and so on—are neither true nor false. They are, like the statements we analyzed above, non-rational . . . Even more, there is nothing to resolve, because there is no 'true' or 'correct' moral or value position, only alternatives."[603]

While I appreciate the straightforward manner of Mackie, Sturgeon, and Eller, yet it is truly breathtaking to see such statements in black and white. Can we really accept the implication of Eller's argument, for instance, that condemnations of Hitler and the holocaust are "neither true nor false"?

Eller referenced Nietzsche's view that moral standards are merely an attempt to control people:

> "Morals cannot be true or false. Morals are not facts, as Nietzsche stated, but rather instructions or orders."[604]

In other words, according to Nietzsche (and Eller), moral values, and particularly, the Christian moral system, are merely attempts at stealing individual freedom and enslaving people to the church, and church leaders.

This is a complete distortion of Christian moral principles. Rather than enslaving, they set men free. No longer are men captive to the temptations of the world, the Devil, and their own sinful nature, but instead find

---

[603]David Eller, *Natural Atheism*, Cranford New Jersey (American Atheist Press, 2004) 101-102.
[604]David Eller, *Natural Atheism*, 102.

true peace and strength in Jesus Christ. They conquer by becoming servants of love in the image of Jesus Christ!

Problems with Relativist' ethics

While relativism seems to offer a *live and let live ethic* that places a high value on freedom and mutual respect, it is ultimately an unworkable system. Consider the relativist' views of Bertrand Russell as explained by S. T. Joshi:

> "Russell, in *Religion and Science*, unequivocally adopts the principle of 'the 'subjectivity' of values'(R 237), with the obvious corollary that 'if two men differ about values, there is not a disagreement as to any kind of truth, but a difference in taste'(R 237-38). Another consequence of the principle is that 'there can be no such thing as 'sin' in any absolute sense; what one man calls 'sin' another may call 'virtue,' and though they may dislike each other on account of this difference, neither can convict the other of intellectual error'(R 238-39)."[605]

Russell can be commended for the straightforward statement of his ethics. Given his atheism, a relativist position is the only honest position. Nevertheless, the implications are startling. A victim of the holocaust would have no basis for condemning the actions of Hitler, for as Russell said, "What one man call sins another may call 'virtue.'" Indeed, any condemnation of Hitler would represent merely "a difference in taste."

Father Copleston attempted to point this weakness out in his famous debate with Bertrand Russell:

---

[605]Bertrand Russell, as quoted by S. T. Josh, *The Unbelievers: The Evolution of Modern Atheism*, Amherst NY (Prometheus Books, 2011) 165.

"Copleston: I think, in fact, that those modern atheists who have argued in the converse way 'there is no God, therefore, there are no absolute values and no absolute law,' are quite logical. Russell: I don't like the word 'absolute.' I don't think there is anything absolute whatever. The moral law, for example, is always changing. At one period in the development of the human race, almost everybody thought cannibalism was a duty."[606]

Russell appealed to the reality of changing ethical standards to suggest that there are, in fact, no objective, absolute, and universally binding ethical standards.

Russell erred by confusing *what is* (descriptive ethics) with *what should be* (prescriptive ethics). Because ethical standards change over time (descriptive) does not prove that they ought (prescriptive) to change. Because acts like theft, adultery, and murder have been present throughout human history (descriptive) is no argument that they ought to occur (prescriptive). Russell's argument, in effect, then, is circular; ethical standards should change because ethical standards change.

Russell's relativism simply left him with no basis for judging even the most egregious acts; the Holocaust and ante-bellum slavery were simply products of their culture, neither objectively right nor wrong, but merely matters of taste.

Consider the insightful comments of C. S. Lewis:

"If 'good' or 'better' are terms deriving their sole meaning from the ideology of each people, then of course

---

[606]Bertrand Russell & F. C. Copleston, *The Existence of God—A Debate* as reprinted in *A Modern Introduction to Philosophy: Readings from Classical and Contemporary Sources,* Third Edition, Paul Edwards & Arthur Pap, Editors, New York, (The Free Press, 1973) 486-487.

ideologies themselves cannot be better or worse than each other. Unless the measuring rod is independent of the things measured, we can do no measuring. For the same reason it is useless to compare the moral ideas of one age with those of another: progress and decadence are alike meaningless words."[607]

Groothius, likewise, showed the self-defeating nature of relativism:

"Relativists thereby contradict themselves by their statements. Despite their relativism, they will issue universal and absolute moral imperatives, such as 1. We should *never* affirm our own moral views as universal and absolute. 2. Moral absolutes are *absolutely* wrong. 3. *Everyone* should be a relativist . . . When relativists make such statements, they show that their moral system is unlivable and contradictory, and therefore false."[608]

Pragmatism

One form of relativism is pragmatism. Stumpf said about pragmatism that:

"The movement was given its initial theoretical formulation by Charles S. Pierce; it was given wide and popular circulation through the brilliant and lucid essays of William James; and it was methodically implemented into the daily affairs of American institutions by John Dewey."[609]

---

[607]C. S. Lewis, *Christian Reflections* (1967; reprint, Grand Rapids: Eerdmans, 1978), p. 73 as quoted by Douglass Groothuis, *Christian Apologetics: A Comprehensive Case for Biblical Faith*, Downers Grove IL (InterVarsity Press, 2011) 338.

[608]Douglass Groothuis, *Christian Apologetics: A Comprehensive Case for Biblical Faith*, Downers Grove IL (InterVarsity Press, 2011) 340.

[609]Samuel Enoch Stumpf, *Philosophy: History & Problems*, Fourth Edition, New York (McGraw-Hill Publishing Company, 1989) 410.

Nicholas Rescher summed up pragmatic belief:

> "The characteristic idea of philosophical pragmatism is
> that efficacy in practical application—'What works out
> most effectively in practice'—somehow provides a standard
> for the determination of truth in the case of statements,
> rightness in the case of actions, and value in the case of
> appraisals."[610]

In perhaps more accessible language, the
Encyclopedia of Ethics defined pragmatism:

> "The position that the meaning or TRUTH of a belief is
> determined by the outcome of adhering to that belief.
> Pragmatism is a theory of truth, which argues that ideas
> are true if they operate effectively in the world . . . James's
> views on pragmatism are particularly important for ethics
> as he held that all beliefs, even a belief in GOD, are true
> insofar as they 'work' in the world . . . The essential point
> is that if a belief in God made for a better life and society,
> then such a belief would be true. Pascal's Wager is also
> frequently cited as an example of a pragmatic religious
> principle. In ordinary ethical language, pragmatism also
> means that what works is true . . . A pragmatist is in this
> sense more interested in consequences than in moral
> rules."[611]

William James himself compared the value of an
ethical judgment to a financial transaction:

> "Pragmatism, on the other hand, asks its usual
> question, 'Grant an idea or belief to be true,' it says, 'what
> concrete difference will its being true make in any one's
> actual life? . . . What, in short, is the truth's cash-value in

---

[610]Nicholas Rescher, *Pragmatism*, in *The Oxford Guide to
Philosophy*, Ted Honderich, Editor, Oxford UK (Oxford University
Press, 2005) 747.

[611]Susan Neiburg Terkel & R. Shannon Duval, Editors, *Encyclopedia
of Ethics*, New York (Facts on File, Inc, 1999) 216-217.

experiential terms?' . . . Truth lives, in fact, for the most part on a credit system. Our thoughts and beliefs 'pass,' so long as nothing challenges them, just as bank-notes pass so long as nobody challenges them."[612]

His example is actually rather troubling, for it would seem to justify actually (and not just as a comparison) using counterfeit currency. Hey, as long as it works, why not? It's not whether it is right or wrong, but just what works.

Now a pragmatist would probably point out that using counterfeit money may work in the short come, but in the long-term it just might wind up putting one in prison for a long time. In other words, it may not work pragmatically for the long-haul.

Fair enough. But that merely highlights the problem with pragmatic ethics. Counterfeiting is not wrong per se, but is only right or wrong based upon how useful it is (or isn't). Again, is adultery wrong on its face or just not advisable because of the consequences of getting caught?

I would argue rather that what gives the public confidence in currency is that it is backed, either by precious metals, or by the full faith and credit of the government that issued it. Likewise, the only ethical system that can have any real authority is one that it is backed by the full faith and credit of Almighty God.

Problems with pragmatic philosophy and ethics

Norman Geisler summed up some of the problems inherent in pragmatism:

"The pragmatic view has been severely criticized because something is not true simply because it works.

[612]Samuel Enoch Stumpf, *Philosophy: History & Problems*, 644, 646.

Lying may 'work' to avoid a negative result or achieve a desired objective at the expense of the other person, but that doesn't make the lies true . . . Neither is something right because it works. Cheating 'works,' but it is not right . . . A pragmatic view of truth also undermines trust. What judge would allow someone to take a courtroom oath to tell, as one philosopher quipped, 'the expedient, the whole expedient, and nothing but the expedient.'"[613]

The problem, then, with pragmatism ironically, is, that it just doesn't work in the real world we all live in. Consider the pragmatic slogan that "if it feels good, do it." One doesn't have to think very hard to see how shortsighted this ideal is.

It might feel good to get high on drugs, but the effects can be devastating. There are many forms of sexual expression that may feel good, but which are nevertheless, unhealthy and destructive.

Likewise, ethical slogans like, "You can do whatever you want so long as you don't hurt anyone" fail to take into account man's great penchant for self-deception. We are often simply blind to the real consequences of our actions and how they impact others, having an amazing ability of justifying our own actions at the expense of others. In this regard, it suffers from the same weaknesses of Utilitarianism (another form of consequentialism).

Emotivism

We have just considered Eller's allusion to Emotivism. It holds that moral statements merely represent the feelings or emotions of the speaker, and do not have any

---

[613]Norman L. Geisler, *Baker Encyclopedia of Christian Apologetics*, Grand Rapids MI (Baker Books, 1999) 606-607.

objective reference. Emotivism grew out of the logical positivist movement, which held that statements were either analytically true or empirically verifiable, or were meaningless.

One of the logical outcomes of this verificationist principle was that *ethical* statements were held to be factually meaningless and, therefore, merely reflected the emotional feelings of the speaker. Evans and Manis explained:

> "A view which is theoretically different but has the same practical result is ethical *emotivism*. The emotivist says that there are no real (that is, objectively binding) moral obligations. When a person says that an act is wrong, she is not stating a fact, but only expressing her individual emotions or attitude about the act."[614]

S. T. Joshi argued for just this viewpoint: "This is because ethical statements are not statements of fact, but emotional responses to facts."[615] Ayer, an important proponent of Emotivism stated:

> "We can now see why it is impossible to find a criterion for determining the validity of ethical judgments . . . It is not because they have an 'absolute' validity which is mysteriously independent of ordinary sense-experience, but because they have no objective validity whatsoever . . . And we have seen that sentences which simply express moral judgments do not say anything. They are pure expressions of feeling and as such do not come under the category of truth and falsehood . . . they do not express genuine propositions."[616]

---

[614]C. Stephen Evans & R. Zachary Manis, *Philosophy of Religion: Thinking About Faith*, Second Edition, Downers Grove IL (Inter Varsity Press, 2009) 90.

[615]S. T. Joshi, *The Unbelievers: The Evolution of Modern Atheism*, Amherst NY (Prometheus Books, 2011) 227.

Emotivism as an ethical theory has largely been abandoned along with the logical positivist philosophy that spawned it, for the good reason that it goes against our deepest intuitive beliefs about right and wrong.

Are ethics derived collectively from one's culture and/or its government?

Many, perhaps without thinking about it, assume that in some sense each culture creates its own morality and are reflected in their civil laws. This was the view held by Thomas Hobbes (1588-1679):

> "With the establishment of the commonwealth through the social contract, Hobbes tells us, the necessary and sufficient condition for morality is present . . . Hobbes thus establishes *civil authority and law as the foundation of morality*."[617]

Reflecting this idea, some simply refuse to do anything illegal. However, if the law were to change, they might do it. This was the case, for instance with alcohol before, during, and after prohibition. So, it is certainly the case that a country's laws do, at least to some extent, reflect the moral feelings of its citizens, and have a restraining effect.

But there are several problems with the idea that ethics are culturally determined. For instance, how can

---

[616]A. J. Ayer, *Language, Truth, and Logic*, New York, Dover Publications, 1950, 108-109, as quoted by Theodore C. Denise, Nicholas P. White & Sheldon P. Peterfreund, *Great Traditions in Ethics*, Tenth Edition, Belmont CA (Wadsworth Thomson Learning, 2002) 271.

[617]Theodore C. Denise, Nicholas P. White & Sheldon P. Peterfreund, *Great Traditions in Ethics*, Tenth Edition, Belmont CA (Wadsworth Thomson Learning, 2002) 91. For Hobbes, the civil authority could be "a monarch or an assembly) (ibid) 101.

there be ethical progress and moral reformers? The very idea of such reforms is the acknowledgement that the culture has been wrong on an issue.

The fact is that the laws of the United States once allowed for, and even protected, the slave trade, treating the enslaved as property rather than respecting their God-given human rights.

Halverson stated:

> "We recognize, for example, that the federal Fugitive Slave Law of 1793, which allowed slave 'owners' to capture and retrieve slaves who had sought freedom in another state, was a profoundly unjust law because it violated the basic principle that every human being has a right to his personal freedom, that compulsory servitude—slavery—is morally wrong."[618]

Now most of us would agree that the laws permitting slavery were immoral. But if ethics are culturally determined, on what basis can the ante-bellum slavery culture of America be judged?

Further, there was a time when slavery was banned in the United Kingdom (England) while it was legal in the United States. If cultural ethos and civil laws are the basis for morality, this would suggest that slavery was ethically acceptable in the United States and wrong in the United Kingdom at the very same time.

Examples like this abound. During the Nazi period in Germany, was it ethical to exterminate Jews? If you were living in Hitler's Germany, and you were an atheist, on what basis could you condemn Hitler? He had the law and the country on his side.

---

[618]William H. Halverson, *A Concise Introduction to Philosophy*, Third Edition, New York (Random House, 1976) 358.

Atheist Kai Nielsen recognized the inherent problems associated with the view that ethics are culturally determined:

> "It is equally true that the fact that my culture approves of something does not establish that it is a good thing to do. The Greeks of Plato's and Aristotle's time (like people in many other cultures) approved of infanticide. That this is so is established by anthropological investigation but this fact does not establish the truth of the moral statement 'infanticide is sometimes a good thing.' What makes the anthropological statement true does not make the ethical statement true. Plato would not be contradicting himself if he said, 'My culture approves of infanticide, but infanticide is evil.'"[619]

Can we each decide our own morality?

Another relativist' idea often advanced is that each person chooses their own moral values. Since, as we are told, there are no absolutes, each individual is bound only by their own ideals of right and wrong.

If this were the case, it would be difficult to establish civil laws since each person could argue, "My ethics allow me to steal from others" or "You have no right to tell me I can't do heroin. There is nothing wrong with it." If we each choose our own morality, then no one can condemn anyone else for their choices.

Let us consider again, how such an ethic would have applied in the context of Nazi Germany. If your neighbor was an SS officer working at a concentration camp, and you suggested to him that exterminating Jews was wrong, he, if he believed each person decides their own

---

[619]Kai Nielsen, *Atheism & Philosophy*, Amherst NY (Prometheus Books, 2005) 198.

morality, could say, "Well, that's just your opinion. Who are you to tell me what I can or cannot do? Who are you to try to impose your morality on others? If you don't want to kill Jews, that's your decision, but you have no right to tell me what to do."

Unfortunately, the moral relativist that denies objective moral standards, and who believes each person determines their own moral standards, would sadly have had no response to offer the SS officer. The truth is that such an ethic is unworkable in the real world. Without objective moral standards, we would simply have moral anarchy.

The very notion of human rights depends upon a God that transcends both individuals and societies. We can only condemn the actions of the Nazi's if ethics are grounded in God, and not in the will of individuals or society collectively.

There will be a price to pay (increased crime, chemical addiction, broken families, breakdown and corruption in governmental institutions) for the West as it increasingly abandons its Christian foundations.

Ayn Rand's ethics

The atheist Ayn Rand's philosophy reflected a rejection of the Christian ethic concerning love of neighbor (not to mention love for one's enemies) when she said: "'And to earn my love, my brothers must do more that to have been born.'"[620]

In other words, Rand's love had to be earned. Rand's egoistic ethics rejected the downtrodden and outcasts of

---

[620]Norman L. Geisler, *Baker Encyclopedia of Christian Apologetics*, 632.

Steve Lagoon

society, the very people that are the objects of God's mercy and grace.

Does it matter what motivates our ethics?

Michael Martin argued that believers have no advantage over unbelievers concerning matters of morality:

> "Historically, atheists have been attacked for flaws in their moral character . . . Many religious people still hold the opinion that religious belief is closely related to moral action. But is there any reason to suppose that religious belief and morality are intimately associated?"[621]

I ask, as a simple matter of reason, whom we may expect to live by higher moral standards—those who believe that they will be held accountable for their choices by God or those whom believe themselves absolutely free to do as they wish? To me, the answer is obvious.

To prove his case that believers are not morally superior to unbelievers, Martin cited the example of David Hume: "David Hume has been described as the saintly infidel."[622] Unfortunately, for Martin, Hume did not profess atheism. Further, Neil Turnbull showed that David Hume "was brought up in a strict Presbyterian family, and the austere world of Scottish Protestantism."[623]

The point is that although many skeptics and atheists have lived exemplary lives, it should be remembered that

---

[621]Michael Martin, *Atheism: A Philosophical Justification,* Philadelphia PA (Temple University Press, 1990) 4, 5
[622]Michael Martin, *Atheism,* 6.
[623]Neil Turnbull, *Get a Grip on Philosophy,* New York (Barnes & Noble Books, 1999) 114.

they were not raised in a vacuum, but were rather raised in cultures saturated with Christianity.

Indeed, many of our greatest thinkers grew up in very devout families, and were formed and molded by the very Christian principles they would later reject. They were in a real sense living off the borrowed capital of Christianity.

Chapter 33: Evolutionary Accounts of Morality

If we tell our young that they are nothing but evolving animals,

we shouldn't be surprised if they act like animals![624]

Richard Dawkins is at the forefront of offering evolutionary explanations, not only for religion in general, but for the origin of the moral sense itself. Walters explained:

> "Richard Dawkins has been one of the most vocal defenders of the increasingly fashionable atheist position that evolution has hardwired human beings to behave."[625]

Michael Ruse also advanced the idea that evolution is to account for the development of morality:

> "Morality is a biological adaption no less than are hands and feet and teeth . . . Considered as a rationally justifiable set of claims about an objective something, ethics is illusory. I appreciate that when somebody says 'Love thy neighbor as thyself,' they think they are referring above and beyond themselves . . . Nevertheless; such reference is truly without foundation. Morality is just an aid to survival and reproduction and has no being beyond or without this."[626]

---

[624] The Author
[625]Kerry Walters, *Atheism: A Guide for the Perplexed*, New York (The Continuum International Publishing Group Inc, 2010) 128.
[626]Michael Ruse, *Evolutionary Theory and Christian Ethics* in *The Darwinian Paradigm* (London: Routledge, 1989), pp. 262, 269 as quoted by Douglass Groothuis, *Christian Apologetics: A Comprehensive Case for Biblical Faith*, Downers Grove IL (InterVarsity Press, 2011) 349.

Indeed, Ruse, along with E. O. Wilson, have suggested that morality is merely something "fobbed off on us by our genes to get us to cooperate."[627]

It is claimed then, that the moral sense in man is an illusion that yet aided man in his evolutionary struggle for survival. There is then no need to search for an objective accounting of ethics; they are not to be found.

Evolutionary Psychology

Wilson is among a group of thinkers that seeks to wed evolutionary science with the social sciences. That is, the insights of Darwinian evolution become explanatory principles in virtually every area of thought. Steven and Hilary Rose explained:

> "Evolutionary psychology . . . claims to explain all aspects of human behavior, and thence culture and society, on the basis of universal features of human nature . . . And of course there are more serious claims, such as those legitimizing men's 'philandering' and women's 'coyness,' our capacity to detect cheaters, to favor our genetic kin, to be aggressive. Evolutionary psychologists claim to have identified and explained all these as biological adaptations—that is, behaviors that have been selected during human evolution to assist in survival and hence the propagation of our ancestors' genes. The main players in this new genre are the psychologists Leda Cosmides and John Tooby, Margo Wilson and Martin Daly, [and] Steven Pinker."[628]

---

[627]Michael Ruse & E. O. Wilson, *The Evolution of Ethics*, in *Religion and the Natural Sciences*, ed. J. E. Huchingson (Orlando: Harcourt Brace, 1993), 310-311 as cited by Paul Copan, *God Naturalism, and the Foundations of Morality*, chapter in *The Future of Atheism: Alister McGrath & Daniel Dennett in Dialogue*, Robert B. Stewart, Editor, Minneapolis MN (Fortress Press, 2008)151.

Rose and Rose added:

"To an uninitiated eye, evolutionary psychology, which seems to have gotten into the cultural drinking water in both the U.S.A. and the U.K., may seem little different from old-style sociobiology, whose exponents, E. O. Wilson, Richard Dawkins, Robert Trivers and David Buss, still find a place in EP's pantheon of intellectual heroes."[629]

Hilary Nelkin warns of the danger of premature acceptance of the arguments of evolutionary psychology on the basis of its seeming scientific authority:

"Evolutionary explanations combine the credibility of science with the certainty of religion."[630]

To explain the powerful ability of evolutionary thought to reshape Western thought:

"One philosopher, Daniel Dennett, has described Darwinism as a 'universal acid' that eats everything it touches."[631]

Dennett's use of the metaphor of acid is telling since he supports the corrosive effect that evolutionary thought has had on the foundations of Western civilization, most prominent among them the influence of Christianity.

---

[628]Hilary Rose & Steven Rose, *Introduction, Alas, Poor Darwin: Arguments Against Evolutionary Psychology*, Edited by Hilary Rose & Steven Rose, New York (Harmony Books, 2000) 2-3.

[629]Hilary Rose & Steven Rose, *Introduction, Alas, Poor Darwin*, 4.

[630]Dorothy Nelkin, *Less Selfish Than Sacred?: Genes and the Religious Impulse in Evolutionary Psychology*, chapter in, *Alas, Poor Darwin: Arguments Against Evolutionary Psychology*, Edited by Hilary Rose & Steven Rose, New York (Harmony Books, 2000) 26.

[631]Hilary Rose & Steven Rose, *Introduction, Alas, Poor Darwin*, 2.

Rape

Rose and Rose have explained how evolutionary psychology has influenced cultural thinking on the issue of rape:

> "Perhaps the nadir of evolutionary psychology's speculative fantasies was reached earlier this year [2000] with the publication of *A Natural History of Rape: Biological Bases of Sexual Coercion*, by Randy Thornhill and Craig Palmer. In characteristic EP style, Thornhill and Palmer argue that rape is an adaptive strategy by which otherwise sexually unsuccessful men propagate their genes by mating with fertile women."[632]

Rose and Rose noted the weakness of this account:

> "As those women's groups, lawyers and feminist criminologists who have confronted rape over the last three decades have documented, victims of rape are often either too young or too old to be fertile. The universalistic explanation offered by Thornhill and Palmer simply fails to address the evidence."[633]

Sam Harris agreed with the evolutionary origin of morality, yet he attempted to distinguish between acts (like rape) that arose during evolutionary history and the desirability or undesirability of those acts today:

> "The practice of rape may have once conferred an adaptive advantage on our species—and rapist of all shapes and sizes can indeed be found in the natural world . . . Does this mean that rape is any less objectionable in human society? *Even if we concede that some number of rapes are inevitable, given how human beings are wired,* how is this different from saying that some numbers of

---

[632]Hilary Rose & Steven Rose, *Introduction, Alas, Poor Darwin,* 3.
[633]Hilary Rose & Steven Rose, *Introduction, Alas, Poor Darwin,* 3.

cancers are inevitable? We will strive to cure cancer in any case. To say that something is 'natural,' or that it has conferred an adaptive advantage upon our species, is not to say that it is 'good' in the required sense of contributing to human happiness in the present."[634]

We begin our response to Harris by noting the false comparison he made between rape and cancer. For while Harris argued that rape "may have once conferred an adaptive advantage" yet, it is hard to conceive how cancer "may have once conferred an adaptive advantage."

But for the sake of argument, if ethics and morals owe their origin to the fact that they had conferred an evolutionary advantage, as is suggested, on what basis, then, does Harris condemn rape today? On what basis can he distinguish between the ethical nature of rape versus monogamy? Harris' attempt to do so is merely arbitrary given his evolutionary hypothesis.

Charles Jenks noted the inconsistency of supporters of such evolutionary psychological explanations when they lead to undesirable conclusions that are abrasive to our modern sense:

> "Even EP-enthusiasts, such as Richard Dawkins and Steven Pinker, when they do not like the message, tell their genes to jump in the lake."[635]

If evolutionary success is defined as leaving progeny, it seems difficult to understand how Harris can condemn

---

[634]Sam Harris, *The End of Faith: Religion, Terror, and the Future of Reason*, New York (W. W. Norton & Company, 2004) 185.

[635]Charles Jencks, *EP, Phone Home*, chapter in, *Alas, Poor Darwin: Arguments Against Evolutionary Psychology*, Edited by Hilary Rose & Steven Rose, New York (Harmony Books, 2000) 53.

serial rapists. Is not the rapist merely acting out of an instinctual evolutionary drive to pass on his genes?

Some try to evade this implication by arguing that the offspring living under the protection of a father in a long-term monogamous relationship had/have a greater chance of survival and reproduction.

But if nature displays both serial rapists (have many offspring and play the odds that one or more will survive) and monogamist (focus on protecting a few children in an intact family), there is, then, no evolutionary argument to favor one over the other, since they have both been successful in evolutionary terms.

The Naturalist Fallacy

Some counter that such arguments (as I have just made) are guilty of the naturalistic fallacy. Wilson, Dietrich, and Clark explain:

> "Evolutionary psychologists frequently cite something called the naturalistic fallacy to describe an erroneous way of thinking about the ethical implications of evolved behaviors. The fallacy is usually summarized by the slogan 'ought cannot be derived from is.' Just because a given behavior evolved by natural selection does not make it ethically acceptable. Again and again, the naturalistic fallacy is invoked in response to those who criticize evolutionary psychology (and before that sociobiology) for its perceived dire ethical implications. Unfortunately, appealing to the naturalistic fallacy is not the drop-dead argument it is often taken to be."[636]

---

[636]David Sloan Wilson, Eric Dietrich, and Anne B. Clark, *On the Inappropriate Use of the Naturalistic Fallacy in Evolutionary Psychology*, Netherlands (Kluwer Academic Publications, 2003) 669.

Wilson, Dietrich, and Clark offered an example of evolutionary psychologists, in this case Gaulin and McBurney, appealing to the naturalistic fallacy:

> "Evolutionary psychology explains behavior; it does not justify it. Imagining that it offers a justification is known as the naturalistic fallacy (e.g., Buss 1990). In a nutshell, the naturalistic fallacy confuses 'is' with 'ought.' It confuses the situation that exists in the world with our ethical judgment about that situation. Earthquakes, volcanic eruptions, floods, pestilence, AIDS, cancer, and heart attacks are all natural phenomena. Yet we study their causes, not to justify them, but to be better able to eradicate them or alleviate their effects. By the same token, we hold that studying the possible evolutionary origins of child abuse or infidelity is a good way to understand and therefore address the problems (p. 16)."[637]

As with Harris, the argument is not legitimate since "earthquakes, volcanic eruptions, floods, pestilence, AIDS, cancer and heart attacks" are not normally advanced as evolutionary adaptations to increase reproductive success.

Then Wilson, Dietrich, and Clark move on to show how the naturalistic fallacy is improperly invoked to avoid the implications involved in evolutionary explanations of rape:

---

[637]S. J. C. Gaulin and D. H. McBurney, *Psychology: An Evolutionary Approach*, Prentice-Hall, Upper Saddle River, NJ, 2001 15-16, as quoted by David Sloan Wilson, Eric Dietrich, and Anne B. Clark, *On the Inappropriate Use of the Naturalistic Fallacy in Evolutionary Psychology*, Kluwer Academic Publishers, Netherlands, 2003, 671-672669. at web address: http://courses.washington.edu/evpsych/Wilson%20et%20al%20on%20naturalistic%20fallacy.pdf

"To see how discussion of the naturalistic fallacy is employed for a contemporary issue, we turn to Thornhill and Palmer's (2000) *The Natural History of Rape*, which discusses the naturalistic fallacy nine times."[638]

Wilson, Dietrich, and Clark explained possible explanations for the evolutionary origin of rape discussed by Thornhill and Palmer. For instance:

"The next time that the fallacy is invoked follows a discussion of the hypothesis that rape is a form of mate choice in women. According to this hypothesis, women evolved to play 'hard to get' so that only the toughest and most fit men would succeed in mating with them. Women may not want to be raped in terms of their psychological motivation, but their very horror insures that they will be impregnated only by the best. They do not regard this as a very plausible hypothesis to explain rape in humans, merely as a theoretical possibility. What would be the ethical implications if the hypothesis turned out to be true?"[639]

Wilson, Dietrich, and Clark warn that evolutionary psychologists cannot simply dismiss the ethical implications of their theories:

"Our point is merely that the naturalistic fallacy cannot be used to ward off ethical debates the way that a crucifix is supposed to ward off vampires."[640]

---

[638] David Sloan Wilson, Eric Dietrich, and Anne B. Clark, *On the Inappropriate Use of the Naturalistic Fallacy in Evolutionary Psychology,* 2003, 673.

[639] David Sloan Wilson, Eric Dietrich, and Anne B. Clark, *On the Inappropriate Use of the Naturalistic Fallacy in Evolutionary Psychology,* 2003, 673.

[640] David Sloan Wilson, Eric Dietrich, and Anne B. Clark, *On the Inappropriate Use of the Naturalistic Fallacy in Evolutionary Psychology,* 2003, 674.

Then they, Wilson, Dietrich, and Clark, asked:

> "If rape is natural, won't that fact be used to justify rape or at least to not judge it as harshly as if rape is abnormal?"[641]

Could not a rapist argue at his trial that his actions have resulted from deep evolutionary drives and should not be judged criminally? Indeed, he may have learned in his college class on evolution that women only resist men's advances so that the strongest among them finally succeeds in impregnating her. This puts Dennett's phrase "Darwin's dangerous idea"[642] in an unflattering light.

Since evolutionary atheists like Dawkins and Dennett have no Archimedean basis for ethics, and even assert that ethical systems are the illusory subterfuge of evolution (see above), they are without recourse to judge the rapist.

In contrast, Christianity recognizes the impulse of sin in human behavior. But this is balanced by a will that is free to resist as much as to yield to dark impulses, and that there are objective and divinely authoritative ethical standards that we are all accountable to.

Dawkins and the evolutionary origin of altruism

One of the questions facing evolutionists is to explain how or why altruism arose within an evolutionary framework. If it is all about the survival of the fittest in a

---

[641]David Sloan Wilson, Eric Dietrich, and Anne B. Clark, *On the Inappropriate Use of the Naturalistic Fallacy in Evolutionary Psychology*, 2003, 675.

[642]Daniel Dennett, *Darwin's Dangerous Idea: Evolution and the Meanings of Life*, New York (Simon & Schuster, 1995).

savage world, what accounts for altruistic behavior? Kerry Walters explained Richard Dawkins' answer:

> "Dawkins argues that selfish genes which favor reciprocal altruism improve their chances of survival and reproduction. Reciprocal altruism is the symbiotic cooperation between members of a different species in which deals are 'brokered' that result in mutual benefit . . . Our genes 'know' that it's in their interest to keep promises so that the behavior will elicit reciprocity."[643]

To begin with, I am not clear how genes can "know" things. Where in the gene is the brain that figures things out; that thinks "Oh, whenever the organism I am in works well with others and helps out the less fortunate, my survivability increases!" Is that really a scientific explanation?

At any rate, Dawkins argued that just as favoring your kin helps to ensure generational reproductive success, so also, developing reciprocal and symbiotic relationships with other does as well. But Dawkins doesn't explain why altruism (giving limited food supplies to the needy) increases the evolutionary advantage over his competitors in the survival of the fittest who for their part, take away food from the weak.

It seems that Dawkins is trying to put a pretty bow on the dog eat dog, survival of the fittest evolutionary theory, without offering any real scientific basis for his evolutionary account of altruism.

Dawkins altruism as misfirings

Dawkins attempted to defend his explanation of the evolutionary advantage of altruism by showing how such

[643]Kerry Walters, *Atheism,* 128.

behavior arose in the first place. We noted that Dawkins' argument that our genes "know" altruistic behavior is to their evolutionary advantage. How they learned this, according to Dawkins, must have been the result of "misfirings."

Kerry Walters explained:

> "But the question immediately arises as to how the in-group behaviors that Dawkins describes made the leap to moral virtues that have wider application. How did our ancestors move from favoring their own kin to universalizing behaviors such as loyalty and generosity? In a move similar to his analysis of religion as an evolutionary by-product, Dawkins' answer is that our 'Good Samaritan urges' are biological misfirings . . . In the case of humans, our ancestor's privileging of kin has misfired into a moral regard for all humans, or at least for a wider range of humans."[644]

Dawkins compares our sense of altruism to the 'unfortunate' lust a man may have for a woman who is unable to conceive. "Both are misfirings, Darwinian mistakes: blessed, precious mistakes."[645]

Although Dawkins tried to use positive terms to describe his idea ("blessed, precious mistakes) I suspect that he used words like" misfiring" and "mistakes" believing them to be less flammable and offensive than 'mutations.' But how else could these new genetic features be passed down in evolutionary terms?

Strictly speaking, evolution is supposed to reward with survival those who outdo their competitors in the battle for life. Therefore, argued Dawkins, altruistic

---

[644]Kerry Walters, *Atheism,* 129
[645]Richard Dawkins, *The God Delusion*, New York (Houghton Mifflin Company, 2006) 221.

behavior, helping others beyond one's own family group is counterproductive in evolutionary terms and must have resulted from some "biological misfiring."

The implication of Dawkins' argument is that all our humanitarian efforts are misguided at best. Rushing famine relief to feed the starving; providing safe-harbor to war refugees; sending aid workers and supplies to help victims of natural disasters, fighting slavery and injustice. All these altruistic activities are contrary to evolutionary forces; merely the result of some biological misfiring.

How very much this stands in contrast to the Christian ethic of loving your neighbor, and of being good Samaritans, compassionately caring for the needy and suffering of the world in the name of Jesus Christ.

If morality resulted from genetic misfirings they are arbitrary

And if Dawkins is correct that moral ideals have resulted from genetic mutations, it follows that our particular beliefs of right and wrong have no objective basis? If altruistic behavior resulted from a genetic misfiring, it follows that some have the altruistic gene, and others don't. Neither can be thought to be "good or bad" per se, but are merely random results of evolutionary history.

The logical implication is that altruistic behavior is no better, morally or ethically, than self-centered behavior. Both have been successful in evolutionary terms and suggesting that one is morally superior is merely arbitrary.

Likewise, some evolutionists have argued that natural selection may have caused different ethical norms for those living in different environments. If this is so, how can we know which, or if any, is correct?

John Haught challenged Dawkins idea of misfiring and altruism:

> "Still the real issue, raised but not answered by Dawkins, is how to justify our moral precepts so that we are bound by them unconditionally . . . Even if our ethical instincts evolved by natural selection, we still have to explain why we are obliged to obey them here and now, especially since they may be evolutionary 'misfirings.'"[646]

How can believing false ideas confer evolutionary advantage?

And if as many evolutionists claim, religious ideas themselves evolved because they offered survival advantages despite the fact they run counter to evolutionary principles, how can we know if the same is not true of or our moral impulses and beliefs? Perhaps they confer some survival advantage and yet are false! If our moral and ethical beliefs are merely the result of the random forces of evolution (mutations and changing environments), how can we trust them? How can we know that they are not, in fact, false?

Dawkins other explanations for altruism

Walters described further aspects of Dawkins' evolutionary account of altruism:

---

[646]John F. Haught, *God and the New Atheism: A Critical Response to Dawkins, Harris, and Hitchens*, Louisville KY (Westminster John Knox Press, 2008) 72-73.

"Kinship and reciprocation, says Dawkins, are the 'twin pillars' of natural altruism, but they give rise to a couple of secondary behavioral qualities that serve to further ground human moral actions. One is reputation, the habitual display of behavior which earns the animal the 'reputation' of being a good reciprocator. The other is advertisement, in which animals behave altruistically as a signal to others of their dominance or superiority. Birds known as Arabian babblers, for example, 'altruistically' donate food to one another to show off. Such displays of superiority are responded to favorably by sexual partners, thereby increasing the likelihood of such altruistic advertisement being passed on to offspring."[647]

Dawkins understandably grounds his argument in kinship and reciprocation. Of course, helping our own aids in the survival of our genetic line (Darwinian fitness).[648] We have seen how Dawkins argued that altruistic behavior beyond our own can be accounted for by genetic misfirings.

As Walters summed up, Dawkins also appealed to other reasons for altruistic behavior. One is reputation. Apparently potential mates are attracted to a mate that has a reputation for altruism. But why would this be so in evolutionary terms? Would a potential mate be attracted to one with a reputation for wasting precious resources (time, energy, food, and even life) on non-kin relations, perhaps hoping that the others would reciprocate? It seems more likely, in cold evolutionary terms, that potential mates would write off the altruistic

---

[647]Kerry Walters, *Atheism,* 128.

[648]Dorothy Nelkin, *Less Selfish Than Sacred?: Genes and the Religious Impulse in Evolutionary Psychology,* chapter in, *Alas, Poor Darwin: Arguments Against Evolutionary Psychology,* Edited by Hilary Rose & Steven Rose, New York (Harmony Books, 2000)18.

babbler as a poor choice on account of its wasteful management of precious resources.

Aczel further challenged Dawkins' explanation:

> "Natural selection tells us that individuals strive to propagate their genes through future generations. Therefore, risking one's own life to save complete strangers from a burning house should be a tendency that would disappear from the world: By doing this, a person increases the probability of removing his or her genes from future generations . . . In fact, how would you use evolution to explain the persistence in our world of people such as soldiers, medics, firefighters, police officers, and first responders who courageously save members of a different race than their own at the risk of losing their lives?"[649]

The problem of what is versus what ought to be.

After describing Dawkins evolutionary account of ethics, Walters raised serious concerns about its usefulness or applicability:

> "Is it legitimate to springboard from the fact that these behaviors enhance survival to the norm that we ought to practice them. This is a question that not only challenges Dawkins's evolutionary account of morality but any ethics that claims to be naturalistic rather than superanaturalistic. How can description be prescription?"[650]

Charles Taylor cited Solovyov's pointed parody of evolutionary accounts of ethics:

[649]Amir D. Aczel, *Why Science Does Not Disprove God*, New York (HarperCollins Publishers, 2014) 202-203.
[650]Kerry Walters, *Atheism: A Guide for the Perplexed*, New York (The Continuum International Publishing Group Inc, 2010) 130.

"There seems to be a strange inference here, caricatured by Solovyov: 'Man descends from the apes, therefore we must love each other.'"[651]

Finally, J. P. Moreland noted Mackie's important rejection of the theory of the evolutionary account of ethics and morality:

"The late J. L. Mackie, who in my opinion may be the best philosophical atheist of this century . . . made the following statement: 'Moral properties constitute so odd a cluster of properties and relations that they are most unlikely to have arisen in the ordinary course of events without an all-powerful god to create them.' Mackie's solution is to just deny the existence of these properties. And he goes on to argue that all we can do is to create values subjectively."[652]

---

[651]Charles Taylor, *A Secular Age*, Cambridge MA (The Belknap Press of Harvard University Press, 2007) 596.

[652]J. P. Moreland, & Kai Nielsen, *Does God Exist?: The Debate Between Theists & Atheists*, Amherst NY (Prometheus Books, 1993) 114.

Section Seven: The Problem of Evil and Suffering

Chapter 34: Feeling the Pain

"There is Auschwitz, and so there cannot be God.

Primo Levi"[653]

"Does anyone know where the love of God goes when waves

turn the minutes to hours."

Gordon Lightfoot[654]

I have placed the problem of evil and suffering in the section concerned with arguments against the existence of God because it is as Peter Kreeft stated: "The strongest argument for atheism has always been the problem of evil."[655]

We see all around us great human misery and suffering from a seemingly endless list of diseases and

---

[653]Primo Levi, as quoted in *Random House Webster's Quotationary*, Leonard Roy Frank, Editor, New York (Random House, 2001) 49.

[654]Gordon Lightfoot, *The Wreck of the Edmund Fitzgerald*, Moose Music LTD/Early Morning Music LTD

[655]Peter Kreeft, Introduction to *Does God Exist?: The Debate Between Theists & Atheists*, J.P. Moreland & Kai Nielsen, Amherst NY (Prometheus Books, 1993) 25.

calamities. We see the scourge of cancer wreaking havoc on our bodies, including even small children. It is hard to see senior citizens racked by age and minds giving way to various forms of dementia.

In addition to suffering, we are well-acquainted with the various atrocities and acts of evil reported in our daily news. Rapes, murders, child abuse; needless and senseless crimes perpetrated by those whom seem to be monsters.

In *The Brothers Karamazov* by Fyodor Dostoevsky, the character Ivan has begun to pour out his soul to his brother Aloysha about the evil and suffering men inflict upon one another. As he recollects some truly brutal mistreatment of children, Ivan suddenly stops to say "I am making you suffer, Aloysha, you are not yourself. I'll leave off if you like.' But Aloysha responds, "Never mind. I want to suffer too."[656]

"I Want to suffer too"

We are moved by Aloysha's response. It is all too easy to bury our heads in the sand and ignore the suffering around us. It genuinely hurts us to hear of it. But we must face the reality of it. All of us, whether believer or unbeliever, must feel the weight of it. We must join Aloysha and feel the suffering too.

In just the last century, some of the greatest atrocities of history were perpetrated including the millions of Russians killed in Stalin's murderous campaigns, the

---

[656]Fyodor Dostoevsky, *The Brothers Karamazov* as excerpted in *A Modern Introduction to Philosophy: Readings from Classical and Contemporary Sources,* Third Edition, Paul Edwards & Arthur Pap, Editors, New York, (The Free Press, 1973) 459.

millions of Jews and other targets that were killed in
Hitler's holocaust, the killing fields of Cambodia, the
rape of Nanking, and the slaughter of Rwanda just to
mention the most notorious.

It is important that we are exposed to the personal
narratives of those who have suffered through these
horrors. For instance, I was deeply moved by the books *A
Cambodian Odyssey* by Haing Ngor[657] and *Night* by Elie
Wiesel.[658]

Haing Ngor and the killing fields of Cambodia

Haing Ngor was a doctor who survived the period of
the killing fields in Cambodia between 1975 and 1979.
He described the thoughts that he wrestled with while he
was being tortured by the Khmer Rouge soldiers:

> "There we saw wooden structures with uprights and
> crosspieces . . . At the far end of the rows, prisoners were
> being punished in a manner I had never heard of before.
> They were tied to the crosses, the weight of their bodies
> sagging against the ropes . . . Smoke and flames rose from
> the fires around the prisoner's feet. I was still on the
> ground and the soldiers were tying my wrists to the cross.
> 'Just shoot me!' I shouted at them. 'Just shoot! Get it over
> with!' I fought them, but they were much stronger and they
> outnumbered me. They . . . hoisted me up until my feet
> were above the pile of wood and rice hulls . . . After the
> guards tied all of the prisoners they went around to each
> pile of rice hulls and lit it with cigarette lighters . . . Fires
> with rice hulls gave off thick, stinging smoke and burns
> slowly, for days . . . Of those who had been crucified longer,

[657]Haing Ngor, *A Cambodian Odyssey*, New York (Macmillan
Publishing Company, 1987).
[658]Elie Wiesel, *Night*, New York (Bantam Books, 1960, 1986).

some had already died from starvation or thirst . . . My feet were about six feet off the ground and three feet above the pile of wood and rice hulls . . . Our group of eighteen prisoners didn't do any more talking. We were too thirsty to talk out loud. We were too busy praying."[659]

At this point, Ngor described the desperate nature of his prayers while under the torture:

"You gods—any gods who can hear. Hindu gods. Jesus. Allah. Buddha. Spirits of the forests and the rice fields. Spirits of my ancestors. Hear me gods . . . Spirits of the wind, I prayed. If the gods cannot hear, then carry the news to them. To any god who has power. Tell the gods what is happening to me."[660]

I grant that it is difficult to take in this account and understand why God did not answer by destroying these enemies of humanity immediately. I do not wish to downplay the question. We shall soon wrestle with such questions, but let us take in one more example.

Elie Wiesel and the Holocaust

Let us hear the troubling recollections of Holocaust survivor Elie Wiesel from his classic book *Night:*

"One day when we came back from work, we saw three gallows rearing up in the assembly place, three black crows. Roll call. SS all around us, machine guns trained; the traditional ceremony. Three victims in chains—and one of them, the little servant, the say-eyed angel. The SS seemed more preoccupied, more disturbed than usual. To hang a young boy in front of thousands of spectators was no light matter. The head of the camp read the verdict. All

---

[659]Ngor, *A Cambodian Odyssey*, 243, 244,
[660]Ngor, *A Cambodian Odyssey*, 246.

eyes were on the child. He was lividly pale, almost calm, biting his lip. The gallows threw its shadow over him. This time the Lagerkapo refused to act as executioner. Three SS replaced him. The three victims mounted together onto the chairs. The three necks were placed at the same moment within the nooses. 'Long live liberty!' cried the two adults. But the child was silent. 'Where is God? Where is He?' someone behind me asked. At a sign from the head of the camp, the three chairs tipped over.

Total silence throughout the camp. On the horizon, the sun was setting. 'Bare your heads!' yelled the head of the camp. His voice was raucous. We were weeping. 'Cover your heads!' Then the march past began. The two adults were no longer alive. Their tongues hung swollen, blue-tinged. But the third rope was still moving; being so light, the child was still alive. For more than half an hour he stayed there, struggling between life and death, dying in slow agony under our eyes. And we had to look him full in the face. He was still alive when I passed in front of him. His tongue was still red, his eyes were not yet glazed. Behind me, I heard the same man asking: 'Where is God now? And I heard a voice within me answer him: 'Where is He? Here He is—He is hanging here on these gallows.'"[661]

In other words, at least for the moment, Wiesel's belief in God hung with the boy on the rope. To put it more to the point, Wiesel couldn't conceive how God could stand by and watch this cruelty without intervening. This then is the difficult question that confronts us.

Wiesel's Wounded Faith

Perhaps it helps to know that Wiesel clung to faith in God despite the horrors he had experienced. In an interview with Antonio Monda [Monda's words are italicized] about God, Wiesel said:

---

[661] Elie Wiesel, *Night*, 61-62.

"'In the end, the existence of God is the only true problem,' *he says, with a severe expression,* 'in which all other problems are subsumed and minimized. At times, I think that we are always talking about God without realizing it. . . . Pascal is one of the thinkers I most admire, and he wasn't the first to speak of a hidden God. The Bible itself speaks of God who covers his face. And my interpretation—it's only mine—is that God covers his face because he can't bear what he sees, what we men do' . . . *Do you believe in God, Professor Wiesel?* 'Yes, of course' . . . *Do you pray?* 'Yes, constantly and simply'. . . *And have you always prayed?* 'No, I've had my moments of crisis, which have led me to study and argue with God, at times dramatically' *How would you define your faith today?* 'I would use the adjective wounded, which I believe may be valid for everyone in my generation. Hasidism teaches that no heart is as whole as a broken heart, and I would say that no faith is as solid as a wounded faith.'"[662]

In another place, Wiesel said, "I have always believed in God, though I have my quarrels with him."[663]

Yancey provided insightful commentary on Wiesel's experience:

"Wiesel lost his faith in God at the concentration camp. For him, God literally hung to death on the gallows . . . But in fact the image that Wiesel invokes so powerfully contains within it the answer to his question. Where was God? The voice within Elie Wiesel spoke truth: in a way, God did hang beside the young *pipel.* God did not exempt even himself from human

---

[662]Elie Wiesel interviewed by Antonio Monda in Antonio Monda, *Do You Believe?: Conversations On God and Religion,* New York (Vintage Books, 2007) 169-170, 173-174.

[663]*Random House Webster's Quotationary,* Leonard Roy Frank, Editor, New York (Random House, 2001)320.

suffering. He too hung on a gallows, at Calvary, and that alone is what keeps me believing in a God of love.

God does not, in the comfortable surroundings of heaven, turn a deaf ear to the sounds of suffering on this groaning planet. He joined us, choosing to live among an oppressed people—Wiesel's own race—in circumstances of poverty and great affliction. He too was an innocent victim of cruel, senseless torture. At that moment of black despair, the Son of God cried out, much like the believers in the camps, 'God, why have you forsaken me.'

Jesus, the Son of God on earth . . . responded with faithfulness, turning attention to the good that his suffering could produce: 'for the joy set before him [Christ] endured the cross' (Hebrews 12:2). What joy? The transformation, or redemption, of humanity."[664]

Sickness, disease, injuries, natural disasters, and the "red in tooth and claw" world

David Eller noted that "Christian apologists in particular have attempted to distinguish two kinds of evil—natural and moral."[665]

We have just considered examples of moral evil, and man's inhumanity to man. As Eller explained, there are also natural evils including natural disasters such as earthquakes, tornados, hurricanes, floods, famines, pestilence, and the like (sometimes called acts of God). Finally, it is not only human suffering that concerns us but animal suffering as well.

---

[664] Philip Yancey, *Where is God When It Hurts*, Revised & Expanded Edition, Grand Rapids MI (Zondervan, 1977, 1990)156.
[665] David Eller, *Natural Atheism*, Cranford New Jersey (American Atheist Press, 2004) 53

So let us consider how we can reconcile the suffering and evil in our "red in tooth and claw world"[666] with the affirmation that there is a loving God.

Theodicy

The attempt to reconcile evil and suffering with the concept of God falls under the category of theodicy:

> "Theodicy. Attempts 'to justify the ways of God to men' by solving the problem that evil presents to the theists. The word derives from the title to the *Theodicy* of Leibniz."[667]

Reese defined theodicy as:

> "From *theos* ('God') and *dike* ('justice'). A term introduced by Leibniz to characterize the topic of God's government of the world in relation to the nature of man. The problem is the justification of God's goodness and justice in view of the evil in the world."[668]

Before we consider a Christian theodicy, we shall consider the classic philosophical challenge to theodicy known as the Epicurus dilemma, which suggests that no such reconciliation is possible.

---

[666]Alfred Lord Tennyson, *In Memoriam A.H.H.*, Cantos 56, 1850

[667]Antony Flew, *A Dictionary of Philosophy*, Revised Second Edition, New York (Gramercy Books, 1979) 352.

[668]William L. Reese, *Dictionary of Philosophy and Religion: Eastern and Western Thought*, Atlantic Highlands, NJ (Humanities Press, 1980) 573.

Chapter 35: The Epicurus Dilemma and the Challenge to Theodicy

The Greek philosopher Epicurus laid down a philosophical challenge related to the perennial question of how to reconcile God's existence with the existence of evil and suffering in the world. Epicurus (341-270) said:

> "Is he [God] willing to prevent evil, but not able? Then he is impotent. Is he able, but not willing? Then he is malevolent. Is he both able and willing? Whence then is evil?"[669]

In his *Dialogues Concerning Natural Religion*, David Hume's character Philo made an allusion to the same:

> "Epicurus' old questions are yet unanswered. Is he willing to prevent evil, but not able? Then is he impotent. Is he able, but not willing? Then is he malevolent. Is he both able and willing? Whence then is evil?"[670]

As Epicurus stated the question, since evil and suffering exist, either God is good and really wants to stop suffering, but is not powerful enough, or He does have sufficient power, but because He is not good, He does not to stop it.

---

[669]Louis P. Pojman, *Philosophy: The Quest for Truth*, Sixth Edition, New York-Oxford, (Oxford University Press, 2006) 109.

[670]David Hume, *Dialogues Concerning Natural Religion* as reprinted in *Introduction to Philosophy: Classical and Contemporary Readings*, Fourth Edition, John Perry, Michael Bratman & John Martin Fischer, Editors, Oxford (Oxford University Press, 2007) 114.

Is a weak God the answer?

There are indeed those who have been driven to conclude that God must surely be lacking the power to stop evil or He most certainly would.

This is the view, for instance, of the Jewish Rabbi Harold S. Kushner in his book *"When Bad Things Happen to Good People."* Rabbi Kushner's position was forged in the fire of watching his own son suffer from a tragic condition and his conclusion is understandable. Kushner could not accept that God could have the power, and yet have allowed his son's suffering. Kushner, therefore, argued that while God is good, He was limited in power.

While such a philosophically weak God may supply emotional comfort to some, nevertheless, such a God is not the God revealed in the pages of Holy Scripture. It certainly is not the God of Anselm, the greatest being that can be imagined. No, this God seems to be kind of wimpy in the face of the forces of evil.

On the other hand, the God of Scripture is the all-powerful ruler of the universe:

> "Have you not known? Have you not heard? The LORD is the everlasting God, the Creator of the ends of the earth. He does not faint or grow weary; his understanding is unsearchable" (Isaiah 40:28).
>
> "All the inhabitants of the earth are accounted as nothing, and he does according to his will among the host of heaven and among the inhabitants of the earth; and none can stay his hand or say to him, 'What have you done?'"(Daniel 4:35).
>
> "For in him all things were created: things in heaven and on earth, visible and invisible, whether thrones or powers or rulers or authorities; all things have been

created through him and for him. He is before all things, and in him all things hold together" (Colossians 1:16-17).

Is God malevolent and unconcerned?

The other option posed by Epicurus is the unpleasant idea that while having the power, God simply doesn't care. He therefore, observes from heaven wholly unconcerned and lacking in compassion at the evil and suffering in the world.

Again, this is not the God revealed in the Scriptures. How could God have shown greater love or compassion than by sending His own Son to die on cruel cross to make forgiveness and peace with Him possible?

> "For God so loved the world, that he gave his only Son, that whoever believed in him, should not perish, but have everlasting life" (John 3:16).
>
> "Praise be to the God and Father of our Lord Jesus Christ, the Father of compassion and the God of all comfort, who comforts us in all our troubles, so that we can comfort those in any trouble with the comfort we ourselves receive from God"(2 Corinthians 1:3-4).
>
> "The LORD is compassionate and gracious, slow to anger, abounding in love" (Psalm 103:8).
>
> "Because of the LORD's great love we are not consumed, for his compassions never fail" (Lamentations 3:22).

Chapter 36: Classical Free-will Theism & the Epicurus Dilemma

Rest assured the Epicurus dilemma is a false dichotomy. There is a way out of the dilemma that preserves both God's goodness and power and reconciles them with the reality of evil and suffering. The way forward is known as "free will theism." While yet an atheist, Antony Flew coined the name by which it has come to be known: "I was, in fact, the first to label this the free-will defense."[671]

The free-will defense affirms each of the attributes of God taught in traditional Christian theology including His omnipotence (all-powerful), omniscience (all-knowing), His goodness, and His justice. This is possible by understanding that although God did not create evil and suffering, He allowed for their possibility, contingent upon how His creatures exercised their God-given free-will. Saint Augustine argued:

> "Since God is supremely good, He would allow bad things to exist in the world only if He were so powerful and good that He could even bring good out of bad."[672]

Or borrowing from Leibniz, God created the "best of all possible worlds" while placing a premium on freedom and love.

---

[671]Antony Flew, *There is a God: How the World's Most Notorious Atheist Changed His Mind*, New York (HarperCollins/HarperOne, 2007) 59.

[672]Augustine, *Enchiridion* in *Introduction to Philosophy: Classical and Contemporary Readings*, Fourth Edition, Edited by John Perry, Michael Bratman & John Martin Fischer, Oxford UK (Oxford University Press, 2007) 82.

The cause of evil and suffering

Part of any biblically-based theodicy, then, is to trace the origin of evil and suffering in the first place. The Bible traces the origin of evil to rebellion against God; both in an angelic revolt led by Satan, and in the rebellion of man in the Garden of Eden.

God made a perfect world for man (Genesis 1:31); a world without evil; a world without suffering. But a world with choice; follow God and enjoy God's blessings or rebel against God, and bring down evil and suffering as a consequence.

The universal and catastrophic effects of the fall.

I don't think most comprehend the truly devastating effects the fall had upon humanity, and upon the world in which they live.

The most important result of the fall was the introduction of sin and death into the world. The curse was to have effects not only on mankind including the introduction of pain at childbirth for mothers (Genesis 3:16), but a curse upon the universe itself. The earth would no longer easily produce for man because of the curse (Genesis 3:17).

Indeed, the apostle Paul declared: "We know that the whole creation has been groaning in labor pains until now"(Romans 8:23).

I believe that this curse on the universe resulted in the loss of the God-centered order of creation and the "red in tooth and claw world."

The world, with all its killing and being killed, for man no less than the animals, displayed the lostness of a universe fallen from Edenic blessing.

The universal reality of original sin

Mark Mittelburg referenced Chesterton's startling statement about the source of evil in the world:

> "British author G. K. Chesterton once replied to the question 'What's wrong with the world?' by simply and honestly saying; '*I am*.'"[673]

Chesterton clearly understood sin, and particular the doctrine of original sin, as the universal malady of mankind. Geisler shared another insightful comment of Chesterton along the same lines: "Chesterton describes the doctrine of original sin as 'the doctrine of the equality of men."[674] The New England spelling primer had it: "In Adam's fall, we sinned all."[675]

Alexander Solzhenitsyn profoundly described the same truth:

> "If only there were evil people somewhere insidiously committing evil deeds, and it were necessary only to separate them from the rest of us and destroy them. But the line dividing good and evil cuts through the heart of every human being."[676]

---

[673]Mark Mittleburg, *Why Faith in Jesus Matters* chapter in William Lane Craig & Chad Meister, Editors, *God is Great, God is Good: Why Believing in God is Reasonable and Responsible,* Downers Grove IL (Inter Varsity Press, 2009) 224.

[674]Norman L. Geisler, *Baker Encyclopedia of Christian Apologetics,* Grand Rapids MI (Baker Books, 1999) 127.

[675]As quoted by Jim and Barbara Willis, *Armageddon Now: The End of the World A to Z,* Canton MI (Visible Ink Press, 2006) 123.

[676]Alexander Solzhenitsyn, *The Gulag Archipelago,* 1973, as quoted

Benjamin Franklin's self-discovery of moral failure

There is a very amusing, and yet informative story, from the life of Benjamin Franklin describing what his biographer Isaacson called "*The Moral Perfection Project.*"[677] Franklin made a list of positive virtues and negative vices, and then attempted to keep track of his "bold and arduous project of arriving at moral perfection."[678] The results: "Mastering all of these thirteen virtues at once was 'a task of more difficulty than I had imagined.'" Franklin recalled . . . "'I was surprised to find myself so much fuller of faults than I had imagined,' he dryly noted."[679]

I think, if we are honest, we should all with Benjamin Franklin, have to admit that we do not live up even to our own moral expectations, let alone those of God.

Man the Sinner / Moral Evil

Sadly, the first people, Adam and Eve, chose the way of rebellion and rather than passing down to their posterity, human natures characterized by goodness (according to God's original design), they instead passed down evil, sin, and death, the result of their rebellion. What was meant for good had been twisted by rebellion into evil.

---

in Anne Rooney, *The Story of Psychology*, London (Arcturus Publishing Limited, 2015) 168.

[677] Walter Isaacson, *Benjamin Franklin: An American Life*, New York (Simon& Schuster Paperbacks, 2003) 89.

[678] Benjamin Franklin, as quoted by Walter Isaacson, *Benjamin Franklin*, 89.

[679]Walter Isaacson, *Benjamin Franklin*, 91.

The Bible teaches that original sin infects all of Adam's children so that there now exists an insuperable gulf between them and their creator (Romans 3:23; 6:23; 5:12).

Denise et al, related about the Greek philosopher Diogenes of Sinope, that he "is reputed . . . to have carried a lighted lantern day and night looking for an honest man."[680] Though he may have lived right down to the present, yet would his search have been in vain, save for Jesus Christ Himself.

Moral evil and man's inhumanity to man

John Hick pointed out:

"An enormous amount of human pain arises either from the inhumanity or the culpable incompetence of mankind. This includes such major scourges as poverty, oppression and persecution, war, and all the injustice, indignity, and inequity which occur even in the most advanced societies. These evils are manifestations of human sin."[681]

Here is where the explanatory power of Christianity is so compelling. That is, it is the Christian worldview that so accurately depicts the real world we all live in as any check of the daily news will confirm.

---

[680]Theodore C. Denise, Nicholas P. White & Sheldon P. Peterfreund, *Great Traditions in Ethics*, Tenth Edition, Belmont CA (Wadsworth Thomson Learning, 2002) 48 (footnote).

[681]John Hick, as cited by Louis P. Pojman, *Philosophy: The Quest for Truth*, Sixth Edition, New York. Oxford (Oxford University Press, 2006) 123.

Civil law as testimony to human sin and wickedness

The Philosopher Moritz Schlick made this excellent observation:

> "It all begins with an erroneous interpretation of the meaning of 'law.' In practice this is understood as a rule by which the state prescribes certain behavior to its citizens. These rules often contradict the natural desires of the citizens (for if they did not do so, there would be no reason for making them)."[682]

In other words, the very existence of civil laws points to an inherent problem in human nature that makes outward coercion necessary for civilized life.

Natural evils

When we consider the tragic loss of life often associated with the destructive forces wrought by natural calamities, one factor should at least partly alleviate our lament.

That is, we should consider the possibility that when all the science is understood, such activities involved in the world's self-regulation (weather, volcanic and seismic activity, mountain building and erosion, fires and floods, and even fluctuations in Earth's temperature) will be shown to have an overall beneficial effect for life on earth.

---

[682]Moritz Schlick, *A Modern Introduction to Philosophy: Readings from Classical and Contemporary Sources,* Third Edition, Paul Edwards & Arthur Pap, Editors, New York, (The Free Press, 1973) 60.

Yeager Hudson explained:

"Perhaps a world governed by natural law in which sentient beings never suffer as a consequence of the operation of that law is simply not possible. If we are to enjoy the positive benefits that result from the operation of natural law, certain dangers inevitably accompany them. If storms did not occur in the earth's atmosphere to stir up gases and drive off the harmful vapors, humans would suffocate in the stagnant air. Storms also pick up moisture from oceans and lakes and transport it in the form of rain and snow to inland areas that, without such precipitation, would dry up and become deserts. To be sure, sometimes humans or animals suffer harm or even death from storms, but the consequences would be vastly worse if there were no storms to bring their beneficent effects."[683]

Why didn't God create free beings who couldn't sin?

Many have asked why God created a world with the possibility of evil and sin to exist. David Eller stated in this way:

"Why, for instance, did God, who should have known better, make such a flawed creature as man, who would likely if not certainly use his free will to his own detriment? There are even philosophers of religion who argue that God could have made an improved human who still possessed free will—one who was more likely to choose freely the course of good."[684]

Nielsen noted Mackie's similar concerns:

---

[683]Yeager Hudson, *The Philosophy of Religion*, Mountain View CA (Mayfield Publishing Company, 1991) 123.

[684]David Eller, *Natural Atheism*, Cranford New Jersey (American Atheist Press, 2004) 53.

"Mackie responds that God, if there is a god, if he can create humans who *sometimes* freely choose good . . . why could he then not create all human beings as beings who always choose good and thus, by God's doing this, there will be no evil."[685]

But this is just the point of the free-will argument; that people are in fact free: free to do good or evil. If God were to restrict the possibility of humans from doing evil, at that very moment, free will disappears into a verbal illusion. Yeager Hudson responded to such questions:

"Certain philosophers such as J. L. Mackie and John McClusky have attempted to argue that God could have created free human beings who always freely choose to do what is good . . . At first glance this proposal appears to be plausible. As Ninian Smart has shown, however, more detailed examination of the claims that God could have created free humans who are wholly good reveals it to be an illusion."[686]

Walters argued that free-will could be preserved by limiting only the exercise of the will

Kerry Walters, likewise, argued that God could have created free beings and yet avoided the evil and suffering in the world by simply limiting man's free exercise of freedom:

"There is a distinction between free will and free act: When a parent prevents a child from playing with a firecracker, all that's obviously been interfered with is the child's freedom of action. Her capacity for free will is undamaged. Similarly, God's intervention to prevent or

---

[685]Kai Nielsen, *Atheism & Philosophy*, Amherst NY (Prometheus Books, 2005) 28.
[686]Yeager Hudson, *The Philosophy of Religion*, 127-128.

forestall evil acts need not damage the human capacity of free will. Hitler's ability to freely will evil endures even if God limits his ability to act on that will."[687]

What kind of world would this be in which we are regularly curtailed from doing our wishes? Of what value is freedom if it is limited only to the will and not too actions? Would America be considered a free country if all its citizens were locked up in prisons, but were free to desire whatever they wanted?

There is no doubt that we can distinguish evil desires from evil actions. Indeed, Jesus did just that noting that one could have a level of guilt simply for desiring to sin, even though they may not have in fact, acted out the sin. For example, he said:

> "You have heard that it was said, 'Do not commit adultery.' But I tell you that anyone that looks at a woman lustfully has already committed adultery with her in his heart" (Matthew 5:27-28).

The apostle John made a similar distinction: "Anyone who hates his brother is murderer" (1 John 3:15).

So there are indeed two levels of sin described. Sins of the heart and sins of action. There is, however, I suggest, a greater degree of guilt in actually carrying out the sin than merely entertaining it in one's heart. Nevertheless, both types are sin since they represent expressions of human freedom. It is simply impossible to conceive of God being able to prevent human actions without correspondingly restricting human freedom.

---

[687]Kerry Walters, *Atheism: A Guide for the Perplexed*, New York (The Continuum International Publishing Group Inc, 2010) 90.

Toward a biblical response as to why God allowed the possibility of evil to arise

As we consider why God allowed for the possibility of evil to come into existence, John Hick begins us in the direction of a biblical answer:

> "Christian thought has always considered moral evil in its relation to human freedom and responsibility. To be a person is to be a finite center of freedom, a (relatively) free and self directing agent responsible for one's own decisions. This involves being free to act wrongly as well as rightly. The idea of a person who can be infallibly guaranteed always to act rightly is self-contradictory . . . Consequently, the possibility of wrongdoing or sin is logically inseparable from the creation of finite persons, and to say that God should not have created beings who might sin amounts to saying he should not have created people."[688]

Hick added,

> "A different objector might raise the question of whether or not we deny God's omnipotence if we admit that he is unable to create persons who are free from the risks inherent in personal freedom . . . It is no limitation upon God's power that he cannot accomplish the logically impossible, since there is nothing here to accomplish, but only a meaningless conjunction of words."[689]

Perhaps none have explained it more lucidly than has C. S. Lewis:

---

[688]John Hick, as cited by Louis P. Pojman, *Philosophy: The Quest for Truth*, Sixth Edition, New York. Oxford (Oxford University Press, 2006) 122.

[689]John Hick, *The Problem of Evil* as reprinted in *A Modern Introduction to Philosophy: Readings from Classical and Contemporary Sources,* Third Edition, Paul Edwards & Arthur Pap, Editors, New York, (The Free Press, 1973) 465-466.

"God created things which had free will. That means creatures which can go either wrong or right. Some people think they can imagine a creature which was free but had no possibility of going wrong; I cannot. If a thing is free to be good it is also free to be bad. And free will is what has made evil possible. Why, then, did God give them free will? Because free will, though it makes evil possible, is also the only thing that makes possible any love or goodness or joy worth having.

A world of automata—of creatures that worked like machines—would hardly be worth creating. The happiness which God designs for His higher creatures is the happiness of being freely, voluntarily united to Him and to each other in an ecstasy of love and delight . . . and for that they must be free. Of course God knew what would happen if they used their freedom the wrong way: apparently He thought it worth the risk . . . If God thinks this state of war in the universe a price worth paying for free will—that is, for making a live world in which creatures can do real good or harm and something of real importance can happen, instead of a toy world which only moves when He pulls the strings—then we may take it is worth paying."[690]

Lewis concluded by arguing that God determined that the value of freedom and real love was worth the price. Soren Kierkegaard agreed: "Love exits only in freedom, only in freedom is there enjoyment and everlasting delight."[691]

Mennsen and Sullivan make the point that:

"We choose to have children . . . even though we can predict that they will undergo substantial mental

---

[690]C. S. Lewis, *Mere Christianity*, New York (Collier Books-MacMillan Publishing Company, 1943, 1960) 52-53.

[691]Soren Kierkegaard, *Either/Or* as cited in Robert Bretall, *A Kierkegaard Anthology*, New York (The Modern Library/Random House,1946) 56.

anguish and serious physical suffering [and] Parents know with certainty that their children will commit moral evil."[692]

In this spirit of Lewis' compelling argument, just as we have children though we know that they will both commit sin and experience suffering in this world because we think it is ultimately worth it, in the same way, though God knew what would come of the world he created, in His infinite wisdom, He thought it was ultimately worth it.

The philosopher Immanuel Kant agreed that human freedom was an essential value:

> "Autonomy is therefore the ground of the dignity of human nature and of every rational nature."[693]

Likewise, Benjamin Franklin's biographer noted that he saw nothing inherently difficult in God's gift of free-will to mankind:

> "But if God is indeed all powerful, Franklin reasoned, he surely is able to find a way to give the creatures he made in his image some of his free will."[694]

---

[692] Sandra Menssen & Thomas D. Sullivan, *The Agnostic Inquirer: Revelation from a Philosophical Standpoint*, Grand Rapids MI (William B. Eerdmans Publishing Company, 2007, 169.

[693] Immanuel Kant, *Groundwork of the Metaphysic of Morals* in *Introduction to Philosophy: Classical and Contemporary Readings*, Fourth Edition, John Perry, Michael Bratman & John Martin Fischer, Editors, Oxford (Oxford University Press, 2007)549.

[694] Walter Isaacson, *Benjamin Franklin: An American Life*, New York (Simon& Schuster Paperbacks, 2003) 87.

Alvin Plantinga's free-will defense

Randy Alcorn noted the influence of Alvin Plantinga's presentation of this free-will defense among professional philosophers:

> "Thanks to Alvin Plantinga's famous free will defense in *God, Freedom, and Evil,* professional philosophers widely regard the idea of God and evil as logically compatible."[695]

Alcorn provided an important quote from Plantinga's important work:

> "A world containing creatures who are significantly free . . . is more valuable, all else being equal, than a world containing no free creatures at all. Now God can create free creatures, but He can't cause or determine them to do only what is right. For if He does so, then they aren't significantly free after all; and they do not do what is right freely. To create creatures capable of moral good, therefore, He must create creatures capable of moral evil; and He can't give these creatures the freedom to perform evil and at the same time prevent them from doing so. As it turned out, sadly enough, some of the free creatures God created went wrong in the exercise of their freedom; this is the source of moral evil."[696]

---

[695]Randy Alcorn, *Is Evil Only a Problem for Christians?*, chapter in Sean McDowell & Jonathan Morrow, *Is God Just a Human Invention? And Seventeen Other Questions Raised by the New Atheists,* Grand Rapids MI (Kregel Publications, 2010) 213

[696]Alvin Plantinga, *God, Freedom, and Evil* (Grand Rapids: Eerdmans, 1977), 30 as quoted by Randy Alcorn, *Is Evil Only a Problem for Christians?*, chapter in Sean McDowell & Jonathan Morrow, *Is God Just a Human Invention? And Seventeen Other Questions Raised by the New Atheists,* Grand Rapids MI (Kregel Publications, 2010) 214

Real freedom versus puppets on a string

As a young man, and new in my Christian faith, the free-will defense spoke powerfully to me. Sure God could have made people like little play dolls that say "I love you" when you pull the string. But that would be anything but real love.

Again, imagine having a spouse that was really a life-like robot built with voice recognition capabilities so that it responded to your words of affection with some pre-programmed words of affection in return. It might sound good, but the words would ring hollow.

Perhaps one of the things it said was, "You're the only one I love!" Of what possible value would those words be since they were spoken by a machine that could not choose another?[697]

Real love, however, requires real freedom to make real choices.

Relative or absolute freedom

In contrast to man's God-given freedom, Samuel Stumpf described Sartre's atheistic expression of man's freedom:

> "Man, says Sartre, is free: man is freedom. In a classic phrase, he says that man is *condemned* to be free. Condemned because he finds himself thrown into the world, yet free because as soon as he is conscious of himself, he is responsible for everything he does."[698]

---

[697]When I first considered this argument, I never imagined that one day people would actually by robotic dolls for 'companionship' which are currently coming on the scene!

[698]Samuel Enoch Stumpf, *Philosophy: History & Problems*, Fourth Edition, New York (McGraw-Hill Publishing Company, 1989) 505.

Stumpf likewise related that "Kierkegaard has similarly spoken of the *dizziness* of freedom."[699]

Sartre believed people were absolutely free because there is no God that determines man's morals and values. The Bible, on the other hand, teaches a relative freedom; freedom within the bounds set by God.

How is free-will compatible with perfect goodness in heaven?

Atheists have challenged this free-will defense by noting that since people have free will in heaven, and yet will not sin, why couldn't the same be true during our earthly sojourn? The implication is that the free-will argument as a theodicy is defective.

H. J. McCloskey, in his excellent discussion of the problem of evil, quoted from Joyce on this question:

> "And all who accept Christian revelation admit that those who attain their final beatitude exercise freedom of the will, and yet cannot choose aught but what is truly good."[700]

How is it, then, that heaven's citizens can be free and yet free from sin? Steele noted Swineburne's views of the matter:

> "Swineburne apparently notices this problem, and suggests that souls in Heaven will be limited in some ways, lacking the fullness of opportunity available to humans today. Swineburne's proposal presumably means that other persons such as angels, who also once had the kind of

[699]Samuel Enoch Stumpf, *Philosophy: History & Problems*, 506.
[700]Father G. H. Joyce, *Principles of Natural Theology*, Chapter 17, as quoted by H. J. McCloskey, *God and Evil*, chapter in *Critiques of God: Making the Case Against Belief in God*, Peter A. Angeles, Editor, Amherst New York (Prometheus Books, 1997)218-219.

free will that God felt he had better not constrain, permitting the rebellion led by Lucifer, will also eventually have permanently limited capacities if they are not to be destroyed."[701]

I would argue that Swineburne is on the right track with his answer; in some way God will restrict the possibility of man's rebellious actions during their heavenly existence. I would argue that free-will *was* exercised in the choice for heaven in the first place.

This can be compared to someone parachuting out of an airplane. The free-will decision to jump is finally made on the airplane; once one jumps, falling is no longer a choice, but a necessary result of their previous decision. Likewise, a heaven without sin is a necessary consequence of a free-decision of faith in the gospel of Jesus Christ.

The idea that once-made, free decisions necessarily restrict future freedom is not really that unusual. In fact, virtually every choice we make limits our future freedom. A freely desired sexual encounter can lead to pregnancy, and the responsibilities of parenthood. A tragic accident can result from one's freely chosen decision to get drunk and drive. Good grades on a report card can be the result of the free decision to focus on studies rather than spending time on entertainment. And, again, the free decision to choose Christian faith necessarily results in limited but real freedom in heaven.

While free, heavenly citizens will cease to face temptation from without or from within. They will no

[701]David Ramsay Steele, *Atheism Explained: From Folly to Philosophy*, Chicago and La Salle, IL (Open Court Publishing Company, 2008) 212.

longer be affected by the sinful nature that had been a constant source of temptation during their earthly sojourn. Nor will they face temptations from without, either from others sinners, or from the demonic influence of fallen angels. That is, there will be no tree of the knowledge of good and evil in the paradise of heaven.

We can illustrate this principle with a hypothetical example of someone threatening suicide by jumping from a skyscraper. Once they jump (leap), the choice has been made. During their fall, they might wish to change their mind, but all that remains is to live with the tragic consequences of their previous decision. Their freedom of will remains, yet it is constrained or limited by their past free decision. In the same way, having freely taken a leap of faith for Christ, those in heaven will be bound by their earlier decision, and glad for it.

The New Testament teaches that Christians, who had formally been slaves to sin, the Devil, and the world, have been redeemed by the blood of Christ. They have been purchased with a price and now belong to God(1 Corinthians 6:20). They have sold themselves to the eternal blessedness of God.

Neither will God tolerate any longer the rebellious among the angels, but will finally judge them as the Bible describes (Revelations 20:7-10; 2 Peter 2:4; Jude 6).

How is free-will compatible with God's own goodness?

Steele further stirred the pot, challenging the free-will theodicy with another intriguing question:

"According to classical theism, God himself cannot possibly do anything evil. Theists also claim that God has free will. If God combines free will with a guarantee against ever committing evil, then it cannot be impossible to combine free will with a guarantee against ever committing evil."[702]

Therefore, Steele felt justified in arguing:

"If God's omnipotent, couldn't he have given people free will and at the same time guaranteed that they would in fact always make the 'right' choices?"[703]

Daniel Howard-Snyder, a theist, raised the same basic question in his discussion of *God, Evil, and Suffering*:

"A question arises: God enters into relationships of love, and yet he is not able to be or do evil; so why can't he make us capable of relationships of love while also making us unable to be and do evil?"[704]

In response, the vast difference between an eternal and necessary being as God is compared to the finite and contingent nature of humanity must be considered. God didn't come into being; He simply is and simply is good and can be no other.

Humanity, on the other hand, is a contingent being; a creation of God, and created with the ability to choose good or evil.

Should we conclude from this that God's love is somehow less than real, or less than man's love for God because He had or has no choice but to love humanity?

I reject that conclusion and note the choice God made to create man. He didn't have to create the universe or

---

[702]David Ramsay Steele, *Atheism Explained,* 199-200.
[703]David Ramsay Steele, *Atheism Explained,* 199.
[704] Daniel Howard-Snyder, *God, Evil, and Suffering*, a chapter in *Reason for the Hope Within*, Edited by Michael J. Murray, Grand Rapids MI (William B. Eerdmans Publishing Company, 1999) 90.

man in it. Rather He chose to make man even with the possibility that they would reject Him.

Indeed, God freely chose to make man despite the fact that He knew that they would reject Him, and that He would Himself suffer on the cruel cross of Calvary to bring them back to Himself.

The apostle Paul declared:

> "But God demonstrates his own love for us in this: While we were still sinners, Christ died for us. Since we have now been justified by his blood, how much more shall we be saved from God's wrath through him! For if, while we were God's enemies, we were reconciled to him through the death of his Son, how much more, having been reconciled, shall we be saved through his life!"(Romans 5:8-10).

Amazing Love, how can it be, that thou,

my God shouldst die for me?[705]

Do miracles nullify the free-will defense?

H. J. McCloskey interacted with the thought of the Jesuit father G. H. Joyce and argued that miracles nullify the free-will argument. If God prevents some evil through miraculous intervention (despite any consequential limits on freedom), shouldn't He intervene more often to prevent more evil. McCloskey explained:

> "It may be argued that free will is compatible with less moral evil than in fact occurs . . . God, if He were all-

---

[705] Charles Wesley, *And Can It Be, That I Should Gain*, 1738

powerful, could miraculously intervene to prevent some or perhaps all moral evil; and He is said to do so on occasions in answer to prayers (for example to prevent wars) or of His own initiative . . . These are all considerations advanced by Joyce, and . . . they establish that God could have conferred free will upon us, and at least very considerably *reduced* the amount of moral evil that would have resulted from the exercise of free will. This is sufficient to show that not all the moral evil that exists can be justified by reference to free will alone. This conclusion is fatal to the account of moral evil in terms of free will alone . . . The difficulty is as fatal to the claims of theism whether all moral evil or only some moral evil is unaccountable."[706]

McCloskey summed up his argument:

"In this paper it has been maintained that God, were He all-powerful and perfectly good, would have created a world in which there was no unnecessary evil . . . It has simply been argued that a benevolent God could, and would, have created a world devoid of superfluous evil . . . Hence we must conclude from the existence of evil that there cannot be an omnipotent, benevolent God."[707]

McCloskey argued that if it is acceptable for God to limit some freedom through miraculous intervention, why not prevent even more (or all) evil on the same grounds? McCloskey seems to think this argument is the Achilles heel of free-will theodicy.

Although I appreciated McCloskey's fair-minded discussion of the question of evil, nevertheless, his argument is without weight. First, it should be

---

[706]H. J. McCloskey, *God and Evil*, chapter in *Critiques of God: Making the Case Against Belief in God,* Peter A. Angeles, Editor, Amherst New York (Prometheus Books, 1997) 219-220
[707]H. J. McCloskey, *God and Evil*, 223.

remembered that God is God, and can intervene in any way He deems appropriate.

More to the point, all of God's actions are consistent with His perfect goodness (omnibenevolence) and perfect knowledge (omniscience). Therefore, God will intervene in ways that are not only in accord with his purposes, but will result in the greatest good.

Again, in accordance with His perfect goodness and knowledge, we can be sure that God has a just purpose for all His actions. He is working all things to the good (Romans 8:28). God limits evil (and free will) precisely in accord with these factors, and therefore McCloskey's argument against free-will theodicy is without merit. He has not proven the existence of "superfluous evil."

A Christian response to suffering

With the foregoing in mind, let us respond to the critics of Christianity that wave the Epicurus Dilemma around as though it is a damning indictment of the Christian faith. As we have seen, Christians have very reasonable answers to the dilemma Epicurus posed.

We acknowledge with sadness and compassion the very real pain and suffering going on in the world. Nevertheless, Christians are comforted by several facts. *First*, that God is with us in our pain, helping us through it. **Second,** that the pain is not in vain, but rather God brings good out of it by building our faith in Him (this is an example of what J. L. Mackie called "'absorbed evils" in contrast to apparent senseless evil which Mackie calls "unabsorbed evil").[708] **Third,** evil will be judged and justice will prevail in the universe. Believers of all time will reside in the New Heavens and the New Earth where pain and suffering are eradicated.

The future and the end of pain

"Then I saw "a new heaven and a new earth," for the first heaven and the first earth had passed away, and there was no longer any sea. I saw the Holy City, the New Jerusalem, coming down out of heaven from God, prepared as a bride beautifully dressed for her husband. And I heard a loud voice from the throne saying, "Look! God's dwelling place is now among the people, and he will dwell with them. They will be his people, and God himself will be with them and be their God. 'He will wipe every tear from their eyes. There will be no more death or mourning or crying or pain, for the old order of things has passed away'" (Revelations 21:1-4).

Pain as a Gift

In his classic book on pain and suffering, *Where is God When it Hurts*, Philip Yancey described pain as "the gift nobody wants."[709] He goes on to explain that great importance that pain plays for our over-all health. He does this by especially explaining how devastating it is for those who cannot feel pain like Leprosy patients.

Yancey said:

"Pain is not an afterthought, or God's great goof. Rather, it reveals a marvelous design that serves our

---

[708]J. L. Mackie as quoted by Michael Martin, *Atheism: A Philosophical Justification,* Philadelphia PA (Temple University Press, 1990) 363.

[709] Philip Yancey, *Where is God When It Hurts*, Revised and Expanded, Grand Rapids MI (Zondervan Publishing House, 1977, 1990) 25.

bodies well. Pain is as essential to a normal life, it could be argued, as eyesight or even good circulation. Without pain, as we shall see, our lives would be fraught with danger, and devoid of many basic pleasures."[710]

To illustrate his point, Yancey shared the story of Dr. Paul Brand and his work at the leprosarium in Carville Louisiana. Yancey explained that Dr. Brand:

"Knew that people with diseases like leprosy and diabetes were in grave danger of losing fingers, toes, and even entire limbs simply because their warning system of pain had been silenced. They were literally destroying themselves unawares."[711]

Indeed, it is heart-braking to read Yancey's account of life for those unable to feel pain. The reality of the positive value of pain does not negate the terrible pain that we must sometimes endure. But it reminds us that pain is a gift because it helps us to avoid much greater damage.

"It is by those who have suffered that the world has been advanced"[712]   Leo Tolstoy

Suffering as Soul-making

---

[710] Philip Yancey, *Where is God When It Hurts*, 31.

[711] Philip Yancey, *Where is God When It Hurts*, 31-32

[712] Leo Tolstoy, as quoted by Philip Yancey, *Where is God When It Hurts*, Revised and Expanded, Grand Rapids MI (Zondervan Publishing House, 1977, 1990) 139.

John Hick stated,

> "If we ask whether the business of soul-making is worth all the toil and sorrow of human life, the Christian answer must be in terms of a future good which is great enough to justify all that has happened on the way to it."[713]

Kerry Walters amplified Hick's position:

> "Suffering, as theologian John Hick (following the third-century Irenaeus) says, is soul-making. It serves as a spiritual catalyst by jolting us out of complacency and obtuseness. It encourages self-examination, deep reflection, and compassion for other suffering beings. Without the presence of suffering, humans would possess less depth and goodness than they do. So suffering is, if you will, a *felix culpa* that hurts us but at the same time tempers us (Hick 2007)."[714]

Dr. Martin Luther King, Jr. understood this truth and lived it out in his life:

> "Christianity has always insisted that the cross we bear precedes the crown we wear. To be a Christian one must take up his cross, with all its difficulties and agonizing and tension-packed content, and carry it until that very cross leaves its mark upon us and redeems us to that more excellent way which comes only through suffering."[715]

"What doesn't destroy me makes me stronger"[716]

---

[713] John Hick, *The Problem of Evil*, 469.`

[714] Kerry Walters, *Atheism*, 90.

[715] Dr. Martin Luther King Jr. as quoted by Philip Yancey, *Where is God When It Hurts*, Revised & Expanded Edition, Grand Rapids MI (Zondervan, 1977, 1990) 141.

[716] Dr. Martin Luther King Jr. as quoted by Philip Yancey, *Where is God When It Hurts*, 141. Some also trace this quote to Nietzsche.

Dr. Martin Luther King Jr.

Philip Yancey provided other examples of the possible benefits of suffering gleaned from a list by a "nun named Monica Hellwig"[717] which includes:

> "Suffering, the great equalizer, brings us to a point where we realize our urgent need for redemption . . . Those who suffer know not only their dependence on God and on healthy people but also their interdependence with one another . . . Those who suffer have no exaggerated sense of their own importance . . . suffering humbles the proud . . . Suffering helps us distinguish between necessities and luxuries."[718]

Soul-making[719] and the example of Children

John Hick is insightful in contrasting the expectations of secularists that if God is all-powerful and all good, the world would be an un-ending party with the biblical view of the world as a place of soul-making. John DePoe quoted Hick in this regard:

> "Antitheistic writers almost invariably assume a conception of the divine purpose which is contrary to the Christian conception. They assume that the purpose of a loving God must be to create a hedonistic paradise; and therefore to the extent that the world is other than this, it proves to them that God is either not loving enough or not powerful enough."[720]

---

[717] Philip Yancey, *Where is God When It Hurts*, 145.

[718] Philip Yancey, *Where is God When It Hurts*, 145.

[719] Philip Yancey, *Where is God When It Hurts*, Revised & Expanded Edition, Grand Rapids MI (Zondervan, 1977, 1990) 94. says: "The notion of earth as a 'vale of soul-making' [is a phrase from] the poet John Keats.' *The quote is slightly adapted for clarity.*

Hick offered, as a better metaphor, the example of parents that choose to have children knowing that they will face a world containing challenges including evil, suffering, pain, and temptations, but consider life worth it and have children anyway.

In the same way, argued Hick, despite the challenges facing mankind, God has judged that from the perspective of eternity, it will have all been worth it.[721]

Soul-making and relief from suffering

Some raise an interesting question about the principle of soul-making. If God is using pain or suffering to teach us moral lessons or to build our faith, is it wrong, then, to seek relief from that pain through modern medicine?

Yancey explained:

"During the Middle Ages, women were burned at the stake for the heretical act of taking pain-relieving medicines for childbirth. 'In sorrow shalt thou bring forth children,' priests admonished as they condemned the women to death. And after Edward Jenner had perfected the smallpox vaccine he faced his strongest opposition from clergy, who opposed any interference with the will of God. Even today some religious sects reject modern medical treatment."[722]

The idea was that it was wrong to escape pain since God used it to build your character and your faith (soul-making). Other Christians have even gone further and

---

[720] John Hick, Evil and the God of Love, 256-257, as quoted by John DePoe, *The Problem of Evil and Reasonable Christian Responses*, chapter in *True Reason: Confronting the Irrationality of the New Atheism,* Tom Gilson & Carson Weitnauer, Editors, Grand Rapids MI (Kregel Publications, 2012) 210.

[721] Ibid.

[722] Philip Yancey, *Where is God When It Hurts*, 96.

sought pain and suffering through the *mortification of the flesh*, earnestly seeking God's approval or blessing.

Does the Bible proscribe medical comfort?

So does the Bible forbid the pain relief provided by modern medicine? When Timothy was having frequent stomach problems, perhaps as a result of the poor quality of his drinking water, the apostle Paul admonished him to: "Stop drinking only water, and use a little wine because of your stomach and your frequent illnesses"(1 Timothy 5:23).

This tells us that faithful Christians cannot expect to escape illnesses or injuries. It also tells us that it is not unbiblical for Christians to seek relief from bodily suffering or to use medications to relieve symptoms associated with illness.

Jesus' ministry was one of healing, delivering people from pain and suffering (Matthew 12:15, 15:30). Likewise, Paul's missionary associate Luke was a physician as well (Colossians 4:14).

Just as Christians shouldn't seek martyrdom but accept it if it is God's will, neither should we seek pain and suffering, but accept it if we can not find relief.

One of the lessons garnered from our Lord's Parable of the Good Samaritan (Luke 10:25-37) is the importance of caring for those in need. Jesus didn't say, "Leave the Samaritan on the road, he must pay for his sins" (Karmic debt) or "Leave him in the ditch because I am using this to build his character."

The point is that it is not for us as Christians to evaluate or determine why someone is suffering. Our job is to compassionately care for all people. We needn't fear that our acts of mercy may prevent a soul from learning some important lesson. There remains yet enough of suffering in our fallen world for these lessons to be learned .

God brings good out of evil

When the biblical Joseph, having been saved by God from their treachery, revealed himself to his brothers, they remembered their evil deeds toward him, and anticipated his wrath. But Joseph looked at the bigger picture and saw the finger of God:

> "Do not be distressed and do not be angry with yourselves for selling me here, because it was to save lives that God sent me ahead of you . . . So then, it was not you who sent me here, but God . . . Joseph said to them, 'Don't be afraid. Am I in the place of God? You intended to harm me, but God intended it for good to accomplish what is now being done to save lives'"(Genesis 45:5,8; 50:19-20).

The apostle Paul comforted believers by telling them: "And we know that in all things God works for the good of those who love him, and who have been called according to his purpose" (Romans 8:28).

At a decisive time in American history while the nation was experiencing the horrors of the civil war, President Abraham Lincoln understood the Christian principle that God can bring good out of evil:

> "The purposes of the Almighty are perfect and must prevail, though we erring mortals may fail to accurately perceive them in advance. We hoped for a happy termination of this terrible war long before this, but God knows best and has ruled otherwise. We shall yet acknowledge His wisdom and our own error therein. Meanwhile we must work earnestly in the best light He gives us, trusting that so working still conduces to the great ends He ordains. Surely, He intends some great good to follow this mighty convulsion, which no mortal could make, and no mortal could stay."[723]

Certainly, at the very least, one of the goods that came out of the Civil War was the final eradication of the slave trade in America and the beginnings of the African-American march to freedom and equality.

The point of the foregoing is that although evil and suffering exist in the world, it is not in our power to understand it all. It is beyond our finite comprehension.

But we know that God is working to set all things straight. Every day and in every way, the Lord is orchestrating the universe of man to bring about the greatest goodness possible from this fallen world.

Our response as Christians is to compassionately seek to comfort the afflicted, to remedy injustice, protect the poor and powerless, and to give of ourselves for others as our Lord did for mankind.

God addressed suffering in the world by suffering Himself

Randy Alcorn argued powerfully that God has dealt with the problem of suffering and evil in the world by becoming human and sharing in it, and setting the stage for its ultimate removal:

> "The incarnation of Jesus demonstrates that God is not aloof or uninvolved in our world. He stepped into our existence, experienced all that we have ever experienced and more, and was crucified in our place to conquer death and evil, to redeem all of creation, and to make all things new . . . The evil in human hearts nailed Christ to that cross. But God took our evil and redeemed it for good, the

---

[723]Abraham Lincoln, *Letter to Eliza P. Gurney*, September 4, 1864, *Random House Webster's Quotationary*, Leonard Roy Frank, Editor, New York (Random House, 2001) 314.

salvation of all who would trust him . . . Christianity boasts the only God who has wounds. Evil and sin have been conquered at the cross and await final destruction at Christ's return; evil will not have the final word."[724]

An illustration of trusting children

I want to share an observation that was inspired by a comment I once heard made by Christian Psychologist James Dobson, and which I believe most parents can identify with.

A very young child, perhaps a year old, is sick and in the intensive care unit of a hospital. All around, from the child's perspective, are strange people with their faces covered by masks, holding him down and sticking him with painful needles. In the midst of the pain and fear, the child wonders, "Why doesn't mom and dad help me?" or worse yet, "Why are mom and dad actually helping these people to hurt me?"

The child is simply too young to understand. At that point, the only thing that the child can do is to look into his or her parents' eyes and trust that what is happening is somehow for their good.

And this is just what we must do. We are like the child, simply not able to fully comprehend why God is allowing our suffering. We must look to our loving heavenly Father, and trust. Trust that He is there with us in our suffering, bringing us comfort, and working all things to the good.

---

[724]Randy Alcorn, Is *Evil Only a Problem for Christians?*, 216-217.

Chapter 37: Challenges to Free Will Theodicy

The Bambi question: What about apparently senseless suffering?

One of the challenges to the free-will theodicy is the supposed senseless suffering in the world, what Mackie called the "unabsorbed evils."[725] The idea is that perhaps God can be excused for allowing suffering that has some possible purpose such as its soul-making or character building qualities.

But, says the skeptics, there is much suffering for which there is simply no such explanation, and for which God cannot be excused. A chief example offered of this senseless suffering is animal suffering sometimes referred to as the Bambi question.

Kerry Walters explained:

> "Suffering in the nonhuman animal world is mind-bogglingly horrible. To what end is *it?* Surely not to stimulate soul-growth in animals. It seems pointless and hence cruel on the part of a Creator to allow it."[726]

In response, I note that in the original creation such suffering didn't exist. The "red in tooth and claw" world resulted as a consequence of man's rebellion. God's creation included a binding connection between humanity and the animal kingdom in which the actions of one effected the other analogous to the relationship

---

[725] J. L. Mackie as quoted by Michael Martin, *Atheism: A Philosophical Justification,* Philadelphia PA (Temple University Press, 1990) 363.

[726] Kerry Walters, *Atheism: A Guide for the Perplexed*, New York (The Continuum International Publishing Group Inc, 2010) 91

between parents and children. Man and animal were tied together at their genesis.

In the beginning, God gave man dominion and responsibility over the world. As a part of the fall, God's curse and punishment fell over every aspect of man's dominion, including the animal kingdom. Man's desire to survive, and manage the world, would be forevermore challenged in the wild and savage post-fall environment.

Nevertheless, Scripture tells us: "Are not two sparrows sold for a penny? Yet no one of them will fall to the ground apart from the will of your Father"(Matthew 10:29). Animal lives, like human lives, are ultimately in God's hands. They are His creation and He is sovereign over them. From the perspective of eternity, we shall understand the suffering of the fallen world. Nevertheless, it is clear that God does not approve of the senseless infliction of suffering and mistreatment of animals.

"The righteous care for the needs of their animals, but the kindest acts of the wicked are cruel"(Proverbs 12:10).

Apparently senseless suffering

In his book, *Why Evil and Suffering?*,[727] C. S. Rodd, provided a fictional account to raise serious objections to *soul-making* or *pain as a gift to prevent worse suffering* arguments as explanations for why God allows suffering:

> "'I know, I know,' replied Dr Mac, and he went on to point out that while pain could be a warning of danger, not all pain could be explained that way. He pointed out that if

---

[727] C. S. Rodd, *Why Evil and Suffering?*, Peterborough, United Kingdom (Epworth Press, 1998).

Frances had felt a pain as bad as the worst toothache when the cancer first started in her breast she would have gone straight away to the doctor. Then she could have been completely cured almost for certain. 'It is sad,' he said, 'that many cancers often give no pain at all until they have advanced so far that they are much more difficult to control. Pain doesn't seem to be linked with the seriousness of the disease." He chuckled, 'Not many people die of toothache.' He was musing now, and Anne listened, completely fascinated. "What was the use of the pain of appendicitis to the peasant in the Middle Ages? It was not much good having the warning before we had modern antiseptics and surgery . . . We can let God off some of the charges, but a vast amount remains. And is it not made worse by the irrationality of the pain? Some pain is pointless. At other times when we need to feel pain to warn us of disease there is none."[728]

Rodd made several points.

Rodd argued that while pain may be helpful in raising awareness of possibly more severe danger to come, this doesn't work as an explanation for all pain. Indeed, pain seems to be out of proportion to the seriousness of the consequences in the human body i.e. great pain for teeth and little pain for cancer (at least early on when a pain warning could be of more help). And of what help was the pain of appendicitis as a warning before the advent of modern surgical procedures?

In response, we note that in most cases, pain does serve as a very helpful warning of danger for our bodies. I ask, however, if it is reasonable to expect that pain be always in proportion to the level of danger to the body?

---

[728] C. S. Rodd, *Why Evil and Suffering?*, 31-32

Pain during the dying experience

But let us frame the question with the reminder that one way or the other we are all going to die[729] (Romans 5:12, 6:23). This is a hard truth.

Pain normally serves the purpose of warning individuals to take steps to protect themselves and preserve health.

But as we are dying, pain is not primarily serving as a warning signal, but is rather an unfortunate by-product of the death of the body. In this case, it can be argued, we can be thankful that the pain of cancer was not like that of "pain as bad as the worst toothache" that Rodd referred to.

Is toothache pain out of proportion?

And what of Rodd's point that toothache pain is out of proportion to its importance as a bodily function, and so senseless? In fact, healthy teeth and gums are quite important to our over-all health. The Mayo Clinic Staff explained:

"Your oral health is more important than you might realize. Learn how the health of your mouth, teeth and gums can affect your general health . . . Did you know that your oral health offers clues about your overall health—or that problems in your mouth can affect the rest of your body? Protect yourself by learning more about the connection between your oral health and overall health . . .

---

[729] My longtime pastor, mentor, and predecessor as president of Religion Analysis Service, Dr. William BeVier used to remind his congregation that the death rate is still one per person!

.Your oral health might contribute various diseases and conditions, including:

Endocarditis. This infection of the inner lining of your heart chambers or valves (endocardium) typically occurs when bacteria or other germs from another part of your body, such as your mouth, spread through your bloodstream and attach to certain areas in your heart. **Cardiovascular disease.** Although the connection is not fully understood, some research suggests that heart disease, clogged arteries and stroke might be linked to the inflammation and infections that oral bacteria can cause. **Pregnancy and birth complications.** Periodontitis has been linked to premature birth and low birth weight. **Pneumonia.** Certain bacteria in your mouth can be pulled into your lungs, causing pneumonia and other respiratory diseases."[730]

The Mayo Clinic article added:

> "Other conditions that might be linked to oral health include eating disorders, rheumatoid arthritis, certain cancers and an immune system disorder that causes dry mouth (Sjogren's syndrome)."

Appendicitis was admittedly a most unfortunate affliction before modern medical procedures. For most of human history, appendicitis was a death sentence for about 50% who came down with it (in America about 7% of the population). In that case, pain served as a warning

---

[730] Mayo Clinic Staff, *Oral Health: A Window to Your Overall Health,* June 4, 2019 at website: https://www.mayoclinic.org/healthy-lifestyle/adult-health/in-depth/dental/art-20047475

sign despite the lack of treatments available in the Middle Ages as Rodd quite correctly noted.

But does this prove Rodd's argument about senseless suffering. I would argue that this suffering was not senseless since it did spur scientists on to eventually find effective treatments beginning in the 18th century.

However, it is not necessary to find a purpose for every type of suffering in the world. This is because all suffering, whether we are personally experiencing it or observing it in others (including in the animal kingdom) serves to teach mankind about the fall and the need for universal redemption.

Chapter 38: The Legacy of the Church

It is common for believers and unbelievers alike to attack each other for the tragedies of history. Fair enough. But we should not forget that there is more than enough guilt to go around.

Surely Bertrand Russell was being facetious when he said of the Church:

> "'I cannot, however, deny that it has made some contributions to civilization.' He listed two contributions: the Gregorian calendar, and the ability of Egyptian priests to predict eclipses. Regarding other useful contributions, he said, 'I do not know of any other.'"[731]

Moreover, it is hard to take the claims of David Mills seriously when he so obviously overstated his case about the Church:

> "For 1500 years, the Christian Church systematically operated torture chambers throughout Europe. Torture was the rule, not the exception."[732]

Likewise, were Mills' hyperbolic comments about the Christian Church's detrimental effect on the development of science:

> "Were it not for religious persecution and oppression of science, mankind might have landed on the moon in the year A.D. 650. Cancer may have been eradicated forever by the year A. D. 800. And heart disease may today be

---

[731]Timothy Morgan, *Thank God for Atheists: How the Greatest Skeptics Led Me to Faith*, Eugene OR (Harvest House Publishers, 2015) 95.

[732]David Mills, *Atheist Universe: The Thinking Person's Answer to Christian Fundamentalism*, Berkeley CA (Ulysses Press, 2006) 48

unknown. But Christianity put into deep hibernation Greek and Egyptian scientific gains of the past."[733]

It is no wonder some are turned off to the Church after being fed such delirious diatribes based upon nothing but far-fetched imaginative speculations.

Yes, the Church has been guilty of shameful acts

Being in the believer's camp, I am ashamed of many things that have been done in the name of Christ. I can only cringe to think of the evils of the witch hunts; the persecution of sects like the Anabaptist and the Waldensians; the evils associated with the crusades and the Spanish inquisition. There are no excuses for these and other sins of the Church. But allow me to offer some alleviating thoughts along with these confessions.

Factors that influenced the sins of the Church

First, a perennial problem challenging the church since the time of Constantine has been the corrupting influence that has resulted whenever the ties between the Church and state have been too close. One of the great Baptist principles, and one enshrined in the United States Constitution, is the principle of the separation of church and state. The civil magistrate was never meant to be the enforcer of church purity; to hunt down and kill apostates and heretics. The Jews under the Mosaic law

---

[733]David Mills, *Atheist Universe,* 49.

lived in a theocracy; Christians, in contrast, are to live under the civil laws of the secular state.

Robert Stewart stated:

> "When the Church follows the example of Jesus, her Master, and serves those who are most needy in this world, and speaks to corrupt powers rather than joining them in their attempts to dominate, the Gospel of Jesus is particularly attractive."[734]

Second, it is a fact that often times, what may have appeared to have been religious wars were not really so. While religion certainly played a factor, it was more often a secondary issue to other issues, whether economic, political, cultural, or ethnic in nature.

Third, Christians have never claimed that being a Christian makes one perfect or without sin. On the contrary, the struggle with the sin nature is a life-long battle. In the meantime, there will be failures, sometimes terrible ones. But these sins and misdeeds are despite the moral teachings of Jesus and the Bible, and not because of them.

Fourth, to reject Christianity because some have abused power in the church is to make the mistake of throwing the baby out with the bathwater. There can be little doubt that the good done in the name of Jesus Christ has far outweighed any of the evil perpetrated by those who failed to live by His message.

Robert Stewart noted that, in the same way, we do not reject secular government despite the massive atrocities that have been committed by them, nor do we

---

[734] *The Future of Atheism: Alister McGrath & Daniel Dennett in Dialogue*, Robert B. Stewart, Editor, Minneapolis MN (Fortress Press, 2008) 10.

reject science because of the many unethical experiments that have caused needless human suffering.[735]

Finally, the atrocities of the church (i.e., the crusades, witch hunts, and the Spanish inquisition) were carried out in clear violation of biblical ideals by those who were twisted by their own evil ends.

About the witch hunts, Mary Midgley made this interesting historical observation:

> "Consider the witch craze that prevailed in Europe from the fifteenth to the seventeenth centuries. This craze was not, as is often supposed, simply a survival of ancient superstition caused by ignorance and finally cured by the rise of science. On the contrary, in the Middle Ages there were few prosecutions for witchcraft because the Church authorities thought that witchcraft was rare (though real) and they discouraged witch-hunting because they saw the danger of false accusation. It was in the Renaissance that things changed."[736]

Midgley then quoted Karen Green and John Bigelow to support her assertion:

> "The [Renaissance] Europeans did three things which set them far apart from most other peoples at most other times and places. Between 1500 and 1700 they set sail in tall ships and colonized the far corner of the globe. They made stunning strides forward in the sciences. And they executed tens of thousands of people, mainly women, as witches."[737]

---

[735] *The Future of Atheism: Alister McGrath & Daniel Dennett in Dialogue*, 10.

[736] Mary Midgley, *Why Memes?*, chapter in, *Alas, Poor Darwin: Arguments Against Evolutionary Psychology*, Edited by Hilary Rose & Steven Rose, New York (Harmony Books, 2000) 97.

[737] Karen Green and John Bigelow, "*Does Science Persecute Women? The Case of the 16th-17th Century Witch-hunts*, Philosophy, Volume 73, No. 284 (April 1998), p. 199 as quoted by Mary Midgley, Why

The Protestant Reformation was a beginning at correcting abuses by the Church, but it has never completed its task, and it is the ongoing work of all true bible-believing Christians to strive toward lives in accord with biblical purity.

19th Century Imperialism and Colonialism

The Christian church is often maligned as an unholy factor in the period of imperialism and colonialism during the late 19th and early 20 centuries.

But the influence of evolutionary thought on the same has not been appreciated. The spirit of the age (*Zeitgeist*) was all about the survival of the fittest, a dog eat dog world, where the strong very properly survive and thrive at the expense of the weak. It is not surprising that in such a philosophical climate, European powers, whom believed they were at the pinnacle of the evolutionary process, thought it their right to subdue and exploit those nations they considered to be weak and inferior.

DeRosa explained:

"Haeckel endorsed German colonialism and annexation of other European territories. The struggle to survive included the taking of lands to preserve the favored race."[738]

DeRosa quoted Haeckel's attitude in this regard:

Memes?, chapter in, *Alas, Poor Darwin: Arguments Against Evolutionary Psychology*, Edited by Hilary Rose & Steven Rose, New York (Harmony Books, 2000) 97.

[738] Tom DeRosa, *Evolution's Fatal Fruit: How Darwin's Tree of Life Brought Death to Millions*, Fort Lauderdale FL (Coral Ridge Ministries, 2006) 155.

> "Even if these races were to propagate more abundantly than the white Europeans, yet sooner or later they would succumb to the latter in the struggle for existence."[739]

The perfect gospel and imperfect believers

One of the truly extraordinary facts of church history is that God has built His church despite the imperfect vessels He has used for the task. He takes sinners, and over time, changes their hearts and lives, a process miraculous in itself.[740]

Francis Collins made an interesting point in this regard:

> "The church is made up of fallen people. The pure, clean water of spiritual truth is placed in rusty containers and the subsequent failings of the church down through the centuries should not be projected onto the faith itself, as if the water had been the problem . . . The Beatitudes spoken by Christ in the Sermon on the Mount were ignored as the Christian Church carried violent Crusades in the Middle Ages and pursued a series of inquisitions afterward."[741]

There was simply no biblical basis or justification for such atrocities. Unfortunately, some Christians have abused their power thinking they were doing God's work.

Gospel singer Mark Heard brilliantly captured the dangers of this out-of-control, blind zeal in his song *Everybody Loves a Holy War*:

---

[739] Tom DeRosa, *Evolution's Fatal Fruit*, 160.

[740] Theology calls this process "sanctification."

[741] Francis S. Collins, *The Language of God: A Scientist Presents Evidence for Belief*, New York (Free Press, 2006) 40-41.

"Some say that God has approved of their mob
Esteeming their purposes alone
Choosing sides with a definite pride
And taking their cause for His own

Everybody loves a holy war
Draw the line and claim divine assistance
Slay the ones who show the most resistance
Everybody loves a holy war

Many's the man with the iron hand
Supposing his own thoughts to be Divine
He will break any bond-
'cause the other man's always wrong
It's a handy excuse for his crimes

Everybody loves a holy war
Draw the line and claim divine protection
Kill the ones who show the most objection
Everybody loves a holy war

Dissident cries are met with cold eyes
And treatment the devil would get
Righteousness and truth
can be weapons in the hands of fools
While innocents go to their deaths

Everybody loves a holy war
Draw the line and claim divine assistance
Slay the ones who show the most resistance
Everybody loves a holy war."[742]

The positive force of Christianity

Nevertheless, I would merely point out that historically, most of the social help institutions in our culture have been the work of Christians and Christian

---

[742]Mark Heard, *Everybody Loves a Holy War, Victims of the Age,* Home Sweet Home Records, 1982

organizations? Indeed, how many hospitals have been called *First Atheist Hospital* rather than names like Saint John's or Saint Joseph's Hospital?

Throughout history, whom do we usually associate with not only hospitals, but orphanages, food shelves, homeless shelters, and other charitable efforts? The answer is too obvious. This is why even Freud could say: "Religion has clearly performed great services for human civilization."[743]

Glenn Sunshine noted some important contributions of Christianity to our modern world:

> "The truth of the matter is that many cultural ideas and goods would not exist had there never been Christianity—women's rights, protection for infants and the unborn, child labor laws. Separation of church and state, liberty and justice, human dignity, abolition of slavery in the western world, universities, modern science, hospitals, musical innovations, and the importance of the written word—just to name a few."[744]

Kerry Walters chimed:

> "There's a shrillness of tone and a tendency to hasty generalizations in the New Atheists . . . They ignore the fact that in the twentieth century, much more violence has been perpetrated by secular totalitarian regimes than by religious repression. They conflate fringe and violence-prone religious groups with mainstream ones . . . And they overlook the complex intermingling of culture, politics, and

---

[743]Sigmund Freud, *The Future of An Illusion* in Christopher Hitchens, *The Portable Atheist: Essential Readings for the Nonbeliever*, Philadelphia PA (De Capo Press, 2007) 152.

[744]Glenn S. Sunshine, *What Good is Christianity?*, chapter in Sean McDowell & Jonathan Morrow, *Is God Just a Human Invention? And Seventeen Other Questions Raised by the New Atheists*, Grand Rapids MI (Kregel Publications, 2010) 224

faith that may lead to violence expeditiously justified by religious rhetoric but actually inspired by quite secular factors."[745]

Can anyone seriously doubt the enormous positive influence Christianity has had upon mankind? Charles Taylor stated:

"Of course, the Christian roots of all this run deep . . . There was the mass-mobilization campaigns of the early nineteenth century—the anti-slavery movement in England, largely inspired and led by Evangelicals; the parallel abolitionist movement in the United States, also largely Christian inspired. Then this habit of mobilizing for the redress of injustice and the relief of suffering world-wide becomes part of our political culture."[746]

Even the atheist Victor Stenger conceded:

"Now, the campaign to end slavery in the United States and elsewhere was led by Christians, to their everlasting credit."[747]

John Haught reminded us:

"In contrast to much previous atheistic bashing of Christianity, the theme of social justice is hardly noticeable as an issue for Dawkins, Harris, and Hitchens. Dawkins does give an uneasy nod to one of the most prophetic figures of our time, Martin Luther King Jr. But he insists that King's message was 'incidental' to his Christianity (271). Hitchens also feels obligated to mention King, but he claims that King's legacy 'has very little to do

[745]Kerry Walters, *Atheism: A Guide for the Perplexed*, New York (The Continuum International Publishing Group Inc, 2010) 120.
[746]Charles Taylor, *A Secular Age*, Cambridge MA (The Belknap Press of Harvard University Press, 2007) 371.
[747]Victor J. Stenger, *God: The Failed Hypothesis, How Science Shows That God Does Not Exist*, Amherst New York (Prometheus Books, 2007) 203.

with his professed theology'(180). Neither critic shows any
sign of ever having read King's "Letter from Birmingham
Jail.' That landmark document in the civil rights
movement clearly cites Jesus and the prophets as the most
authoritative voices in support of what others had called
the 'extremism' of King's protest against the injustice of
racism."[748]

---

[748]John F. Haught, *God and the New Atheism: A Critical Response to
Dawkins, Harris, and Hitchens*, Louisville KY (Westminster John
Knox Press, 2008) 94.

Chapter 39: The Legacy of Atheism

Despite its notable failures, the Church has always been guided by the moral and ethical teachings of the Bible, and particularly the teachings of Jesus. These have surely acted as a restraint and prevented great evils during the times in which barbarism was on the march across the Middle Ages.

The consequences of atheism unleashed

But it is fair to ask what it is that would restrain atheistic movements, most especially when they have gained power. This is the point made by Francis Collins:

> "In fact, by denying the existence of any higher authority, atheism has the now-realized potential to free humans completely from any responsibility not to oppress one another."[749]

In other words, without any foundation for ethics, atheism has the potential of releasing the most destructive forces and committing the greatest atrocities the world will ever know. Hitler, Stalin and Mao, unrestrained by any moral standards, and unconcerned about post-mortem judgment, committed their heinous crimes with impunity.

The atheist David Steele offered this assessment:

> "I do conclude, sadly, that atheists are morally no better than Christians or Muslims, and that the propensity of people to commit atrocities at the behest of unreasonable ideologies is independent of whether those ideologies include theism or atheism."[750]

---

[749]Francis S. Collins, *The Language of God: A Scientist Presents Evidence for Belief*, New York (Free Press, 2006) 42.

Steele makes the important point that any human institution is going to suffer embarrassment at the hands of some of its followers simply because all humans are by nature flawed. In light of this fact, it is important to be as fair as possible in our judgments and to be honest about our failures.

Atheism's double-standard

Timothy Morgan pointed to atheism's double-standard concerning the judgment of history:

> "When I investigated atheism, I found a double standard. A very broad definition was applied to Christianity, one that made it culpable for the actions of every religious nut job. In contrast, a very narrow definition was applied to atheism that essentially excused it from any wrong ever committed by any atheist."[751]

The well-known and agnostic attorney Vincent Bugliosi agreed:

> "I'll give this to Hitchens. When, in speaking of the pernicious influence of religion, he says, 'Religion kills,' I agree. He fails to add, however, that secularism and science don't do too bad a job in this area either."[752]

S. T. Joshi provided an example of just such a double-standard by Richard Dawkins:

---

[750]David Ramsay Steele, *Atheism Explained: From Folly to Philosophy*, Chicago and La Salle, IL (Open Court Publishing Company, 2008) Preface xii.

[751]Timothy Morgan, *Thank God for Atheists: How the Greatest Skeptics Led Me To Faith*, Eugene OR (Harvest House Publishers,2015) 71.

[752]Vincent Bugliosi, *Divinity of Doubt: The God Question*, New York (Vanguard Press, 2011) 45.

"As for Stalin, he was indeed an atheist, but Dawkins remarks, 'Individual atheists may do evil things but they don't do evil things in the name of atheism.'"[753]

That is, atheism should not be held responsible for the atrocities of Stalin since Stalin wasn't a good atheist or that he wasn't acting in accordance with the true principles of atheism.

This may or may not be true, but in fairness, the same grace or courtesy ought to be extended both ways. That is, Christianity should not be held responsible for the evil deeds of those who, although taking the name of Christ, acted in a manner completely contrary to His teachings and ideals.

Nevertheless, the reality remains that many of the greatest mass murderers in history were atheists bent on eradicating religious belief.

Alister McGrath reminded us that:

"Communism was a 'tragedy of planetary dimensions' with a grand total of victims variously estimated by contributors to the volume [*The Black Book of Communism*] at between 85 million and 100 million . . . Communism promised liberation from the illusion of religion; it ended up with a body count exceeding anything previously known in history."[754]

Understandably, Sam Harris also sought to distance atheism from the evils of Communism:

"Consider the millions of people who were killed by Stalin and Mao: although these tyrants *paid lip service* to

[753]S. T. Joshi, *The Unbelievers: The Evolution of Modern Atheism*, Amherst NY (Prometheus Books, 2011) 209.
[754]Alister McGrath, *The Twilight of Atheism: The Rise and Fall of Disbelief in the Modern World*, New York (Doubleday, 2004) 233.

Steve Lagoon

rationality, communism was little more than a political religion. At the heart of its apparatus of repression and terror lurked a rigid ideology . . . Even though their beliefs did not reach beyond this world, they were both cultic and irrational."[755]

Harris cleverly attempted to pull a rabbit out of a hat with the implication that all the atrocities of the likes of Stalin and Mao were actually the fault of *religion*. Why? Because, as Harris subtly suggested, the Communists' totalistic commitment to their principles was "cultic" and "a political religion."

But that's just the point. The *religion* they were committed to was *atheism,* and no double-speak can evade that fact. David Mills made a similar attempt to distance atheism from the atrocities of the atheistic states under Stalin and Mao:

> "Undeniably, some Communists nations, such as Stalinist Russia and Maoist China, have been guilty of horrible human rights abuses. *No atheist I ever met defends such political repression!* . . . These past human rights abuses invariably stemmed from the leadership's power-mad political ambitions . . . Is it really fair to condemn a school of thought for perversions and abuses of its teachings?"[756]

I am sympathetic to Mills' desire to rescue atheism from the connection of such atrocities, but I could only

---

[755]Sam Harris, *The End of Faith: Religion, Terror, and the Future of Reason*, New York (W. W. Norton & Company, 2004) 79. See his similar argument in Sam Harris, *Letter to a Christian Nation*, New York (Alfred A. Knopf, 2006) 39-43

[756] David Mills, *Atheist Universe: The Thinking Person's Answer to Christian Fundamentalism*, Berkeley CA (Ulysses Press, 2006) 63-64.

wish that Mills would extend the same courtesy to the Church as he does to atheistic communism.

As Mills said, "Is it really fair to condemn a school of thought for perversions and abuses of its teachings?" Yes, Mr. Mills, is it really fair of you to condemn the Christian faith because of the, "perversions and abuses of its teachings"? For I promise Mr. Mills, *no Christian I ever met defends atrocities* like the inquisition, witch hunts, or the crusades.

Alister McGrath summed up this concern:

"In their efforts to enforce their atheist ideology, the Soviet authorities systematically destroyed and eliminated the vast majority of churches and priests during the period 1918-1941. The statistics make for dreadful reading. This violence, repression and bloodshed were undertaken in pursuit of an atheist agenda—the elimination of religion. Atheists can be just as repressive, brutal and bloodthirsty as any other ideology. Atheism is just fine when it remains nothing more than ideas, discussed in university seminar rooms. But when it grasps political power, it turns out to be just as bad as anything else."[757]

Militant Atheism

Julian Baggini warned of the dangers of militant atheism:

"The fact that the Soviet Union was atheist is no more reason to think that atheism is necessarily evil than the fact that Hitler was a vegetarian is a reason to suppose that all vegetarians are Nazis. The mere existence of millions of humane atheists in Western democracies . . .

---

[757]Alister McGrath, *Is Religion Evil?* Chapter in William Lane Craig & Chad Meister, Editors, *God is Great, God is Good: Why Believing in God is Reasonable and Responsible,* Downers Grove IL (Inter Varsity Press, 2009) 127.

shows that there is no essential link between being an atheist and condoning the gulags. However, there is I believe a salutary lesson to be learned from the way in which atheism formed an essential part of Soviet communism . . . This lesson concerns what can happen when atheism becomes too militant and Enlightenment ideals too optimistic."[758]

Baggini followed with this rather chilling statement:

"What happened in Soviet Russia is one of the reasons why I personally dislike militant atheism. When I heard someone recently say that they really thought religious belief was some kind of mental illness and that they looked forward to a time in the future when religious believers would be treated, I could see an example of how militant atheism can lead to totalitarian oppression . . . There is, however, a need to remember that militant or fundamentalist atheism, which seeks to overturn religious belief by force, is as dangerous as any other form of fundamentalism."[759]

Sam Harris shows that Baggini's concerns are not unfounded:

"In fact, it is difficult to imagine a set of beliefs more suggestive of mental illness than those that lie at the heart of many of our religious traditions."[760]

Such statements are indeed alarming and destructive to constructive debate and philosophical inquiry.

---

[758]Julian Baggini, *Atheism,* New York (Sterling, 2003) 128.
[759]Julian Baggini, *Atheism,* 131-132, 133.
[760]Sam Harris, *The End of Faith: Religion, Terror, and the Future of Reason,* New York (W. W. Norton & Company, 2004) 72.

What about Hitler and Nazism?

Atheist apologists seek to evade the association of atheistic ideology with Hitler, the Nazis, and the Holocaust. Instead they place the guilt at the step of the church. Undeniably, the Roman Catholic and Protestant churches of Germany had a mixed record during the period. Yet, not given to subtlety, Sam Harris sought to lay the blame at the feet of the church:

> "The Holocaust is relevant here because it is generally considered to have been an entirely secular phenomenon. It was not. The anti-Semitism that built the crematoria brick by brick—and still thrives today—comes to us by way of Christian theology. Knowingly or not, the Nazis were agents of religion."[761]

Is this a fair critique? It is certainly true that a stream of anti-Semitism has been a stain on the church, most regrettably in the German reformer Martin Luther.[762] Lingering anti-Semitism was exploited by Hitler to advance his deadly aims. It is regrettably true that many in the churches of Germany had compromised themselves and failed to uphold Christian principles.[763] All this is true, and no attempt is made to cover it up. We can only ask God's forgiveness and stand by His grace.

---

[761]Sam Harris, *The End of Faith,* 79.

[762]Late in his life, and frustrated with the lack of response of the Jews to the gospel, Martin Luther wrote the anti-Semitic work *On the Jews and Their Lies* in 1543, a most unfortunate stain upon his otherwise amazing career.

[763] There were of course, many courageous Christians in the "Confessing Church" that opposed Hitler and remained true to their Christian convictions, often paying a high price for their faithfulness.

The atheistic influence on the Holocaust

That said, let us consider the other side of the coin, and the atheistic influences that played a role in the tragedy of the Holocaust.

Nietzsche's ethical influence on Hitler and Nazism[764]

Nietzsche was quite ahead of his times in feeling the full power of the eclipse of God in the West. He felt that Christianity had dominated the scene for too long and had been a corrupting influence on Western culture. He favored a radical rejection of Christian ethical standards which he felt had enslaved men and restricted their freedom. In brief, Christian morality had made men soft and weak.

What was needed was for men to take the initiative, to be manly, to be strong, and to have the will to power to exert themselves forcefully to success, and never mind the collateral damage.

Norman Geisler summed up Nietzsche's ethics:

"The shocking realization of God's death brought Nietzsche to the conclusion that all God-based values and absolutes were also dead . . . Hence, Nietzsche rejected

---

[764] Samuel J. Youngs, *A Sun to See By—Christianity, Meaning, and Morality,* chapter in *True Reason: Confronting the Irrationality of the New Atheism,* Tom Gilson & Carson Weitnauer, Editors, Grand Rapids MI (Kregel, 2012) 170. noted "that even Bertrand Russell condemned [Nietzsche's philosophical system] as a motivator of Nazism and fascism" citing Russell's *History of Western Philosophy* (New York: Routledge, 2004) 687-691.

traditional Judeo-Christian values in an almost violent manner. Nietzsche questioned even general principles such as 'Injure no man' (*Beyond Good and Evil,* 186-87). He ridiculed the Christian principle of love . . . In place of traditional Christian values, he proposed that modern people go 'beyond good and evil.' He suggested a transevalutation that would reject the 'soft' feminine virtues of love and humility and seize the 'hard' male virtues of harshness and suspicion."[765]

Some of Nietzsche's defenders (the 'gentle Nietzscheans'[766]) suggest that he often used hyperbole, and that some of his harshest comments were not meant to be taken literally. Perhaps that is partially the case, but it is impossible to deny his contempt for and rejection of Christian values, or to deny the tragic influence of Nietzsche's ethics during Hitler's despotic rule.

Martin Rhuel, a history professor at the University of Cambridge, explained how Nietzsche opposed advancing human rights in his day:

> "But a note in his unpublished papers, known as the *Nachlass,* casts doubt on these apolitical readings. In a topical entry from 1884, he condemns the emancipatory movements that were transforming western societies in the 19th century. Nietzsche lists their objects with palpable disdain: women, slaves, workers, 'the sick and corrupt.' The fragment leaves little doubt that its author considers the emancipation of these groups a disastrous mistake bound to exacerbate the 'leveling of European man' and the decay of contemporary culture."[767]

---

[765]Norman L. Geisler, *Baker Encyclopedia of Christian Apologetics,* Grand Rapids MI (Baker Books, 1999) 539.

[766]Martin A. Ruehl, *In Defense of Slavery: Nietzsche's Dangerous Thinking,* The U.K. Independent, January 2, 2018, at web address: https://www.independent.co.uk/news/long_reads/nietzsche-ideas-superman-slavery-nihilism-adolf-hitler-nazi-racism-white-supremacy-fascism-a8138396.html

Timothy Morgan showed the direct influence Nietzsche had upon Nazi thought:

"Though his supporters have tried to downplay Nietzsche's influence on Hitler, 150,000 special durably designed copies of his book *Thus Spoke Zarathustra* were distributed to German soldiers during World War I. Hitler also paid homage to his memory, was a frequent visitor to the Nietzsche museum in Weimar, used Nietzsche's expressions in *Mein Kampf,* and publicized photos of himself staring in rapture at a bust of Nietzsche."[768]

Hitler clearly believed himself to be the very embodiment of Nietzsche's philosophy, the uberman/superman with the will to power to seize power. Denise, White & Peterfreund tried to downplay Nietzsche's negative influence upon Hitler and the Nazis.

"Nietzsche's works are frequently, but erroneously regarded as philosophical support for the National Socialist (Nazi) movement in Germany. A few themes from his philosophy may support the Nazi doctrines, but there are fundamental differences—for example, in the opposition of Nietzsche's principle of radical creative individualism to the Nazi principle of the priority of the state over the individual."[769]

Well, well. Where do we start? First, note the important concession that "a few themes from his philosophy may support the Nazi doctrines." And this is

---

[767]Martin A. Ruehl, *In Defense of Slavery; Nietzsche's Dangerous Thinking,* The U.K. Independent

[768]Timothy Morgan, *Thank God for Atheists: How the Greatest Skeptics Led Me To Faith,* Eugene OR (Harvest House Publishers,2015) 51-52.

[769]Theodore C. Denise, Nicholas P. White & Sheldon P. Peterfreund, *Great Traditions in Ethics,* Tenth Edition, Belmont CA (Wadsworth Thomson Learning, 2002) 214.

quite an understatement. But Denise et al try to soften the blow of their concession by making a distinction between Nietzsche's promotion of individualism versus the Nazis' emphasis on the individual *as a servant of the state.*

But this defense cannot bear the weight of the facts. Nietzsche's superman was an individual with the will to power and dominate over others. Denise et al themselves stated:

> "However, Nietzsche does not intend this doctrine of the transevaluation of values for the 'common herd,' but for the few 'free spirits' of the day who are intellectually fit to receive it."[770]

Surely Hitler saw himself as this superman, this free spirit, intellectually ready to control the common herd. So it is not really the case that Nietzsche supported individualism in general, but only for those who were prepared to dominate others to advance themselves.

The influence of evolutionary thought on Hitler and Nazism

Likewise, Denise et al tried to avoid the clear influence of Darwinian evolution on Hitler's thinking, via Nietzsche:

> "Although the conception of evolution is fundamental in Nietzsche's ethical system, his interpretation of it departs from the widely accepted Darwinian hypothesis. In Darwin's theory, evolution is conceived as passive and mechanical adaption to the environment, but Nietzsche finds the true meaning of evolution in an aggressive 'will to

---

[770]Theodore C. Denise, Nicholas P. White & Sheldon P. Peterfreund, *Great Traditions in Ethics*, 214.

power' to dominate the environment: 'The strongest and highest Will to Life does not find expression in a miserable struggle for existence, but in a Will to War, a Will to Power, a Will to Overrpower!' There is in evolution no progress toward a goal: Each thing in the universe manifests a ceaseless, blind striving for power, shifting back and forth between success and failure in the competition for mastery."[771]

Again, Denise et al began with the major concession that "evolution is fundamental in Nietzsche's ethical system." They attempt to soften the concession, however, by making a distinction between Darwin's version of evolution in contrast to the more purposeful and dominating version of Nietzsche. But again, the defense is without merit. Did not Darwinian evolutionary theory advance the idea of the survival of the fittest, a dog eat dog world where the strong prevail over the weak?

Indeed, the Denise et al description of Nietzsche's evolutionary philosophy could not better describe Hitler's own narcissistic mentality and messianic complex. Nietzsche (and Hitler) conceived of the races of man as a part of an evolutionary development, and that the strong needed to eliminate the weak in order to preserve the superior race.

Ruehl explained:

"Slaves, Nietzsche remarked, hailed from 'useless and harmful stock' and belonged to an altogether different and invariably subordinate species."[772]

Again, Ruehl stated:

---

[771]Theodore C. Denise, Nicholas P. White & Sheldon P. Peterfreund, *Great Traditions in Ethics*, 215.
[772]Martin A. Ruehl, *In Defense of Slavery: Nietzsche's Dangerous Thinking*,

"In *The Gay Science*, he [Nietzsche] significantly mentions 'subhumans' as the natural attendants of heroes and supermen."[773]

Nietzsche had no regard for the Christian system of ethics which he considered "slave-morality." Rather, man was to be a law unto himself. This is quite in the spirit of Nietzsche's affirmation that "the noble type of man regards himself as a determiner of values, he does not require to be approved of; he passes the judgment."[774]

Ernst Haeckel, a prominent early evolutionist said:

"That immense superiority which the white race has won over the other races in the struggle for existence is due to Natural Selection . . . That superiority will, without doubt, become more and more marked in the future, so that fewer races of man will be able, as time advances, to contend with the white in the struggle for existence."[775]

Amazingly, De Rosa explained how Darwin advanced the same theory:

"Darwin displayed his assumptions of racial superiority in *Descent of Man* in a discussion about the evolutionary future of man . . . he refers to the 'civilized races' and the 'savage races' of man and expresses the confidence that 'civilized' men will, in the future, 'certainly exterminate and replace the savage races.'"[776]

[773]Martin A. Ruehl, *In Defense of Slavery; Nietzsche's Dangerous Thinking*.

[774]Friedrich Nietzsche, *Beyond Good and Evil*, no. 260, as quoted by Theodore C. Denise, Nicholas P. White & Sheldon P. Peterfreund, *Great Traditions in Ethics*, Tenth Edition, Belmont CA (Wadsworth Thomson Learning, 2002) 216.

[775]Ernst Haeckel, *The Pedigree of Man and Other Essays*, Translated by Edward Aveling (London: Freethought, 1883), p. 85., as quoted by Ted Benton, *Social Causes and Natural Relations*, in *Alas, Poor Darwin: Arguments Against Evolutionary Psychology*, Edited by Hilary Rose & Steven Rose, New York (Harmony Books, 2000) 249.

The legacy of Social Darwinism[777]

Shawn Stevens explained the destructive nature of social Darwinism; the attempt to understand and frame social and cultural issues within an evolutionary framework:

> "Darwin's influence spread into Germany, partly because of the influence of a man named Ernst Haeckel. Haeckel was a huge fan of Darwin and had the pleasure of meeting Darwin in 1866 . . . Haeckel believed in the superiority of the Germanic people and, also, in combating Christian faith . . . While Darwinian evolution affected the world view of communists from Lenin to Stalin to Mao, it also influenced and provided a foundation for the naziism of Adolf Hitler."[778]

Stevens also quoted Richard Weikart's comments about social Darwinism:

> "Many social Darwinists and eugenicists consigned most of the world's population to the realm of the 'inferior.' They regarded non-European races as varieties of the human species—or sometimes as completely separate species—that were not as advanced in their evolutionary development as Europeans."[779]

Again, Stevens explained:

---

[776] Tom DeRosa, *Evolution's Fatal Fruit: How Darwin's Tree of Life Brought Death to Millions*, Fort Lauderdale FL (Coral Ridge Ministries, 2006) 126-127.

[777] DeRosa noted that phrase "social Darwinism" was coined by Herbert Spencer. Tom DeRosa, *Evolution's Fatal Fruit, 132.*

[778] Shawn Stevens, *Darwin and the Races of Man*, reprinted in *The Discerner,* April-June, 2015, 21, 23.

[779] Richard Weikart, as quoted by Shawn Stevens, *Darwin and the Races of Man*, reprinted in *The Discerner*, April-June, 2015, 24.

"With the entrance of Adolf Hitler into German history, Darwinism was catapulted to an even uglier height. By Hitler's time a whole new generation of social Darwinists had risen up. . . Hitler taught that the triumph of the strong over the weak was simply a process of nature. Even more offensive still are his words, taken from *Mein Kampf,* in which he says . . . 'A stronger race (*Geschlecht*) will supplant the weaker, since the drive for life in its final form will decimate every ridiculous fetter of the so-called humanness of individuals, in order to make place for the humanness of nature, which destroys the weak to make place for the strong.'"[780]

Finally, Stevens summed up Hitler's social Darwinian agenda:

"His policy, wherever naziism was established, was Darwinian eugenics. Findley and Rothney write: 'Hitler was a 'social Darwinist,' who applied to human life the evolutionary vision of nature as a struggle amongst species for the survival of the fittest. For Hitler, history was a struggle for survival among biologically distinct races.'"[781]

John Eidsmoe explained how the American system of thought based upon Christian belief contrasted with the godless evolutionary philosophy of Nazism:

"The framers of the [United States] Constitution had a firm basis for believing in equality for they believed in a Creator: 'All men are *created* equal.' If one accepts the evolutionary humanist model, what is to prevent one from concluding that some men, or some races, have evolved to a point of superiority over others? Lest that notion sound far-fetched, let us remember that the Nazis believed exactly that."[782]

---

[780]Shawn Stevens, *Darwin and the Races of Man,* reprinted in *The Discerner,* April-June, 2015, 27
[781]Shawn Stevens, *Darwin and the Races of Man,* 27-28
[782]John Eidsmoe, *Christianity and the Constitution: The Faith of*

Sarah Gordon showed how Hitler put his atheistic evolutionary ideas into practice:

> "In his ethnic theory all 'subhumans' (including Poles and Russians) must be conquered and their leaders exterminated to prove the historical superiority of 'Aryans.' All Jews ('nonhuman parasites') must be exterminated . . . His murder of millions of non-Jews, however, did not result so much from paranoia as from his belief that 'subhumans' who had been conquered in the past did not deserve anything better than enslavement and selective extermination."[783]

Responding to Richard Dawkins, David Robertson wrote of Hitler's true motives:

> "You want to cite Hitler as a Christian, although even you know that is going a bit far . . . If we really want to know what Hitler thought, his actions and above all his private words are the most compelling evidence . . . Hitler's *Table Talk*, which tells us conclusively what Hitler thought about Christianity: 'The heaviest blow that ever struck humanity was the coming of Christianity.' Even more interesting is the following from Traudl Junge, Hitler's personal secretary: He was not a member of any church, and thought the Christian religions were outdated, hypocritical institutions that lured people into them. The laws of nature were his religion. He could reconcile his dogma of violence better with nature than with the Christian doctrine of loving your neighbor and your enemy . . . 'We are probably the highest stage of development of some mammal which developed from reptiles and moved on to human beings, perhaps by way of the apes. We are

---

Our Founding Fathers, Grand Rapids MI (Baker Books, 1987, 1995) 365.

[783]Sarah Gordon, *The Fate of German Jews*, in *The Nazi Revolution: Hitler's Dictatorship and the German Nation*, Third Edition, Allan Mitchell, Editor, Lexington MA (D. C. Heath a   nd Company, 1990) 176-177.

part of creation and children of nature, and the same laws apply to us as to all living creatures. And in nature the law of the struggle for survival has reigned from the first. Everything incapable of life, everything weak is eliminated. Only mankind and above all the church have made it their aim to keep alive the weak, those unfit to live, and people of an inferior kind."[784]

DeRosa quoted the evolutionist Niles Eldredge (who famously advocated for the theory of punctuated evolution along with Stephen Jay Gould) as acknowledging the unfortunate fruits of social Darwinism:

"Eldredge does, however, acknowledge that 'social Darwinism' . . . 'has given us the eugenics movement and some of its darkest outgrowths, such as the genocidal practices of the Nazis in World War II—where eugenics was invoked as a scientific rationale to go along with whatever other 'reasons' Hitler and his fellow Nazis had for the holocaust."[785]

Geisler reported Voltaire's prophetic statement about the fruits of atheism:

"With theists Voltaire spoke against atheism. He wrote: 'I have always been convinced that atheism cannot do any good, and may do very great harm. I have pointed to the infinite difference between the sages who have written against superstition and the madmen who have written against God. There is neither philosophy nor morality in any system of atheism' (*Philosophical Letters*, 33). He adds, 'It would not be difficult to prove from history that atheism may sometimes produce as much evil as the most barbarous superstitions' (ibid., 29)."[786]

---

[784]David Robertson, *The Dawkins Letters: Challenging Atheist Myths*, Great Britain (Christian Focus Publications, 2007) 110-112.

[785] Tom DeRosa, *Evolution's Fatal Fruit*, 140-141, quoting from Niles Eldredge, *Darwin: Discovering the Tree of Life*, W. W. Norton & Company, New York/London, 2005, p. 13.

The atheist response to evil and suffering

When the problem of suffering and evil is discussed, it is almost always in the context of theodicy. That is, believers are asked to defend how or why God allows the evil and suffering present in the world. We have acknowledged the gravity of the problem and wrestled with Christian responses.

But what is often overlooked in the discussion is the lack of an explanation for evil and suffering offered by atheists. It is easy for atheists to sit on their high horse and cast aspersions upon Christianity for the existence of suffering and evil. But what alternative do they offer? What great wisdom do they impart to the world? Only this; evil and suffering are brute facts, so deal with it.

For the atheist, there is simply no inherent meaning or purpose for the universe or for man's place in it. "All we are is dust in the wind."[787] We owe our existence to a random cosmic incident. It's a dog eat dog world; the survival of the fittest; the strong trample over the weak.

Nor is there purpose in suffering. Just endure it because that's the way the world is and the sooner you understand that the better. There is no hope for ultimate justice in the face of evil. There is no hope of eternal life and heavenly bliss; a world devoid of injustice and suffering. Nope. Just death. That's the atheist's answer to the presence of evil and suffering in the world.

---

[786]Norman L. Geisler, *Baker Encyclopedia of Christian Apologetics*, Grand Rapids MI (Baker Books, 1999) 766.
[787]Kerry Livgren, Kansas, *Dust in the Wind*, Kirshner Records, 1977

Millard Erickson closes our discussion of the problem of evil and suffering by reminding us of the God that Christians worship:

"That God took sin and its evil effects on himself is a unique contribution by Christian doctrine to the solution of the problem of evil. It is remarkable that, while knowing that he himself would become the major victim of the evil resulting from sin, God allowed sin to occur anyway . . . But even more to the point is the fact of the incarnation. The Triune God knew that the second person would come to earth and be subject to numerous evils: hunger, fatigue, betrayal, ridicule, rejection, suffering, and death. He did this in order to negate sin . . . God is a fellow sufferer with us of the evil in this world . . . What measure of love is this! Anyone who would impugn the goodness of God for allowing sin and consequently evil must measure the charge against the teachings of Scripture that God himself became the victim of evil so that he and we might be victors over evil."[788]

---

[788]Millard J. Erickson, *Christian Theology*, Second Edition, Grand Rapids MI (Baker Books, 1998) 456.

Section Eight: The Origin of Religious Beliefs

Chapter 40: Explanations for Religious Beliefs

The ubiquitous nature of religious belief must be explained

One of the facts of life is that most of the people whom have ever lived have believed in some form of divinity; a god or gods. This presents a challenge to atheism. How can they account for the nearly ubiquitous belief in God?

For Bible-believing Christians the origin of religion is no mystery. God is the source of the universe, and of all life in it. We have an inner drive to be in fellowship with God and we reach are fullest potential only as we walk with Him. Without God, we continually attempt fulfillment in substitutes unworthy and unable to satisfy our deepest needs.

Rejecting this explanation, atheists and skeptics search for alternative explanations for man's religious nature. Indeed, Michael Martin explained that the nearly universal belief in God itself has been used as an argument for the existence of God:

> "Philosophers and theologians such as Cicero, Seneca, the Cambridge Platonists, Gassendi, and Grotius have appealed to the common consent of humankind (*the consensus gentium*) as support for belief in the existence of God. Such an appeal is usually referred to as the argument from common consent."[789]

---

[789]Michael Martin, *Atheism: A Philosophical Justification,* Philadelphia PA (Temple University Press, 1990) 210.

James Thrower agreed:

"It was common practice until quite recently for apologetic theologians to begin their discussion of the evidence for a religious, and more particularly, a theistic world view with reference to what is known as the *argumentum e consensu gentium,* the argument from the general consent of mankind. It is an extremely venerable argument . . . More recently, Professor John Baillie evokes it as the first argument of his theistic apologia, stating quite categorically 'that we know of no human society, however savage and backward, which does not already find itself confronted by the divine.'"[790]

The fact of the near universal belief in God

Is religious belief really so universal? Kerry Walters stated:

"All this leaves the atheist with a puzzle. If religious conviction—whose broad but essential definition is belief in the supernatural—is so irrational, why is it still so prevalent? After all, as we saw in Chapter 1, it's still the majority opinion in the world today."[791]

Yeager Hudson stated:

"So pervasive is the phenomenon we call religion that some have suggested that the proper name for human beings is *homo religious.* There seems to be no societies, ancient or modern, from which religion is absent."[792]

---

[790]James Thrower, *Western Atheism: A Short History*, Amherst NY (Prometheus Books, 2000) 1.

[791]Kerry Walters, *Atheism: A Guide for the Perplexed*, New York (The Continuum International Publishing Group Inc, 2010) 95.

[792]Yeager Hudson, *The Philosophy of Religion*, Mountain View CA (Mayfield Publishing Company, 1991) 251.

Hans Küng agreed: "Religion has always existed. Both historically and geographically religion is ubiquitous."[793] Geisler related the words of Camus and Kaufmann:

> "The French atheist Albert Camus added, 'Nothing can discourage the appetite for divinity in the heart of man.' . . . Walter Kaufmann reaches the point that he confesses . . . 'Whether he worships idols or strives to perfect himself, man is the God-intoxicated ape."[794]

Anthony Layng said:

> "All human cultures appear to include faith in supernatural power . . . all human cultures today include faith in some spiritual beings and forces."[795]

Morton Hunt continued the idea:

> "Why have nearly all human beings in every known culture believed in God or gods and accepted the customs, dogmas, and institutional apparatus of an immense array of different religions? . . . Yet while this indicates that the human mind is basically pragmatic, nearly every human being during recorded history (and to judge from archaeological evidence much of prehistory) has held religious beliefs based on no empirical evidence whatever."[796]

---

[793]Hans Küng, *Freud and the Problem of God*, Enlarged Edition, New Haven & London (Yale University Press, 1990) 73.

[794]Norman L. Geisler, *Baker Encyclopedia of Christian Apologetics*, Grand Rapids MI (Baker Books, 1999) 281.

[795]Anthony Layng, *Supernatural Power and Cultural Evolution*, in *Science and Religion: Are They Compatible?*, Paul Kurtz, Editor, Amherst New York (Prometheus Books, 2003) 291, 292.

[796]Morton Hunt, *The Biological Roots of Religion,* in *Science and Religion: Are They Compatible?*, Paul Kurtz, Editor, Amherst New York (Prometheus Books, 2003) 299, 300.

Robert Morey suggested that the argument from consent must be frustrating to atheists who wonder how belief in God continues to have its hold:

> "Abstract philosophical arguments have little meaning for the average person because the existence of God has always been, for most people, a matter of common sense. Thus when atheism competes with theism in the open marketplace of ideas, it never convinces the average people who make up the bulk of the population."[797]

Toward an atheist's response to the ubiquitous nature of religious belief

Religious belief is culturally conditioned

A common atheistic response is that religious beliefs are not arrived at through a process of reason, but are rather accepted through a process of acculturation; people just accept what is dominant in their culture.

Bugliosi makes such a case:

> "Likewise, does any Christian reading this book really doubt that if he were a Jew born in Jerusalem that he would most likely be a member of the Jewish religion? And that if he were an Arab born somewhere in Saudi Arabia, he would most likely be a Muslim? Or if he were an Indian born in India that he would most likely be a member of the Hindu faith? Isn't it comforting for people to know that their very firmly held religious beliefs have nothing to do with the quality and merit of the beliefs, and everything to do with geography?"[798]

---

[797]Robert A. Morey, *The New Atheism and the Erosion of Freedom*, Minneapolis MN (Bethany House Publishers, 1986) 28.

[798]Vincent Bugliosi, *Divinity of Doubt: The God Question*, New York (Vanguard Press, 2011) 231.

To add insult to injury, Bugliosi adds that: "Our sense of superiority over all other religions is a form of prejudice."[799]

There can be no doubt that Bugliosi's point is a fair criticism of popular religion. Just as Socrates stated that "the unexamined life is not worth living,"[800] so in the present case we can argue that the *unexamined religion may not be worth believing.*

To the point, it is important that everyone examines their own religious beliefs. Nevertheless, while Bugliosi's point is well-taken, it does not take into account the nature of religious pluralism in America. We live in what can be compared to a supermarket of religious choices; where conversions occur regularly, and in which younger generations increasingly reject the beliefs of their parents.

In light of the increase in knowledge, the increase in travel, and the increase in the speed of communication, the argument that we each merely accept the beliefs of our own culture is simply untrue.

Further, the tidy picture of religious geography Bugliosi painted does not match the religious pluralism on the ground; for in each of the countries he mentioned there exists strong religious minority communities.

David Mills: All children are born atheists and conditioned to become believers

The atheist David Mills also promoted the idea that religion results from enculturation, most especially in the

---

[799]Vincent Bugliosi, *Divinity of Doubt,* 2011) 231.
[800]Samuel Enoch Stumpf, *Philosophy: History & Problems,* Fourth Edition, New York (McGraw-Hill Publishing Company, 1989) 546.

family of origin, and that children would otherwise be atheists. He insisted: "We should recognize that all children are born atheists. There is no child born with religious beliefs."[801]

But if all children are born atheists (as Mills' argued), then we naturally wonder why most of them become God believers? Mills' explanation is simple, their parents (and culture in general) brainwash them into God belief:

> "Because, again, they were taught to believe as small children and because almost everybody they know believes in God also."[802]

Mills' argument is confused, for if everyone is born an atheist, why do they grow up to indoctrinate their own children? If religious belief is so irrational, what compels generation after generation to first accept belief in God, and then willingly brainwash their own children?

Mills stated that "almost everybody they know believes in God." But again, why is this so, if they are all born atheists? Mills has a simple if not flattering answer; they conform to God-belief because they are essentially spineless cowards:

> "Few adults—and literally no children—have the independence of mind to dismiss the prevailing majority opinion as being total nonsense."[803]

This is an amazing claim in light of the fact that virtually every generation challenges the beliefs and ideals of their parents. As the song says, "Every

---

[801]David Mills, *Atheist Universe: The Thinking Person's Answer to Christian Fundamentalism*, Berkeley CA (Ulysses Press, 2006) 29.
[802]David Mills, *Atheist Universe,* 29.
[803]David Mills, *Atheist Universe,* 29.

generation blames the one before."[804] Mills claim is simply breathtaking; most of the people who have ever lived simply lack the convictions and courage of David Mills and his atheistic friends.

Kai Nielsen shared a similar perspective. He traced the ubiquitous nature of religious faith to childhood indoctrination:

> "I recall a psychiatrists once saying to me, after I had given a lecture on psychoanalysis and religion, that while he didn't need religion, while many people didn't need religion, a significant number of people who came to him for help very much needed their religion to attain psychological stability. Their chance of finding any significance in their lives, and no doubt their ability to hold onto any effective moral orientation, was tied for all practical purposes to their holding onto their religious beliefs. But he also agreed that if they had been differently *indoctrinated*, soberly educated without these religious myths, they would not need this religious crutch . . . I should not like to see it apologetically overplayed into the Pascalian theme that all men need religion to give significance and moral orientation to their lives."[805]

Note how Nielsen used the word 'indoctrinated' in a pejorative sense when referring to the religious training of youth. But is it any less 'indoctrinating' to raise children without religious beliefs and feeding them a steady diet of atheism and naturalism instead?

At bottom, Nielsen's argument, like Mills, is circular. Junior is religious because mom and dad indoctrinated him in God belief. *Why* did mom and dad indoctrinate

---

[804]B. A. Robertson & Mike Rutherford, Mike and the Mechanics, *In the Living Years*, EMI Music Publishing/ Imagem Music Inc.

[805]Kai Nielsen, *Atheism & Philosophy*, Amherst NY (Prometheus Books, 2005) 153.

junior in religion? Because they were likewise indoctrinated by their parents, and so forth and so on. But the question Nielsen's theory never explains is how the chain of God belief began or arose in the first place and remains so compelling generation after generation.

If, as Nielsen suggests, God is the ultimate emperor who has no clothes, that is, if God belief rests on such shaky intellectual grounds, then why, pray tell, Mr. Nielsen, does it have such universal appeal?

God belief as delusion

Let us consider the very prevalent idea that religious belief is the ultimate delusion of man. God is merely a delusional projection of man to help him cope with the frightening world in which he lives.

Feuerbach and projection

We can trace this modern idea back to Ludwig Feuerbach. He was a powerful initiator and popularizer of the idea that "God" was merely a human projection. Barnes explained:

> "Ludwig Feuerbach (1804-1872). In a work entitled, *The Essence of Christianity*, Feuerbach said that we humans tended to 'project' into the sky above us some of our own ideas about ourselves. We create God in the human image and likeness . . . Our sense of the infinite allows us to dream up the possibility of a Supreme Reality that is infinitely perfect. We call it 'God.' In order to imagine the perfection of this Infinite God we look to the best aspects of our human nature, exaggerate those aspects into perfection, and then attribute those aspects to God . . But it is really our own idealized selves we are worshipping when we worship God, said Feuerbach . . . By this we sacrifice our autonomy and make ourselves dependent on an imaginary God. Feuerbach called this a

kind of self-alienation, whereby we come to treat our own abilities and strengths as alien to us."[806]

Yeager Hudson added:

"What we worship as gods are what Feuerbach calls *Wunschwesen*, 'wish-beings,' and our religious behavior represents the acting out of a delusion."[807]

We shall address projection theories below as we consider the views of Freud who had adopted much of Feuerbach's projection views.

Karl Marx

Karl Marx agreed with the thrust of Feuerbach's ideas:

"Man makes religion, religion does not make man . . . Religion is the sigh of the oppressed creature, the heart of the heartless world, and the soul of the soulless conditions. It is the opium of the people. The abolition of religion as the *illusory* happiness of the people is the demand for their *real* happiness."[808]

Barnes elaborated on the views of Marx concerning religion:

"Marx said relatively little about religion. His most famous statements appear in an 1844 article on Hegel's *Philosophy of Right*. Religion is an illusion, Marx said . . .

---

[806]Michael Horace Barnes, *Understanding Religion and Science: Introducing the Debate*, New York (Continuum International Publishing Group, 2010) 93-94.

[807]Yeager Hudson, *The Philosophy of Religion*, Mountain View CA (Mayfield Publishing Company, 1991) 137.

[808]Karl Marx, as quoted by Michael Horace Barnes, *Understanding Religion and Science: Introducing the Debate*, New York (Continuum International Publishing Group, 2010) 95.

used by people to express their misery caused by the condition of life in this world. They do this by contrasting this life with an idealized world to come, and by contrasting the callous rulers of this world with an idealized otherworldly leader who is God. Religion is therefore the cry of the oppressed, an expression and sign of their distress. Religious otherworldliness promises pie in the sky in the great by and by: it thus becomes the opium by which people dull their awareness of their current pains in this world."[809]

Marx's concern for the oppression of the poor at the hands of those who have abused the Christian faith for their own purposes is commendable. It is certainly the case that Church leaders cannot ignore the plight of the poor and needy in this life and place all their focus on heavenly glories to come. The old saying that someone can be so heavenly minded that they are no earthly good comes to mind.

Indeed, throughout the Bible, the prophets cried out against such injustice. It was in part His bold challenge of the exploitations of the powers that be that led to Jesus' crucifixion. The history of mankind since the time of Christ shows the greatest army of caregivers have marched to the cross of Christ, feeding the hungry, providing drink to the thirsty, clothing to the naked, homes to orphans, visits to the prisoner, and a multitude of other caring ministries to those in need.

This is in contrast to the fruits of Marxist's communistic philosophy, which despite whatever good intentions Marx may have had, have been an instrument of massive suffering in this world.

---

[809]Karl Marx, as quoted by Michael Horace Barnes, *Understanding Religion and Science,* 95.

Further, Marx's theory doesn't explain why religious belief remains so popular amongst prosperous nations like America. With perhaps the highest standard of living ever known to mankind, yet American commitment to religious devotion is as strong as ever. Belief in God, then, is not merely the opium of the desperate masses seeking some hope amidst despair. It is the ever-present conviction of the most advanced and comfortable generation of human history.

Freud's theories on the origin of religion

Sigmund Freud was indeed an atheist, and yet one with a life-long interest in religion. Kerry Walters described Sigmund Freud as:

> "Fascinated by religion . . . He wrote three books devoted to exploring the psycho-history of religious belief: *Totem and Taboo* (1913), *The Future of an Illusion* (1927), and *Moses and Monotheism* (1939)."[810]

Küng added: "Freud, from his eightieth year, continued to study religion intensively and devoted to it almost the greater part of the remaining five years of his life."[811]

Walters described Freud's view of religion as springing from totemism:

> "The first and third of Freud's studies of religion are provocative but bizarre. In *Totem and Taboo*, he argued that God-belief is an attempt to deal with the ancient traumatic memory of sexual rivalry between sons and father which culminates in patricide. After the patricide,

---

[810]Kerry Walters, *Atheism,* 105.
[811]Hans Küng, *Freud and the Problem of God,* Enlarged Edition, New Haven & London (Yale University Press, 1990) 52.

the sons are burdened with guilt and the need for expiation. So they endow a totem, or animistic spirit with the qualities of the slain father (who after all, is the only person capable of bestowing on them the forgiveness they crave). Sexual conflict and unresolved guilt, then, are the bases of religion."[812]

Hans Küng elaborated: "Thus religion is based entirely on the Oedipus complex of mankind as a whole. For Freud this is the psychological explanation of the origin of religion."[813]

Freud on religion as expression of fear and wish fulfillment

Kai Nielsen explained how Freud borrowed from Feuerbach in developing his ideas on religion:

"Ludwig Feuerbach, from whom Freud took the projection theory, wanted to substitute a humanist perspective for a theological one. He wanted theology to become anthropology."[814]

Küng agreed:

"Freud took over from Feuerbach and his successors the essential arguments for his personal atheism: 'All I have done—and this is the only thing that is new in my exposition—is to add some psychological foundation to the criticisms of my great predecessors.'"[815]

---

[812]Kerry Walters, *Atheism,* 106.
[813]Hans Küng, *Freud and the Problem of God*, Enlarged Edition, New Haven & London (Yale University Press, 1990) 39.
[814]J. P. Moreland, & Kai Nielsen, *Does God Exist: The Debate Between Theists & Atheists*, Amherst NY (Prometheus Books, 1993) 81.
[815]Hans Küng, *Freud and the Problem of God*, 75.

More to the point, Walters showed Freud's agreement that belief in God does not arise from reason or revelation, but rather from man's fears:

> "In short, religion for Freud, as for Hume and Marx, is consolatory. It helps humans deal with fears which otherwise would be too burdensome to endure . . . What makes Freud's account of religion unique is his insistence that God-belief isn't merely erroneous (as Hume suggested) or oppressive (as Marx said), but a form of psychopathology. To be more precise, Freud diagnoses religious belief as an infantile obsessive neurosis. Religion is infantile because the deity to whom believers pay homage is actually a father substitute . . . The earthly father is replaced by a heavenly one purified of the former's weaknesses and foibles."[816]

Hans Küng elaborated on Freud's position:

> "Religion, then, arose out of the oldest, strongest, and most urgent wishes of mankind. Religion is wishful thinking, illusion. 'Illusion' means that religion is not a deliberate lie in the moral sense . . . [it] is motivated by wish-fulfillment."[817]

One common theme that Freud adopted was the idea of God as a perfect projection of our imperfect human fathers:

> "The common man cannot imagine this Providence otherwise than in the figure of an enormous exalted father. Only such a being can understand the needs of the children and be softened by their prayers and placated by the signs of remorse. The whole thing is so patently infantile, so foreign to reality . . . it is painful to think that the great majority of mortals will never rise above this view."[818]

---

[816]Kerry Walters, *Atheism,* 107.
[817]Hans Küng, *Freud and the Problem of God,* 46.
[818]Sigmund Freud, *Civilization and Its Discontents* (New York: W.

Freud's education for reality

Küng explained Freud's view concerning mankind's need to move on from the childish need for religion, to be educated for reality, and to transition to a world without God, very much like the world that Nietzsche envisioned:

> "One thing we must not do and that is to abolish religion by force and at one stroke, 'Education for reality.' Both for the individual human being and for mankind as a whole religion is a pubertal, transitional phase of human development. Neither as individual nor as species can man remain child forever. He must grow up, he must master reality with his own resources and with the aid of science and at the same time learn to resign himself to the inescapable necessities of fate. To leave heaven to the angels and the sparrows . . . abandon expectations of a hereafter and concentrate all the resources thus liberated on earthly life, this is the task of the mature, adult human being."[819]

Freud's psychoanalysis neutral on existence of God

However, Küng showed that although Freud was a convinced atheist himself, his theories were not primarily intended to disprove the existence of God, but rather to explain the psychological aspects of religious belief:

> "It should be noted that Freud is concerned with the psychological nature of religious ideas (as illusions), not with their truth content (as reality). 'To assess the truth-value of religious doctrine does not lie within the scope of the present enquiry. It is enough for us that we have

W. Norton, 1961) p. 21 as quoted by Yeager Hudson, *The Philosophy of Religion*, Mountain View CA (Mayfield Publishing Company, 1991) 138.
[819]Hans Küng, *Freud and the Problem of God*, 48-49.

recognized them as being, in their psychological nature, illusions."[820]

Kung added:

"This too is what Freud constantly maintained, that psychoanalysis does not necessarily lead to atheism. It is a method of investigation and healing and can be practiced by atheists and theists."[821]

Summing up Freud's theories on religion

Let us then, sum up Freud's theories about religion. It had its start in the mythic past, in which sons battled their father for their mother's affection. This competition ultimately resulted in the boys murdering their father. Now racked with guilt, and seeking atonement, the boys transferred their allegiance to a totem. They sought from the totem the forgiveness unavailable from their slain father, and this is the source of mankind's religious nature. This aspect (the source of the Oedipus complex) of Freud's ideas on religion is perhaps less-known.

More well-known are Freud's ideas that religion represents an infantile state of men in which they project onto this totem/divinity their need for a father figure to comfort them in the face of their fear of the terrifying aspects of life. Religion is then, nothing more than a delusion or illusion for the immature. What is needed, then, is education for reality; men need to learn to face life as it is and not fall prey to foolish myths.

---

[820]Hans Küng, *Freud and the Problem of God*, 46-47. Freud's quote is from the *Future of an Illusion*, 9:167.
[821]Hans Küng, *Freud and the Problem of God*, 75.

Responding to Freud's theories on religion

It is difficult to respond to Freud's very imaginative and highly speculative theory about the Oedipus complex and totemism as the source for religion. Are we to believe that both the source and ongoing need for religion springs from our guilt complex resultant from forbidden familial eroticism and the need to find appeasement for that guilt? Freud was an intellectual giant, no doubt, but his reductionist theory greatly simplifies and distorts a fundamental aspect of the human condition.

Wishful Thinking and projection

"If the triangles made a god, they would give him three sides."[822]

Joseph Ernest Renan

Of course, Trinitarians often use the triangle as an illustration of the doctrine of the Trinity (I'm just saying!).

One of the most common assumptions among atheists and skeptics is that rather than God being the creator of the universe, God is a creation of man. For instance, in *The Brothers Karmazov* by Fyodor Dostoevsky, Ivan Karamazov says, "As for me, I've long resolved not to think whether man created God or God man."[823] Paul Edwards put it well:

---

[822]Joseph Ernest Renan, as quoted in *The Concise Columbia Dictionary of Quotations*, Robert Andrews, Editor, New York (Columbia University Press, 1989) 110.

[823]Louis P. Pojman, *Philosophy: The Quest for Truth*, Sixth Edition, New York. Oxford (Oxford University Press, 2006) 111.

"Since the days of the German Philosopher Feuerbach (1804-1872) and more especially since the publication of the theories of Freud and certain of his disciples, many unbelievers have reasoned on this topic roughly along the following lines. People whose lives are devoid of certain forms of earthly love and warmth tend to escape into a world of dreams and make believe. Not finding satisfaction for some of their deepest and most powerful longings in their physical and human environment, they seek consolation and substitute–gratification in a world of their own making which can be managed more easily than the hard and cold universe around them."[824]

Likewise, Kai Nielsen said:

"We must cure man of his need for religion, and not just show the intellectual absurdity of it. We must, as Feuerbach and Marx stressed, transform society so that men will no longer need to turn to religious forms to give inspiration to their lives."[825]

Peter Kreeft stated the problem with a bit of wit:

"For either God created us in His image, or we created Him in ours. (It could be both options, of course; as one wag put it, 'God created us in His image and we've been returning the compliment ever since.')."[826]

As with Feuerbach, Freud's ideas about religion as wishful thinking must be rejected. Religion as wish-fulfillment advocated by Feuerbach and Freud has been very influential in modern thinking.

---

[824]Paul Edwards, *A Modern Introduction to Philosophy: Readings from Classical and Contemporary Sources,* Third Edition, Paul Edwards & Arthur Pap, Editors, New York, (The Free Press, 1973) 390.

[825]Kai Nielsen, *Atheism & Philosophy,* 161.

[826]Peter Kreeft, Introduction to *Does God Exist?: The Debate Between Theists & Atheists,* J.P. Moreland & Kai Nielsen, Amherst NY (Prometheus Books, 1993)18-19.

Responding to religion as wish-fulfillment and projection

Küng responded to Freud's argument concerning religion as wishful thinking:

> "All human believing, hoping, loving—related to a person, a thing, or God—certainly contains an element of projection. But its object need not, for that reason, be a mere projection . . . The mere fact of projection, therefore, does not decide the existence or non-existence of the object to which it refers . . . Is religion human *wishful thinking*? And must God for that reason be merely a human wishful structure, an infantile illusion or even a purely neurotic delusion? As we have argued elsewhere against Feuerbach, a real God may certainly correspond to the wish for God. This possibility is one which even Freud did not exclude. And why should wishful thinking be entirely and universally discredited?"[827]

Küng further elaborated on this point:

> "Why in fact should I not be permitted to wish? Why should I not be allowed to wish that the sweat, blood, and tears, all the suffering of millennia, may not have been in vain, that definitive happiness may finally be possible for all men—especially the despised and downtrodden? . . . May I not too feel aversion to the idea that the life of the individual and of mankind is ruled only by pitiless laws of nature, by the play of chance and by the survival of the fittest, and that all dying is a dying into nothingness? . . . Perhaps this being of our longings and dreams does actually exist. Perhaps this being who promises us eternal bliss does exist."[828]

---

[827]Hans Küng, *Freud and the Problem of God*, 77, 78.
[828]Hans Küng, *Freud and the Problem of God*, 78-79.

The bottom line, for Küng, is that Freud's anti-theistic beliefs are just that, beliefs, not facts:

"Freud's atheism, of which he was quite certain long before any of his psychological discoveries, thus turns out to be a pure hypothesis, an unproved postulate, a dogmatic claim."[829]

For Küng, then, man's intense desire for God, his wish, need not be merely an empty illusion. It just might be that there is a God that corresponds to our need and satisfies it.

Evans and Manis agreed:

"Once more, it appears that even if Freud's account is accepted, it does not follow that religious belief is false. It is not surprising to the religious believer that religion fulfils important psychological functions. If Freud is right, then humans have a deep need to believe in God. But surely the existence of such a need does not show that God does not exist. Indeed, many religious believers would accept much of Freud's account of the importance of early childhood experiences—and of one's relationship to one's father, in particular—in developing beliefs about God. For them the human family is a divinely designed institution, whose function may be, in part, to give humans some idea of what God is like and some inclination to believe in him."[830]

Likewise, Robert Morey stated:

"It is erroneous to assume that the object of man's desires or wishes cannot exist . . . This is the basic error of Feuerbach in his *Essence of Christianity* (1853). He argues that since God was something that man wished to believe

---

[829]Hans Küng, *Freud and the Problem of God*, 80.
[830]C. Stephen Evans & R. Zachary Manis, *Philosophy of Religion: Thinking About Faith*, Second Edition, Downers Grove IL (Inter Varsity Press, 2009) 150.

in, something he felt he needed, therefore God was only the projection of man's wish or desire. God does not exist *per se.* Freud and many others have followed Feuerbach into this logical error."[831]

A man known much less as a philosopher, the former governor of Minnesota, Jesse Ventura, made headlines repeating the same mantra "Organized religion is a sham and a crutch for weak-minded people."[832] I liked Christian comedian Mike Warnke's retort to such claims. He said, "a crutch ain't bad if you're crippled."[833] That is, mankind has a crippling problem with the reality of sin, and Jesus Christ is the cure.

The biblical God is not the kind of God men would project

In a debate with Kai Nielsen, J. P. Moreland reiterated R. C. Sproul's point in this regard:

> "Further, as R. C. Sproul has pointed out, the biblical God is not the kind of a God that one would want to project. One would want to project a much more tame being and not a being quite so holy, so demanding, so awesome as the triune biblical God."[834]

C. S. Lewis made a similar point in his own winsome way:

> "We want, in fact, not so much a Father in Heaven as a grandfather in Heaven—a senile benevolence who, as they

---

[831]Robert A. Morey, *The New Atheism and the Erosion of Freedom*, 26.

[832]Jesse Venutra, November 1999 *Playboy,* as quoted in David Mills, Atheist Universe: *The Thinking Person's Answer to Christian Fundamentalism*, Berkeley CA (Ulysses Press, 2006) 190.

[833]https://en.wikiquote.org/wiki/Mike_Warnke

[834]J. P. Moreland, & Kai Nielsen, *Does God Exist?*, 79.

say, 'liked to see young people enjoying themselves,' and whose plan for the universe was simply that it might be truly said at the end of each day, 'a good time was had by all.'"[835]

Yes, it seems that the kind of God we would want to project would be some kind of big daddy God that protects us and give us the things we desire. A combination of a cosmic ATM machine and personal security guard.

Such a 'god' is more the stuff of mythology and idolatry than the God of the Bible, who not only loves us, but is a just and holy judge before whom we shall all appear one day to give an account for our lives.

Further, that man has an innate need for God is no more an argument against His existence than man's thirst is an argument against the existence of water.

Freud's shoe on the other foot

"An atheist cannot find God for the same

reason a thief cannot find a policeman."[836]

If it is fair to speculate concerning the psychological reasons for man's belief in God, it should be equally fair to speculate the concerning the psychological reasons that may motivate atheists to deny the existence of God. Sure, it is possible that man has created the idea of God

---

[835]C. S. Lewis, *The Problem of Pain*, New York (Macmillan, 1962, 1975) 40.

[836]*20,000 Quips & Quotes*, Evan Esar, Editor, New York (Barnes & Noble Books, 1995) 48.

to fulfill psychological needs and to provide comfort as he faces a scary world.

But may it not also be just as possible that those who deny the existence of God have unconscious or hidden reasons for doing so. For instance, in his autobiography, Wilhelm Stekel said, "Fervid atheism is usually a screen for repressed religion."[837]

Evans and Manis likewise commented:

> "Sociologists of knowledge can give accounts of the social origins of atheistic beliefs, as well as religious beliefs. If believers sometimes show a deep psychological need to believe in God, nonbelievers sometimes show an equally psychological need to reject any authority over them and to assert themselves as their own lords and masters."[838]

Alister McGrath agreed:

> "It was also pointed out that if belief in God was a response to human longing for security, might it not also be argued that atheism was a response to the human desire for autonomy?"[839]

Could not man's desire for unrestricted freedom display itself as an unconscious motivation for the denial of God's existence? Peter Kreeft continued this line of reasoning, turning Freud's totemism and Oedipus complex theories against him:

---

[837] *The Encyclopedia of Religious Quotations*, Frank S. Mead, Editor, Westwood NJ (Fleming H. Revell Company, 1965) 12.

[838] C. Stephen Evans & R. Zachary Manis, *Philosophy of Religion.* 151.

[839] Alister McGrath, *The Twilight of Atheism: The Rise and Fall of Disbelief in the Modern World,* New York (Doubleday, 2004) 58-59.

"Thus the Freudian argument begs the question. The God-question cannot be settled that way, psychologically. The theist could fairly turn the argument around and psychoanalyze the atheist's motives as the atheist has analyzed his. He could argue, for example, that Freud had a bad relationship with his father, and explain that that was why he became an atheist: it was the Oedipus complex. Instead of killing his earthly father, Freud took vengeance on his heavenly Father. Such an 'argument' has no more (and no less) validity than Freud's own explanation of the heavenly Father as a substitute for the lost earthly father."[840]

J. P. Moreland argued along the same lines:

"I would like to say, in addition, that if anyone is engaging in some sort of projection or defense mechanism, then a good case could be made that it might be the nontheist and not the theist . . . Paul Vitz, who is a psychologist, I think at New York University, studied the lives of several atheists and he just came out with a book on Freud. He concluded that most of them had bad relationships with their fathers, and, in fact, if anyone was not approaching the God-question fairly, then it was the atheist who desired to kill the father and who was afraid to have someone control his or her life."[841]

Orlo Strunk Jr. provided a fascinating summary of possible psychological motives, conscious or unconscious, for atheism:

"A psychologist, for example, might like to believe that a person becomes an atheist because he was unable to develop a sense of trust in his formative years . . . Yet, we would suppose, if belief can be explained in psychological

[840]Peter Kreeft, *Introduction, Does God Exist?: The Debate Between Theists & Atheists*, J.P. Moreland & Kai Nielsen, Amherst NY (Prometheus Books, 1993) 24.
[841]J. P. Moreland, & Kai Nielsen, *Does God Exist?*,79.

terms, so too can atheism. Psychologists have identified at least four psychological motives which help explain the atheistic position. First, atheism may be the result of a *revolt against authority*. Many a young man desperately desires to overthrow his father. *In the process he might also cast down the God of his father* . . . Second, atheism may have its roots in a man's *deep yearning for power* . . . Third, atheism may be the result of *projection*, the tendency to avoid blame by placing the responsibilities upon others . . . Fourth, atheism may be the end result of the conquest of desire over reason, of what the psychologists call rationalization. Inner and outer forces may drive an individual to formulate all kinds of explanations in order to overcome psychological discomfort."[842]

As Strunk described, "many a young man" in attempt to cast aside their father, also cast down their father's God as well. This was in fact, the very experience of Soren Kierkegaard. His biographer Walter Lowrie stated:

"He [Kierkegaard] recognized a few years later that his state of mind meant not only revolt against his father but against God."[843]

To the point, Küng asked:

"Atheists accuse religion of being wishful thinking. But we for our part may ask whether atheism too might not be wishful thinking, projection?"[844]

---

[842]Orlo Strunk, Jr., *The Choice Called Atheism: Confronting the Claims of Modern Unbelief*, Nashville TN (Abingdon Press, 1968) 38, 41-42.

[843]Walter Lowrie, *A Short Life of Kierkegaard*, New York City (Anchor Books/Doubleday & Company, Inc, 1961) 73.

[844]Hans Küng, *Freud and the Problem of God*, 85.

Confession time for former skeptics who didn't want to believe in God

That is, is it possible that atheists hope and wish that God doesn't exist as much as a theist may hope and wish that God does exist? Groothius quotes Aldous Huxley:

> "I had motives for not wanting the world to have meaning; consequently, I assumed that it had none . . . Most ignorance is vincible ignorance. We don't know because we don't want to know. It is our will that decides . . . Those who detect no meaning in the world generally do so because, for one reason or another, it suits their books that the world should be meaningless."[845]

In the same book, Huxley added:

> "For myself, as, no doubt, for most of my contemporaries, the philosophy of meaninglessness was essentially an instrument of liberation. The liberation we desired was simultaneously liberation from a certain political and economic system and liberation from a certain system of morality. We objected to the morality because it interfered with our sexual freedom."[846]

Francis Collins referred to his own agnosticism as a young man:

---

[845] Aldous Huxley, *Ends and Means, An Inquiry into the Nature of Ideals and into the Methods Employed for Their Realization* 3rded. (New York: Harper & Brothers, 1937), p. 312 as quoted in Douglass Groothuis, *Christian Apologetics: A Comprehensive Case for Biblical Faith*, Downers Grove IL (InterVarsity Press, 2011) 143.

[846] Aldous Huxley, *Ends and Means, An Inquiry into the Nature of Ideals and into the Methods Employed for Their Realization* (New York: Harper & Brothers, 1937), 273 as quoted by Carson Weitnauer, *The Irony of Atheism*, chapter in *True Reason: Confronting the Irrationality of the New Atheism,* Tom Gilson & Carson Weitnauer, Editors, Grand Rapids MI (Kregel Publications, 2012) 30.

"Though I did not know the term at the time, I became an agnostic . . . some arrive at this position after intense analysis of the evidence, but many others simply find it to be a comfortable position that allows them to avoid considering arguments they find discomforting on either side. I was definitely in the latter category. In fact, my assertion of 'I don't know' was really more along the lines of 'I don't want to know.' As a young man growing up in a world full of temptations, it was convenient to ignore the need to be answerable to any higher spiritual authority. I practiced a thought and behavior pattern referred to as 'willful blindness' by the noted scholar and writer C. S. Lewis."[847]

Collins confession reminds me of the one Augustine made in his great work appropriately called *Confessions:*

"But I still postponed my renunciation of this world's joy . . . As a youth I had been woefully at fault, particularly in early adolescence. I had prayed to you for chastity and said *'Give my chastity and continence, but not yet'* For I was afraid that you would answer my prayer at once and cure me too soon of the disease of lust, which I wanted satisfied, not quelled."[848]

Walters shared Thomas Nagel's interesting self-confession in this regard:

"The naturalist *wants* the universe to be all there is, just as the supernaturalist *wants* there to be a God. Each has a personal, emotional stake in his respective position that goes beyond intellectual assent. Philosopher Thomas Nagel offers a forthright confession of this role of personal desire in choosing worldviews. 'I want atheism to be true and am made uneasy by the fact that some of the most

[847]Francis S. Collins, *The Language of God: A Scientist Presents Evidence for Belief,* New York (Free Press, 2006) 16.
[848]Augustine, *Confessions,* Harmondsworth, Middlesex, England (Penguin Books, 1984) 169.

intelligent and well-informed people I know are religious believers. It isn't just that I don't believe in God and, naturally, I hope that I'm right in my belief. It's that I hope there is no God! I don't want there to be a God; I don't want the universe to be like that."[849]

Likewise, Lennox shared the comment of Sir Arthur Eddington:

"One such was Sir Arthur Eddington (1882-1944), who reacted as follows: 'Philosophically, the notion of a beginning of the present order of Nature is repugnant . . . I should like to find a genuine loophole."[850]

Roy Varghese shared a story from the life of famed philosopher Bertrand Russell, as told by his daughter Katherine Tait, that perhaps speaks to early influences and hidden motives for his skepticism:

"Russell's rejection of God was not motivated just by intellectual factors. In *My Father, Bertrand Russell,* his daughter, Katherine Tait, writes that Russell was not open to any serious question of God's existence: 'I could not even talk to him about religion.' Russell was apparently turned off by the kind of religious believers he had encountered. "I would have liked to convince my father that I had found what he had been looking for, the ineffable something he had longed for all his life. I would have liked to persuade him that the search for God does not have to be in vain. But it was hopeless. He had known too many blind Christians, bleak moralists who sucked the joy from life and persecuted their opponents; he would never have been able to see the truth they were hiding. Tait, nevertheless, believes that Russell's 'whole life was a search for God . . . Somewhere at the back of my father's mind, at the bottom of his heart, in the depths of his soul, there was an empty

---

[849]Thomas Nagel as quoted by Kerry Walters, *Atheism,* 49-50.
[850]John C. Lennox, *God's Undertaker: Has Science Buried God?,* New Updated Edition, Oxford England (Lion Books, 2009) 67.

space that had once been filled by God, and he never found anything else to put in it.'"[851]

Atheism and the quest for autonomy

There is a longing among many to be free and to do what they will. They are repelled by the idea that they will one day have to stand before God and give an account for their lives. Weitnauer calls this desire to be free of God's watchful eyes and accountability the "cosmic authority problem."[852]

None has been clearer in their passionate desire to escape from God's sovereignty than Friedrich Nietzsche, as this quote from his work *Thus Spoke Zarathustra* reflected:

"But he had to die: he saw with eyes that saw everything: he saw man's depths and ultimate grounds, all his concealed disgrace and ugliness. His pity knew no shame: he crawled into my dirtiest nooks. This most curious, overobtrusive one had to die. He always saw me: on such a witness I wanted to have my revenge or not live myself. The god who saw everything, even man—this god had to die! Man cannot bear it that such a witness should live."[853]

---

[851]Roy Abraham Varghese, *Preface* p. 20-21 in Antony Flew, *There is a God: How the World's Most Notorious Atheist Changed His Mind*, New York (HarperCollins/HarperOne, 2007)

[852] Carson Weitnauer, *The Irony of Atheism*, chapter in *True Reason: Confronting the Irrationality of the New Atheism,* Tom Gilson & Carson Weitnauer, Editors, Grand Rapids MI (Kregel Publications, 2012) 31.

[853]Friedrich Nietzsche, *Thus Spoke Zarathustra*, in the *Portable Nietzsche*, ed. Walter Kaufman (New York: Viking Press, 1975), p. 379 as quoted by Douglass Groothuis, *Christian Apologetics: A Comprehensive Case for Biblical Faith*, Downers Grove IL (InterVarsity Press, 2011) 144.

David Mills expressed this desire for absolute freedom, untainted by any divine obligation:

"By eliminating a very burdensome obligation to appease a nonexistent God, an individual thereby gains maximum freedom to choose his own goals and ideas for a satisfying life . . . Atheism is synonymous with freedom."[854]

Those attracted to the freedom atheism offers may one day find themselves standing before the tribunal of the living God and having to give an account of how he used that freedom. Kai Nielsen expressed this same desire for autonomy:

"We do not need a God to *give* meaning to our lives by making us for His Sovereign Purpose and thereby arguably robbing us of our freedom . . . Moreover, is it really compatible with human dignity to be *made* for something? . . . Finally, is it not *infantile* to go on looking for some Father, some Order, that will lift all the burden of *decision* from you? Children follow rules blindly, but do we want to be children all our lives?"[855]

Nielsen is passionate concerning his cry for human autonomy. He feels God belief robs man, not only of his freedom, but also of his dignity.

But why should this be so? Could it be that one can "be all you can be" in the fullest sense as a consequence of being in union with, rather than in rebellion against, their creator? For if we are all God's creation, then, we are foolish to rebel against His authority.

Paul Moser pointed out that God cannot just be wished out of existence:

[854]David Mills, *Atheist Universe,* 33.
[855]Kai Nielsen, *Atheism & Philosophy,* 222.

"Likewise, people cannot define or postulate God out of existence, as if a mere definition could block the actual existence of God."[856]

Again, God's moral guidance is for our benefit in the same way that our human parents' guidance (avoid drugs and crime) is meant for our own good. To reject this moral guidance, then, is only to hurt ourselves.

If we have been made to be in relationship with God, as Christianity suggests, then our cries for absolute freedom are about as puzzling as a hammer complaining about having to pound in nails. It is not infantile to live for the purpose for which you were created. It is infantile, however, to throw tantrums because you can't have it their own way or do their own thing.

I am convinced that the greatest joy and fulfillment experienced in life is enjoyed by those who embrace their God-given purpose in life. There is no greater excitement that can be gained than by using our gifts, our creativity, and our passions for the journey of life given us as a gift of God.

The Biblical assessment for full autonomy

Groothius quite rightly highlights the apostle John's assessment of man's predicament:

"This is the verdict: Light has come into the world, but people loved darkness instead of light because their deeds were evil. Everyone who does evil hates the light, and will not come into the light for fear that their deeds will be exposed. But whoever lives by the truth comes into the

---

[856]Paul K. Moser, *Evidence of a Morally Perfect God*, chapter in William Lane Craig & Chad Meister, Editors, *God is Great, God is Good: Why Believing in God is Reasonable and Responsible*, Downers Grove IL (Inter Varsity Press, 2009) 51.

light, so that it may be seen plainly that what they have done has been done in the sight of God" (John 3:19-21).

Turned off to faith by the mistakes of the faithful

Further, it is also quite reasonable to suppose that many have been turned off to God because of negative experiences they have had with the church.

For example, I worked with a man who was a really nice guy. When I talked to him about things of faith, he had no time for the discussion. His reason was clear. He told me that he had been in the United States Navy, and once while getting into a boat with a Navy chaplain, he accidently upset the boat, causing the chaplain to slip, which was followed by a nasty curse-filled rebuke by the said chaplain. My friend said he decided then and there that if that is what Christianity was about, he wasn't interested.

Others have been alienated by their treatment at a church; turned off by constant appeals for donations; or perhaps have even been abused as children. All of these and many other examples could very well be conscious or unconscious motivations in a persons' rejection of God, and understandably so.

Kerry Walters acknowledged these factors:

"Other people may disbelieve in God because they endured unhappy religious experiences as children or because an especially traumatic incident in which God didn't answer their prayer persuaded them of God's nonexistence . . . Still others may find the moral hypocrisy of some religious leaders distasteful enough to wash their hands of religion altogether."[857]

---

[857]Kerry Walters, *Atheism,* 13, 14.

No doubt, it is disturbing and troubling to see the faith trampled upon by those who hypocritically abuse it for personal gain. But like any human institution, the good can be used and abused by those with dark motives, and it is, therefore, imperative that we do not as it were, throw the baby of good faith out with the bathwater of phony preachers and hypocrites in the pews.

Neither should we forget, however, that the church is made up of imperfect people. This side of eternity, Christians will struggle with the sin and unfortunately hurt others along the way. It is hoped that they will repent and seek forgiveness from those they have hurt.

But we should not think of Christians as having reached sinless perfection, but rather as sinners being changed and sanctified day by day through their faith in Christ, becoming increasingly conformed to the image of Christ (Romans 8:29).

Those contemplating the Christian faith should keep these facts in mind. Rather than to focus on the failings of Christians, they do better to focus on the holy and perfect God of Heaven that will never disappoint them.

Freud, repression, and God substitutes

After a thorough examination of Sigmund Freud's ideas concerning religion, and the effects of his ideas in the field of psychoanalysis in particular, and the culture in general, Hans Küng asked an important question:

> "I, as a theologian, dare to ask this question: Shouldn't psychiatrists in particular, indeed educated people in general, ask whether a phenomenon of repression may not be at work here . . . If Freud's own analysis of religious ideas is correct—that is, that religion fulfills the 'oldest, strongest, most urgent wishes of humanity'. . . and if 'the

secret of their strength is the strength of these wishes,'
then their repression must have consequences. And these
consequences could be highly destructive."[858]

This is at the same time both a profound and startling
question raised by Küng. Forgetting for the moment the
source or origin of man's religious nature, and even the
question of God's existence, Küng asked a very pragmatic
question. If believing in God has always held such a
pivotal place in man's psyche, is there not some
psychological price to be paid for God repression?

Küng continued this line of thought by noting how
repressed needs for religion often find expression in
substitutes:

> "Substitute fulfillment does not solve the problem but
> rather aggravates it. A modern form of suppression occurs
> when religious wishes are fulfilled in a 'secular' fashion (in
> such partial spheres as career, family, or political, cultural,
> social, or athletic activity). When relative values (such as
> money, career, sex, knowledge, party, or leader) are made
> formally absolute, we speak of a 'cult' or 'substitute
> religion.'"[859]

But, argued Küng, these substitutes cannot finally
fulfill our deepest needs and longings:

> "Couldn't some (but not all!) of the neuroses of our
> times and their symptoms be diagnosed as products of
> spiritual traumata? Because *homo patiens* in modern times
> no longer admits and embraces his deepest, hidden
> religious wishes, emotions, affects . . . but rather has
> shifted them to the unconscious by means of a defense
> mechanism and fixed them there—in short, 'repressed'
> them? This leads to substitute satisfactions, daydreams,

---

[858]Hans Küng, *Freud and the Problem of God*, 134, 140.
[859]Hans Küng, *Freud and the Problem of God*, 140.

parapraxias, and pathological symptoms or to projection onto substitute objects (persons, ideas, movements) that often take on a fanatical, absolute significance."[860]

Küng concluded that much of the maladies in modern living can at least be partially traced to this religious repression:

"The characteristic neurosis of our times is probably no longer repressed sexuality (what is there left to be repressed?) but rather the *lack of orientation, lack of norms, want of meaning, and emptiness* suffered by countless people. Isn't the whole critical development in modern times—right up to the problem of susceptibility, even among the young, to alcohol, drugs, and criminality on the one hand, and to practical nihilism, terroristic anarchism, and suicide on the other—isn't this development related to the severing of our ethical-religious convictions, norms, and communities?"[861]

Küng's description speaks powerfully and prophetically to our age and times.

Religion invented to control People

Another explanation for religion is that it is simply a tool invented to control the masses. It gives the priestly caste power over the lives of their followers. It is hard to take such a theory seriously. If there is no legitimate reason to believe in God, how do these sinister religionists get people under their spell?

Try this where you live. Tell everyone in your town that you have a 300 foot invisible dragon, and that unless people stop by your house to worship the dragon and leave offerings for it, the dragon will make their lives

---

[860]Hans Küng, *Freud and the Problem of God*, 142
[861]Hans Küng, *Freud and the Problem of God*, 143-144.

difficult and at their deaths devour their souls in his lair. It is most likely that you would get laughed out of your town for your bizarre claims.

Yet, in contrast to my proposal, most people find the evidence for God's existence compelling.

Dawkins: Evolution and religion as a Meme/Memes

Richard Dawkins has developed a concept known as a *meme* or *Memes* to describe the prevalence of ideas in human culture. He compared the spread of ideas to the spreading of viruses, and that just as natural selection and evolutionary forces have acted upon the natural world, so also, they act upon and affect the spread of ideas. Daniel Dennett explained:

> "It's ideas, not worms, that hijack our brains—replicating ideas. Ideas that we rehearse and think about, and decide that we like, pass them on to somebody else, who passes them on to somebody else. They make copies; they spread like a virus. These themes are what Richard Dawkins calls *memes*. Dawkins, who wrote *The Selfish Gene* in 1976, introduced the idea that cultural items had an evolutionary history too. They could replicate. They could differentially replicate, and the fittest were the ones that would get us to make the most copies. He pointed out that they are analogous to genes or to viruses."[862]

After initially defining memes, Dennett moved on to suggest that *the origin of religion* can be explained by the concept of memes:

---

[862]Daniel Dennett in *The Future of Atheism: A Dialogue*, Daniel Dennett & Alister McGrath, Robert B. Stuart, Editor, Minneapolis MN (Fortress Press, 2008) 24.

"When I started working on my book on the evolution of religion, people said very often, 'Oh, you're working on the evolution of religion. That's an interesting question. What do you think religions are for? Because after all, every human group that's ever been studied has some form of religion, so it must be good for something.' And I said, 'Well, yeah, that's a possibility, but that's a false inference.' 'Well, why?' And I said, 'Well, every human group that's ever been studied also has the common cold. What's that good for?' It's good for itself. It replicates because it can. I'm not saying religion is like the common cold; I'm saying it *might* be. I'm saying that some religious ideas could be like the common cold; they spread because they can spread. They are fit and we can't get rid of them anymore than we can get rid of the common cold . . . The fact that it's still here only shows that it is benefiting the fitness of something, but it might be only itself."[863]

There is nothing wrong with the meme concept per se. There is certainly a reasonable analogy to be made between the spreading (replicating, mutating) of ideas with the spreading of a virus. Likewise, we have all witnessed and experienced such and readily identify with it (fads, fashions, ideals).

But for Dawkins and Dennett, religion is an undesirable meme that is actually destructive to those who accept it (akin to the common cold), and to the cultural context in which they live. How shall we respond?

To begin with, Dawkins and Dennett's explanation of the spread of religion as a virus-like meme does not say anything about the origin of religion in the first place.

Second, while the meme concept can be useful as an analogy, it is a mistake to take it literally. This is

---

[863]Daniel Dennett in *The Future of Atheism,* 24-25.

because the spreading of a virus is an entirely natural and thoughtless process. But the spreading of ideas occurs through sentient beings weighing the value of the ideas they spread, ignore, or reject. Alister McGrath made this point in a debate with Daniel Dennett:

> "And what about the cognitive model that underlies the meme? . . . It seems to me that Dennett seems to buy into Dawkins's curious idea, set out in 1976, of memes 'leaping from brain to brain.' This seems to posit cognition as an essentially passive reception of the memes. But cognition is an active process. *Anyway, has anyone actually seen these things, whether leaping from brain to brain, or just hanging out?*"[864]

Dennett seeks to evade this crucial distinction by noting that man has the ability to alter the course of evolution and natural selection through processes like breeding and genetic engineering. Therefore, strictly speaking, evolution, although usually a random and mindless process, at times does involve sentient input. Summing up this argument, Dennett seeks to show McGrath's point as misguided:

> "Then we have memes that are unconsciously selected and we have memes that are completely wild—we didn't even know we were doing it. So there's no contradiction."[865]

With this comparison, Dennett clouds the issues involved. Dennett is trying to show that religion is an example of a rogue destructive meme similar to a common cold. However, the fact that men can intervene in natural processes through genetic engineering or

---

[864] *The Future of Atheism,* 31.
[865] *The Future of Atheism,* 47.

breeding is besides the point. The spread of the common-cold is a random and thoughtless process in stark contrast to the spread of ideas.

Dennett seems to want to have his cake and eat it too. That is, on the one hand, memes are just words, and language, and ideas, fads, and cultural expressions. Dennett responded to McGrath's skepticism concerning memes:

> "Alister's skepticism about memes is seriously misguided. First of all, he doubts the very existence of memes . . . Words are memes. If you're baffled about whether memes exist, just ask yourself if words exist. If you think words exist, then the case for memes is pretty clear."[866]

Well, the obvious question then, is, what's the big deal? If memes are just another way of speaking about words, then what was the big contribution of Dawkins with the concept of memes in 1976? Haven't we always known that ideas spread through language and cultures and are responsive to various forces, foremost that the ideas were accepted by rational people?

Mary Midgley asked:

> "What is now the point of the proposal? If memes really correspond to Dawkinsian genes they must indeed be fixed units—hidden, unchanging causes of the changing items that appear round us in the world. But all the examples we are given correspond to phenotypes. They are the apparent items themselves."[867]

---

[866] *The Future of Atheism,* 36.
[867] Mary Midgley, *Why Memes?,* chapter in, *Alas, Poor Darwin: Arguments Against Evolutionary Psychology,* Edited by Hilary Rose & Steven Rose, New York (Harmony Books, 2000) 91.

Midgley asked further penetrating questions about the alleged memes:

> "So what, if anything, does this leave of the original parallel with genetics? How seriously is that parallel now intended? If memes are indeed something parallel to genes . . . if they are hidden causes of culture rather than its units—what sort of entities are these causes supposed to be? They are not physical objects. But neither are they thoughts of the kind that normally play any part in our experience. They seem to be occult causes of those thoughts. How then do they manifest themselves? How do we know that they are there? It does not help to say that they are bits of information located in the infosphere (p. 347). Information is not a third kind of stuff, not an extra substance added to Cartesian mind and body or designed to supersede them. It is an abstraction from them. Invoking such an extra stuff is as idle as any earlier talk of phlogiston or animal spirits or occult forces."[868]

At the bottom, aren't Dawkins and Dennett just saying that they don't like religion, in language dressed up to sound scientific? Further, Dawkins and Dennett haven't explained why the religious meme has been so universally successful. People don't choose to get a cold virus, but they do choose to believe in and practice their religions.

How do Dawkins and Dennett distinguish a good from a bad meme; good ideas from bad? Why, for Dawkins and Dennett, are religious ideas bad, but tolerance is good? Is not Dawkins' rejection of the religious meme merely arbitrary?

---

[868]Mary Midgley, *Why Memes?*, chapter in, *Alas, Poor Darwin: Arguments Against Evolutionary Psychology*, Edited by Hilary Rose & Steven Rose, New York (Harmony Books, 2000) 91-92.

In response to McGrath, Dennett agreed that atheism is itself a meme: "Is atheism a meme? Of course it's a meme."[869]

How, then, does Dennett know that it is not atheism rather than theism that is the parasitic virus that just keeps hanging around for its own good, and not for the good of the host? In sheer numbers, it seems odd to consider something believed by an overwhelming majority of earth's residents as the destructive meme. Wouldn't it be more sensible to consider the minor variant of atheistic belief the oddball parasitic meme?

Further, if there is no God, and the spread of ideas is simply a natural process (like evolutionary changes) then how are moral judgments of ideas possible? In that case, racism and tolerance are just natural evolutionary variations with no moral character or aspect.

On the other hand, if there is a God, and an objective platform to make moral judgments, then memes can also be judged. And if God has created man as an agent with true freedom, then memes are the result of thoughtful and free processes and enjoy a moral status.

Religion an evolutionary advantage?

One of the leading ideas among atheists today is to suggest that religious beliefs, though false, offered a survivability advantage to believers through evolutionary history. For instance, Gerald Benedict stated:

> "Belief in God lingers so persistently and universally that we must consider if it is somehow built into our make-up, and indispensable to our survival . . . it is possible that at the deepest level there is a basic need at work."[870]

---

[869] *The Future of Atheism,* 37.

Notice the subtle suggestion that religious belief may be "indispensable to our survival." Other commentators are equally direct. For instance, Barnes stated:

> "Some claim that the social bonding and sense of dedication religion promotes provides a strong advantage to a group that shares a religion . . . Religion thereby helps to preserve the group, and along with it the religion it holds."[871]

Paul Kurtz agreed:

> "The hypothesis that I wish to offer is that belief in the efficacy of prayer and the submission to divine power persists because it has had some survival value in the infancy of the race; powerful psycho-social-biological factors are thus at work, predisposing humans to submit to the temptation [to religious beliefs] . . . This is an evolutionary explanation; that is, belief in the transcendental has adaptive value, and those tribes or clans which believed in unseen myths and forces to whom they propitiated by ritual and prayer had a tendency to pass on this genetic predisposition to their offspring. Thus religiosity is a 'heritable' factor within the naked human ape."[872]

Kurtz cited E. O. Wilson for support of this theory:

> "E. O. Wilson also maintains that there is some biological basis for religiosity; though one cannot locate this in a specific gene . . . He [Wilson] argues that theological overbeliefs offer consolation in the face of

[870]Gerald Benedict, *The God Debate: A New Look at History's Oldest Argument,* London (Watkins Publishing, 2013) 25.
[871]Michael Horace Barnes, *Understanding Religion and Science: Introducing the Debate*, New York (Continuum International Publishing Group, 2010) 31.
[872]*Science and Religion: Are They Compatible?*, Paul Kurtz, Editor, Amherst New York (Prometheus Books, 2003) 284-285

adversity, and that these religious overbeliefs—whether true or false—provide a functional means of adaptation."[873]

Anthony Layng agreed with Kurtz on the evolutionary origin of religious belief:

> "Evolution of [religious or supernatural] beliefs has come to determine which populations had the greatest capacity to survive . . . From an evolutionary perspective, this universality suggests that such beliefs must have played some essential role in ensuring the well-being of human populations."[874]

Michael Martin was likewise convinced by this idea:

> "One could argue that a much simpler explanation of the facts is to maintain that belief in God has survival value for humans. Thus the disposition to believe in God can be accounted for in terms of evolutionary theory . . . Once again, the yearning for God may have survival value and hence may be explainable in evolutionary terms without any need to postulate a real object of yearning."[875]

False beliefs helpful?

Since so many atheists accept the theory that religious beliefs and practices have provided a survivability advantage in evolutionary terms, we should consider the rather startling implications of that view. *For instance, if atheism is true, it suggests that evolution favored those who held false beliefs!* Natural selection conferred an advantage to those who held to the delusion of a non-existent God.

---

[873] *Science and Religion: Are They Compatible?*, 285.

[874] Anthony Layng, *Supernatural Power and Cultural Evolution*, in *Science and Religion: Are They Compatible?*, Paul Kurtz, Editor, Amherst New York (Prometheus Books, 2003) 292.

[875] Michael Martin, *Atheism: A Philosophical Justification*, Philadelphia PA (Temple University Press, 1990) 211, 212.

The atheist George Smith argued that holding to false beliefs is normally not beneficial:

> "It is my firm conviction that man has nothing to gain, emotionally or otherwise, by adhering to falsehood [about the existence of God]."[876]

If, as George Smith argued, false beliefs are unproductive today, one wonders why they should have conferred an advantage through evolutionary history? Atheist Michael Martin also failed to explain this disconnect:

> "If there is no connection between evidence and truth, it is difficult to see how the human race has survived to date. We base the actions that we need to perform in order to survive on what we believe to be true, and we believe this latter on the evidence. But then, if there were no connection between truth and evidence, our survival would be a mystery."[877]

Steven Pinker pressed the point:

> "It only raises the question of why a mind would evolve to find comfort in beliefs it can plainly see are false. A freezing person finds no comfort in believing he is warm; a person face-to-face with a lion is not put at ease by the conviction that it is a rabbit."[878]

Good questions. Further, one would think that religious beliefs, if truly false, would have been more a

---

[876]George H. Smith, *Atheism: The Case Against God,* Amherst NY (Prometheus Books, 1979, 1989) *Introduction,* x.

[877]Michael Martin, *Atheism: A Philosophical Justification,* Philadelphia PA (Temple University Press, 1990) 36.

[878]Steven Pinker, *Whence Religious Belief?,* in *Science and Religion: Are They Compatible?,* Paul Kurtz, Editor, Amherst New York (Prometheus Books, 2003) 309-310.

detriment to survival given the investment of time and energy devoted to religious activities (praying, senseless rituals and ceremonies, worship etc.), thus diverted from positive efforts at survival.

The skeptic Michael Scriven stated:

> "In general, beliefs without foundations lead to an early grave or to an accumulation of superstitions, which are usually troublesome and always false beliefs."[879]

The theory that evolution favored God believers proposed by many atheists leaves many questions unanswered. For instance, it seems almost too obvious to ask; but, if as suggested, religious beliefs have been an aid to evolutionary survivability, on what basis would it make sense to abandon them now?

Further, we wonder if there are other areas of belief that have had similar survivability value despite there being untrue?

Finally, if it is true that evolution favored those who held to religious beliefs, does that explain why atheists are always in the minority, being less favored through the process of natural selection?

Faith as an innate need in man

We have considered various attempted explanations by atheists for the central place religion has always played for humanity and found them wanting. We move now to a Christian explanation for the same, first by noting that God belief is an innate and essential aspect of man's being.

---

[879]Michael Scriven, *God and Reason*, chapter in *Critiques of God: Making the Case Against Belief in God,* Peter A. Angeles, Editor, Amherst New York (Prometheus Books, 1997) 101.

Let us begin with the passionate expression of this theme by Blaise Pascal:

> "There was once in man a true happiness of which there now remain to him only the mark and empty trace, which he in vain tries to fill from his surroundings, seeking from things absent the help he does not obtain in things present? But these are all inadequate, because the infinite abyss can only be filled by an infinite and immutable object, that is to say, only by God himself."[880]

Descartes agreed, describing this desire for God as an innate need:

> "All that's left is to explain how I have gotten my idea of God from Him . . . The idea must therefore be innate in me, like the idea of myself. And it's not at all surprising that in creating me God put this idea into me, impressing it like a craftsmen's mark on His work."[881]

Saint Augustine began his great work *Confessions* with this theme:

> "Man is one of your creatures, Lord, and his instinct is to praise you. He bears about him the mark of death, the sign of his own sin, to remind him that you thwart the proud. But still, since he is a part of your creation, he wishes to praise you. The thought of you stirs him so deeply that he cannot be content unless he praises you, because you made us for yourself and our hearts find no peace until they rest in you."[882]

---

[880]Blaise Pascal, *Pascal's Pensées*, New York (E.P. Dutton & Co, INC, 1958), *Pensées Section* 7(425) on page 113.

[881]René Descartes, *Meditations on First Philosophy* in *Introduction to Philosophy: Classical and Contemporary Readings*, Fourth Edition, Edited by John Perry, Michael Bratman & John Martin Fischer, Oxford UK (Oxford University Press, 2007) 182.

[882]Saint Augustine, *Confessions*, Middlesex England (Penguin Books, 1961) 121 (from Book 1:1 in traditional format).

Samuel Stumpf commented on Augustine's thought and how this theme affects every area of our lives:

"Consequently, man always bears the marks of his creation . . . It is not by accident that man *seeks* happiness. That he seeks it is a consequence of his incompleteness, his finitude. That he can find happiness only in God is also no accident, since he was made by God to find happiness only in God . . . Man inevitably loves . . . There is a wide range of objects that man can choose to love, reflecting the variety of ways man is incomplete . . . Therefore, each thing is a legitimate object of love, one must not expect more from it than its unique nature can provide. The basic need for human affection cannot be satisfied by things. But this is particularly the case with man's spiritual need. Man was made, said Augustine, to love God. God is infinite. In some way, then, man's nature was made so that only God, the infinite, can give him ultimate satisfaction or happiness . . .

Man's pride, which turns him away from God, leads him to many forms of overindulgence, since he tries to satisfy an infinite need with finite entities. He therefore loves things more than he should . . . His love for another person can become virtually destructive of the other person, since he tries again to derive from that relationship more that it can possibly give . . . It does not take long for disordered love to produce disordered persons, and disordered persons produce a disordered community . . .

Indeed, Augustine argued that we can love a person properly only if we love God first, for then we will not expect to derive from human love what can be derived only from our love of God. Similarly, we can love ourselves properly only as we subordinate ourselves to God, for there is no other way to overcome the destructive consequences of pride than by eliminating pride itself."[883]

---

[883]Samuel Enoch Stumpf, *Philosophy: History & Problems*, Fourth Edition, New York (McGraw-Hill Publishing Company, 1989) 144-146.

The Reformer John Calvin also reflected this biblical theme: "A sense of Deity is inscribed on every heart."[884] Jay Richards added: "Some theologians, like John Calvin, add that individuals have an intuitive capacity, a *sensus divinitas*, which produces belief in God."[885]

Surely, the *sensus divinitas* is a creation of God who has "set eternity in their hearts" (Ecclesiastes 3:11). Unfortunately, atheists try to suppress this deep need, to their own poverty.

D. E. Trueblood stated: "Herein lies part of the deep significance of the ancient saying that it is hard to believe, but harder still to disbelieve."[886]

The atheist Michael Martin argued against the idea that God-belief is innate in man:

> "There is no good reason to suppose that belief in God is innate . . . the theory that belief in God is innate does not account for the presence of millions of atheists . . . Moreover, the theory that there is an innate yearning for God cannot account for those atheists who do not have such a yearning."[887]

The Christian answer to Martin's argument is simple. Despite the atheist's objections to the contraire, they do

---

[884] *The Encyclopedia of Religious Quotations*, Frank S. Mead, Editor, Westwood NJ (Fleming H. Revell Company, 1965) 168.

[885] Jay Wesley Richards, *Proud Obstacles and a Reasonable Hope*, included in William A. Demski, Introduction, *Signs of Intelligence: Understanding Intelligent Design*, Edited by William A. Demski & James M. Kushiner, Grand Rapids MI (Brazos Press, 2001) 53.

[886] D. E. Trueblood, *The Evidential Value of Religious Experience*, as reprinted in *A Modern Introduction to Philosophy: Readings from Classical and Contemporary Sources,* Third Edition, Paul Edwards & Arthur Pap, Editors, New York, (The Free Press, 1973) 445.

[887] Michael Martin, *Atheism: A Philosophical Justification,* Philadelphia PA (Temple University Press, 1990) 211.

have an innate need and desire for God, which they suppress and redirect to other objects (idolatry). Perhaps, just maybe, as Hans Küng has suggested, many of the problems of modern life are a consequence of this suppression of our deep need for God.

Men may deny God and yet the hunger yearns. They sense it; they feel it. They try desperately to fill this infinite need with finite things; things incapable of satisfying the need. And so, they drink in excess, they do drugs for escape; they run wild after physical lust and pleasure, always coming up short. They agree with Mick Jagger that they "can't get no satisfaction." Just as our hunger drives us to eat and our thirst drives us to drink; so, this need drives us to the God that we have tried to ignore.

Menssen and Sullivan argued:

"It has sometimes been remarked that, while the fact that a person is hungry does not prove the cupboard is full of bread, the fact that human beings are capable of hunger may point to the existence of such a thing as food. Whether or not that is true, if you believe you are dying of hunger, surely it is eminently reasonable for you to search the cupboard for food—indeed, it would be incomprehensible if you were not to."[888]

Like one trying to put the wrong battery in a child's toy are those who attempt to run their lives on the wrong source. Yet God calls out to them, "Come, all you who are

---

[888] Sandra Menssen & Thomas D. Sullivan, *The Agnostic Inquirer: Revelation from a Philosophical Standpoint*, Grand Rapids MI (William B. Eerdmans Publishing Company, 2007, 17.

thirsty, come to the waters" (Isaiah 55:1). Jesus said: "Everyone who drinks this water will be thirsty again, but whoever drinks the water I give them will never thirst. Indeed, the water I give them will become in them a spring of water welling up to eternal life" (John 4:13-14).

The persistence of faith in a committed atheist family

It is interesting to consider the persistence of faith in the example of perhaps the best-known atheist of the past generation, Madeline Murray O Hare. She raised her son William to be an atheist, and yet he became a Christian believer.[889] Though this is an anecdotal example, it is interesting that faith survived despite the parental onslaught against God belief, or maybe because of it.

Indeed, O'Hair felt the emptiness of the atheism as journalist Lee Strobel explained. In his book, *The Case for Faith*, Strobel described a chilling message left by Madalyn Murray O'Hair:

> "'Somebody, somewhere, love me.' written repeatedly in the diary of the late atheist Madalyn Murray O'Hair."[890]

Can faith be eradicated from a whole society?

Let us consider a larger sample size. For generations atheism was the official doctrine of the former Soviet

---

[889]You can read his story in his book *My Life Without God*, William J. Murray, Eugene OR (Harvest House Press, 1982).

[890]Madalyn Murray O' Hair, as quoted by Lee Strobel, *The Case for Faith: A Journalist Investigates the Toughest Objections to Christianity*, Grand Rapids MI (Zondervan, 2000)343.

Union, and faith was severely suppressed and persecuted. Despite generations taught atheism, yet, as soon as freedom broke forth with the fall of the former Soviet Union, there was an explosion in religious expression.

Man the worshiper

This suggests that religious belief is indeed innate in man. Men will risk everything including their very lives to be faithful to this inward call. They will accept beatings and torture rather than abandon this inward compulsion. Why will they do this if religious ideas are so devoid of logic and reason?

The fact is that man is a worshipping being. He will either worship the true God, or he will worship what is not God, substitutes. Evans and Manis stated:

> "Calvin writes, 'There is within the human mind, and indeed by natural instinct, an awareness of deity . . . Therefore, since from the beginning of the world there has been no region, no city, in short, no household, that could do without religion . . . this conviction, namely, that *there is some God*, is naturally inborn in all, and is fixed deep within, as it were in the very marrow.'"[891]

Kai Nielsen discussed this issue by noting the argument of Will Herberg, a proponent of this idea:

> "Will Herberg, reasoning . . . about these matters . . . argues there are 'on the existential level . . . no atheists.' Why not? Because, according to Herberg, 'the structure of a human being is such that man cannot live his life, or understand himself, without some ultimate concern . . .

---

[891]C. Stephen Evans & R. Zachary Manis, *Philosophy of Religion: Thinking About Faith*, Second Edition, Downers Grove IL (Inter Varsity Press, 2009) 194.

That is indeed his god . . . In this sense every man, by virtue of being human, is *homo religiosus*; every man has his religion and his god. On the existential level, then, the question is not god or no god, religion or no religion; but rather: what *kind* of God? What *kind* of religion.' Luther remarks that 'whatever your heart clings to and confides in, that is your God.'"[892]

After fairly presenting the argument, Nielsen responded that simply having an ultimate concern:

"Does not make him religious, except in the perfectly trivial sense that to be religious about anything is to be involved with it and the like; it does not give him a religion or a god, except in another *metaphorical* sense."[893]

Strictly speaking, Nielsen is correct. Atheism is logically the denial of the existence of God, and so it seems strange on the face of it to accuse them of being worshipers. Yet, Herberg is not arguing that atheists *intend* to be worshipers. He is arguing, instead, that they are *unwitting* worshipers of things not divine; worshipers by default.

I appreciate Kai Nielsen's frank acknowledgment that this does sometimes happen:

"But Herberg goes beyond this, for according to him atheism is not only religious, it is an idolatrous religion for it deifies man . . . I think it must be admitted that *some* atheists, not sufficiently emancipated from religious thinking, did stupidly deify man."[894]

While acknowledging that some atheists have been guilty of this pseudo-worship, notice that Nielsen blames

---

[892]Kai Nielsen, *Atheism & Philosophy*, 162.
[893]Kai Nielsen, *Atheism & Philosophy*, 163.
[894]Kai Nielsen, *Atheism & Philosophy*, 164.

it on the fact that these bumbling atheists have only made this mistake because they have not been "sufficiently emancipated from religious thinking."[895]

Nielsen concludes that such thinking is an aberration and that "no atheist *must* think this way; no atheist should think this way; and most atheists do not think in this confused way."[896]

Contrary to Nielsen's assertion, the apostle Paul expressed the divine assessment of the matter:

> "Since the creation of the world God's invisible qualities—his eternal power and divine nature—have been clearly seen, being understood from what has been made, so that men are without excuse. For although they knew God, they neither glorified him as God nor gave thanks to him, but their thinking became futile and their foolish hearts were darkened. Although they claimed to be wise, they became fools and exchanged the glory of the immortal God for images made to look like mortal man and birds and animals and reptiles . . . They exchanged the truth of God for a lie, and worshipped and served created things rather than the creator—who is forever praised. Amen (Romans 1:20-23, 25)."

And that is just how it has been; men have worshipped everything from the stars above to the earth below, and most everything in between. Most abhorrently, man has gone so far as to deify himself at the expense of God. This is sheer idolatry, the concern of the first of the ten commandments: "You shall have no other gods before me" (Exodus 20:3).

---

[895]Kai Nielsen, *Atheism & Philosophy*, 164.
[896]Kai Nielsen, *Atheism & Philosophy*, 164.

Section Nine: What Happens Next: To be or not to be?

I don't want to achieve immortality through my work ... I want

to achieve it through not dying.[897]   *Woody Allen*

Chapter 41: What's Next: Afterlife or Extinction?

"There are only two sure things in life, death and taxes!"

Benjamin Franklin

"If you believe in forever, then life is just a one-night stand"[898]

We move now to consider the idea of an afterlife. Is this life all there is, or will we have a continued existence beyond the grave? This understandably has been a burning question in the hearts of men and a common theme in the arts.

For instance, Freddie Mercury of Queen, wrote and sang, "I don't want to die. I sometimes wish I'd never been born at all."[899] A lighter attitude was expressed by

---

[897]Woody Allen, as quoted by *The Macmillan Dictionary of Quotations*, John Daintith, Editor, New York (Macmillan Publishing Company, 1989) 275
[898]Alan O' Day and Johnny Stevenson, *Rock and Roll Heaven*, popularized by the Righteous Brothers, 1973

the character of Peter Pan: "'To die,' said Barrie's Peter Pan, 'would be an awfully big adventure.'"[900] With a sense of optimism, James Drummond Burns, with his last words said: "I have been dying for twenty years, now I am going to live."[901]

The inescapability of death

Vincent Bugliosi referred to Shakespeare's comment: "Shakespeare said that 'every person owes God a death,"[902] which mirrors the Bible statement that "Just as man is destined to die once, and after that to face judgment" (Hebrews 9:27).

Samuel Stumpf explained the existentialist philosopher Martin Heidegger's description of man's response to impending death:

> "We know time, he says, because we know we are going to die. Man's existence is therefore temporal. Man attempts to deny his temporality, to evade the inevitability of his limited existence . . . Of his many moods, man's fundamental mood, says Heidegger, is the mood of anxiety. Anxiety arises out of man's awareness of the precarious nature of his Being."[903]

---

[899]Freddie Mercury, Queen, *Bohemian Rhapsody* lyrics © Sony/ATV Music Publishing LLC.

[900]Quoted by J. I. Packer in Foreward, p. 7, of Larry Dixon, *The Other Side of the Good News*, Wheaton IL (BridgePoint, 1992).

[901]*The Encyclopedia of Religious Quotations*, Frank S. Mead, Editor, Westwood NJ (Fleming H. Revell Company, 1965) 245.

[902]Vincent Bugliosi, *Divinity of Doubt: The God Question*, New York (Vanguard Press, 2011) 188.

[903]Samuel Enoch Stumpf, *Philosophy: History & Problems*, Fourth Edition, New York (McGraw-Hill Publishing Company, 1989) 499-500.

Man's desire for life beyond the grave

The Bible tells us that "He has set eternity in our hearts" (Ecclesiastes 3:11). Joseph Addison expressed this firm desire in man:

> "Whence this pleasing hope, this fond desire, this longing for immortality? Tis the divinity that stirs within us; Tis heaven itself that points out an hereafter, and intimates eternity to man."[904]

Likewise, Spinoza described that need within all men to "persevere in our being . . . (through) indefinite time."[905] Vincent Bugliosi described man's passionate desire to live:

> "Most of us know, from firsthand experience, how much of a struggle life is with its constant trials and tribulations. No matter. I'm told there is a passage in a novel by Fyodor Dostoevsky in which a character in the story exclaims, 'If I were condemned to live on a rock, chained to a rock on the lashing sea, and all around me were ice and gales and storm, I would still want to live. Oh God, just to live, live, live! . . . American Revolutionary War hero Ethan Allen tried [to lighten the moment] when his physician told him, 'I feel the angels are waiting for you,' 'Waiting are they? Waiting are they: Allen said. 'Well, let 'em wait.'"[906]

---

[904] *The Encyclopedia of Religious Quotations*, Frank S. Mead, Editor, Westwood NJ (Fleming H. Revell Company, 1965) 244.
[905] Benedict de Spinoza, *Ethics*, part III, prop. VI and VIII, in John Wild (ed.), *Spinoza Selections* (New York: Scribner, 1930), pp. 215-216, as quoted by William H. Halverson, *A Concise Introduction to Philosophy*, Third Edition, New York (Random House, 1976) 300.
[906] Vincent Bugliosi, *Divinity of Doubt: The God Question*, New York (Vanguard Press, 2011) 184.

The common belief in the afterlife

As with the question of the existence of God itself, whether there is or is not an afterlife for mankind is beyond the realm of scientific investigation. Nevertheless, there are good reasons to suppose that death is not the end, but merely the beginning of eternal life.

Corliss Lamont stated:

"That in practically all cultures, at least until recently, there is to be found belief in some sort of after-existence is not to be questioned."[907]

The Bible clearly affirms the reality of the afterlife for all, in the bliss of heaven or the judgment of hell. Jesus said:

"Very truly I tell you, a time is coming and has now come when the dead will hear the voice of the Son of God and those who hear will live . . . Do not be amazed at this, for a time is coming when all who are in their graves will hear his voice and come out—those who have done what is good will rise to live, and those who have done what is evil will rise to be condemned(John 5:25, 28-29)."

Clarence Darrow's attack on the belief in immortality

Of course, atheists and skeptics deny biblical teaching concerning the reality of the afterlife. For instance, Clarence Darrow mocked the idea of the immortality of

---

[907]Corlis Lamont, *The Illusion of Immortality* (New York: Frederick Ungar, 1965), as reprinted as a chapter in *Critiques of God: Making the Case Against Belief in God,* Peter A. Angeles, Editor, Amherst New York (Prometheus Books, 1997) 260.

the soul, of the afterlife, and belief in a personal resurrection. For him, all of life can be characterized as:

"The best we can do is to be kindly and helpful toward our friends and fellow passengers who are clinging to the same speck of dirt while we are drifting side by side to our common doom."[908]

One of Darrow's chief attacks was to ridicule those whom although they claimed to believe in life after death, nevertheless, seem to fear the approach of death:

"If people really believed in a beautiful, happy, glorious land waiting to receive them when they died; if they believed that their friends would be waiting to meet them; if they believed that all pain and suffering would be left behind: why should they live through weeks, months, and even years of pain and torture while a cancer eats its way to the vital parts of the body? Why should one fight off death? Because he does not believe in any real sense: he only hopes."[909]

The fight for life is a natural instinct given us by God, and doesn't in any way diminish the reality of our belief in our heavenly reward.

Death as the consequence of man's rebellion

As to death itself, let it be understood that it was not this way in the beginning. Rather, death is a curse for

---

[908]Clarence Darrow, *The Delusion of Design and Purpose* as reprinted in *A Modern Introduction to Philosophy: Readings from Classical and Contemporary Sources,* Third Edition, Paul Edwards & Arthur Pap, Editors, New York, (The Free Press, 1973) 453..

[909]Clarence Darrow, *The Myth of Immortality* in Paul Edwards, *A Modern Introduction to Philosophy: Readings from Classical and Contemporary Sources,* Third Edition, Paul Edwards & Arthur Pap, Editors, New York, (The Free Press, 1973) 262.

man's rebellion in the Garden of Eden: "But you must not eat from the tree of the knowledge of good and evil, for when you eat of it you will surely die" (Genesis 2:17). The apostle Paul wrote: "Therefore, just as sin entered the world through one man, and death through sin, and in this way, death came to all men" (Romans 5:12).

The curse of death

Vincent Bugliosi powerfully expressed the kinds of concerns that Darrow was raising about the woes of death:

> "Not only is our death too horrible for most of us to even contemplate for more than a few moments, but the loss of our loved ones, if possible, is even worse. How do you say the final good-by to the love of your life? How can you do it when you have become a part of each other's life, and in the process a part of each other, for forty, fifty, sixty years? You're losing your lifetime partner, with whom you've gone through everything together, the highs, the lows, the happiness, the tears, the memories (oh, those old photographs). And now one has to leave the other behind. How do you, how can you, say the last good-bye? And how are you going to be able to go on without him or her? There are no words.
>
> Your parents, your father young and virile and your mother young and beautiful in their wedding photographs. As a child, you always knew your father was the strongest and greatest man in the world and your mother the sweetest and most wonderful woman. The strong legs and back of your father that carried you piggyback in the backyard when you were a child cannot even bear the weight of his own body any longer, brought low and weakened by the ravages of life. You talk to him at his bedside and tell him how much you love him, but his eyes closed, and breathing heavily, he does not answer, though he somehow lets you know he can hear you. You and your

family can't bear the thought of losing 'Papa' or 'Dad,' a father you knew would have given his life for you, and you are helpless to stop what is taking place before your eyes."[910]

A little later, Bugliosi made a heartfelt objection to death:

"And shouldn't you curse God when you yourself are on your deathbed and want desperately to stay alive, not die, yet you know that you are very close to making the terrifying leap into everlasting darkness, pondering the incredibly terrifying thought that shortly you will no longer exist, never to experience life and see your loved ones again?"[911]

Thank you, Vincent, for your poignant expression of the psychological state of those facing mortality.

Death as an enemy to be defeated

Although death has resulted from man's rebellion against God, yet, in His mercy, God has overcome death through the death and resurrection of Jesus Christ, and made it possible for us to live again, and to be reunited with our loved ones.

Death is indeed an enemy and a curse to man; it is not natural, and we instinctively resist it. Dylan Thomas said: "Do not go gentle into that good night. Rage, rage against the dying of the light."[912]

---

[910]Vincent Bugliosi, *Divinity of Doubt*,185-186
[911]Vincent Bugliosi, *Divinity of Doubt,* 189.
[912]Dylan Thomas, *Do Not God Gentle into That Good Night*, Collected Poems (New Direction, 1946), as quoted by Corlis Lamont, *The Illusion of Immortality* (New York: Frederick Ungar, 1965), as reprinted as a chapter in *Critiques of God: Making the Case Against Belief in God,* Peter A. Angeles, Editor, Amherst New York (Prometheus Books, 1997) 271.

The good news is that death has been overcome by Jesus Christ:

> "The last enemy to be destroyed is death . . . When the perishable has been clothed with the imperishable, and the mortal with immortality, then the saying that is written will come true: 'Death has been swallowed up in victory. Where, O death, is your victory? Where, O death, is your sting? The sting of death is sin . . . But thanks be to God. He gives us the victory through our Lord Jesus Christ" (1 Corinthians 15:26, 54-56)."

We have the sure promise of God that in the resurrection, God "will wipe every tear from their eyes. There will be no more death or mourning or crying or pain, for the old order of things has passed" (Revelation 21:4).

These truths give us comfort and hope while we walk through the valley of the shadow of death (Psalm 23:4).

The past and the future of eternity

Clarence Darrow asked why we should believe in an eternal future absent of an eternal past. He put it this way:

> "If I did not exist in the infinite past, why should I, or could I, exist in the infinite future?"[913]

I am not sure what the relevance of non-existence in the past has to do with existence in the future. We could just as well ask why we are here at all since there was a time in which mankind did not exist.

---

[913]Clarence Darrow, *The Myth of Immortality* 264.

Blaise Pascal, however, anticipated just such a question:

> "Atheists—What reason have they for saying that we cannot rise from the dead? What is more difficult, to be born or to rise again; that what has never been should be, or that what has been should be again? Is it more difficult to come into existence than to return to it?"[914]

Along the same lines, Roy L. Smith said, "it should be no more difficult to believe that life will go on than to understand how it began."[915] And again, Edward Young:

> "Seems it strange that thou shouldst live forever? Is it less strange that thou shouldst live at all? This is a miracle; and that no more."[916]

Norman Geisler showed that even such a rationalist as Thomas Paine had no objection to the Christian doctrine of the resurrection and the afterlife:

> "As for immortality, Paine could simply say, 'I hope for happiness beyond this life' (*Age of Reason*, 1.3). He added, 'I trouble not myself about the manner of future existence. I content myself with believing, even to positive conviction, that the Power that gave me existence is able to continue it, in any form and manner he pleases, either with or without this body . . . It appears more probable to me that I shall continue to exist hereafter than I should have had existence, as I now have, before that existence began."[917]

---

[914]Blaise Pascal, *Pascal's Pensées*, New York (E.P. Dutton & Co, INC, 1958), *Pensées* 222, on page 63.

[915] *The Encyclopedia of Religious Quotations*, Frank S. Mead, Editor, Westwood NJ (Fleming H. Revell Company, 1965) 253.

[916] *The Encyclopedia of Religious Quotations*, 255.

[917]Norman L. Geisler, *Baker Encyclopedia of Christian Apologetics*, Grand Rapids MI (Baker Books, 1999) 573.

The problem of resurrection and the dissolution of bodily elements

Darrow raised a similar argument by mocking the possibility of the bodily resurrection in the face of the dissolution of the body following death in the form of a *reductio ad absurdum* argument:

> "Every dead body, no matter whether consumed by fire or buried in the earth, has been resolved into its elements, so that the matter and energy that once formed human beings has fed animals and plants and other men. As the great naturalist, Fabre has said: 'At the banquet of life each is in turn a guest and a dish.' Thus the body of every man now living is in part made from the bodies of those who have been dead ages. Yet we are still asked to believe in the resurrection of the body. By what alchemy, then, are the individual bodies that have successfully fed the generations of men to be separated and restored to their former identities?"[918]

Again, the great philosopher and theologian Augustine anticipated such arguments that questioned the credibility of the resurrection:

> "At the resurrection the substance of our bodies, however disintegrated, will be reunited. We maintain no fear that the omnipotence of God cannot recall all the particles that have been consumed by fire or by beasts, or dissolved into dust and ashes, or decomposed into water, or evaporated into air."[919]

---

[918]Clarence Darrow, *The Myth of Immortality* in Paul Edwards, *A Modern Introduction to Philosophy: Readings from Classical and Contemporary Sources,* Third Edition, Paul Edwards & Arthur Pap, Editors, New York, (The Free Press, 1973) 266-267.

[919]Saint Augustine, *The City of God,* 22:2, as quoted in *The Great Quotations,* Edited by George Seldes, New Jersey (Castle Books, 1966) 70.

In this context, it should be remembered that men were made from the dust in the very beginning: "The Lord God formed the man from the dust of the ground" (Genesis 2:7).

What is difficult in believing that just as God has made man from the dust in the past, he can do it again?

The implications of the dissolution of the body and regular replacement of cells.

Science teaches us that the cells that compose our body are constantly dying and being replaced. Benjamin Radford of *LiveScience* explains:

> "It's a neat idea, and one that has caught the popular imagination. Here's how the story goes: Every seven years (or 10, depending on which story you hear) we become essentially new people, because in that time, every cell in your body has been replaced by a new cell. Don't you feel younger than you were seven years ago?
>
> It is true that individual cells have a finite life span, and when they die off they are replaced with new cells. As *The New York Public Library's Science Desk Reference* (Stonesong Press, 1995) notes, "There are between 50 and 75 trillion cells in the body.... Each type of cell has its own life span, and when a human dies it may take hours or days before all the cells in the body die." (Forensic investigators take advantage of this vaguely morbid fact when determining the cause and time of death of homicide victims.)
>
> Red blood cells live for about four months, while white blood cells live on average more than a year. Skin cells live about two or three weeks. Colon cells have it rough: They die off after about four days. Sperm cells have a life span of only about three days, while brain cells typically last an entire lifetime (neurons in the cerebral cortex, for example, are not replaced when they die).

There's nothing special or significant about a seven-year cycle, since cells are dying and being replaced all the time. It's not clear where this myth began."[920]

Since the fact that our bodily cells are constantly dying and being renewed raises no problems concerning our personal identity, neither should cellular changes associated with death and resurrection raise any concerns about the continuity or identity of our bodies.

A person being charged with a crime years in the past cannot escape prosecution based on the fact that most of the cells that composed his body at the time of the crime no longer exist. The government cannot deny social security benefits to a man since just about every cell of his body is different from when he received his social security card number.

There remains, then, no objection to the Christian doctrine of the bodily resurrection despite the disintegration of at least some of the cells that originally made up the person's body.

Surprising support for belief in the afterlife and immortality

Augustine and Pascal were not alone in supporting the belief in the afterlife and immortality. Some of the greatest minds in human history shared their belief. For instance, John Haynes Holmes explained:

"Thus, Voltaire declared that 'reason agrees with revelation . . . that the soul is immortal.' Thomas Paine

[920]Benjamin Radford, *Does the Human Body Really Replace Itself Every Seven Years?*, April 4, 2011, at website address: https://www.livescience.com/33179-does-human-body-replace-cells-seven-years.html

affirmed that he did not 'trouble (himself) about the manner of future existence,' so sure he was that 'the Power which gave existence is able to continue it an any form.'"[921]

Johann Wolfgang von Goethe said: "Those who hope for no other life are dead even in this."[922] I love Benjamin Franklin's clever expression of faith in the future resurrection as told by his biographer Walter Isaacson:

"Franklin had written Polly that she must come see him soon, for he was now like a building that required 'so many repairs that in a little time the Owner will find it cheaper to pull it down and build a new one."[923]

The great rocket scientist Werner von Braun said:

"Everything science has taught me—and continues to teach me—strengthens my belief in the continuity of our spiritual existence after death."[924]

Even atheists can believe in the afterlife

Kai Nielsen conceded that even atheists can believe in the afterlife:

"I'll say something that might surprise some of you. There's a famous Cambridge philosopher, John Ellis McTaggart, who was an atheist *and* believed in immortality. There's no logical impossibility of believing that you survive the death of your body, even though you do not believe in God . . . But my point is that the two beliefs are not logically linked. I could be an atheist who

[921]John Haynes Holmes, in *A Modern Introduction to Philosophy: Readings from Classical and Contemporary Sources*, Paul Edwards & Arthur Pap Editors, New York (The Free Press, 1973) 254.
[922] *The Encyclopedia of Religious Quotations*, 248.
[923]Walter Isaacson, *Benjamin Franklin: An American Life,* New York (Simon& Schuster Paperbacks, 2003) 431
[924] *The Encyclopedia of Religious Quotations*, 244.

believes that he will survive the death of his body in a godless world. The two beliefs are only linked traditionally. There's no logical connection between believing in the afterlife and believing in God."[925]

In his response to Nielsen during their debate, J. P. Moreland added: "C. J. Ducasse is another atheist who believes in immortality without God."[926] The foregoing shows that belief in an afterlife is not the exclusive property of God-believers.

A personal testimonial of the comfort of faith through tragedy

I close this section on a personal note. My family suffered a horrible tragedy when our 17-year-old son, Kyle Brandon Lagoon, was killed in a car crash in 2001. There was not even a chance to express our love or to say goodbye. It was simply devastating. I am not sure how we could have gotten through it without the hope our faith in Christ provided.

In the days and weeks that followed, my family attended a grief support group at a local hospital, for families suffering loss. I will never forget what happened at one such session. As we went around the table, each person poured out their grief and the comfort they found in their faith.

Then it was the turn of a middle-aged woman whose eyes were filled with tears. She said:

---

[925]J. P. Moreland, & Kai Nielsen, *Does God Exist?: The Debate Between Theists & Atheists*, Amherst NY (Prometheus Books, 1993) 87. See also, A. J. Ayer, *That Undiscovered Country*, in Christopher Hitchens, *The Portable Atheist: Essential Readings for the Non-believer*, Philadelphia PA (Da Capo Press, 2007) 274.
[926]J. P. Moreland, & Kai Nielsen, *Does God Exist?*, 88.

"You all have been talking about your faith in God and the comfort you have in the hope of seeing your loved one again. But my father and I were atheists. We didn't have that hope to comfort us. As he lay there dying, he kept saying 'I am scared" and I didn't know what to say."

Her words were chilling to those gathered and marked a contrast between the hope of believers and the hopelessness of atheism. And so, the apostle Paul said:

"Brothers, we do not want you to be ignorant about those who fall asleep, or to grieve like the rest of men, who have no hope . . . we will be with the Lord forever. Therefore encourage each other with these words" (1 Thessalonians 4:13, 17-18).

The lyrics to the Brooks and Dunn song *Believe* express so well my convictions about the hope of an afterlife:

"I can't quote the book, the chapter or the verse.
You can't tell me it all ends, in a slow ride in a hearse.
You know I'm more and more convinced,
the longer that I live.
Yeah, this can't be, no this can't be,
no this can't be all there is.
When I raise my hands, bow my head.
I'm finding more and more truth
in the words written in red.
They tell me there's more to life
than just what I can see.
I believe, Oh I believe."[927]

---

[927]Ronnie Dunn & Craig Wiseman, *Believe*, Brooks and Dunn, *Hillbilly Deluxe*, 2005

Chapter 42: What About Hell?

Many have rejected the belief in God because of being troubled by the doctrine of Hell. They simply can't accept that a God of goodness could banish people to eternal torment. They feel it is unfair that someone would suffer forever for the sins of a lifetime.

In response, it should be remembered that the doctrine of Hell need not be connected to the more important question of whether God exists. One can reject the doctrine of Hell without rejecting belief in God. Each question should be logically examined and judged upon their own merit.

C. S. Lewis on Hell

The great author and apologists C. S. Lewis had keen insight into the Christian doctrine of Hell. Douglass Groothuis described Lewis' view on the motives that lead souls into Hell:

> "As a character in C. S. Lewis's novel *The Great Divorce* puts it, 'There are only two kinds of people in the end: those who say to God, 'Thy will be done,' and those to whom God says, in the end, 'Thy will be done.'"[928]

Lewis shined a spotlight on the fact that Hell is just God honoring people's freely-made decisions. They have rejected God both in life, and for eternity. Lewis added that:

---

[928]Douglass Groothuis, *Christian Apologetics: A Comprehensive Case for Biblical Faith*, Downers Grove IL (InterVarsity Press, 2011) 89.

"I willingly believe that the damned are, in one sense, successful, rebels to the end; that the doors of hell are locked on the *inside*."[929]

This speaks to the final rebellion of Hell's citizens, damned by their own obstinance. But the C. S. Lewis quote that most captured my own feelings about Hell is this:

"There is no doctrine which I would more willingly remove from Christianity than this [hell], if it lay in my power . . . I would pay any price to be able to say truthfully: 'All will be saved.'"[930]

Lewis expressed our natural aversion to the doctrine of Hell. Yet, truth is not determined by our wishes, but by the sovereign King of the universe.

The imagery of Hell includes both utter darkness and fiery light. It includes unnatural images such as worms that die not and fires that never burn out, both inconsistent with our normal experience. These images for Hell suggest that Jesus had a less than literal interpretation in mind.

William V. Crockett pointed out:

"Physical fire works on physical bodies with physical nerve endings, not on spirit beings. We see in Matthew 24:41 that the eternal fire was created for spirit beings like the devil and his angels. The fire must in some sense be a spiritual fire, which is another way of acknowledging it to be a metaphor for God's punishment for the wicked."[931]

---

[929]C. S. Lewis, *The Problem of Pain*, New York (Macmillan, 1962, 1975) 127.

[930]C. S. Lewis, *The Problem of Pain*, New York (Macmillan, 1962, 1975) 118.

[931]William Crockett, *Four Views On Hell*. William Crockett, Editor,

Now, the Bible clearly teaches the physical resurrection of all men, saved or lost (Daniel 12:2; John 5:28-29), but since the Devil and the demonic host will be in Hell (without physical bodies) the fire seems superfluous for them for whom it was created. Therefore, as Crockett has suggested, there seems to be something else going on here besides what some have called making God a "Cosmic cook"[932] maintaining an "everlasting Auschwitz."[933]

I do not know exactly what Hell will be like. However, given the descriptions of it in the Scriptures, it will not be pleasant. My personal view is that the imagery of fire and brimstone is metaphorical of the conscious suffering of the unbeliever, especially of the regret of having rejected God and not being able to revise that decision.

Ravi Zacharias captured this ideal:

> "What is hell but the absence of God? And for me to live my life with the absence of God is to already be on the road to hell."[934]

Whatever is meant by the imagery of Hell, it served as a dire warning of the consequences of rejecting God's grace and mercy. Again, C. S. Lewis captured this idea:

> "The prevalent image of fire is significant because it combines the ideas of torment and destruction. Now it is quite certain that all these expressions are intended to

---

Grand Rapids MI (Zondervan Publishing House, 1992) 30.

[932]*Four Views On Hell.* William Crockett, Editor, Grand Rapids MI (Zondervan Publishing House, 1992) 50.

[933]*Four Views On Hell.* William Crockett, Editor, 149.

[934]Ravi Zacharias, Interview with Lee Strobel, *The Case for Faith: A Journalist Investigates the Toughest Objections to Christianity*, Grand Rapids MI (Zondervan, 2000) 223.

suggest something unspeakably horrible, and any interpretation which does not face that fact is, I am afraid, out of court from the beginning."[935]

The bottom line is that Hell is a place of judgment, eternal, for those who reject Jesus Christ.

Doctrine from above or below

As I have already alluded to, for Christians, doctrines are not selected by personal preference. Rather, believers in Christ are bound by His word. We are compelled to subject our personal feelings to the omniscient judgment of God. The liberal easily rejects the doctrine of Hell as not in line with his tastes. But for conservative Bible-believing Christians, truth is not a supermarket of preferences, but rather is something fixed by the creator and ruler of the universe. It doesn't matter how we feel about it, the truth is the truth.

All this is to say that there is in my mind a certain revulsion to the idea of eternal conscious punishment. I don't understand it. That is, I don't understand why God would not simply put the finally wicked and obstinate rebels of the universe out of existence. But I am not God. I must accept God's Word on the matter. To reject the doctrine, I would have to show that it is unbiblical. Yet, a careful study of the relevant texts make a powerful case for the reality of hell (Matthew 25:46; 2 Thessalonians 1:6-10; Revelations 14:10-11, 20:11-15).

J. P. Moreland makes this interesting observation on the purpose of Hell:

---

[935] C. S. Lewis, *The Problem of Pain*, New York (Macmillan, 1962, 1975) 125.

"Hell was not part of the original creation. Hell is God's fall-back position. Hell is something God was forced to make because people chose to rebel against him and turn against what was best for them and the purpose for which they were created. You know, when people founded the United States, they didn't start out by creating jails . . . They were forced to create them because people would not cooperate. The same is true for hell."[936]

Is Hell a case where the punishment doesn't fit the crime?

It is often asked if hell is fair since one is punished infinitely for the sins of a finite lifetime. Several responses are appropriate. I am comforted by the fact that God is just, and His punishments will be just. "Will not the Judge of all the earth do right?" (Genesis 18:25).

J. P. Moreland commented on this question:

"We all know that the degree to which a person warrants punishment is not a function of the length of time it took to commit a crime. For example, a murder can take ten seconds to commit . . . My point is that the degree of someone's just punishment is not a function of how long it took to commit the deed; rather, it's a function of how severe the deed itself was."[937]

The penalty for assassinating the President of the United States must be correspondingly greater than a typical murder sentence in virtue of the greater impact of the crime. How much more, then, should the penalty be for a crime against our eternal creator?

[936]J. P. Moreland, Interview with Lee Strobel, *The Case for Faith: A Journalist Investigates the Toughest Objections to Christianity*, Grand Rapids MI (Zondervan, 2000) 243.

[937]J. P. Moreland, Interview with Lee Strobel, *The Case for Faith*, 251-252.

Section Ten: Epistemology and the Problem of How We Know

Plato, Hume, and Kant

Chapter 43: Plato's Cave Allegory and the Blindness of Men

We move now to consider the area of philosophy known as epistemology. This concerns questions about how we know things and includes what the nature of reality is.

This is a concern in discussions about the existence of God for several reasons. For instance, if as Christians claim, God is transcendent and not a part of the universe, then how can we know He exists?

We have seen that there are many good arguments for believing in God. These can be compared to the current scientific evidence for black holes; they can't be detected directly, but are rather known indirectly.

Plato's allegory of the cave challenges us to question some of our deepest assumptions about the nature of reality and what we think we know. Is it possible that there is more going on than just what we can take in with our senses or can measure with scientific equipment? Is it possible that we are missing the supernatural forest for the natural trees?

Plato's cave allegory

Delius, Gatzemeier, Sertcan & Wünscher explain:

"Plato's 'simile of the cave' is to be found in his dialogue *The Republic*. People chained up for life in a cave constantly see in the firelight the shadows of things which they cannot see, and they regard the shadows as the things themselves. However, the things themselves are mere images of an idealized existence, represented by the sun shining outside the cave. Plato uses the simile to describe the path to recognition of the ideas, which, as real originals, are superordinate to the world of concrete, visible things which are mere copies of them."[938]

Bryan Magee put it like this:

"The most famous passage in all Plato's writings occurs in the *Republic*, and is known as the Myth of the Cave. In it Plato puts into symbolic form his view of the human condition, and especially of human knowledge in relation to reality as a whole. Imagine, he says, a big cave, connected to the outside world by a passage long enough to prevent any day light from penetrating into the cave itself. Facing the far wall, with their backs to the entrance, is a row of prisoners. Not only are their limbs chained, they are also fastened by their neck so that they cannot move their heads, and therefore cannot see one another, indeed cannot see any part of themselves.

All they can see is the wall in front of them. And they have been in this situation all their lives, and know nothing else. In the cave behind them there is a bright fire. Unknown to them there is a rampart as high as a man between the fire and them; and on the other side of this rampart are people perpetually passing to and fro carrying things on their heads. The shadows of these objects are cast on the wall in front of the prisoners by the light of the fire, and the voices of

[938]Christoph Delius, Matthias Gatzemeier, Deniz Sertcan & Kathleen Wünscher, *The Story of Philosophy from Antiquity to the Present*, Germany (KÖNEMANN, 2005)12.

the people carrying them are echoed back from this wall to the prisoners' ears. Now, says Plato, the only entities that the prisoners ever perceive or experience in the whole of their existence are those shadows and those echoes. In these circumstances it would be natural for them to assume that shadows and echoes constitute all the reality there is; and it would be to this 'reality,' and to their experiences of it, that all their talk would refer.

If one of the prisoners could shake off his chains, so cramped would he be by a lifetime of entrapment in the half-dark, that merely to turn around would be painful and awkward for him, and the fire would dazzle his eyes. He would find himself confused and uncomprehending, and would want to turn back again to face the wall of shadows, the reality understood. If he were dragged up out of the cave altogether into the world of blazing sunlight he would be blinded and bewildered, and it would be a long time before he was able to see or understand anything. But then, once he was used to being in the upper world, if he were to return to the cave he would be temporarily blinded again, this time by the darkness. And everything he said to the prisoners about his experiences would be unintelligible to those whose language had reference only to shadows and echoes. The way to begin understanding this allegory is to see us human beings as imprisoned in our own bodies, with only other such prisoners for company, and all of us unable to discern the real selves of one another, or even our own real selves. Our direct experience is not of reality, but what is in our minds."[939]

Samuel Stumpf described further implications of Plato's cave allegory as it relates to human knowledge:

---

[939]Bryan Magee, *The Story of Philosophy: 2500 Years of Great Thinkers from Socrates to the Existentialist and Beyond,* New York (Barnes & Noble, 2006) 31.

"Before one can go from false knowledge to true knowledge, he must somehow become aware that he is in a state of ignorance. It is as if one must be awakened from a 'sleep of ignorance.' . . . In his allegory, Plato depicted how men moved from darkness to light, from ignorance to knowledge. But in this allegory he portrays the mood of self-satisfaction among the prisoners; they do not know that they are prisoners, that they are chained by false knowledge and dwell in the darkness of ignorance. Their awakening must come through some external agent."[940]

Now, with his cave allegory, Plato was defending his teaching about an ideal world of forms which he believed existed in some heavenly abode, and in which existed perfect prototypes of all earthly things. Having forgotten truths known in their pre-existence, learning for men is essentially the process of recollection.

Setting aside Plato's intentions concerning his theory of learning, I offer a different lesson derived from the cave allegory. Indeed, it can be read in the light of biblical teaching concerning man's lost condition, being in trapped in sin and blind to the truth, and in desperate need for the redemption that comes from Christ, the 'external agent' of light.

Toward the conclusion of the allegory, Plato said:

"On the contrary, our own account signifies that the soul of every man does possess the power of learning the truth and the organ to see it with; and that, just as one might have to turn the whole body round in order that the eye should see light instead of darkness, so the entire soul must be turned away from this changing world, until its eye can bear to contemplate reality and that supreme

[940]Samuel Enoch Stumpf, *Philosophy: History & Problems*, Fourth Edition, New York (McGraw-Hill Publishing Company, 1989) 66-67.

splendor which we have called the good. Hence there may well be an art whose aim would be to affect this very thing, the conversion of the soul . . . to ensure that, instead of looking in the wrong direction, it is turned the way it ought to be."[941]

I call on my skeptical readers to consider the possibility that they may actually be strapped to the back side of a cave, not seeing things as they really are; seeing only a part of reality and mistaking it for the whole. Jesus has broken your chains; turn your eyes from the darkness of the cave; seek forth the light that can illuminate all of reality.

Consider the message from God contained in the Bible and let it lead to the "true light that gives light to every man" (John 1:9), Jesus Christ!

I plead with you to consider these words:

"This is the verdict: Light has come into the world, but men loved darkness instead of light because their deeds were evil. Everyone who does evil hates the light for fear that his deeds will be exposed. But whoever lives by the truth comes into the light" (John 3:19-21).

---

[941]Plato, *The Republic, The Allegory of the Cave*, as quoted by Samuel Enoch Stumpf, *Philosophy: History & Problems*, Fourth Edition, New York (McGraw-Hill Publishing Company, 1989) 609.

Chapter 44: Epistemology: Is Absolute Truth a Reasonable Standard for Determining Truth?

In this section, we shall consider what should count as a reasonable standard or test for establishing the claim that God exists. In discussions about the existence of God, skeptics will often raise the bar so high, that even the most persuasive arguments are simply brushed aside.

As we have mentioned earlier, the standards used in our courts do not require absolute proof in deciding cases, since such is usually not possible. Rather, the evidence is weighed using reasonable standards that necessarily fall short of certainty.

In the question of God's existence, neither side of the argument has absolute and conclusive proofs to settle the case. Therefore, it is incumbent upon each of us to honestly evaluate the evidence for the existence of God.

Some, however, object to this suggestion and demand absolute certainty and undeniable proof before they would believe in the existence of God. But is that a reasonable demand, especially when we accept many other things, important things, on less than certain grounds.

Epistemological skepticism

For instance, philosopher Louis Pojman summed up other areas where there is epistemological skepticism among philosophers:

> "*Skepticism* is the theory that we do not have any knowledge; that we cannot be completely certain of any of our beliefs, not even the belief that we cannot be completely certain of any of our beliefs. For all we know, the universe and everything in it could have doubled in

size last night while we were sleeping. We cannot check this by measuring our height with a ruler because the ruler has also doubled in size. How could we prove that the world didn't double in size or become 27 percent smaller? How can we prove that the world and ourselves were not created seven minutes ago with all our apparent memories of the past built into our minds, fossils built into the stones, and buildings artificially aged?

Could the world all be an illusion? How can we prove there are indeed other minds, that the other beings in our classroom are not just cleverly constructed robots programmed to speak and smile and write exams? How do you know that you are not the only person who exists and that everything else is merely part of a long dream you are dreaming? Soon you will awaken and be surprised to discover that what you thought were dreams were really mini-dreams within one grand and glorious maxi-dream? Or perhaps you are simply a brain suspended in a tub full of chemical solutions in a laboratory and wired to a computer that is causing you to have your apparent experiences?"[942]

Pojman showed that skepticism is easy. *It is always easier to doubt things than to prove things.* As it relates to the question of God's existence, skeptics may take comfort that there are not absolute proofs for the existence of God. But such arguments may prove too much since similar arguments can be used to cast doubts on the most basic beliefs we hold. Christopher Grau elaborated:

"This is the kind of perplexing thought that Descartes forces us to confront. It seems we have no justification for the belief that we are not dreaming. If so, then it seems we similarly have no justification in thinking that the world we experience is the *real* world. Indeed, it becomes

[942]Louis P. Pojman, *Philosophy: The Quest for Truth*, Sixth Edition, New York. Oxford (Oxford University Press, 2006) 164-165.

questionable whether we are justified in thinking that *any* of our beliefs are true."[943]

Descartes' evil demon

We shall take a closer look at the implications of such philosophical skepticism. In his search for a ground of true knowledge, Rene Descartes discussed the thought experiment of an evil demon:

> "I shall then suppose, not that God who is supremely good and the fountain of truth, but some evil genius not less powerful than deceitful, has employed his whole energies in deceiving me; I shall consider that the heavens, the earth, colors, figures, sound, and all other external things are nought but the illusions and dreams of which this genius has availed himself in order to lay traps for my credulity; I shall consider myself as having no hands, no eyes, no flesh, no blood, nor any senses, yet falsely believing myself to possess all these things."[944]

How, then, wondered Descartes, could we know if what we perceive to be reality was really the machinations and deceptions of an evil demon? The answer is that we can't really disprove the supposition, yet most people do not trouble themselves with it, and go on living as if our senses are reliable.

---

[943]Christopher Grau, *Bad Dreams, Evil Demons, and the Experience Machine: Philosophy and The Matrix* in *Introduction to Philosophy: Classical and Contemporary Readings*, Fourth Edition, Edited by John Perry, Michael Bratman & John Martin Fischer, Oxford UK (Oxford University Press, 2007) 196.

[944]René Descartes, *The Sphere of the Doubtful*, Arthur Pap, *A Modern Introduction to Philosophy: Readings from Classical and Contemporary Sources,* Third Edition, Paul Edwards & Arthur Pap, Editors, New York, (The Free Press, 1973) 126.

Putman's brain in the vat

Ben Dupré showed how Descartes' evil demon was the inspiration for similar modern versions of the same thought experiment:

> "'Imagine that a human being has been subjected to an operation by an evil scientist. The person's brain has been removed from the body and placed in a vat of nutrients which keeps the brain alive. The nerve endings have been connected to a super-scientific computer which caused the person to have the illusion that everything is perfectly normal. There seem to be people, objects, the sky etc.; but really all the person is experiencing is the result of electronic impulses travelling from the computer to the nerve endings.'
>
> The classic modern telling of the brain-in-a-vat story above was given by the American philosopher Hilary Putman in his 1981 book *Reason, Truth, and History,* but the germ of the idea has a much longer history. Putman's thought experiment is essentially an updated version of a 17th-century horror story—the evil demon (*malin génie*) conjured up by the French philosopher René Descartes in his 1641 *Meditations on First Philosophy.*"[945]

The Matrix

Dupré then drew the line that started with Descartes and Putman to the movie *The Matrix:*

> "Ideas such as the brain in the vat have proved so thought-provoking and suggestive that they have led to numerous popular incarnations. One of the most successful was the 1999 movie *The Matrix,* in which computer hacker Neo (played by Keanu Reeves) discovers that the world of 1999 America is in fact a virtual simulation created by a

---

[945]Ben Dupré, *50 Philosophy Ideas You Really Need to Know*, London (Quercus Publishing Plc, 2007) 4-5.

malign cyber-intelligence and he and other humans are kept within fluid-filled pools, wired up to a vast computer."[946]

Descartes famously found his grounding for knowledge in the maxim: *"I think therefore I am."*[947] But how to prove the reality of the world beyond our own thoughts remains heretofore, a difficult philosophical problem.

More to the point, is it reasonable to enforce a higher standard of proof for believing in the existence of God than we expect for other philosophically challenging propositions?

Assumptions in all worldviews

Is it true that naturalism is strictly empirical and that all of its assertions are built upon rock-solid evidence? This is hardly the case. Naturalists, like adherents of any other worldview have their own foundational assumptions.

Kerry Walters spoke to worldviews:

> "The German word for worldview, *weltanschauung*, literally means 'looking at the world.' As mentioned earlier, a worldview is a core of basic **assumptions,** beliefs, values, and commitments about reality that colors the way we think about the world and the things in it."[948]

---

[946]Ben Dupré, *50 Philosophy Ideas You Really Need to Know*, 5.

[947]René Descartes, as quoted by James K. Feibleman, *Understanding Philosophy: A Popular History of Ideas*, New York (Horizon Press, 1973) 103. Stumpf traced this idea back to Saint Augustine: "In addition, he said that even the Skeptics would have to admit that the act of doubting is itself a form of certainty, for a person who doubts is certain that he doubts. Here, then, is another certainty, the certainty that I exist, for if I doubt I must exist." from Samuel Enoch Stumpf, *Philosophy: History & Problems*, Fourth Edition, New York (McGraw-Hill Publishing Company, 1989) 137.

[948]Kerry Walters, *Atheism: A Guide for the Perplexed*, New York

Walters suggested that worldviews (from whatever perspective) are at bottom, circular in nature:

> "Every worldview is circular to the extent that it presupposes certain basic beliefs and then interprets facts about the world by appealing to those beliefs. The rock-bottom belief of naturalism is that any explanation about the world must come from within the world because the world is all there is."[949]

As Walters showed, naturalism, which purports to be an impartial and scientific search after truth has at its base, an unprovable assumption that the material world is all that exists. Just as supernaturalism has an assumption of God's existence, so naturalism has the assumption that God does not exist.

Properly basic beliefs

Going further with this concept, philosopher Alvin Plantiga has popularized the idea of properly basic beliefs. William Lane Craig explained:

> "Philosophers call beliefs such as this 'properly basic beliefs.' They aren't based on some other beliefs; rather, they are part of the foundation of a person's system of beliefs. Other properly basic beliefs [beyond belief in God] include the belief in the reality of the past, the existence of the external world, and the presence of other minds such as your own. When you think about it, none of these beliefs can be proven . . . Thus, my basic beliefs are not arbitrary but appropriately grounded in experience. There may be no way to prove such beliefs, and yet it is perfectly rational to hold them . . . In the same way, belief in God is for those who seek him a properly basic belief grounded in our

(The Continuum International Publishing Group Inc, 2010) 34.
[949]Kerry Walters, *Atheism,* 46-47.

experience of God, as we discern him in nature, conscience, and other means."[950]

Evans and Manis further explained Plantinga's properly basic belief concept:

"Rather than trying to show that religious belief enjoys evidential support, one can instead challenge the assumption that beliefs require the support of evidence to be rationally justified. Alvin Plantinga has developed at length this line of response . . . called *Reformed epistemology:* it follows in the tradition of the Protestant Reformer and theologian John Calvin in its view that belief in God can be rationally justified apart from any arguments or evidence because it is (or can be) *properly basic.* A belief is *basic* for a person if he does not hold it on the basis of other beliefs that he holds; it is *properly* basic . . . If every belief requires other beliefs to support it, then we are headed for an infinite regress of justifying beliefs, which seems to imply that ultimately no belief can be rationally justified. But this is absurd; surely many of our beliefs *are* justified. Therefore, there must be some properly basic beliefs."[951]

Stumpf traced this idea as far back as Aristotle:

"If it were necessary to demonstrate every premise, this would involve an infinite regress, since each prior premise would also have to be proved, in which case the enterprise of knowledge could never get started. Aristotle, referring again to the *archai* or primary premises, said that 'not all knowledge is demonstrative: on the contrary, knowledge of the immediate premises is independent of demonstration.'"[952]

---

[950]William Lane Craig, *Why I Believe God Exists*, chapter in Norman L. Geisler & Paul K. Hoffman, *Why I Am a Christian: Leading Thinkers Explain Why They Believe*, Grand Rapids MI (Baker Books, 2001) 79.

[951]C. Stephen Evans & R. Zachary Manis, *Philosophy of Religion: Thinking About Faith*, Second Edition, Downers Grove IL (Inter Varsity Press, 2009)191-192.

After his conversion to theistic belief, Antony Flew reflected upon the cogency of the idea of properly basic beliefs:

> "By far, the headiest challenge to the argument came from America. The modal logician Alvin Plantinga introduced the idea that theism is a properly basic belief. He asserted that belief in God is similar to belief in other basic truths, such as belief in other minds or perception (seeing a tree) or memory (belief in the past). In all these instances, you trust your cognitive faculties, although you cannot prove the truth of the belief in question. Similarly, people take certain propositions (e.g., the existence of the world) as basic and others as derivative from these basic propositions."[953]

Atheists support of properly basic beliefs

As we have been arguing, properly basic beliefs are not unique to believers. Orlo Strunk Jr. stated:

> "The most powerful kind of contemporary atheism does not spend a great deal of time debating the issue of God's existence or nonexistence. Whole systems of modern atheism simply *start with the assumption that there is no God* . . . Contemporary atheism begins its witness with the conviction that there is no God and that we had best get on with things."[954]

Walters elaborated:

[952]Samuel Enoch Stumpf, *Philosophy: History & Problems*, 88.

[953]Antony Flew, *There is a God: How the World's Most Notorious Atheist Changed His Mind*, New York (HarperCollins/HarperOne, 2007) 55.

[954]Orlo Strunk, Jr., *The Choice Called Atheism: Confronting the Claims of Modern Unbelief*, Nashville TN (Abingdon Press, 1968) 29-30.

"All worldviews inevitably include some fundamental beliefs that either are not provable or are justified circularly, and so bootstrapping from first principles is a necessity. Naturalism is no exception to this rule."[955]

Atheists' inconsistency concerning properly basic beliefs

It is, then, simply unfair for naturalists and atheists to attack believers for believing in God (without absolute proof) when their worldview is likewise built on unproven assumptions. Nevertheless, Martin challenged the propriety of theists arguing that belief in God was properly basic:

"There may not at present be any clear criterion for what can be a basic belief, but belief in God seems peculiarly inappropriate for inclusion in the class since there are clear disanaologies between it and the basic beliefs allowable by classic foundationalism."[956]

Winfried Corduan answered Martin's point:

"In fact, we can turn the table on the person making such demands on us and point out that the demand is not even legitimate. It implies the thesis that in order to be true a belief must be able to withstand any conceivable doubt. No belief can withstand that requirement— including the belief that in order to be true a belief must be able to withstand any conceivable doubt."[957]

In other words, what's good for the atheists' goose should be good for the believer's gander.

---

[955]Kerry Walters, *Atheism,* 49.

[956]Michael Martin, *Atheism: A Philosophical Justification,* Philadelphia PA (Temple University Press, 1990)273-274.

[957]Winfried Corduan, *No Doubt About It: The Case for Christianity,* Nashville TN (Broadman & Holman Publishers, 1997) 42.

Chapter 45: Atheists Must Have Faith Too— David Hume and the Problem of Induction

One form of skepticism is known by philosophers as the problem of induction. How can we know that the future will be like the past? How can we be sure of the idea of cause and effect? Arthur Pap noted:

> "The time-honored 'problem of induction' whose apparent insolubility has been called by some 'the scandal of modern philosophy.'"[958]

Pap traced the discussion concerning the problem of induction from Descartes, Hume, to the present:

> "Hume raised the problem whether we can ever be justified in accepting the conclusion of an inductive argument . . . he questioned not only whether inductive conclusions can ever be certain but even whether they can ever be so much as probable. A position which is less critical of common-sense beliefs about matters of fact is that of the philosophers who maintain that no empirical proposition can ever be absolutely certain. The most we can ever obtain is a high degree of probability . . . Ever since Descartes claimed—at least as critical philosopher, if not as devout Christian—that the only thing which indubitably exists is his own doubt of the existence of anything else, and therewith his own mind ('I think, therefore I exist'), many philosophers have denied that any propositions about the physical world . . . are ever certain."[959]

Arthur Pap also described the issues Hume raised concerning the problem of induction:

---

[958]Arthur Pap, *A Modern Introduction to Philosophy: Readings from Classical and Contemporary Sources,* Third Edition, Paul Edwards & Arthur Pap, Editors, New York, (The Free Press, 1973) 121.

[959]Arthur Pap, *A Modern Introduction to Philosophy,* 120-121.

"Is it that we infer that nature *will be* uniform from the fact that it *has been* uniform? But to justify this inference and to prove the alleged presupposition of the uniformity of nature is one and the same thing; hence we beg the question if we attempt to prove that nature must be uniform by relying on the inference from what has happened to what will happen . . . Conclusion: induction cannot be logically justified at all; it is not even a process of reasoning, but a *habit* of expecting what has happened in such and such circumstances to happen again in similar circumstances."[960]

Hume had illustrated this point with the example of bread:

"The bread which I formally ate nourished me; that is, a body of such sensible qualities was, at that time, endued with such secret powers. But does it follow that other bread must also nourish me at another time, and that like sensible qualities must always be attended with like secret powers? The consequence seems nowise necessary . . . But if you insist that the inference is made by a chain of reasoning, I desire you to produce that reasoning."[961]

That is, Hume argued that there is no philosophical or logically necessary justification for assuming that past experiences can be used to determine future behavior.

Arthur Pap clarified:

"It should be noted that neither Hume nor other skeptics deny the *psychological* fact that we are strongly inclined to believe that the future will be like the past. They and other philosophers discussing the subject are not

[960]Arthur Pap, *A Modern Introduction to Philosophy,* 117.
[961]David Hume, Section 4 of *An Inquiry Concerning Human Understanding,* as produced in *A Modern Introduction to Philosophy: Readings from Classical and Contemporary Sources,* Third Edition, Paul Edwards & Arthur Pap, Editors, New York, (The Free Press, 1973) 134-135

concerned with questions of psychology but with *logical* problems—with the question of the justification or validity of inductive inferences."[962]

Antony Flew made clear that Hume's skepticism could not be lived out in life:

"Hume's Skepticism about cause and effect and his agnosticism about the external world are of course jettisoned the moment he leaves his study."[963]

Hume himself admitted as much:

"None but a fool or madman will ever pretend to dispute the authority of experience or to reject that great guide of human life, it may surely be allowed a philosopher to have so much curiosity at least to examine the principle of human nature which gives this mighty authority to experience."[964]

Yes, someone would have to be a fool or madman to attempt to live life ignoring the voice of experience. W. C. Salmon stated:

"It is not difficult to appreciate the response of the man engaged in active scientific research or practical affairs who says, in effect, 'Don't bother me with these silly puzzles; I'm too busy doing science, building bridges, or managing affairs of state.' No one, including Hume, seriously suggests any suspension of scientific investigation or practical decision pending a solution of the

[962]Arthur Pap, *A Modern Introduction to Philosophy: Readings from Classical and Contemporary Sources,* Third Edition, Paul Edwards & Arthur Pap, Editors, New York, (The Free Press, 1973) 117.

[963]Antony Flew, *There is a God: How the World's Most Notorious Atheist Changed His Mind,* New York (HarperCollins/HarperOne, 2007) 58.

[964]David Hume, Section 4 of *An Inquiry Concerning Human Understanding,* 136.

problem of induction. The problem concerns the foundations of science."[965]

The problem of induction and the possibility of science

Indeed, the problems raised by Hume impact the most basic foundations of modern science. Bertrand Russell stated:

> "The business of science is to find uniformities, such as the laws of motion and the law of gravitation, to which, so far as our experience extends, there are no exceptions."[966]

Nevertheless, Russell supported Hume's primary point:

> "It must be conceded, to begin with, that the fact that two things have been found often together and never apart does not, by itself, suffice to *prove* demonstratively that they will be found together in the next case we examine. The most we can hope is that the oftener things are found together, the more probable it becomes that they will be found together another time, and that, if they have been found together often enough, the probability will amount *almost* to certainty. It can never reach certainty."[967]

Stumpf says:

---

[965]W. C. Salmom, *The Problem of Induction* in *Introduction to Philosophy: Classical and Contemporary Readings*, Fourth Edition, Edited by John Perry, Michael Bratman & John Martin Fischer, Oxford UK (Oxford University Press, 2007) 270.

[966]Bertrand Russell, *A Modern Introduction to Philosophy: Readings from Classical and Contemporary Sources,* Third Edition, Paul Edwards & Arthur Pap, Editors, New York, (The Free Press, 1973) 141.

[967]Bertrand Russell, *A Modern Introduction to Philosophy,* 142.

"Hume's most striking philosophical argument was that since all our knowledge comes from experience, we cannot have any knowledge of 'causality' or necessary connections because we do not experience causality, and, therefore, we cannot infer or predict any future event from our experience of the present. What we call *causality,* said Hume, is simply our habit of associating two events because we experience them together, but this does not justify the conclusion that these events have any necessary connection. Thus, Hume denied inductive inference. And yet, it is precisely upon the notion of causality and inductive inference that science is built, for it assumes that our knowledge about an indefinite number of smaller events in the present gives us reliable knowledge about an indefinite number of similar events in the future. The logical outcome of Hume's empiricism was that there cannot be any scientific knowledge, and this leads to philosophical skepticism."[968]

How to respond to the problem of induction

The pragmatic response to the problem of induction is to simply acknowledge the philosophical problem but press on anyway. We may not be able to prove, in a philosophical sense, cause and effect, or that the future will be like the past and present but believing in these concepts has been a very reliable guide for science and for life in general.

Thomas Reid represented the Scottish Philosophy of Common-sense. In contrast to epistemological skepticism, Reid argued that our senses are essentially reliable. Geisler explained:

"We know these faculties are trustworthy because, however we try to refute these principles, they prevail. Further, all thinking depends on the assumption that they

[968]Samuel Enoch Stumpf, *Philosophy: History & Problems,* 301.

are reliable. In response to skeptics who distrust their faculties, Reid observes that even Hume trusted his senses in practice and is guilty of pragmatic inconsistency."[969]

Aristotle himself stated the same idea which he called the *Archai:*

> "Demonstrative reasoning must therefore lay hold of reliable premises, principles, or what Aristotle calls *archai,* i.e. 'first things.' . . . How are these first principles or *archai* arrived at? Aristotle answers that we learn these *archai* from observation and induction. When we observe certain facts many times, 'the universal that is there,' he says, 'becomes plain.' . . . If one then asks the additional question whether and how we can know that the *archai* or principles are true, Aristotle says we know they are true simply because the mind, working with certain facts, recognizes and 'sees' their truth."[970]

The fact that Hume raised difficult problems about induction did not necessitate abandoning inductive reasoning. Else, we would have had to abandon the scientific endeavor along with it.

Likewise, we do not need to abandon belief in God merely because skeptics have raised difficult philosophical questions. As we have seen, the problem of induction proves that even the most ardent skeptic must have faith to live in this world, trusting that he will not suddenly fly off into space or be crushed by a huge boulder that suddenly materializes above his head.

---

[969]Norman L. Geisler, *Baker Encyclopedia of Christian Apologetics,* Grand Rapids MI (Baker Books, 1999) 638.
[970]Samuel Enoch Stumpf, *Philosophy: History & Problems,* 87-88.

The faith of atheists

Hence, Mark Mittelberg argued that even the atheist's denial of God's existence rests upon faith:

"Even the person who casually says, 'Oh, I never worry about things like that!' lives by faith that people need not concern themselves about these matters [salvation or the existence of God]. This might surprise you, but even atheists live by faith—including the so-called New Atheists. They operate in the belief that there is no Creator, no higher moral law to which they are accountable, no divine judgment and no afterlife. They can't prove these things. They don't *know* for a fact that there is no God, spiritual standard, day of reckoning or existence after death."[971]

Evans and Manis agreed:

"The basic convictions that shape the conclusions of the atheist in these matters are equally subjective. Atheism can no more be proved by valid arguments with uncontroversially true premises than can theism."[972]

Francis Collins, who served as the director of the Human Genome Project, said of atheism:

"The major and inescapable flaw of Dawkin's claim that science demands atheism is that it goes beyond the evidence. If God is outside of nature, then science can neither prove nor disprove His existence. Atheism itself must therefore be considered a form of blind faith, in that

---

[971]Mark Mittelburg, *Why Faith in Jesus Matters*, chapter in William Lane Craig & Chad Meister, Editors, *God is Great, God is Good: Why Believing in God is Reasonable and Responsible,* Downers Grove IL (Inter Varsity Press, 2009) 218.

[972]C. Stephen Evans & R. Zachary Manis, *Philosophy of Religion: Thinking About Faith*, Second Edition, Downers Grove IL (Inter Varsity Press, 2009) 187-188.

it adopts a belief system that cannot be defended on the basis of pure reason."[973]

Alister McGrath added:

"The belief that there is no God is just as much a matter of faith as the belief that there is a God. If 'faith' is defined as 'belief lying beyond proof,' both Christianity and atheism are faiths."[974]

The term 'faitheist' was coined for just this reason.

---

[973]Francis S. Collins, *The Language of God: A Scientist Presents Evidence for Belief,* New York (Free Press, 2006) 165.

[974]Alister McGrath, *The Twilight of Atheism: The Rise and Fall of Disbelief in the Modern World,* New York (Doubleday, 2004) 180.

Chapter 46: Solipsism and the Problem of Other Minds

Hello? Hello? Hello?

Is there anybody in there?

Just nod if you can hear me

Is there anyone at home?[975]

A specific example of philosophical skepticism is called solipsism, or *the problem of other minds*. It is similar to Descartes' evil demon problem in that it raises questions about our most basic assumptions about the world. Antony Flew explained the issue of solipsism:

> "The theory that I am the sole existent. To be a solipsist I must hold that I alone exist independently, and that what I ordinarily call the outside world exists only as an object or content of my consciousness. This doctrine, though doubtless psychologically very difficult, if not impossible, to hold, is philosophically interesting in that many thinkers have thought it necessary to attempt refutations, or even to admit that, however bizarre, it is strictly irrefutable . . . It is indeed questionable whether we can argue validly to the existence or nature of a mind-independent external world."[976]

---

[975]Pink Floyd, *Comfortably Numb*, David John Gilmour & Roger Waters, © Warner/Chappell Music, Inc, BMG Rights Management US, LLC, Imagem Music Inc

[976]Antony Flew, *A Dictionary of Philosophy*, Revised Second Edition, New York (Gramercy Books, 1979) 330.

C. S. Rodd's pragmatic Christian response to the problem of solipsism

In his book *Is There A God*, C. S. Rodd had his character Geoff argue that just as the problem of solipsism does not prevent anyone from believing in the reality of other persons, neither should philosophical arguments raised against God's existence prevent belief in God:

> "'We all know that you can't prove that we've got minds if you stick to what can be weighed and measured. We just know we have' . . . 'You can't prove that Tim has a mind, but you are quite confident that he has. Nothing is likely to shake your belief. Isn't that exactly like our position with God? We have seen that we can't prove that God exists. But if we believe that other people have minds, why not believe that God exists?'. . . 'My point is that just because none of the so-called 'proofs' of God's existence provide a knock-down argument that will convince an atheist, there is no reason to be ashamed of our own belief in God. It is quite as reasonable as believing in other people's minds.'"[977]

Kai Nielsen referred to this as the parity argument i.e., that belief in other minds and belief in God are comparable?[978] He provides a very good explanation of it and then proceeds to undermine its validity:

> "We may not be able to prove that there is a God it has been argued, we cannot prove that there are other minds, that the sun will come up tomorrow, that time is real, that there are real causal powers, or that there is an external world . . . People arguing out of this tradition often invoke a kind of *parity argument*. The secularist, it is claimed, has

---

[977]C.S. Rodd, *Is There a God?* From the *Thinking Things Through* series, no. 9, Peterborough (Epworth Press, 2002) 50, 52.
[978]Kai Nielsen, *Atheism & Philosophy*, Amherst NY (Prometheus Books, 2005) 259.

to take a lot of things on faith, too. If it is demonstration you are after, it has been said, you can no more demonstrate the existence of other minds, the presence of causes, the existence of the external world, or the reliability of your senses, than you can the existence of God. If it is irrational to believe in God because we cannot demonstrate His existence, then it is equally irrational to believe in other minds, induction, the external world, the reality of time, causal powers, and the like . . . Science, the claim might go, rests just as much or just as little on faith as does religion."[979]

Nielsen moved on to refute the parity argument:

"After listening with comprehension . . . to a careful demonstration that we cannot know that other people have minds, the simple atheist, or indeed the simple believer, is surely justified in believing, no matter how good the metaphysical argument . . . For other minds, the problem is simply *how* we know, not *that* we know, that others have minds . . . The correct outcome of the puzzle is not in the slightest in dispute or in doubt. After all, the chap in philosophical perplexity about other minds . . . is addressing his argument to others . . . Our doubts about whether God exists . . . pose conceptual puzzles as well, but . . . we have, as Peirce stressed, real doubts here, not merely Cartesian doubts parading as genuine doubts."[980]

With a mere verbal wave of the hand, Nielsen sought to set aside hundreds of years of sophisticated philosophical argumentation, "Cartesian doubts parading as genuine doubts." He made no attempt to refute the problem of solipsism; we just know there are other minds and that's all there is to it. Thus, Nielsen offered no rebuttal of the parity problem; he simply dismissed it as so obviously true it needed no refutation.

---

[979]Kai Nielsen, *Atheism & Philosophy*, 256-257.
[980]Kai Nielsen, *Atheism & Philosophy*, 257-258.

Nielsen further argued:

> "Even, if all of that were rejected by someone, the parity argument would still be a bad one for it would only show . . . that religious belief is not uniquely irrational . . . we still would have to say that the theist was even more irrational than the atheist, for he not only has all the atheist's irrational beliefs [i.e. belief in other minds etc.], he has some additional ones as well of a very strange sort—beliefs that Ockham's razor would justify us in shaving away. The other 'irrational beliefs' he shares with the atheist are not so shaveable, for they, humanly speaking, as both theists and atheist acknowledge, are not beliefs they can do without. But his theistic beliefs are not so indispensable. By sticking to them, he exhibits an even greater irrationality than does the atheist."[981]

With this argument, Nielsen grants, for sake of argument, that both belief in God and belief in other minds cannot be proved, and so have logical parity. Yet, he argued that the theist case is the more irrational since in addition to the philosophically unproven concepts that atheists accept i.e., solipsisms, he adds to them all, the unprovable belief in the existence of God.

Nielsen is like a criminal denying he has parity with another criminal because whereas he stole only $500.00 the other guy stole $700.00.

But the bottom line remains; from a strictly philosophical basis, there is parity in the belief in other minds and the belief in God, since both are unproven philosophical assertions. Neither is Nielsen's appeal to Ockham's razor convincing since believing that the universe is a result of an intelligent designer is at least

---

[981]Kai Nielsen, *Atheism & Philosophy*, 259.

as simple as believing that random chance is to account for everything.

Kerry Walters acknowledged the point made by theists that:

> "After all, the truth of the naturalist perspective is no more 'provable' than that of supernaturalism. Opting for it, then, must involve a leap of faith."[982]

While acknowledging the place that faith holds, even for naturalists, yet, Walters hints that belief in God tips the scales too far toward irrationality:

> "All understandings of faith include some degree of believing without full proof. The question is at what point believing without full proof becomes irrational."[983]

I agree. There must certainly be some point where it becomes irrational to believe something without sufficient evidence. But God-belief is both coherent and supported by powerful arguments.

This examination of the problems raised by philosophers concerning epistemological issues, how we know things, has shown that no matter how one may attempt to answer these perennial questions, we simply don't have all the answers to the questions raised, and faith necessarily remains for believers and unbelievers alike.

Most of us just go on living according to common sense, blissfully ignorant of the skeptical concerns of the philosophers. Indeed, even the philosophers themselves

---

[982]Kerry Walters, *Atheism: A Guide for the Perplexed*, New York (The Continuum International Publishing Group Inc, 2010) 48.

[983]Kerry Walters, *Atheism: A Guide for the Perplexed*, New York (The Continuum International Publishing Group Inc, 2010) 48.

spend most of their lives assuming that the world is pretty much as it appears to be. Julian Baggini summed up the idea well:

> "The crux of the issue is the very fact I have stressed throughout my argument, that absolute proofs are not available for the vast majority of our beliefs, but that a lack of such proof is no grounds for the suspension of belief."[984]

This is true for the unbeliever no less than for the believer.

---

[984]Julian Baggini, *Atheism,* New York (Sterling, 2003) 45.

Chapter 47: The Inductive Leap and Reasonable Faith

The fact is that in virtually every area of our life, we operate with a certain degree of faith. In a discussion of the problem of induction, philosopher Max Black noted the irony involved for philosophers who though they have no philosophical justification for believing the basic law of cause and effect (which serves as a foundation for modern science), nevertheless make the *inductive leap*:

> "He [the philosopher] finds it hard to understand how the 'inductive leap,' which seems to involve a plain logical fallacy, could ever be justified . . . It seems that unless induction can be justified, our claims to have scientific *knowledge* must be rejected as unfounded and science will have to count as no better than any other unsubstantiated *faith.*"[985]

The irony, then, is, that the same philosophers who require absolute proof for the existence of God, and who mock the necessity of faith, find that they themselves must also take the inductive leap of faith to make sense of the world.

Faith must fill the gap.

I don't know that my car will not suddenly float off into space; I must have faith that my future experience will be like my past experiences. Faith indeed!

Kant's Copernican revolution: Reality filtered through the brain

---

[985]Max Black, *A Modern Introduction to Philosophy: Readings from Classical and Contemporary Sources,* Third Edition, Paul Edwards & Arthur Pap, Editors, New York, (The Free Press, 1973) 158.

These are not merely the idle speculations of philosophers. It was Immanuel Kant's skeptical argument about human knowledge that he felt had launched a Copernican revolution in philosophy and has had a lasting impact into the present. Andrew Fiala explained:

> "The *Critique of Pure Reason* is one of the most important philosophical texts ever written. Like Copernicus, Kant dared to question the ordinary perspective from which we habitually view the world. While we usually imagine that knowledge occurs when the mind corresponds to objects, Kant argues that knowledge is made possible by the fact that objects must conform to the shape of our minds. This results in a moderate form of skepticism, known as 'transcendental idealism,' whose primary tenet is that we cannot know things as they are in themselves because we only know things as they appear to us."[986]

The significance of Kant's claims is truly breathtaking; we can never know the world as it actually is (the thing in itself). Rather, we can only know the world after it has been filtered through our minds which have sifted and shaped the data according to its own categories (the thing as it appears to us). Samuel Stumpf explained:

> "Kant did not mean to say that the mind creates objects, nor did he mean that the mind possesses innate ideas. His Copernican revolution consisted rather in his saying that the mind brings something to the objects it experiences. With Hume, Kant agreed that our knowledge begins with experience, but unlike Hume, Kant saw the

---

[986]Andrew Fiala, *Introduction to Immanuel Kant, Critique of Pure Reason*, Translated by J.M.D. Meiklejohn, New York (Barnes & Noble, 1781, 2004) *Introduction*, 7

mind as an active agent doing something with the objects it experiences. The mind, says Kant, is structured in such a way that it imposes its way of knowing upon its objects. By its very nature, the mind actively organizes our experiences . . . Knowledge is, therefore, a cooperative affair between the knower and the thing known . . . I can never know that thing as it is in itself, for the moment I know it, I know it as my structured mind permits me to know it. If colored glasses were permanently fixed to my eyes, I should always see things in that color and could never escape the limitations placed on my vision by those glasses. Similarly, my mind always brings certain ways of thinking to things, and this always affects my understanding of them."[987]

Stumpf further showed that Kant believed that this distortion of the mind includes knowledge of even our selves:

"Kant calls it the 'transcendental unity of apperception,' what we should call the *self* . . . Our self-consciousness, however, is affected by the same faculties that affect our perception of the external objects. I bring to the knowledge of myself as an object of knowledge the same 'lenses' through which I see everything."[988]

Kant denied the possibility of direct knowledge of the world

James Feibleman explained the implications of Kant's system on human knowledge and everyday experience:

"For instance, given the pair, *appearance-and-reality*, Kant made of his act of experience merely one of appearance. Like Locke, he said that the reality of the

---

[987]Samuel Enoch Stumpf, *Philosophy: History & Problems*, Fourth Edition, New York (McGraw-Hill Publishing Company, 1989) 307-308.

[988]Samuel Enoch Stumpf, *Philosophy: History & Problems*, 309.

material object, the chair, the *thing-as-it-is-in-itself*, is forever unknowable. In this way, he ruled out all reliable knowledge of the external world, which may or may not correspond to its appearance. If the appearance is the reality there would be no need to distinguish between them, but since we do distinguish, it suggests a difference. And so what Kant was saying about reliable knowledge of reality was that it cannot be had."[989]

Stumpf showed how Kant attempted to save science within his system:

> "Science is possible because all men, having the same structure of mind, will always and everywhere order the events of sense experience the same way . . . We can have scientific knowledge of phenomena but cannot have scientific knowledge of the noumenal realm, or the realm that transcends experience."[990]

On the one hand, if everyone makes the same mistakes, we might be tempted to ask why then does it matter? Or we can ask, if we don't (and can't) have direct knowledge of the world, how could Kant know that all of our minds are similarly structured, or how their structured, or that things aren't just as we sense them?

Further, even if it is argued that science is possible because all of our minds are similarly-structured, it still leaves the possibility that while all the laws of science are uniform, they are uniformly wrong since they do not correspond to the world as it actually is.

Geisler raised the same issue concerning Kant's epistemology:

---

[989]James K. Feibleman, *Understanding Philosophy: A Popular History of Ideas*, New York (Horizon Press, 1973) 141.
[990]Samuel Enoch Stumpf, *Philosophy: History & Problems*, 311.

"The argument that we cannot know the real world is self-defeating. The very statement 'We cannot know reality' is a statement that presupposes knowledge about reality."[991]

Stumpf elaborated on the problems inherent in Hume's system:

"The idealists, especially Fichte, quickly recognized the glaring contradictions in Kant's argument concerning the thing-in-itself. How is it possible to say that something exists but that we can know nothing about it? Do we not already know something about it when we say that it exists? Moreover, Kant has asserted the existence of the thing-in-itself in order to account for our experiences of sensation, saying in effect that the thing-in-itself is the *cause* of any given sensation."[992]

Geisler explained the implications of Kant's epistemology:

"The price of the Kantian synthesis was high: Lost in his model of the knowing process was the ability to know reality. If Kant was right, we know how we know, but we no longer know. For if all knowledge is formed or structured by *a priori* categories, we can only know things as they appear *to us,* not as they are in *themselves.* We can know *phenomena* but not *noumena.* Thus the net epistemological gain was the ultimate loss. Reality or the thing-in-itself, including God, is forever beyond us. What is left for us is the thing to me, which is appearance but not reality. Thus, Kant's view ends in philosophical agnosticism."[993]

---

[991]Norman L. Geisler, *Baker Encyclopedia of Christian Apologetics*, Grand Rapids MI (Baker Books, 1999) 404.

[992]Samuel Enoch Stumpf, *Philosophy: History & Problems*, 327.

[993]Norman L. Geisler, *Baker Encyclopedia of Christian Apologetics*, 402.

Kant's radical epistemological skepticism raised interesting issues, but it is riddled with inconsistencies. Science shows every day that there is no reason to doubt the reality of the world as it is in itself. Nor is there any reason for Christians to doubt God as He is in Himself.

Section Eleven: The Leap of Faith
Chapter 48: A Reasoned Faith

"Go to him he calls you; you can't refuse

When you ain't got nothing, you got nothing to lose

You're invisible now, you've got no secrets to conceal.[994]"

Fideism

When we talk about faith, we are not talking about blind faith. Rather, we are talking about *a reasoned faith*. Nevertheless, skeptics often attack Christianity for being hostile to reason. For instance, Nietzsche, perhaps with Kierkegaard in mind, said: "'Faith' means not wanting to know what is true."[995]

Kai Nielsen agreed:

> "Religious belief—or at least belief in God—should be impossible for someone living in our century, who thinks carefully about these matters and who has a tolerable scientific education and good philosophical training."[996]

I find these attacks amazing in light of the many outstanding theistic believers in academia and science through the ages. A frequent target of such charges are

---

[994]Bob Dylan, *Like a Rolling Stone*, © Bob Dylan Music Obo Special Rider Music
[995]Friedrich Nietzsche, as quoted by Walter Kaufmann, *Existentialism From Dostoevsky To Sartre*, Revised and Expanded, New York (Meridian, 1975) 19.
[996]Kai Nielsen, *Atheism & Philosophy*, Amherst NY (Prometheus Books, 2005) 79.

those Christians identified with fideism, which at least as the movement is popularly understood, encouraged belief despite what any contrary evidence might show.

Paul Edwards explained this type of fideism:

> "We have not so far considered a viewpoint which has become increasingly influential among pro-religious philosophers in recent years. This is the position known as 'fideism'—belief in God (or other religious propositions) on the basis of faith alone . . . Fideistic believers are ready to concede that the arguments for the existence of God are not valid, but they commonly add that this is not necessarily a cause for concern. Faith, in the words of John Hick, 'stands ultimately upon the ground of religious experience and is not a product of philosophical reasoning.' A person either has faith in which case he does not need any logical arguments or else he does not in which case no amount of arguments will give it to him . . . Kierkegaard, a leading figure in the fideist tradition, went so far as to maintain that those who tried to prove the existence of God are enemies of true faith."[997]

What I can appreciate in the ideas of fideism is that coming to faith in God is not merely an intellectual exercise, but is also a matter of the will. That is, our wills are involved. At base we are rebels against God. Yet, in

---

[997]Paul Edwards, *A Modern Introduction to Philosophy: Readings from Classical and Contemporary Sources,* Third Edition, Paul Edwards & Arthur Pap, Editors, New York, (The Free Press, 1973) 391. Evans and Manis clarify types of fideism: "It should be noted that the term 'fideism' is used in multiple ways in philosophy of religion, and many different perspectives have been described as fideistic . . . Evans distinguishes what he terms 'irrational fideism' . . . from what he terms 'responsible fideism,' which is defended as a reasonable position."(C. Stephen Evans & R. Zachary Manis, *Philosophy of Religion: Thinking About Faith*, Second Edition, Downers Grove IL (InterVarsity Press, 2009) 219. Presumably, it is considered responsible fideism because it still values the place of apologetics in defense of the Christian faith.

the gospel, God offers peace with Himself through the cross of Christ. This is grace; not only that Christ died for our sins, but also that He also works in our hearts to draw us to Himself.

On the other hand, fideism is troubling. Is it true that faith is based upon experience alone, despite any contrary evidence? There is an aspect of faith that can take us beyond, but not contrary to the evidence. Our faith should be a reasoned faith, an examined faith if you will, but not an irrational faith.

Kierkegaard on faith and reason

Barnes has categorized Soren Kierkegaard as a representative of the Fideist' perspective in which it is supposed that "Faith is contrary to reason."[998] However, I believe this is based upon a misunderstanding of Kierkegaard's views.

Norman Geisler noted Kierkegaard's acceptance of orthodox Christian teachings:

> "Theologically Kierkegaard was orthodox . . . He believed in inspiration of Scripture . . . the virgin birth, miracles, the substitutionary atonement, the bodily resurrection, and the final judgment."[999]

Barnes summarized Kierkegaard's view of faith and reason:

---

[998]Michael Horace Barnes, *Understanding Religion and Science: Introducing the Debate*, New York (Continuum International Publishing Group, 2010) 16.

[999]Norman L. Geisler, *Baker Encyclopedia of Christian Apologetics*, Grand Rapids MI (Baker Books, 1999) 406.

"True faith is blind commitment. The ideal Christian is a 'knight of faith' who gallops to the edge of the cliff and leaps."[1000]

Bretall noted that Kierkegaard reacted to Hegel's system of rationalism and thus:

"It was against that [Hegel's rationalism] S.K. reacted so violently, and for this reason he sometimes swings to the opposite extreme and appears to be a fideist who would cut himself off completely from the intellect and its claims . . . but his considered viewpoint was not fideistic . . . As Lowrie says, he was essentially a 'Catholic Christian' in its broadest sense."[1001]

Lowrie explained it this way:

"It is very easy to misapprehend, even to caricature, S.K.'s notion of the 'leap,' more especially when it is a leap into the paradoxically religious sphere which S.K. characterizes as 'the absurd.' The leap is indeed a decisive choice . . . But this does not imply an antithesis between the intellect and the will, for the whole man, intellect, feeling, and will, is involved in the choice."[1002]

This characterization of Kierkegaard's beliefs need not be seen as holding faith and reason in tension. Rather, for the Christian, they are complimentary; faith based upon reason, believing what is not seen by what is seen (Hebrews 11:1).

Kierkegaard's "knight of faith"[1003] does indeed charge boldly forward for Christ ignoring all the slinging arrows

[1000]Michael Horace Barnes, *Understanding Religion and Science,* 16.
[1001]Robert Bretall, *A Kierkegaard Anthology,* New York (The Modern Library/Random House,1946) *Introduction* 24.
[1002]Walter Lowrie, *A Short Life of Kierkegaard,* New York City (Anchor Books/Doubleday & Company, Inc, 1961) 144.
[1003]Michael Martin, *Atheism: A Philosophical Justification,*

of skepticism, toward the city of God. As with any soldier going forth into battle, he does so trusting in the battleplan and mission of his commander.

Geisler further explained Kierkegaard's view in this regard:

> "Reason, however, plays the negative role of helping to distinguish nonsense from paradox. The Christian is prevented by reason from believing sheer nonsense (*Postscripts,* 504) . . . Kierkegaard was not an irrationalist, as some have claimed . . . Kierkegaard has been widely misunderstood."[1004]

It is important to remember that Kierkegaard was not opposed to rational justification for faith. Martin wrote:

> "Adams is careful to note that Kierkegaard was not arguing that historical propositions about Christianity . . . cannot be established with a high degree of probability by objective reasoning."[1005]

Rather, Kierkegaard recognized that at some point one must take leave of endless arguments about Christianity and make a choice, take a leap of faith.

A rational faith and a reasoned leap

The Christian faith does indeed involve a leap of faith. But it is not a blind leap, but a leap in response to the Word of God, which provides a rational basis of belief on which to justify the leap. Yes, there is necessarily a leap "into the abyss, trusting that God is there."[1006]

Philadelphia PA (Temple University Press, 1990) 251-252.

[1004]Norman L. Geisler, *Baker Encyclopedia of Christian Apologetics*, 408, 410.

[1005]Michael Martin, *Atheism,* 254.

[1006]Soren Kierkegaard as quoted by Michael Horace Barnes,

The atheist believes that at the conclusion of his earthly life, he will make a leap into the abyss of nothingness. But that remains a leap of faith, for he knows not with certainty whether he may actually awaken to another plane of existence, and perhaps even before a cosmic judge.

Reasoned faith

The great Reformed theologians made a helpful distinction to illuminate the relationship between faith and reason. They spoke of *notitia* as referring to the intellectual content of Christian faith, of *assensus* as the intellectual agreement with this *Notitia* or content, and of *fiducia,* the actual exercise of faith in the gospel of Jesus Christ.

There is, then, information to be believed and intellectual content to be accepted. The Christian gospel is not merely emotional experiences. Rather, it involves rational propositions that form the basis of belief for the simplest child and the most profound philosophers and theologians.

This perspective differs from the fideistic "Don't confuse me with the facts, I've already made up mind" mentality.

In stark contrast to that type of Fideism, Jesus taught us to "Love the Lord your God with all your heart and with all your soul and *with all your mind"* (Matthew 22:37). Peter admonished Christians to "Always be prepared to give an answer to everyone who asks you to give the reason for the hope you have" (1 Peter 3:15).

Understanding Religion and Science, 27.

Tertullian on faith and reason

In an attempt to portray Christianity as irrational, some atheists have charged the early church father Tertullian with an extreme or irrational form of fideism. For example, David Eller argued:

> "As Tertullian, an early church father, stated clearly, Christianity is true because it is absurd—because there is no evidence for it and nothing else like it in human experience."[1007]

Tertullian was a brilliant thinker and writer. He certainly did not disdain the importance of rational arguments in support of Christianity as Eller suggested. Rather, Tertullian, was playing off the skeptics' accusation that the Christian gospel message was foolish, and rejoicing to be thought a fool for Christ.

Ted McDonald explained:

> "We should notice that Tertullian's remarks did not include the word, absurd. This mistranslation results in an erroneous representation of Tertullian's true views. According to *Webster's New World Dictionary,* absurd means "so clearly untrue or unreasonable as to be laughable or ridiculous." But Tertullian did not use the Latin word "*absurdum,*" he used the Latin word, "*ineptum.*" The Latin word, *ineptum,* should have been translated "foolish." From the context, we see that Tertullian was commenting upon the phrase, "the foolishness of God" as found in 1 Corinthians. He was not affirming that he was attracted to Christianity because of its absurdity, i.e. because of its laughably untrue nature. Rather, he was commenting upon 1 Corinthians Chapter 1."[1008]

[1007]David Eller, *Natural Atheism,* Cranford New Jersey (American Atheist Press, 2004) 168.

Here are some relevant portions of 1 Corinthians 1 that formed the basis for Tertullian's comments:

"For the message of the cross is foolishness to those who are perishing, but to us who are being saved it is the power of God. For it is written: 'I will destroy the wisdom of the wise: the intelligence of the intelligent I will frustrate.' Where is the wise man? Where is the philosopher of this age? Has not God made foolish the wisdom of the world? . . . But we preach Christ crucified: a stumbling block to the Jews and foolishness to Gentiles, but to those whom God has called, both Jews and Greeks, Christ is the power of God and the wisdom of God. For the foolishness of God is wiser than man's wisdom" (1 Corinthians 1: 18-20, 23-25).

McDonald provided a fuller context of Tertullian's quote from the *Anti-Nicene Fathers* volumes. Reading them in context in the light of Paul's words in 1 Corinthians makes his intent clear:

"For which is more unworthy of God, which is more likely to raise a blush of shame, that *God* should be born, or that He should die? that He should bear the flesh, or the cross? be circumcised, or be crucified? be cradled, or be coffined? be laid in a manger, or in a tomb? *Talk of 'wisdom!'* You will show more of *that* if you refuse to believe this also. But, after all, you will not be "wise" unless you become a 'fool' to the world, by believing 'the foolish things of God.'. . .

The Son of God was crucified; I am not ashamed because men must needs be ashamed *of it.* And the Son of God died; it is by all means to be believed because it is absurd. And He was buried, and rose again; the fact is certain, because it is impossible. But how will all this be true in Him, if He was not Himself true--if He really had

[1008]Ted J. McDonald, *Tertullian: Is the Gospel Absurd*, 2012, at Web Address: http://www.christiantreasury.org/content/tertullian-gospel-absurd

not in Himself that which might be crucified, might die, might be buried, and might rise again?"[1009]

Tertullian was an avid apologist for the Christian faith and far from a fideist, despite claims to the contrary. Tertullian, as a lawyer, regularly used reason in defense of the faith, and in opposition to those that mocked Christianity. Indeed, Tertullian captured this idea in his famous quote:

"What has Jerusalem to do with Athens, the Church with the Academy, the Christian with the heretic?"[1010]

In light of the foregoing, Michael Barnes misleading characterization of Tertullian's beliefs is disappointing. He suggested that Tertullian turned to faith when "rational knowledge fails":

"In the 2nd century CE the Christian philosopher–lawyer Tertullian . . . invoked faith as the answer, even saying at one point "I believe [rather than know] because it is absurd.' Where rational knowledge fails, faith is the answer, said Tertullian."[1011]

[1009]Tertullian, *De Carne Christi 5.4* in *The Anti-Nicene Fathers, Volume 3, Latin Christianity: It's Founder Tertullian*, p. 525, as quoted by Ted J. McDonald, *Tertullian: Is the Gospel Absurd?*, 2012, at Web Address:
http://www.christiantreasury.org/content/tertullian-gospel-absurd
[1010]Tertullian, *Prescription Against Heretics*, Chapter 7, as quoted by David Eller, *Natural Atheism*, Cranford New Jersey (American Atheist Press, 2004) 173.
[1011]Michael Horace Barnes, *Understanding Religion and Science: Introducing the Debate*, New York (Continuum International Publishing Group, 2010) 1. Brackets are Barnes

Barnes goes further, mischaracterizing Tertullian's approach as "Faith against reason."[1012] It is clear that Tertullian was not opposed to reason, but only to secularized godless philosophy. In light of this evidence, I appreciate the atheist David Steele's clear statement in defense of Tertullian:

"It's [fideism] often attributed to the fourth-century Christian Tertullian, who is notorious for having said 'I believe because it is absurd' or 'I believe because it's impossible.' In fact, these quotations are torn out of context, and Tertullian took almost exactly the opposite view. Tertullian very definitely defended the claim that Christianity is reasonable and not at all absurd."[1013]

Peter Grice provided this quote by Tertullian:

"'Obviously reason is something that belongs to God, because there is nothing which God, the creator of all things, did not foresee, arrange and determine by reason. Nor is there anything he does not want to be investigated and understood by reason' (*De Poenitenia 1.2, Patrologia Latina 1:1227).*"[1014]

These are hardly the sentiments of a hardened Fideist.

Further, I disagree with the fideist' contention that apologetics are neither necessary nor effective. To the contrary, the history of Christianity is filled with

---

[1012]Michael Horace Barnes, *Understanding Religion and Science,* 16.

[1013]David Ramsay Steele, *Atheism Explained: From Folly to Philosophy,* Chicago and La Salle, IL (Open Court Publishing Company, 2008) 121.

[1014] Peter Grice, *Reason in a Christian Context,* chapter in *True Reason: Confronting the Irrationality of the New Atheism,* Tom Gilson & Carson Weitnauer, Editors, Grand Rapids MI (Kregel Publications, 2012) 134.

examples of those whose spiritual journey included being powerfully persuaded by intellectual arguments in favor of the Christian faith. "For the message of the cross is foolishness to those who are perishing, but to us who are being saved it is the power of God" (1 Corinthians 1:18). Indeed, for me (and so many others), the rational and logical nature of Christianity is what we found so compelling and attractive in the first place.

Pascal's Wager

Perhaps you recall these lyrics from the Blood, Sweat, and Tears song *When I Die*:

My troubles are many, they're as deep as a well

I can swear there ain't no heaven but I pray there ain't no hell

Swear there ain't no heaven and pray there ain't no hell,

But I'll never know by living, only my dying will tell[1015]

These lyrics reflect the kind of gamble some play with eternity. As a matter of sheer logic, neither the existence of God nor the reality of the afterlife can be absolutely proven or disproven. This should drive every person to a serious contemplation of their own mortality and the afterward to their book of life. And this is at the heart of Pascal's wager.

While Pascal advocated wagering on the existence of God, those who don't believe in an afterlife are engaged in a roll of the dice as well.

[1015]Blood, Sweat, and Tears, Laura Nyro, *And When I Die*, © Sony/ATV Music Publishing LLC, Warner/Chappell Music, Inc.

Pascal's wager is named after the famed French philosopher and mathematician Blaise Pascal (1623-1662). After he passed away, a collection was made of notes Pascal had made concerning the truths of the Christian religion and these eventually formed the work we know as the *Pensées.*

His "wager" argument is found most specifically in *Pensées* 233:

> "Let us then examine this point, and say, 'God is, or He is not.' But to which side shall we incline? Reason can decide nothing here . . . A game is being played at the extremity of this infinite distance where heads or tails will turn up. What will you wager? According to reason, you can do neither the one thing nor the other; according to reason, you can defend neither of the propositions . . . Yes; but you must wager. It is not optional. You are embarked. Which will you choose then? . . . Let us weigh the gain and the loss in wagering that God is. Let us estimate these two chances. If you gain, you gain all; if you lose, you lose nothing. Wager, then, without hesitation that He is . . . The end of this discourse.—Now, what harm will befall you in taking this side? You will be faithful, honest, humble, grateful, generous, a sincere friend, truthful. Certainly you will not have those poisonous pleasures, glory and luxury; but will you not have others?"[1016]

I love how Pascal showed the necessity of the choice we all face: "You are embarked." None will avoid their appointment with the angel of death. Now, as Pascal argued, after we die, we will find the truth. If we have bet **for God** and we were right, we will be most blessed indeed. But if we were wrong, we have lost very little.

[1016]Blaise Pascal, *Pensées*, New York (E. P. Dutton & Company Inc.,1943) 66-68

On the other hand, if we have bet **against God**, and we were right, we have gained very little. However, if we were wrong, we shall be damned for eternity.

Pascal reasoned that the most logical thing to do, given the options available to us, is to believe in (bet on) God. If one finds that difficult, he should be as open as possible to belief in God, even taking the time to seriously pursue the possibility, since the consequences of betting against God are so profound.

Pascal suggested that one struggling with faith give it every opportunity to take root:

> "Endeavor then to convince yourself, not by increase of proofs of God, but by the abatement of your passions. You would like to attain faith, and do not know the way; you would like to cure yourself of unbelief, and ask the remedy for it. Learn of those who have been bound like you, and now stake all their possessions . . . Follow the way by which they began; by acting as if they believed . . . What have you to lose?"[1017]

Can you make yourself believe what you don't?

Some stumble over Pascal's advice of "Endeavoring then to convince yourself." Dawkins' is representative of this concern:

> "But none of that can make me actually believe it if I don't. Pascal's wager could only ever be an argument for *feigning* belief in God."[1018]

Carl Van Doren expressed a similar sentiment:

[1017]Blaise Pascal, *Pensées*, 68.
[1018]Richard Dawkins, *The God Delusion*, New York (Houghton Mifflin Company, 2006) 104.

"An honest unbeliever can no more make himself believe against his reason than he can make himself free of the pull of gravitation."[1019]

It seems certain, however, that Pascal was not advising a course of self-delusion. Martin responded to such concerns:

"As many scholars have pointed out, Pascal was not so naïve as to suppose that one could delude themselves into God-belief. However, he did think that belief could be developed by acting in certain religious ways."[1020]

I take Pascal to be challenging those struggling with ultimate issues to give faith a real chance, setting aside for a time all of their customary objections. They could begin, perhaps, by reading the Bible, not as a critic, but as one open to hear from God. They could humbly consider the possibility that there just might be a being greater than themselves. They could visit a church. They could pray, sincerely asking God to reveal Himself to them. As Pascal said, "What have you to lose?"

C. S. Rodd made reference to the experience of Studdert Kennedy:

"Studdert Kennedy experienced the darkest side of life in the trenches during the first world war, and in one of his poems he says: 'How do I know that God is good? I don't. I gamble like a man, I bet my life upon one side in life's great war. I must, I can't stand out. I must take sides.' And he ends up with some words that I have always kept in my

[1019]Carl Van Doren, *Why I Am an Unbeliever* in Christopher Hitchens, *The Portable Atheist: Essential Readings for the Nonbeliever*, Philadelphia PA (De Capo Press, 2007) 141.
[1020]Michael Martin, *Atheism: A Philosophical Justification,* Philadelphia PA (Temple University Press, 1990) 230.

inner heart as a kind of anchor for my own faith: 'You want to argue? Well, I can't. It is a choice. I choose the Christ.'"[1021]

In the struggle with faith, we can cry out to God like the man who cried out to Jesus, "I believe; help my unbelief" (Mark 9:24, NKJV).

William James and "the will to believe"

William James had a similar argument to Pascal's wager with his argument of *the will to believe*. Martin explained:

> "James's general strategy is to maintain that under certain circumstances, if the intellect cannot decide some issue, we have the right to believe on nonintellectual grounds . . . Under certain conditions we should believe on the basis of beneficial, not epistemic, reasons . . . In other words, when it is real, forced, and momentous *and* the decision cannot by its nature be decided on intellectual grounds, it should be influenced by our passionate nature. To leave the question [of religious faith] open is, according to James, itself a 'passional decision' and 'is attended with the same risk of losing the truth.' . . . James . . . maintains that sometimes the possible gain of achieving truth outweighs the risk of falling into error."[1022]

So, for James, if one is torn somewhere between faith and unbelief, and paralyzed by the choice facing him, it is reasonable to choose belief even at the risk of being wrong, for the benefits of the life of faith should not be missed due to indecision. Despite claims to the contrary, James' will to believe is essentially the same argument as Pascal's wager, with perhaps slightly more emphasis

---

[1021]C.S. Rodd, *Is There a God?* From the *Thinking Things Through* series, no. 9, Peterborough (Epworth Press, 2002) 43.

[1022]Michael Martin, *Atheism,* 238-239. My brackets in quote.

on the this-worldly benefits of faith and not just the eternal benefits (heaven rather than hell).

William James argued that a naturalistic account of the world likely misses a whole amazing aspect of reality, as Yeager Hudson explained:

> "James believes that it is the 'sick souls,' keenly sensitive to both the surface and the hidden dimensions of human life, who are really in touch with reality . . . James argues at length for what he calls the 'reality of the unseen' and suggests that if sanity means being in touch with reality, then those who are conscious both of the surface and the depths of reality are surely at least as sane as those who know only the world's façade."[1023]

James was by any standard a brilliant thinker and his will to believe, like Pascal's wager, should at least inspire in us the desire to give faith a real chance in our lives.

Pojman's experimental faith for the atheist

Perhaps one of the truly unique proposals for faith is that which philosopher Louis Pojman called experimental faith. Martin explained:

> "If Pojman's thesis is correct, perhaps a person who does not believe in God but who nevertheless hopes that God exists could still have faith in God's existence . . . To have faith in God, he says, is not necessarily to believe that God exists. Faith in God can be what he calls experimental faith. Such a faith is open to new evidence that would confirm or disconfirm the hypothesis on which the hope is based. Although faith in God does not entail the belief that God exists, it does entail belief in the possibility that God exists and commitment to living *as if* God exists. Pojman maintains that whether it is rational to have faith in God

---

[1023]Yeager Hudson, *The Philosophy of Religion*, Mountain View CA (Mayfield Publishing Company, 1991) 200.

in this sense 'depends on the outcome of an analysis of comparative values in relationship to probable outcomes. It is the sort of assessment that goes on in any cost-benefit analysis.' As a consequence of his analysis Pojman maintains that agnosticism and 'even an interested type of atheism' are possible religious positions."[1024]

It is difficult to see how Pojman's experimental faith differs in essence from Pascal's wager or James' will to believe. I must say, however, that I take Pojman's proposal very seriously, in that my coming to faith was similar. When I prayed to receive Christ as my savior, I began my prayer with something like "Lord, if you are real, and this gospel message is true, I want to know you and give my life to you. Please reveal yourself to me."

Indeed, I have heard many similar testimonies from Christians who had asked God to reveal Himself to them as well. I am convinced that God honors these sincere cries of faith with more light on the journey to faith.

Doubt and faith

But what is one to do if they have considered issues related to the existence of God, but lingering doubts remain? Further, *what about those who do believe in God, yet have moments of doubt?* They wonder: "What if there is no God?" "What if life is just a cosmic accident without meaning?" "What if Jesus wasn't really God, but was just a man?" "What if Jesus didn't really rise from the dead?"

[1024]Louis Pojman, *Faith Without Belief?, Faith and Philosophy,* 3, 1986, pp. 157-176, as quoted by Michael Martin, *Atheism: A Philosophical Justification,* Philadelphia PA (Temple University Press, 1990) 264-265

Those struggling with such questions and doubts can be very troubled by them, and even fearful that God will be displeased with them. Others have been chastised by church leaders for expressing their concerns and told that they must simply trust the Church. It is just that kind of advice that inspired Mark Twain's quip, "Faith is believing what you know ain't so."[1025]

I am convinced, however, that we need not check our brains at the church door. Many of the greatest intellects of human history were Christian believers. Christianity doesn't consist in blind faith, but in reasoned faith.

Rather, Christians understand that reason, as much as revelation, is a gift of God. Doubts are normal and questions welcome. Struggling with doubts has often been the pathway to the very throne of God. Even for believers, doubts can help reinvigorate faith as one re-examines the powerful evidence for the faith.

C. S. Rodd related:

> "Indeed, doubting may be the first step in gaining a personal faith for ourselves, a faith that we can hold with a clear conscience."[1026]

We should always be willing to hear what others believe and to hear their criticisms of our faith. It would be better to be shown where we have been wrong than to go on blindly and blissfully believing what isn't true! Truth has no fear of being examined; it is only darkness that flees from the light (John 3:19-21).

Do atheists have doubts?

[1025]Mark Twain, *Pudd'head Wilson*, 1894
[1026]C.S. Rodd, *Is There a God?* 77-78.

In this light, I have sometimes asked atheists if they have doubts. I would say to them: "Haven't you ever had a moment where you stopped and thought to yourself, 'What if they are right; what if there is a God?'" It would be perfectly normal if they did, but they tend to deny it.

But the honest seeker after God can admit doubts and ask questions. God is big enough to handle them. I am convinced that God would rather have an honest doubter seeking truth than pretended believers. Anyway, there is no sense in pretending since God knows our hearts. Give your doubts, questions, and fears to the Lord and ask Him to help you. He will!

We should, however, be careful not make the mistake of waiting for absolute proof before we decide, for such is simply not possible. Gary Parker has well said:

"In my own pilgrimage, if I have to choose between a faith that has stared doubt in the eye and made it blink, or a naïve faith that has never known the firing line of doubt, I will choose the former"[1027]

His point is well-taken. It is better to build our lives around ideas that we have seriously investigated than to merely believe what we have been taught or told. In this way, and through this crucible, they become *our* beliefs.

Gerald Benedictine referred to Paul Tillich's comments on the relationship between faith and doubt:

"Paul Tillich thought that doubt and faith were not necessarily in conflict: 'Doubt isn't the opposite of faith; it is an element of faith."[1028]

[1027]Gary Parker, *The Gift of Doubts, Harper Collins,* 1990.
[1028]Gerald Benedict, *The God Debate: A New Look at History's*

I heard somewhere that the tree facing the greatest wind has the deepest roots. James Feibleman said:

> "For it is the beliefs which have demonstrated that they can withstand doubt, not those we have never doubted, which are entitled to carry a seal of evidence."[1029]

Why doesn't God provide an undeniable proof of His existence?

We have made the point that the existence of God can neither be philosophically proven nor disproven in an absolute sense. Nevertheless, we have also argued that the arguments in favor of the "God Hypothesis" are clear, convincing, and true beyond a reasonable doubt.

Yet, skeptics sometimes ask why God doesn't just write His name across the sky in some fantastic miracle that simply can't be ignored.

Some refer to the absence of total or absolute proof for God's existence *Divine Hiddenness* or *Divine Silence*. They want an explanation as to why God doesn't simply make His existence undeniable. They ask why God doesn't come out from behind the screen and reveal Himself directly.

Kerry Walters explained:

> "Some atheists argue against God's existence on the grounds of divine hiddenness: If God really existed, surely God would make his existence more apparent."[1030]

Richard Dawkins made the same point:

Oldest Argument, London (Watkins Publishing, 2013) 133.

[1029]James K. Feibleman, *Understanding Philosophy: A Popular History of Ideas*, New York (Horizon Press, 1973) 74.

[1030]Kerry Walters, *Atheism: A Guide for the Perplexed*, New York (The Continuum International Publishing Group Inc, 2010) 74.

"If he existed and chose to reveal it, God himself could clinch the argument, noisily and unequivocally, in his favour."[1031]

Likewise, Bugliosi asked:

"So why not give these millions proof that they will accept and cannot deny, such as appearing to us in the sky? Since it would be so easy for him to do, why not? They have no answer to this because there is no answer."[1032]

Carl Sagan agreed:

"God could have engraved the Ten Commandments on the Moon. Large. Ten kilometers across per commandment . . . Or why not a hundred-kilometer crucifix in Earth orbit? God could certainly do that. Right! . . . Why didn't God do things of that sort?"[1033]

John O' Leary-Hawthorn said:

"As an atheist I once knew put it, 'He [God] would be calling us up on the telephone.'"[1034]

The epistemic distance for belief or unbelief

Contrary to these arguments, I believe there is a very good reason why God hasn't provided this type of undeniable evidence or proof of His existence. It would

[1031]Richard Dawkins, *The God Delusion*, New York (Houghton Mifflin Company, 2006) 50.

[1032]Vincent Bugliosi, *Divinity of Doubt: The God Question*, New York (Vanguard Press, 2011) 268.

[1033]Carl Sagan, *The God Hypothesis* in Christopher Hitchens, *The Portable Atheist: Essential Readings for the Nonbeliever*, Philadelphia PA (De Capo Press, 2007) 238.

[1034] John O' Leary-Hawthorn, *Arguments for Atheism*, Chapter in *Reasons for the Hope Within*, Michael J. Murray Editor, Grand Rapids MI (William B. Eerdman's Publishing Company, 1999)122.

remove the element of both faith and freedom. Philosopher John Hick called this gap between absolute proof versus adequate proof (which entails the need for faith) "epistemic distance."[1035]

Sandra Menssen and Thomas Sullivan similarly called the requirement to bridge this gap "resolute belief" which involves "a firmness disproportionate to the evidential warrant for the belief."[1036]

As it is, there is more than enough reason to believe, but a gap remains for faith, the epistemic distance. This is by God's design; to separate lovers of truth from lovers of self. Faith has the sifting quality of drawing those sincere and hungry for truth while repelling those too devoted to themselves and their idols. C. S Lewis understood this when he said:

> "It is safe to tell the pure in heart that they shall see God, for only the pure in heart want to."[1037]

Paul Edwards recorded the sentiments of John Hick and Alasdair MacIntyre on this issue:

> "If the existence of God were unquestionably certain like a physical fact, writes John Hick, it 'would leave no

---

[1035] John Hick, *The Philosophy of Religion*, Englewood Cliffs (Prentice Hall, Inc., 1990) 37. As cited by Victorino Raymundo T. Lualhati, *On Epistemic Distance and Faith*, June 2018 at web address: https://www.dlsu.edu.ph/wp-content/uploads/pdf/conferences/research-congress-proceedings/2018/tph-16.pdf

[1036] Sandra Menssen & Thomas D. Sullivan, *The Agnostic Inquirer: Revelation from a Philosophical Standpoint*, Grand Rapids MI (William B. Eerdmans Publishing Company, 2007, 293.

[1037] C. S. Lewis, *The Problem of Pain*, New York (Macmillan, 1962, 1975) 145.

ground for a free human response of trust, self-commitment and obedience.' If we could produce logically coercive arguments, in the words of Alasdair MacIntyre, 'we should be as bereft of the possibility of making a free decision to love God as we should be if every utterance of doubt and unbelief was answered by thunder-bolts from heaven.'"[1038]

Martin noted the similar thoughts of Kierkegaard:

"Kierkegaard maintains that with objective certainty comes lack of personal growth and spiritual stagnation. But with faith there is risk, danger, and adventure—all essential for spiritual growth and transcendence."[1039]

Consider also, the similar sentiments of C. S. Lewis:

"The Irresistible and the Indisputable are the two weapons which the very nature of God's scheme forbids Him to use. Merely to over-ride a human will . . . would be for Him useless. He cannot ravish. He can only woo."[1040]

Lewis, we recall, argued that God did not create mere robots programmed to believe in Him. That would have been illusory rather than real love, like a child's doll that says "I love you" when you pull its string.

Menssen and Sullivan argued that:

"A super-abundantly convincing revelation from on high would need to tear the veil off mysteries of freedom, sin, satisfaction,, and grace . . . suppose . .

[1038]Paul Edwards, *A Modern Introduction to Philosophy: Readings from Classical and Contemporary Sources,* Third Edition, Paul Edwards & Arthur Pap, Editors, New York, (The Free Press, 1973) 391.

[1039]Michael Martin, *Atheism,* 252.

[1040]C. S. Lewis, *Screwtape Letters*, New York (Macmillan, 1961) 128, as quoted by Timothy Morgan, *Thank God for Atheists: How the Greatest Skeptics Led Me to Faith*, Eugene OR (Harvest House Publishers, 2015) 223.

. that God could make the evidence in this world irresistible, so strong that we would have no real choice but to assent. It is quite easy to think of a reason God would not want to do that. It is the same reason given earlier, one endorsed by Kant: such a revelation would destroy all freedom of action."[1041]

God does not want heavenly prisoners forced or dragged into His kingdom against their will. Hence, God has made it possible for people to believe in Him, but He does not demand it of them. God has provided more than enough evidence for belief, but He has left an element of faith lest the freedom of choice be removed and entrance into His Kingdom be compelled. God has provided the way of salvation as a gift through faith in His Son Jesus Christ. Yet, in the final analysis, whether we receive the gift is left to our choice.

Kierkegaard's parable of the King and the Maiden

We shall now consider Kierkegaard's parable of *The King and the Maiden* to further illustrate the point:

"Suppose there was a king who loved a humble maiden. The king was like no other king. Every statesman trembled before his power. No one dared breathe a word against him, for he had the strength to crush all opponents.
And yet this mighty king was melted by love for a humble maiden who lived in a poor village in his kingdom. How could he declare his love for her? In an odd sort of

---

[1041] Sandra Menssen & Thomas D. Sullivan, *The Agnostic Inquirer: Revelation from a Philosophical Standpoint*, Grand Rapids MI (William B. Eerdmans Publishing Company, 2007, 311.

way, his kingliness tied his hands. If he brought her to the palace and crowned her head with jewels and clothed her body in royal robes, she would surely not resist-no one dared resist him. But would she love him?

She would say she loved him, of course, but would she truly? Or would she live with him in fear, nursing a private grief for the life she had left behind? Would she be happy at his side? How could he know for sure? If he rode to her forest cottage in his royal carriage, with an armed escort waving bright banners, that too would overwhelm her. He did not want a cringing subject. He wanted a lover, an equal. He wanted her to forget that he was a king and she a humble maiden and to let shared love cross the gulf between them. For it is only in love that the unequal can be made equal.

The king, convinced he could not elevate the maiden without crushing her freedom, resolved to descend to her. Clothed as a beggar, he approached her cottage with a worn cloak fluttering loose about him. This was not just a disguise – the king took on a totally new identity–He had renounced his throne to declare his love and to win hers."[1042]

While the primary purpose of Kierkegaard's parable was to illustrate the incarnation of the Son of God for the purpose of man's redemption (*Kenosis*) as taught in Philippians 2, nonetheless, we can take a further lesson from the parable as well.

We take note of the parable's description of the king's concern that his maiden's love be real and not coerced. *Just as the King could not ride up in all his kingly glory with his impressive retinue to seek the love of the maiden, so God has not given spectacular and undeniable signs in the heavens compelling men to believe.* For such

---

[1042]Soren Kierkegaard, *The King and the Maiden, Philosophical Fragments*, 31-42, as quoted at https://bearskin.org/2015/04/03/the-king-and-the-maiden/

an act would denigrate man's free response to God's offer of salvation.

Would unbelievers be persuaded by spectacular signs?

Further, it is a fair question whether unbelievers would be persuaded by even the most spectacular signs in the heavens (Compare Luke 16:27-31). Just like skeptics today, Jesus confronted "a wicked and adulterous generation" asking Him for just such a sign. Notice Jesus' response to their demand:

> ""Then some of the Pharisees and teachers of the law said to him, 'Teacher, we want to see a miraculous sign from you.' He answered, 'A wicked and adulterous generation asks for a sign! But none will be given it except the sign of the prophet Jonah. For as Jonah was three days and three nights in the belly of a huge fish, so the Son of Man will be three days and three nights in the heart of the earth" (Matthew 12:38-40).

In other words, He would give them the sign of His own resurrection from the dead. While many have believed the sign, Christ's hardened enemies obstinately refused to believe despite the powerful evidence of His appearances and the empty tomb.

The heavenly sign at Christ's second coming to earth

It is interesting that Jesus has actually promised to provide the kind of sign in the heavens that skeptics have demanded. But this cosmic sign will be universally manifested upon God's timetable, particularly accompanying Christ's still future second coming to earth. At the time, said Jesus, there will be a powerful sign in the heavens:

"At that time the sign of the Son of Man will appear in the sky, and all the nations will mourn. They will see the Son of Man coming in the clouds of the sky, with power and great glory" (Matthew 24:30).

The apostle John described the same event:

"Look, he is coming on the clouds, and every eye will see him; even those who pierced him; and all the peoples of the earth will mourn because of him. So shall it be! Amen"(Revelations 1:7).

Both passages mention the mourning of the people of the earth at the second coming of Christ. This is because when he returns, Jesus will be coming as a judge to separate the good from evil, the sheep from the goats (Matthew 25:31-46).

There are already powerful signs in the heavens

Further, *there already are signs in the heavens above* that reflect the majesty and grandeur of God. David declared by the Holy Spirit:

"The heavens declare the glory of God; the skies proclaim the work of his hands. Day after day they pour forth speech; night after night they display knowledge" (Psalm 19:1-2).

Who has not been awestruck and inspired by a clear dark-night's survey of the heavens and wondered about ultimate meaning and the existence of God?

The God who seeks

Let's bring this down to the personal level. Let there be no doubt that God loves you and wants a relationship with you. The Bible is clear that God wants all men to be saved. The apostle Paul said: "This is good, and pleases

God our savior, who wants all men to be saved and to come to a knowledge of the truth" (1 Timothy 2 3-4). Likewise, the apostle Peter said:

> "The Lord is not slow in keeping his promises, as some understand slowness. He is patient with you, not wanting anyone to perish, but everyone come to repentance" (2 Peter 3:9).

Speaking of God's prevenient grace, Merton said, "We could not seek God unless He were seeking us."[1043] Jesus said, "But I, when I am lifted up from the earth, will draw all men to myself"(John 12:32). God is seeking you as a shepherd seeks a wayward sheep. Francis Thompson described God's graceful call using the metaphor of the *Hound of Heaven*:

> "I fled him down the nights and down the days; I fled Him, down the arches of the years: I fled Him, down the labyrinthine ways of my own mind; And in the midst of my tears I hid from Him."[1044]

And again:

> "All the messages you've heard,
> about Jesus and His word.
> But still you keep on running from His love.
> When you gonna open your eyes and see,
> that it's Him your really need.
> Tell me why do you keep running from His love?
>
> Why do you keep running from His love?
> If you only knew how much He cares for you.
> Don't you know He cries a tear inside,

[1043]Thomas Merton, *Random House Webster's Quotationary*, Leonard Roy Frank, Editor, New York (Random House, 2001) 317.

[1044] *The Encyclopedia of Religious Quotations*, Frank S. Mead, Editor, Westwood NJ (Fleming H. Revell Company, 1965) 188.

every time you run and hide?
Tell me why do you keep running from His love?"[1045]

Please remember that Jesus said He: "came to seek and save what was lost" (Luke 19:10).

Kierkegaard's leap of faith

We can shut our eyes to the overwhelming evidence for God, and stubbornly go on doing our own thing, or we can humble ourselves and take the leap of faith into God's kingdom. This leap of faith is the idea that Soren Kierkegaard emphasized; that at the end of the day, coming to faith requires one to finally leap.

Kierkegaard's parable of the young maiden contemplating marriage

Elmer Duncan explained how Kierkegaard used an illustration of a young maiden contemplating a marriage proposal to explain the leap of faith necessary for Christian salvation.

> "[Kierkegaard] said that we become Christians, that we move into the religious sphere from the ethical, by a 'leap of faith.' As he put it, 'reflection can be halted only by a leap . . . When the subject does not put an end to his reflection, he is made infinite in reflection, i.e., he does not arrive at a decision' . . . Whether we are deciding to become Christians, or to get married, or anything else, we finally must put reflection aside, and make our decision . . . Here I think Kierkegaard can be defended. He did not say that reasons cannot be given for a choice. The young girl asks for reasons, and should have them, before she decides to marry. But, in the very nature of the case, she can never know *all* the facts. She must decide on less than complete

---

[1045]The author

evidence, and so must the Christian. If we wait for complete knowledge, we shall never decide."[1046]

Kierkegaard himself put it like this:

> "Without risk there is no faith. Faith is precisely the contradiction between the infinite passion of the individual's inwardness and the objective uncertainty. If I am capable of grasping God objectively, I do not believe, but precisely because I cannot do this I must believe."[1047]

For Kierkegaard, it is precisely because we don't have absolute proof of God's existence that makes real faith possible. As we have seen, this has the result of separating the faithful from the faithless. So, rather than desponding this lack of certainty, join Kierkegaard in making the leap!

Socrates "Risk" of faith

Menssen and Sullivan have shown that Socrates was in fact a believer, "he was deeply religious" and was "certain that the gods exist, are good, and care for human beings. That certainty governed his whole life."[1048]

[1046]Elmer H. Duncan, *Soren Kierkegaard, Makers of the Modern Theological Mind*, Bob E. Patterson, Editor, Waco TX (Word Books, 1976) 88-89.

[1047]Soren Kierkegaard, *Eternal Happiness, Subjectivity and Truth*, as reprinted in, *A Modern Introduction to Philosophy: Readings from Classical and Contemporary Sources,* Third Edition, Paul Edwards & Arthur Pap, Editors, New York, (The Free Press, 1973) 501.

[1048] Sandra Menssen & Thomas D. Sullivan, *The Agnostic Inquirer,* 318. Likewise, we are told about Aristotle that he had a "belief in a supernatural god," Gerald Schroeder, *The Science of God: The Convergence of Scientific and Biblical Wisdom,* New York (The Free Press, 1997) 6.

How did Socrates face the gap between evidence and certainty? Menssen and Sullivan explained:

> "This paradigmatic lover of wisdom, this progenitor of a long succession of Western philosophers, closes the evidential gap by his will . . . he risks belief on behalf of the good. As Plato's Socrates puts it at the end of Phaedo . . . 'I think it is fitting for a man to risk the belief—for the risk is a noble one.'"[1049]

Don Francisco and a "Step Across the Line"

Don Francisco wrote these words:

> "You got to take a step across the line.
> Let Jesus fill your heart and mind.
> I can show you where to look,
> but you got to seek to find.
> You got to take a step across the line."[1050]

Barry McGuire and the big leap

Barry McGuire, in his song *Cosmic Cowboy* caught the same idea:

> "Somehow without a sound, I heard Him call my name.
> Lookin up, I saw we was high up on this ridge.
> He took me by my hand: led me right to the edge.
> I was so scared I couldn't find a single word to say.
> I mean, there's 10,000 feet in the air,
> and it's just about an inch away.
> But a million miles was out beyond the waving of his hand.
> And I was looking through His eyes,

[1049] Sandra Menssen & Thomas D. Sullivan, *The Agnostic Inquirer,* 320.

[1050] Don Francisco, *Step Across the Line, Forgiven,* Newpax, 1977.

right in to another land.

He said, 'This is my Father's ranch,
as far as you can see.
He made it out of nothing;
every branch and every tree.
The stars, and mountain,
the rivers and the streams.
The oceans and the fountains,
and the valley of your dreams.

That's right, I know that place you long to be.
Truth is, I'm the only door,
you're going to have to pass through me.'
Bending back, I tipped my hat
so I could look Him in the eye.
He just smiled and gave me confidence.
He said, 'go ahead and try.'

Well, it was now or never,
and I knew I had to start.
So I took that step and I went falling,
straight into his heart.
The first thing that I noticed
coming out the other side;
all my fears had vanished,
he taught me how to fly!

There's a Cosmic Cowboy,
and He rides the starry range.
He's a supernatural plowboy,
and he is dressed up kind of strange.
To think I nearly missed him,
being out there on the run.
Ah, but that old hat He was wearing,
was shining brighter than the sun.
And when my eyes adjusted,
to the flashing of His smile;
Hey, I saw His invitation,
He said, 'Come on, Me and you,

we'll go ridin for a while'"[1051]

The way of faith

Mark Mittelburg provided a practical illustration concerning the relationship between reason and faith:

> "Think in terms of flying. It's not enough to just believe in aviation, to spend time in airports, to affirm the skills of pilots. No, that will not get you to Pittsburgh. You need to act on those beliefs by actually climbing on board an airplane. That's real faith, and it can get you where you want to go."[1052]

Hans Küng offered a similar metaphor for saving faith;

> "I have always thought of this attitude of trust as being like learning to swim, which doesn't happen by standing in a riverbank, reading a textbook, or taking a dry swimming course, but rather by taking the venture, perhaps aided by others, of trusting oneself to the enigmatic water that not only supports those who trust in it and don't go rigid, but also moves."[1053]

John F. Haught said: "At some point in the validation of every truth claim or hypothesis, a leap of faith is an escapable ingredient."[1054] Indeed, Haught is insightful in reminding us of the paradox of faith:

[1051]Barry McGuire, *Cosmic Cowboy*, Sparrow Records, 1978.

[1052]Mark Mittelburg, *Why Faith in Jesus Matters*, chapter in William Lane Craig & Chad Meister, Editors, *God is Great, God is Good: Why Believing in God is Reasonable and Responsible,* Downers Grove IL (Inter Varsity Press, 2009) 226.

[1053] Hans Küng, *The Beginning of All Things: Science and Religion,* Grand Rapids MI (William B. Eerdmans Publishing Company, 2005) 81.

[1054]John F. Haught, *God and the New Atheism: A Critical Response to Dawkins, Harris, and Hitchens,* Louisville KY (Westminster John Knox Press, 2008) 47.

"The life of faith is one in which 'there is no knowing without going': 'unless you change and become like children, you will never enter the kingdom of heaven' (Matt. 18:3)."[1055]

Humble before the Lord

That is, we must finally make this leap of faith absent of absolute or total proof, trusting in God as a child instinctively trusts its parents. You must humble yourself, then, if you are to find the king of the universe.

George MacDonald said:

"He [God] can be revealed only to the child; perfectly, to the pure child only. All the discipline of the world is to make men children, that God may be revealed to them."[1056]

Paul Moser stated:

"The Key question will thus become 'who is enquiring about the existence of God? More specifically, what *kind* of person is inquiring about divine reality—a person willing or unwilling to yield to a perfectly loving God? . . . Inquirers about God's existence typically overlook this important cognitive consideration about a God worthy of worship."[1057]

[1055]John F. Haught, *God and the New Atheism*, 46.

[1056] George MacDonald, Life Essential, as quoted by Philip Yancey, *Where is God When It Hurts*, Revised and Expanded, Grand Rapids MI (Zondervan Publishing House, 1977, 1990) 127.

[1057]Paul K. Moser, *Evidence of a Morally Perfect God*, chapter in William Lane Craig & Chad Meister, Editors, *God is Great, God is Good: Why Believing in God is Reasonable and Responsible*, Downers Grove IL (Inter Varsity Press, 2009) 56-57.

Some may find this admonition an offense. But the issue isn't whether we like it, but whether, in fact, it is true. About truth, Bugliosi said:

"An old Turkish proverb says that whoever tells the truth is chased out of nine villages. And a Yugoslavian proverb echoes, 'Tell the truth and run.'"[1058]

The apostle Paul said, "Have I now become your enemy by telling you the truth?" (Galatians 4:16).

If, for the sake of argument, there is an Almighty God, Creator of the universe, and Lord over all, does that not give one pause to consider that reverence toward this Being would be appropriate?

C. S. Lewis' leap of faith

Gerald Benedict described C. S. Lewis' own conversion experience:

"C. S. Lewis became an atheist at the age of fifteen. In *Surprised by Joy*, he said he was 'very angry with God for not existing.' He confessed to being brought to Christianity like a prodigal, 'kicking, struggling, resentful . . .'. You must picture me alone in that room in Magdalen night after night, feeling, whenever my mind lifted even for a second from my work, the steady, unrelenting approach of Him whom I so earnestly desired not to meet. That which I greatly feared had at last come upon me. In the Trinity Term of 1929 I gave in, and admitted that God was God, and knelt and prayed; perhaps, that night, the most dejected and reluctant convert in all England.'"[1059]

[1058]Vincent Bugliosi, *Divinity of Doubt: The God Question*, New York (Vanguard Press, 2011) 218-219.

[1059]Gerald Benedict, *The God Debate: A New Look at History's Oldest Argument,* London (Watkins Publishing, 2013) 113.

My leap

In 1979, a young lady shared the Christian gospel message with me. I initially resisted, but as the conversation continued, I found myself losing resistance, and even to find faith in Christ appealing. But how could I be sure? I got alone and prayed something like this: "Lord, I don't know for sure that this is real, but if it is, I want to know you and live for you. Thank for dying for my sins on the cross. I want to be born-again."

I can only say that for me, that moment was decisive. I was changed and never the same again. Indeed, it was for me as though the scales had fallen from my eyes and I could see and understand the world as if for the first time. A new meaning and passionate purpose for life burst before me. The gospel musician and singer Carman beautifully captured the wonder of the conversion experience.

The Master's Hand[1060]
By Carmen Licciardello
"I walked into the church that night
Thought that I'd drop by the side
So I sat down
I laughed in spite of all my blues
It's really not the type of place
I'm used to hanging around

I looked ahead and saw a man
And watched him close as he began to speak

[1060]Carmen Licciardello, *The Master's Hand* from the album *Some-O-Dat,* Preference Music BMI, New York, 1982.

that certain day
And it seemed like something deep inside
Had seized my soul and though I tried
to shake it
It wouldn't go away

It was as though the words he said
Would echo back inside my head
I almost cried
I'd be a fool so I supposed
Then somehow got myself composed
And held it inside

I felt the blood rush through my wrists
The tighter that I squeezed my fists
Determined not to let conviction start
Then with all my wisdom left behind
I somehow saw that I was blind
And slowly let His presence fill my heart

As everyone stood to their feet
I managed somehow to repeat the prayer
That they were praying
Then I dropped my head and I dropped my eyes
As suddenly I realized
Just what I was saying

Through trembling lips
and streaming tears
I ended all those wasted years
of dreams I'd built on sand
Unloading all my guilt and wrong
I somehow felt both weak and strong

The night I took the Master's hand

As I look back remembering
I still recall how everything just
seemed different than before
How every house and bird and tree
Was strangely beautiful to me
and people were even more

How could I have been so blind
To rush through life and never find
This rock on which I stand
But when I whispered deep that name
I knew I'd never be the same
The night I took the Master's hand
But when I whispered Jesus' name
I knew I never be the same
The night I took the Master's hand"

The God hypothesis

When the apostle Paul testified before Herod Agrippa
II and Festus the Roman Governor, he passionately
shared his story and the gospel of Jesus Christ. Agrippa
responded to Paul: "Do you think that in such a short
time you can persuade me to be a Christian?" Paul
answered Agrippa, "Short time or long—I pray God that
not only you but all who are listening to me today may
become what I am, except these chains."

It is my hope that this book has moved the reader
closer to the kingdom of God and faith in Jesus Christ. I
have shared with you why I believe the God Hypothesis

is a live option and I invite you to share in the living faith
of Christianity.

The Author

Steve Lagoon is the President of Religion Analysis Service, a Christian apologetics and counter-cult ministry located in Minnesota since 1946, and publisher of the *Discerner* (www.ras.org).

He is the co-author of *Blood, Medicine, and the Jehovah's Witnesses* with Steve Devore in 1995 and *Oneness Pentecostalism: New Truth or Old Heresy* in 2000 with Thomas Sheehey.

Steve has a Bachelor's degree in Biblical Studies and a Master of Divinity degree, both from the University of Northwestern-St. Paul.

Made in the USA
Coppell, TX
19 September 2021

62552154R00356